MCSE

IN A NUTSHELL

The Windows 2000 Exams

MCSE
IN A NUTSHELL

The Windows 2000 Exams

Michael Moncur & Paul Murphy

O'REILLY®

Beijing • Cambridge • Farnham • Köln • Paris • Sebastopol • Taipei • Tokyo

MCSE in a Nutshell: The Windows 2000 Exams
by Michael Moncur and Paul Murphy

Copyright © 2001 O'Reilly & Associates, Inc. All rights reserved.
Printed in the United States of America.

Published by O'Reilly & Associates, Inc., 101 Morris Street, Sebastopol, CA 95472.

Editor: Troy Mott

Production Editor: Catherine Morris

Cover Designer: Ellie Volckhausen

Printing History:

February 2001:   First Edition.

Tim O'Reilly was the editor of *MCSE: The Core Exams in a Nutshell, MCSE: The Core Exams in a Nutshell, Second Edition,* and *MCSE: The Electives in a Nutshell,* on which this book is based.

ISBN: 0-596-00030-8

[M]

Table of Contents

Part 3: Active Directory

Part 5:   Designing Active Directory

Part 6:   Designing Network Infrastructure

Part 7: Designing Security

Preface

The MCSE (Microsoft Certified Systems Engineer) program is a rigorous testing and certification program for Windows 2000 system and network administrators. This book is a concise, comprehensive study guide to the areas covered on the core MCSE exams.

If you're an experienced system administrator—whether the experience is with Windows NT, Windows 2000, UNIX, NetWare, or another system—this book will help you codify your knowledge, understand Microsoft's view of the universe, and prepare for the MCSE exams.

If you are a beginner, this book should also prove useful. Of course, you'll need real-world experience that no book can provide. Depending on your needs, you may also need help from other books or classes. Nevertheless, this book will provide a useful framework for your studies.

If you have already made some progress along the MCSE path, you probably have a number of MCSE-related books lining your shelves. Although this book can't replace all of them, it can remain on your desk as a handy reference to the subjects covered on the core MCSE exams. It also includes several features—such as review items and practice tests—that will help you prepare to take the actual exams.

Contents

This book covers the four core (required) exams for the Windows 2000 MCSE certification, along with three Designing exams, one of which you may choose as the fifth required exam. The two Designing exams you do not use as a core exam may be used to fulfill your elective requirements. This book includes the following sections:

About the MCSE Exams
> Introduces the MCSE 2000 program, with information about the content of the exams and study tips

Part 1, Windows 2000 Professional
> Covers Exam 70-210, *Installing, Configuring, and Administering Microsoft Windows 2000 Professional*

Part 2, Windows 2000 Server
> Covers Exam 70-215, *Installing, Configuring, and Administering Microsoft Windows 2000 Server*

Part 3, Active Directory
> Covers Exam 70-217, *Implementing and Administering a Microsoft Windows 2000 Directory Services Infrastructure*

Part 4, Network Infrastructure
> Covers Exam 70-216, *Implementing and Administering a Microsoft Windows 2000 Network Infrastructure*

Part 5, Designing Active Directory
> Covers Exam 70-219, *Designing a Microsoft Windows 2000 Directory Services Infrastructure*

Part 6, Designing Network Infrastructure
> Covers Exam 70-221, *Designing a Microsoft Windows 2000 Network Infrastructure*

Part 7, Designing Security
> Covers Exam 70-220, *Designing Security for a Microsoft Windows 2000 Network*

Conventions Used in This Book

Each Part within this book corresponds to a single MCSE exam and consists of five sections:

Exam Overview
> This is a brief introduction to the exam's topic. The key aspects of the topic are listed, each broken down into two lists of objectives to help direct your preparation. The *Need to Know* list identifies areas you should understand in depth because they will probably be on the exam. The *Need to Apply* list outlines tasks you should be able to perform and should practice during your studies. The objectives in both of these lists include cross-references to the Study Guide.

Study Guide
> This, the largest portion of each Part, is a comprehensive study guide for the areas covered on the exam. It can be read straight through or referred to for areas in which you need further study.

Suggested Exercises
> This is a numbered list of exercises you can perform, usually with a small test network, to gain experience in the exam's subject areas.

Practice Tests

> This section includes a comprehensive practice test to assess your knowledge of the current exam topic, along with a case study and questions that are similar to the format of the Windows 2000 MCSE exams.

Highlighter's Index

> Here we've attempted to compile the facts within the exam's subject area that you are most likely to need another look at—in other words, those you might have highlighted while reading the Study Guide. This will be useful as a final review before taking an exam.

Within the "Study Guide" section, the following elements are included:

On the Exam

> These boxed tips provide information about areas you should study for the exam.

In the Real World

> These tips provide informative asides in cases where reality and the MCSE exams don't necessarily coincide.

The following typographical conventions are used in this book:

Constant width

> Used to indicate keyboard keys, commands, and other values to be typed literally

Italic

> Used for URLs, email addresses, to introduce new terms, and to indicate menu and dialog box options

---

Other MCSE Resources

Depending on your current knowledge and experience, you may need resources beyond this book for your MCSE studies. The one resource all MCSE candidates should be aware of is Microsoft's Training and Certification web page:

> *http://www.microsoft.com/train_cert/*

We recommend that you refer to this page regularly during your certification progress, because changes may be announced that will affect your exam choices.

A wide variety of MCSE study guides are available from other vendors, chief among them the MOC (Microsoft Official Curriculum) study guides. If you need a book for further study, choose the one that best fits your needs.

Other useful resources, although not specifically for the MCSE curriculum, include the various Resource Kits published by Microsoft. These are available for Windows 2000 Professional and Windows 2000 Server and go into great detail about each product. Each kit includes a CD-ROM with useful utilities, some of which are described in this book.

A number of practice MCSE test programs are available. See Microsoft's web page, listed earlier, for information about one such program. See this book's web site (listed in the next section) for links to several third-party test software providers.

Comments and Questions

We have tested and verified the information in this book to the best of our ability, but you may find that features have changed (or even that we have made mistakes!). Please let us know about any errors you find, as well as your suggestions for future editions, by writing to:

O'Reilly & Associates, Inc.
101 Morris Street
Sebastopol, CA 95472
1-800-998-9938 (in the U.S. or Canada)
1-707-829-0515 (international/local)
1-707-829-0104 (FAX)

You can also send us messages electronically. To be put on the mailing list or request a catalog, send email to:

elists@oreilly.com

To ask technical questions or comment on the book, send email to:

bookquestions@oreilly.com

We have a web site for the book, where we'll list examples, errata, and any plans for future editions. The site also includes a link to a forum where you can discuss the book with the author and other readers. You can access this site at:

http://www.oreilly.com/catalog/mcseian/

For more information about this book and others, see the O'Reilly web site:

http://www.oreilly.com

Acknowledgments

We would like to thank everyone involved in the production of this book. Tim O'Reilly, the editor of the "In a Nutshell" series, came up with the original concept and has provided much useful input as the book has evolved through several versions. Troy Mott, Katie Gardner, and Bob Herbstman made sure the project and the authors moved along smoothly, not always an easy task.

The manuscript was also reviewed for technical accuracy at various stages by Pawan Bhardwaj, Matthew Strebe, and Charles Perkins. Their input has helped make this a better book. We would also like to thank the long list of reviewers and editors who worked on previous editions.

Michael would like to thank everyone at Studio B for their help with this project. He would also like to thank his wife, Laura, and the rest of his family and friends. Last, but not least, thanks to Paul Murphy for sharing the load of writing this book.

Paul would like to thank Andy Cerio, Marie Cerio, Lorinda Leshock, and Scott Brennan for all their help over the years. He would also like to thank Troy Mott and Michael Moncur.

About the MCSE Exams

Microsoft's MCSE (Microsoft Certified Systems Engineer) program is one of the oldest and most respected computer certifications. The newest program, MCSE Windows 2000, is expected to be equally popular.

You must pass seven exams to attain the MCSE 2000 certification: five required exams and two electives. This volume covers the available choices for required exams and can also be used to satisfy the elective requirements.

This section describes the details of the MCSE certification, summarizes the exams covered in this book, and provides information about the examination process.

The MCSE 2000 Program

The MCSE certification—the subject of this book—is currently the most sought-after credential for network administrators. The Windows 2000 MCSE certification requires passing seven exams: five core requirement exams and two electives.

Required Core Exams

The required core MCSE 2000 exams include the following:

- Exam 70-210, *Installing, Configuring, and Administering Microsoft Windows 2000 Professional*

- Exam 70-215, *Installing, Configuring, and Administering Microsoft Windows 2000 Server*

- Exam 70-217, *Implementing and Administering a Microsoft Windows 2000 Directory Services Infrastructure*

- Exam 70-216, *Implementing and Administering a Microsoft Windows 2000 Network Infrastructure*

This book covers all of these exams. The exams are described in more detail later in this chapter and in their corresponding chapters (Parts 1-4, respectively).

Optional Core Exams

Along with the required core exams listed above, you must choose one additional core exam from the following list:

- Exam 70-219, *Designing a Microsoft Windows 2000 Directory Services Infrastructure*

- Exam 70-221, *Designing a Microsoft Windows 2000 Network Infrastructure*

- Exam 70-220, *Designing Security for a Microsoft Windows 2000 Network*

These exams are covered in Parts 5, 6, and 7 of this book, respectively. After you have taken one of these exams to fulfill the fifth core exam requirement, you can use the remaining two as elective exams if desired.

Elective Exams

Along with the Designing exams covered in the previous section, a wide variety of elective exams is available to fulfill your elective requirements. These include the following:

- Exam 70-085, *Implementing and Supporting Microsoft SNA Server 4.0*

- Exam 70-086, *Implementing and Supporting Microsoft Systems Management Server 2.0*

- Exam 70-019, *Designing and Implementing Data Warehouses with Microsoft SQL Server 7.0*

- Exam 70-229, *Designing and Implementing Databases with Microsoft SQL Server 2000 Enterprise Edition*

- Exam 70-228, *Installing, Configuring, and Administering Microsoft SQL Server 2000 Enterprise Edition*

- Exam 70-056, *Implementing and Supporting Web Sites Using Microsoft Site Server 3.0*

- Exam 70-224, *Installing, Configuring, and Administering Microsoft Exchange 2000 Server*

- Exam 70-088, *Implementing and Supporting Microsoft Proxy Server 2.0*

- Exam 70-227, *Installing, Configuring, and Administering Microsoft Internet Security and Acceleration (ISA) Server 2000*

- Exam 70-080, *Implementing and Supporting Microsoft Internet Explorer 5.0 by Using the Internet Explorer Administration Kit*

- Exam 70-222, *Migrating from Microsoft Windows NT 4.0 to Microsoft Windows 2000*

- Exam 70-223, *Installing, Configuring, and Administering Clustering Services by Using Microsoft Windows 2000 Advanced Server*

- Exam 70-225, *Designing and Deploying a Messaging Infrastructure with Microsoft Exchange 2000 Server*
- Exam 70-226, *Designing Highly Available Web Solutions with Microsoft Windows 2000 Server Technologies*

Note that this is an abbreviated list, because many exams are available for older versions of the software listed here (for example, SQL Server 6.5 and 7.0). However, most of these exams are scheduled to be retired.

MCSE 2000 Core Exams

The MCSE 2000 program requires four core exams plus a fifth exam that can be chosen from the three optional core Designing exams. This book covers all seven of the Designing exams; the Designing exams you do not use as a core exam can be used as electives. The seven Designing exams covered in this book are described in the sections below.

Windows 2000 Professional

Windows 2000 Professional is Microsoft's entry-level version of Windows 2000 and the successor to Windows NT Workstation 4.0. Windows 2000 Professional is designed to work as a standalone workstation or as a network client. It is the same core operating system as Windows 2000 Server, but has a more restrictive license and does not include some of the more advanced features.

MCSE Exam 70-210, *Installing, Configuring, and Administering Microsoft Windows 2000 Professional*, covers basic aspects of Windows 2000 in general and Windows 2000 Professional in particular. Its emphasis is on the use of Windows 2000 Professional as a network client. This exam is covered in Part 1 of this book.

Windows 2000 Server

Microsoft Windows 2000 Server is one of four Windows 2000 operating systems: Windows 2000 Professional, Windows 2000 Server, and two upscale server versions, Windows 2000 Advanced Server and Datacenter Server.

Microsoft's Exam 70-215, *Installing, Configuring, and Administering Microsoft Windows 2000 Server*, will measure your ability to administer Windows 2000 Server primarily as a member server in an Active Directory environment. You will also need to be familiar with using Windows 2000 Server as a file, application, print, and web server.

Active Directory

Windows 2000 simplifies the management of network resources across multiple domains with the introduction of Active Directory. Active Directory creates a hierarchical structure for every resource in the enterprise. Administration of user accounts, files, and printers from all your domains can be easily managed from a single, all-encompassing directory of network resources.

MCSE Exam 70-217, *Implementing and Administering a Microsoft Windows 2000 Directory Services Infrastructure*, will test your knowledge of how to install, configure, and secure an Active Directory environment. This exam is covered in Part 3 of this book.

Network Infrastructure

Windows 2000 includes a wide variety of networking features, some of which are not available in previous versions of Windows NT. MCSE Exam 70-216, *Implementing and Administering a Microsoft Windows 2000 Network Infrastructure*, focuses on the protocols and services used in Windows 2000 networks. This exam is covered in Part 4 of this book.

Designing Active Directory

Microsoft has added the Designing series of exams as a judge of real-world skills in designing, planning, and implementing networks. Exam 70-217, *Implementing and Administering a Microsoft Windows 2000 Directory Services Infrastructure*, covers the design and implementation of Active Directory in Windows 2000 networks. This exam can be used as a fifth core exam or as an elective and is covered in Part 5 of this book.

Designing a Network Infrastructure

If you are a network administrator or consultant, your job can involve planning, analyzing, and designing networks as much as implementing them. This may include choosing protocols and services to use, designing addressing and Internet access schemes, and providing other services, such as remote access.

MCSE Exam 70-221, *Designing a Microsoft Windows 2000 Network Infrastructure*, deals with the high-level design and planning of network protocols and services. This exam can be used as an optional core exam or as an elective and is covered in Part 6 of this book.

Designing Security

A network administrator or consultant's job can often involve planning, analyzing, and designing networks. Security should be a major consideration in any network design.

MCSE Exam 70-220, *Designing Security for a Microsoft Windows 2000 Network*, deals with the design and planning of network security services and protocols. This exam can be used as an optional core exam or as an elective; it is covered in Part 7 of this book.

The Examination Process

All of the MCSE exams are similar in format, and a certain amount of preparation will help you pass any of them. The following sections look at ways to prepare for the exams and the actual process of taking the exams.

Notes About the Windows NT 4.0 MCSE Track

Because the Windows 2000 MCSE program is new, a few notes about the previous Windows NT 4.0 exams are in order. The previous program required a total of six exams, consisting of four core exams and two electives. Although the first two exams, Windows NT Workstation and Windows NT Server, are roughly equivalent to the Windows 2000 Professional and Windows 2000 Server exams, the rest of the exams have changed significantly.

Microsoft has retired all of the NT 4.0 exams effective December 31, 2000. If you are already certified as an MCSE under the NT 4.0 track, you have until December 31, 2001, to upgrade to the Windows 2000 track or lose your certification.

To make upgrading your certification easier, Microsoft has released Exam 70-240, *Microsoft Windows 2000 Accelerated Exam for MCPs Certified on Microsoft Windows NT 4.0*. This single exam is equivalent to the four required Windows 2000 core exams.

This accelerated exam is only available to candidates who've passed the three core Windows NT exams (Windows NT Workstation, Windows NT Server, and Windows NT Server in the Enterprise). It's available only through December 31, 2001.

ON THE EXAM

The single most important change from the NT 4.0 to Windows 2000 MCSE tracks is that Microsoft now expects you to have at least one year of hands-on experience in order to pass an exam. Although it was possible to attain a "paper MCSE" certification for NT 4.0 by studying books and other documentation, you absolutely need real-world experience with Windows 2000 to complete this certification.

Preparing for Exams

The exams currently cost $100 apiece to take, and the cost applies whether you pass or fail. Thus, it's a good idea to prepare as thoroughly as possible before attempting to take an exam. It's best to concentrate on a single exam at a time.

This book will obviously be helpful in preparing for the MCSE exams. Depending on your understanding of the subject matter, it may be useful to study other materials. Microsoft's documentation, such as the Windows NT Resource Kits, the online books, and the help files included with various utilities, may be helpful.

It is also very important to have real-world experience with the items covered in each exam. It's nearly impossible to pass a Microsoft exam just by studying. You should have access to a network with a minimum of two Windows NT computers to experiment with, and access to a larger network would be even more useful.

A number of free practice exams are available, including the PEP tests free for download from Microsoft at *http://www.microsoft.com/train_cert/*. These are not comprehensive and may not cover all of the exam topics, but can be a good meter on which to test your preparedness. Commercial tests are available from several third-party companies. A practice test is also included in each of the parts of this book.

Scheduling and Payment

Microsoft's exams are administered by Sylvan Prometric and Virtual University Enterprises (VUE). Call (800) 755-3926 to schedule an exam with Sylvan Prometric. Online registration is also available at the Prometric web site (*http://www.prometric.com*). For information about registering with VUE and online registration, see their web site *http://www.vue.com/ms/*. You can register entirely over the phone with a credit card. If you pay by check, you must first mail the check to the testing provider, then call to schedule the exam. Call for the address to which you should send payments.

Your registration ID is your social security number or, if you are outside the U.S., a number assigned by the testing provider. Use this number in all communications with the testing provider and write it on any checks you send.

You usually need to schedule an exam at least 24 hours in advance. After you've scheduled an exam, you must call 24 hours before the scheduled time if you wish to cancel or reschedule.

How the Exams Work

You take the exams at a local testing center. The tests are administered by computer. Most of the answers are multiple-choice, but many are complex and include detailed scenarios and diagrams. Some of the newer exams include simulation questions, requiring you to perform a task with a simulated utility.

Microsoft now offers some of the MCSE tests as adaptive tests. Adaptive testing uses a computer program to analyze your responses and to choose the remaining questions. An adaptive test may ask progressively more difficult questions in an area to determine your level of expertise, or progressively easier questions to determine where your knowledge level lies.

With a standard test, you are given a set time limit for the test (usually 1.5 hours) and must answer a number of questions (between 40 and 100). You can mark questions to return to later if you're not sure of the answers. Adaptive tests have a smaller number of questions (typically 15–30), with the exact amount depending on your responses. Adaptive tests do not allow reviewing of past answers, and they have a shorter time limit.

Many of the core and elective NT 4.0 MCSE exams are now available in adaptive versions. However, Microsoft does not officially announce which tests are adaptive, and you should be prepared for either a standard or adaptive version of any test you take.

When you are finished with an exam, you receive a passing or a failing score. Each exam has its own passing percentage, between 60% and 85%.

The questions generally fall into several categories. Their descriptions follow:

Single answer

These are basic multiple-choice questions requiring a single answer and are generally the easiest. Here is an example:

1. How many nodes can be used on a single segment in an Ethernet 10Base2 network?

    a.   1

    b.   32

    c.   30

    d.   90

Answer: c

These questions often address facts and figures included in the exam objectives. Although these are relatively easy questions, many of them are worded to be confusing or to encourage jumping to conclusions. Be sure to read the questions carefully and double-check your answers.

Multiple answer

These are multiple-choice questions where one or more of the answers is correct, and you must choose all that apply. The following is an example:

1. Which network connectivity devices operate at the physical layer of the OSI model? (Select all that apply.)

    a.   Hubs

    b.   Routers

    c.   Transceivers

    d.   Repeaters

Answer: a, c, d

These questions can be tricky. Although they often address the same type of definitions and facts as the simpler questions, the multiple answers increase the possibility of mistakes. In addition, these questions often describe a network and ask you to answer questions based on its configuration.

Rather than look for one or more obvious answers to these questions, you may find it useful to consider them as a series of true/false questions, evaluating each of the possible choices separately. Otherwise, it's easy to overlook a correct answer.

Be sure to read these questions carefully. Many of them explicitly state the number of correct answers, such as "Select two answers." If you mark the incorrect number of items, the answer is considered incorrect.

Scenario

These questions present a scenario about a need or problem and the steps taken to resolve it. You have to determine whether the solution meets the required result or the optional results. Here is a sample of this type of question.

1. You are installing a network in a training room, to be used temporarily for a period of 30 days. You must connect 10 workstations running Windows NT Workstation and 2 servers running Windows NT Server.

   Required Result: The network must have a transmission speed of 10 Mbps or higher.

   Optional Result: The network should be inexpensive.

   Optional Result: The network should be easy to install.

   Solution: Install 10Base2 Ethernet in a bus topology.

   a. The solution meets the required result and both of the optional results.

   b. The solution meets the required result and only one of the optional results.

   c. The solution meets the required result only.

   d. The solution does not meet the required result.

   Answer: a

These are the most complex questions and can be difficult. They present a complex scenario that you will need to analyze and understand before you answer the question.

As with the multiple answer questions, these are best regarded as a series of true/ false questions. Analyze the scenario and the proposed solution, then compare the required result and the optional results to see which ones are satisfied.

Be sure to double-check your answers to these questions—not only to check your work, but also to ensure you've selected the choice that matches the appropriate set of results.

It is also helpful to look for key phrases in these questions. For example, the question above mentions that the network is temporary, and one of Ethernet 10Base2's strong points is that it can be quickly set up and taken down. The 10-Mbps transmission speed mentioned in the required result is also an indication that Ethernet is the correct choice.

Most of these questions come in sets of two or more questions using the same scenario and different proposed solutions. You may find it helpful to examine all of the questions for a scenario before answering them.

Simulation questions

Some of the newest exams include simulation questions. These provide a simulated version of a utility and require you to perform a task (for example: create a user or copy a file). Simpler simulations show a dialog from a utility and ask you to click the appropriate button for a particular function.

These questions should be easy if you are experienced with the exam's subjects. You cannot mark these questions to return to them later, so be careful to perform the task correctly the first time.

Select and Place, Create a Tree

These new exam types are exclusive to the Windows 2000 exams. They require you to drag and drop items into a list in the correct order or configuration. Like simulation questions, they cannot be returned to later, so answer them carefully.

Many of these questions, as well as multiple-choice questions, are based on *case studies*, extended examples and details about network configurations. Often a number of questions are based on the same case study.

Test-Taking Tips

It's best to study and prepare for one test at a time. Schedule the test on a day when you won't be under stress because of your job or other factors, and give yourself plenty of time to study for the test. Rest well the night before and review your test-preparation materials (such as this book) one last time before taking the test.

Use test-preparation software, or have someone ask you questions, to be sure you're prepared for the test. Don't be satisfied if you merely know 95% of the topics the exam covers. As few as 5–10 incorrect answers can lead to a failing score, and you will make mistakes.

Because the MCSE exams are timed, pacing is important for success. Non-adaptive tests include Forward and Back buttons to review the questions and change your answers if necessary; in addition, you can check a box to highlight a question for later review.

Using these tools, you will find that a good strategy is to first review all of the questions, answering those you are sure of. Then take a second pass through the questions, answering all you can. Mark the questions that you may be able to answer with more time.

The exam scoring process does not deduct points for wrong answers, so it's beneficial to guess rather than leaving an answer blank. You can usually eliminate some of the choices to make your guess more educated. Be aware of the time limit and set aside the last 5–10 minutes to double-check your answers and guess if necessary.

Adaptive tests are more difficult, and to pass these tests it is important that you know all of the exam's topics. If you know someone who has passed the test, don't expect the same questions on your test—even standard tests vary, and adaptive tests will be unique for each individual who takes them.

Don't let the scenario questions take too much of your time—remember, they count for the same score as the other types of questions. On standard tests, you may wish to mark these and come back to them later.

You may not bring any material (papers, calculators, books, etc.) into the exam room with you. However, you are provided with a writing surface. If you have memorized critical items for the test, it may be helpful to write these down when you enter the testing room for reference during the exam.

If you should fail a test, ask the test administrator for a detailed report. This lists the topics of the questions you missed and will be useful for further study. In addition, write down the questions you remember having trouble with so you can study those areas more carefully. You are allowed to repeat an exam as many times as necessary, although you will need to pay each time.

Continuing Education

To maintain your MCSE certification, you must continue to meet the MCSE requirements as Microsoft updates them. Existing exams are often retired or replaced with new versions, and exams for new products are added.

Retired Exams

Microsoft usually retires (discontinues) an exam when the product it refers to becomes obsolete or is replaced by a new version. For example, the Windows NT 3.51 exams were retired in June 2000. The NT 4.0 exams were retired on December 31, 2000.

When one of the exams you took for the MCSE is retired, you are given time (usually six months to a year) to take a new exam to keep your certification. This can be the exam for a new version of the same product or another exam in the same category (i.e., elective exam). For the NT 4.0 exams, you have until December 31, 2001, to upgrade to the Windows 2000 certification, and you can take the accelerated exam to replace the four required core Windows 2000 exams.

When you need to take the new version of an exam to replace a retired exam, Microsoft usually offers a 50% discount if you take the new exam within 6 months.

New Exams

Microsoft periodically releases new exams. These may cover new products or new versions of old products. Microsoft may require that new exams be taken for MCSEs to retain their certification status.

If you take a new version of an exam you passed the previous version of within 3 months after the new version is released, you are given a 50% discount on the price.

Beta Exams

When a new exam is first developed, it is offered as a beta exam. These exams are available for 50% of the normal price. They include a large list of questions; after the beta period, some of these questions will be compiled into the real exam. Beta exams do not usually use adaptive testing.

You receive credit for passing a beta exam, but you don't receive the results immediately; they are sent to you by mail after the beta period ends. Microsoft uses the results to develop the scoring to be used in the final version of the exam.

Recently, Microsoft has changed their beta program so that only a select number of candidates, chosen by Microsoft, can take beta exams. You cannot take most beta exams unless you have been explicitly invited.

PART 1

Windows 2000 Professional

Exam Overview

Windows 2000 Professional is Microsoft's entry-level version of Windows 2000 and the successor to Windows NT Workstation 4.0. Windows 2000 Professional is designed to work as a standalone workstation or as a network client. It is the same core operating system as Windows 2000 Server, but has a more restrictive license and does not include some of the more advanced features.

MCSE Exam 70-210, *Installing, Configuring, and Administering Microsoft Windows 2000 Professional*, covers basic aspects of Windows 2000 in general and Windows 2000 Professional in particular. Its emphasis is on the use of Windows 2000 Professional as a network client.

This is the first required MCSE exam for the Windows 2000 track and should be the first exam you take. In particular, the Windows 2000 Server exam, covered in Part 2 of this book, builds on the foundation of the Windows 2000 Professional curriculum.

There is some overlap in Microsoft's objectives between the Windows 2000 Professional and Windows 2000 Server exams; therefore, we recommend that you make at least a cursory study of Part 2, *Windows 2000 Server*, before taking the Professional MCSE exam.

To prepare for this chapter and the Windows 2000 Professional exam, you should have a basic familiarity with computers and with PC-compatibles in particular and have experience managing Windows 2000 Server in a small network.

Areas of Study

Windows 2000 Basics

Need to Know	Reference
Basic computer and network terminology	"Terminology" on page 18
History of Windows 2000 and other operating systems	"Operating Systems" on page 19

13

Need to Know	*Reference*
Differences between client/server and peer-to-peer networks	"Networking Basics" on page 22
Steps in the Windows 2000 boot process	"The Boot Process" on page 23

Need to Apply	*Reference*
Modify BOOT.INI options	"The BOOT.INI file" on page 24
Log on to Windows 2000 and perform basic functions	"Using Windows 2000" on page 27

Installing Windows 2000 Professional

Need to Know	*Reference*
Windows 2000 Professional hardware requirements	"Hardware requirements" on page 28
Filesystems supported by Windows 2000	"Disk partitions" on page 29
Phases of the Windows 2000 installation	"Performing the Installation" on page 30

Need to Apply	*Reference*
Install Windows 2000 Professional	"Performing the Installation" on page 30
Check hardware compatibility before upgrading	"Checking hardware compatibility" on page 32
Upgrade Windows 95/98 to Windows 2000	"Upgrading from Windows 95/98/Me" on page 33
Upgrade Windows NT to Windows 2000	"Upgrading from Windows NT" on page 33
Install service packs during or after installation	"Using Service Packs" on page 36

Configuring Windows 2000 Professional

Need to Know	*Reference*
Control panel applets and their purposes	"Control Panel" on page 40
Registry subtrees and their primary functions	"The Registry" on page 42

Need to Apply	*Reference*
Use MMC to manage Windows 2000 and manage snap-ins within MMC	"Microsoft Management Console (MMC)" on page 37
Schedule tasks for system maintenance	"Task Scheduler" on page 38
Modify settings using the Control Panel	"Control Panel" on page 40
Edit the registry	"Registry editors" on page 43

Managing Disk Storage

Need to Know	Reference
Differences between basic and dynamic disks	"Basic Disks" on page 47
Components of dynamic disks	"Dynamic Disks" on page 48
Backup methods	"Backing up files" on page 53

Need to Apply	Reference
Partition and format basic disks	"Partitioning" on page 49
Create dynamic disk volumes	"Disk Management" on page 49
Convert disks and partitions from basic to dynamic storage	"Converting basic to dynamic storage" on page 50
Defragment NTFS and FAT partitions	"Defragmenting disks" on page 51
Set and monitor disk quotas	"Disk Quotas" on page 52
Encrypt and decrypt files on an NTFS volume	"EFS (Encrypted Filesystem)" on page 52
Back up and restore files	"Managing Backups" on page 53
Schedule regular backups	"Scheduling backups" on page 55

Managing Network Components

Need to Know	Reference
TCP/IP basics and IP addressing	"TCP/IP" on page 55
Other common protocols supported by Windows 2000	"Other Protocols" on page 57
Basic Active Directory concepts and terminology	"Active Directory" on page 58

Need to Apply	Reference
Configure network protocol settings	"Managing Network Components" on page 55
Configure TCP/IP settings	"Managing TCP/IP" on page 57

Administration and Security

Need to Know	Reference
Default Windows 2000 Professional users and groups	"Default users and groups" on page 62
NTFS security permissions	"NTFS Security" on page 65
Windows 2000 printer terminology	"Managing Printers" on page 68

Need to Apply	Reference
Configure account policies, security options, and auditing	"Security Policies" on page 64

Need to Apply	Reference
Share files and set permissions	"File Sharing" on page 66
Monitor use of shared files	"Monitoring Users and Shares" on page 67
Install printers	"Monitoring Users and Shares" on page 67
Configure print pools	"Print pools" on page 69
Schedule and prioritize print jobs	"Scheduling and priorities" on page 69
Pause, resume, and delete print jobs	"Managing print jobs" on page 69

Optimization and Troubleshooting

Need to Know	Reference
Common performance counter objects	"Performance Console" on page 70
Purpose of system, application, and security logs	"Event Viewer" on page 70
Boot menu options and their purposes	"Boot options" on page 71

Need to Apply	Reference
Monitor system performance	"Performance Console" on page 70
View error messages and audit results	"Event Viewer" on page 70
Troubleshoot problems with the boot process	"Troubleshooting Boot Problems" on page 71

Study Guide

This chapter includes the following sections, which address various topics covered on the Windows 2000 Professional MCSE exam:

Windows 2000 Basics

Describes Windows 2000 and compares it with other Microsoft operating systems. Windows 2000's architecture and boot process are described in detail. This section also covers the basics of using Windows 2000 and the basics of networking.

Installing Windows 2000 Professional

Discusses the planning necessary before installing Windows 2000 Professional, installation methods, and the installation process. This section also describes methods of automating the installation.

Configuring Windows 2000 Professional

Introduces essential Windows 2000 management tools, such as Microsoft Management Console and the Control Panel. This section also describes configuration tasks for hardware devices, power management, and mobile systems.

Managing Disk Storage

Discusses the possible disk configurations, how to implement and manage them, and disk management tools. Disk compression, disk quotas, encryption, and backup methods are also covered.

Managing Network Components

Discusses the network protocols, services, and other components used with Windows 2000, including methods of remote access and the basics of the Active Directory.

Administration and Security

Describes how to manage users, groups, policies, and other aspects of Windows 2000 access control and security. This section also discusses file sharing, printer management, and network auditing.

Optimization and Troubleshooting
Describes several useful utilities for monitoring the performance of Windows 2000 and optimizing performance. Typical troubleshooting procedures are described, along with solutions to common problems.

Windows 2000 Basics

For years, Windows NT (New Technology) was Microsoft's premier operating system for businesses and networks. Windows 2000, released in early 2000, is the latest version of this operating system, replacing Windows NT 4.0.

This section compares Windows 2000 with other Microsoft operating systems and provides basic information about Windows 2000 architecture, networking, and operating system features.

Terminology

The following terms relating to operating systems will be useful in understanding the remainder of this section:

Cooperative multitasking
A system for allowing multiple applications to execute at the same time in an operating system. Applications must cooperate, periodically giving up control of the processor for use by other applications.

Memory protection
A feature that prevents applications from accessing memory belonging to other applications or the operating system itself. Windows NT and Windows 2000 provide a greater degree of memory protection than previous versions.

Multiprocessing
The ability of an operating system to use multiple processors (CPUs) in a computer at the same time. Windows NT and Windows 2000 are the only Windows versions that support multiprocessing.

Multithreading
The ability of an operating system to allow multiple functions (threads) within an application to execute at the same time. In a multiprocessor system, these may be executed on different processors.

Plug and Play
A Microsoft specification for hardware devices and operating systems that support automatic hardware configuration, preventing the need for manual assignment of IRQs, I/O addresses, and other settings. Windows 95, Windows 98, Windows Me, and Windows 2000 support Plug and Play.

Preemptive multitasking
A system for allowing multiple applications to execute at the same time in an operating system. Unlike cooperative multitasking, preemptive systems are able to divide processor time between all applications, regardless of the application's behavior.

> **ON THE EXAM**
>
> You should know all of these terms for the Windows 2000 Professional MCSE exam and understand which Windows versions they apply to (described in the next section).

Operating Systems

Microsoft has released a variety of operating systems over the years, ranging from DOS to Windows 2000. These are summarized in Table 1-1, and the latest ones are described in the following sections.

> **ON THE EXAM**
>
> For the most part, Microsoft's operating systems are backward compatible. Windows 2000 can run 32-bit (Windows 95/98/Me) Windows applications, 16-bit (Windows 3.1x) applications, and DOS applications. However, there may be incompatibilities with programs that require specific device drivers or attempt to access hardware directly.

Table 1-1: Operating System Requirements and Key Features

Operating System	RAM	Disk Storage Required	Multi-tasking?	Multi-processing?	Plug and Play?
DOS	256K	None	No	No	No
Windows 3.1x	2 MB	10 MB	Cooperative	No	No
Windows 95	4 MB	40 MB	Preemptive	No	Yes
Windows 98	16 MB	175 MB	Preemptive	No	Yes
Windows Me	32 MB	480 MB	Preemptive	No	Yes
Windows NT Workstation 4.0	12 MB	117 MB	Preemptive (protected)	Yes (two processors)	No
Windows NT Server 4.0	16 MB	124 MB	Preemptive (protected)	Yes	No
Windows 2000 Professional	32 MB	650 MB	Preemptive (protected)	Yes	Yes
Windows 2000 Server	64 MB	671 MB	Preemptive (protected)	Yes	Yes

Windows 3.1x

Windows 3.1 was the first version of Windows to gain widespread popularity and was the first with specific support for Intel's 16-bit 80386 processor. Two additional versions were released: 3.11, a version with minor corrections, and Windows for Workgroups, a version with support for workgroup networking.

Windows 3.1x is a 16-bit operating system with support for cooperative multitasking. It runs as a shell on top of DOS and requires DOS to run.

Windows 95/98/Me

Windows 98, released in August 1998, is the successor to Windows 95, Microsoft's original 32-bit consumer operating system. Windows 98, like Windows 95, is a 32-bit operating system that supports DOS, 16-bit Windows, and 32-bit Windows applications. Windows 95 and 98 are popular for standalone desktop machines and as network clients for Windows NT or other networks. A built-in peer-to-peer network system allows simple networks to be constructed using only Windows 95 or 98.

Windows 95 improved upon Windows 3.11 with greater stability, better multitasking, support for 32-bit applications, support for long filenames, more customization options, a versatile desktop and file management system, and built-in dial-up networking support.

Windows 98 updated Windows 95 with support for new hardware, including USB and FireWire (IEEE 1394); an improved installation program; support for a number of new network protocols; and improved utilities for configuration and troubleshooting.

A later release, Windows 98 Second Edition (SE), added a number of features to Windows 98. Among the improvements were Internet Connection Sharing (ICS), improved support for hardware, and improved VPN support.

Windows Me (Millenium Edition) was released in August 2000. Windows Me is a minor update to Windows 98 that includes support for the latest hardware, improved recovery from crashes, and Internet Explorer 5.5.

Windows NT

Up to Version 4.0, Windows NT was Microsoft's business-oriented operating system. Windows NT is a 32-bit operating system that supports preemptive multitasking with memory protection, multiprocessing, and multithreading. Windows NT was designed for networking and is generally more reliable than previous Windows versions.

Windows NT 3.51 and earlier versions used the same user interface as Windows 3.1x, but Version 4.0 used the newer Windows 95/98 interface. Unlike Windows 98, NT 4.0 does not support the Plug and Play specification.

Windows 2000 Professional

Windows 2000 Professional is the base version of Windows 2000 and is thus equivalent in purpose to the previous Windows NT Workstation. Windows 2000 Professional uses an updated version of the Windows 98-style user interface; most of these updates were integrated into Windows Me.

Windows 2000 improves on Windows NT 4.0 with some features similar to Windows 98, including Plug and Play and support for the Advanced Power Management (APM) and Advanced Configuration and Power Interface (ACPI) power-management standards. Windows 2000 supports multiprocessing with up to two processors.

Windows 2000 also adds support for the Active Directory, Microsoft's new directory services architecture. Windows 2000 Professional can act as an Active Directory client, but does not maintain a directory services database; Windows 2000 Server is required for this purpose.

Other new features include user interface improvements; additional hardware support, including support for USB and FireWire; support for virtual private networks (VPNs); the Internet Printing Protocol (IPP); and support for Encrypted Filesystem (EFS). Windows 2000 also supports the FAT32 filesystem that originated in Windows 98.

ON THE EXAM

For the Windows 2000 Professional MCSE exam, you should be familiar with the new features of Windows 2000 and the differences between Windows 2000 Professional and Windows 2000 Server.

Windows 2000 Server

As with Windows NT Server, Windows 2000 Server improves on Windows 2000 Professional with support for unlimited Internet connections and support for multiprocessing with four processors (Windows 2000 Professional supports only two processors).

Additionally, Windows 2000 Server supports the Active Directory service and includes server software for DNS (Domain Name Service), DHCP (Dynamic Host Configuration Protocol), and other services.

Windows 2000 Server is further extended by two premium versions: Windows 2000 Advanced Server, which supports up to 8 processors and 2-way clustering; and Windows 2000 Datacenter Server, which supports up to 16 processors and 8-way clustering.

ON THE EXAM

Clustering allows two or more Windows 2000 Server computers to run a single clustered application, providing improved server performance and reliability. Clustering is not covered on the Windows 2000 Professional MCSE exam; it is covered in Part 2.

Networking Basics

There are two basic types of networks: server-based networks, which use dedicated servers; and peer-to-peer networks, which share files between workstations. These are explained in the following sections.

Server-based networks

Server-based networks, also called *client/server networks*, use a dedicated computer called a *server*. Files, printers, and other resources and services on this computer are made available to network workstations, called *clients*. Client machines are simply used by network users and usually do not share files or printers.

Windows 2000 Server is typically used as a server operating system for this type of network. Windows 2000's security model for server-based networks is called the *domain model*. Servers are organized into domains, with one or more computers (the domain controllers) providing centralized authentication.

Peer-to-peer networks

A peer-to-peer network (sometimes simply called a peer network) consists solely of workstations called *peers*. Each workstation can be operated by a user and can also make shared files or printers available to users at other workstations. This system is best suited to smaller networks. Microsoft's term for peer-to-peer networks is *workgroups*.

A workgroup configuration can be used for networks consisting solely of Windows 2000 Professional computers. For a server-based network, one or more computers running Windows 2000 Server are required.

The main disadvantage of a workgroup network is the lack of central control. Each user controls access to their own workstation's shared files and printers. In a large network, this is difficult to manage without compromising security. A workstation that is being accessed by peers can also be slowed down, inconveniencing the user at the workstation.

The advantages of workgroups include their ease of installation and ease of use. They are also less expensive than server-based networks, because a dedicated server is not required. If users are able to manage resource sharing, an administrator may not be required.

ON THE EXAM

Microsoft generally draws the line between peer-to-peer networks and client/server networks at 10 workstations. Exam questions that ask which type of network should be used in a given situation are often easily answered based on the number of users. Be sure to take other factors, such as network growth, security, and administration, into account.

Computer types

In a workgroup network, all of the computers are the same type: peers, also called clients. In a domain-based Windows 2000 network, several different types of computers are typically included:

Domain controllers

> These computers run Windows 2000 Server. Each domain controller maintains a copy of the user account database (Active Directory). Multiple controllers synchronize periodically to maintain the same Directory.

Member servers

> These computers run Windows 2000 Server, but are not configured as domain controllers. Member servers do not maintain a copy of the Directory database, but can share files, printers, and other resources.

Clients

> Clients typically run Windows 2000 Professional or another operating system, such as Windows 95/98/Me or NT Workstation. These computers can log in to the domain and are allowed access to its resources.

ON THE EXAM

Although you should be familiar with these types of computers, for the Windows 2000 Professional MCSE exam you will be dealing strictly with client or peer computers running Windows 2000 Professional.

The Boot Process

As with other PC-based operating systems, the Windows 2000 OS is stored on disk and loaded each time the computer is booted. Windows 2000's boot process is similar to that of Windows NT and more complex than that of earlier versions of Windows. The following are the processes involved when Windows 2000 boots on an Intel-based computer:

1. The computer performs a pre-boot sequence. This includes the Power-On Self Test (or POST) in which the computer determines if the minimum hardware required to boot (video adapter, RAM, and a keyboard) is present. The computer also detects the floppy disk drives, hard disk drives, and (in newer computers) CD-ROM drives from which it can boot. It then selects a boot device (usually the hard disk) according to its stored preferences.

2. The computer's BIOS (in ROM) reads the master boot record (MBR) from the hard disk. The MBR, in turn, loads the boot sector on the default partition. This contains the OS loader, NTLDR. If a SCSI controller without its own BIOS is in use, a driver is loaded from the NTBOOTDD.SYS file at this point.

3. NTLDR switches the processor to 32-bit (enhanced) mode, then loads a mini-filesystem driver to access NTFS or FAT partitions.

4. NTLDR reads the BOOT.INI file and displays a menu of available operating systems. Configuring this file is described in the installation section of this chapter.

5. If DOS or a previous version of Windows was chosen, a DOS boot sector is read from the BOOTSECT.DOS file and executed. Otherwise, Windows 2000 begins to load.

6. NTLDR calls NTDETECT.COM. This program tests and detects some of the computer's hardware, and displays an error message if any hardware problems are found.

7. If more than one hardware profile has been configured, NTLDR displays a menu of available profiles. Otherwise, the default profile is used.

8. NTLDR then transfers control to NTOSKRNL.EXE, the Windows NT kernel. Once the kernel starts, the screen changes from black to blue. A module that handles the hardware abstraction layer, HAL.DLL, is loaded by the kernel.

9. The kernel initializes by creating the HKEY_LOCAL_MACHINE\HARDWARE registry subkey, based on the NTDETECT results. It then copies the current control set (described later in this chapter) to the HKEY_LOCAL_MACHINE\ SYSTEM\Select subkey.

10. The kernel then loads low-level device drivers and filesystems. Once the kernel has started all the drivers, the user-mode subsystem and GUI are started. The screen changes to a graphical display with a slate-blue screen.

11. The kernel then begins the services start phase, where the system services are loaded. After the Winlogon service starts, the logon screen is displayed.

The boot process uses two special disk partitions, referred to as the *boot partition* and the *system partition*. These may be (and typically are) the same volume. These names are misleading: the boot files used in steps 1–4 above are stored in the root directory of the system partition, and NTOSKRNL.EXE and other operating system files are stored on the boot partition. Table 1-2 summarizes the files found on each of these partitions.

Table 1-2: Files Contained in the Boot and System Partitions

System Partition	Boot Partition
NTBOOTDD.SYS	NTOSKRNL.EXE
NTLDR	HAL.DLL
BOOT.INI	\WINNT files
BOOTSECT.DOS	
NTDETECT.COM	

The BOOT.INI file

The entries in the boot menu displayed at startup are based on the BOOT.INI file, located in the root directory of the system partition. A typical Windows 2000 Professional BOOT.INI file, including a dual-boot entry for MS-DOS, looks like this:

```
[boot loader]
timeout=30
default=multi(0)disk(0)rdisk(0)partition(1)\WINNT
[operating systems]
multi(0)disk(0)rdisk(0)partition(1)\WINNT="Windows 2000" /fastdetect
C:\="MS-DOS"
```

ON THE EXAM

The BOOT.INI file has the Hidden, Read-only, and System attributes by default, and cannot be edited. Use `attrib -s -r -h boot.ini` from the command line to remove these attributes. You can reset the attributes after editing, although this is unnecessary.

The file consists of the [boot loader] section with information about defaults, followed by the [operating systems] section with individual entries for each operating system.

The [boot loader] section can include two entries:

timeout
> The number of seconds before the default OS will be selected. A timeout of 0 causes the default OS to boot immediately; a timeout of –1 causes the boot loader to wait indefinitely for a selection.

default
> An entry in the same format as the OS entries below for the default OS.

The entries in the [operating systems] section can include bootable FAT partitions (such as C:\ in the example) for DOS or earlier versions of Windows and Advanced RISC Computing (ARC) entries for Windows NT or Windows 2000. ARC is a standard also used for booting other operating systems on RISC machines. ARC entries use the following format:

> `adapter(x)disk(x)rdisk(x)partition(x)\directory = description`

adapter
> Specifies the disk controller the boot volume is attached to. This value is always either `multi(x)` or `scsi(x)`. The `multi` keyword is used for most disks, including IDE and most SCSI drives; the `scsi` keyword is used strictly for SCSI controllers without a built-in BIOS. The value in parentheses is an index assigned to the controller. Controllers are typically numbered from highest to lowest IRQ assignment.

disk
> For `scsi` entries, indicates the boot drive's SCSI ID number. For `multi` entries, this value is unused and should be set to 0.

rdisk
> For `multi` entries, specifies the SCSI ID or IDE unit number of the boot drive. This entry is unused with `scsi` entries and should be set to 0.

partition
> Specifies the partition within the hard disk. Partitions are numbered sequentially from 1.

directory
> Specifies the path within the boot partition for the system files. This is typically \WINNT for Windows NT or Windows 2000.

description
> Describes the operating system corresponding with the boot entry. These descriptions are displayed in the boot loader menu.

ON THE EXAM

You should know what each field in an ARC path refers to for the Windows 2000 Professional exam. You may be expected to identify the purpose of a particular ARC entry or to describe how to change one to correspond with a change in hardware configuration.

ARC entries for Windows 2000 can be followed by one or more of these options:

/basevideo
> This and the following options can be used after an OS entry. This option forces Windows NT to use VGA mode instead of the defined video driver. The VGA mode entry in the default BOOT.INI file uses this option.

/fastdetect=ports
> Disables scanning for a serial mouse on the COM ports specified. This scan can delay booting and can cause some UPS systems to shut down. This option replaces the /noserialmice option in Windows NT 4.0 and is enabled by default in Windows 2000.

/maxmem:number
> Limits the amount of memory visible to Windows 2000 to the specified number of bytes.

/noguiboot
> Disables the graphical boot status screen.

/sos
> Specifies verbose mode for device drivers.

ON THE EXAM

You should be familiar with all of these options and their uses for the Windows 2000 Professional exam, especially the commonly used /fastdetect option.

Using Windows 2000

Windows 2000's basic user interface is similar to that of Windows 95/98/Me, but various utilities for managing the system are similar to those of earlier versions of Windows NT. Some basics of using Windows 2000 Professional are described in the following sections.

The Logon dialog

The Logon dialog is displayed at the completion of the boot process. This dialog includes fields for username and password and an option to use a dial-up connection. If the computer is configured as a domain client, you can choose the domain to log on to.

The desktop

As with Windows NT 4.0, the initial Windows 2000 display includes a desktop with various icons. The My Computer icon provides access to the computer's disk drives through the Windows NT Explorer, and the Start menu allows access to installed applications.

ON THE EXAM

New to Windows 2000 is a Start menu that can be rearranged with drag-and-drop, similar to Windows 98. The Start menu also automatically hides seldom-used applications and places frequently used applications at the top of lists; this feature is also present in Windows Me.

You can configure options for Windows 2000's Start menu by right-clicking the taskbar and selecting *Properties*. In this dialog you can enable or disable the personalized menus. In addition, you can choose to have the *Control Panel* and *Documents* options in the Start menu expand into submenus.

The My Network Places icon, similar to the Network Neighborhood icon in NT 4.0, displays a list of commonly accessed network locations. You can browse the entire network with the Entire Network icon or browse the local workgroup or domain with the Computers Near Me icon.

Management utilities

Windows 2000 includes a variety of utilities for managing operating system features. The following are some of the most commonly used utilities, all of which are explained in detail later in this chapter:

Microsoft Management Console (MMC)
  A utility that consolidates the functions of many previous Windows NT management utilities. You can access disks, log files, services, applications, and performance monitoring from MMC consoles.

Control Panel

As in Windows NT 4.0, the Control Panel contains a number of applets that you can use to manage various components of the computer.

Task Scheduler

A new Windows 2000 utility that lets you schedule regular maintenance tasks.

Registry Editor

Allows you to display and modify the registry, a database used by Windows 2000 to store settings relating to hardware, the operating system, and applications.

Installing Windows 2000 Professional

Windows 2000's installation process is largely automated and relatively simple and includes a number of improvements over previous versions of Windows NT. This section examines the Windows 2000 installation process, from simple installations to large-scale automated installations.

Planning the Installation

Before installing Windows 2000 Professional on a computer, you should determine the computer's compatibility with Windows 2000. You should also have an idea of the type of network and filesystems that will be used and the method of installation. These considerations are discussed in the sections that follow.

Hardware requirements

Before installing Windows 2000 Professional, be sure the computer meets the minimum hardware requirements. You should also consider the requirements of your users and network in selecting a machine. The minimum and recommended hardware for Windows 2000 Professional on Intel-based computers are described in Table 1-3.

Table 1-3: Windows 2000 Professional Requirements

Item	Minimum	Recommended
CPU	Pentium 133 MHz	Pentium 200 MHz or faster
RAM	32 MB	64 MB or more
Display	VGA	Super VGA or better
Hard disk	SCSI or IDE; 650 MB of space required for OS	2 GB or more
CD-ROM	SCSI or IDE (not required for network installations)	12X speed or faster
Network interface card	Not required	Any supported by NT; only required for network access

There are more specific requirements for each of these devices: for example, certain CD-ROM drives or video adapters may not be supported by Windows 2000.

Each version of Windows 2000 includes a hardware compatibility list (HCL) that describes hardware that has been tested and verified to work with that version.

The HCL is included on the Windows 2000 Professional CD-ROM as HCL.TXT in the \SUPPORT directory. An updated version is always available from Microsoft's web or FTP sites.

ON THE EXAM

Windows 2000 Professional's hardware requirements are a common subject for MCSE test questions. Be sure you know all of the previously mentioned information and know where to access the HCL for specific information.

Disk partitions

Windows NT can be installed in a FAT, FAT32, or NTFS partition. The installation program is able to create either of these if there is empty space available on a hard disk. If you have existing partitions on the disk, you can delete them from the installation program. You can also choose to install in an existing partition; this may overwrite data in the partition.

Another factor in planning Windows NT installations is the filesystem or filesystems to be used. Windows 2000 supports three different filesystems:

FAT (file allocation table)
> The filesystem originally implemented by DOS. It is limited to 8-character filenames with 3-character extensions and supports partitions up to 2 GB (Windows 95/98/Me) or up to 16 GB (Windows NT 4.0/2000).

FAT32
> A new version of the FAT system implemented by Windows 95 (OSR2 and later), Windows 98, and Windows Me. This system is not backward compatible with FAT. It provides more reliable storage and more efficient use of space and raises the partition size limit to 4 TB (terabytes).

NTFS (NT filesystem)
> An improved filesystem, supported only by Windows NT 4.0 and Windows 2000. NTFS is not based on the FAT system. It supports long filenames, partitions as large as 16 EB (exabytes), fault tolerance, security, and compression. Windows 2000 uses NTFS Version 5, which is compatible only with Windows 2000 and Windows NT 4.0 with Service Pack 4 or later.

When installing Windows 2000, you will need to choose among these three filesystems. Here are some guidelines:

- FAT or FAT32 should be used for dual-boot systems, because they can be accessed by DOS or earlier versions of Windows. These systems also have a lower overhead than NTFS and are more efficient for small volumes. FAT is compatible with DOS and supports partitions up to 2 GB; FAT32 is compatible with Windows 95 OSR2 and later, Windows 98, and Windows Me, and supports partitions up to 4 GB.

- NTFS has many advantages: it stores files more efficiently, supports file-level security, is more reliable, and supports Windows 2000's more advanced fault-tolerant features, such as disk striping. NTFS is particularly more efficient with larger drives; Microsoft recommends using NTFS exclusively with partitions 400 MB or larger.

Another factor to consider is the ability to convert between filesystems. Windows 2000 includes a utility, CONVERT.EXE, to convert FAT or FAT32 partitions to NTFS without loss of data. Windows 2000 cannot convert NTFS partitions to FAT or FAT32 without backing up data and reformatting (and permissions will be lost in this process).

IN THE REAL WORLD

Although Windows 2000 does not include this capability, several third-party utilities, such as Partition Magic from PowerQuest, can convert partitions from NTFS to FAT or FAT32 without reformatting.

Installation Methods

The Windows 2000 operating system is provided on a single CD-ROM. The OS can be installed using one of two basic methods:

CD-ROM installation
The SETUP.EXE program can be started from the CD-ROM from an existing operating system (Windows 95/98/Me or NT). If no operating system is installed, setup can be started with boot disks or by booting the CD-ROM if the computer's BIOS supports this feature.

Network installation
If the CD-ROM or a copy of the Windows 2000 Professional installation files can be accessed over the network, this can be used to complete the installation. This option requires an existing operating system and access to the network. Similarly, Windows 2000 can be installed from installation files that reside on the computer's local hard disk if an existing operating system is present.

ON THE EXAM

The Windows 2000 CD-ROM supports the El Torito standard for bootable CD-ROMs, which is supported on many newer computers with IDE or SCSI CD-ROM drives; however, many computers and BIOS versions still do not support this feature.

Performing the Installation

The installation program is called SETUP.EXE and is located in the root directory of the Windows 2000 Professional CD-ROM. If you use boot disks or boot the CD-ROM, Setup will start automatically. If you are starting the installation from an existing OS, run SETUP.EXE manually. On Windows 95/98/Me systems, Setup will start when the CD is inserted if the Auto Insert Notification feature is enabled.

You can also start the Windows 2000 setup from the winnt.exe (DOS or Windows 3.1/95/98/Me) or winnt32.exe (Windows NT) programs in the \i386 directory on the CD-ROM. This is convenient for network or file-based installations.

The setup process consists of a brief text-mode phase, after which the GUI components of Windows 2000 load and the Setup Wizard completes the installation. The steps involved in each phase are described in the following sections.

ON THE EXAM

If you are creating a temporary copy of the Windows 2000 installation files or a network share, all of the files you need are in the \I386 directory of the Windows 2000 CD-ROM.

Text-mode phase

The text-mode phase performs some basic tasks before starting the Setup Wizard. These include the following:

1. Start the SETUP.EXE program using one of the methods described earlier. The Setup welcome screen is displayed; press Enter to continue.

2. If an existing operating system is installed, choose whether to upgrade to Windows 2000 or install a new copy (referred to as a clean install).

3. The Windows 2000 Professional license agreement is displayed. Press F8 to accept the agreement and continue; press Esc to abort the installation.

4. Select a partition for the installation. You can press C to create a new partition or D to delete an existing partition.

5. The setup program scans the installation partition for errors or formats if a new partition was created. Installation files are then copied to the hard disk. This may take several minutes.

6. Restart the computer to continue the installation.

GUI phase (Setup Wizard)

After you restart the computer, the GUI phase of installation begins and the Setup Wizard appears. Follow these steps to complete the installation:

1. Click *Next* at the initial Setup Wizard screen to continue the installation.

2. The setup program detects and installs drivers for hardware devices. This may take several minutes.

3. You are now prompted for regional settings. Use the *Customize* button to change settings for the locale, language, and keyboard layout.

4. Specify the name and organization for the user of this computer.

---

5. You are now prompted for the Windows 2000 Professional product key, which is printed on the CD-ROM package. You must have a valid key to continue the installation.

6. Specify a name for the computer and a password for the local Administrator account.

7. Next, you are prompted for modem dialing information. Specify the region, area code, any keys needed to obtain an outside line, and tone or pulse dialing.

8. You are prompted for the date, time, and time zone. You can also choose whether to automatically account for daylight savings time changes.

9. The setup program now detects and installs network components. This may take several minutes. Choose *Typical* or *Custom* settings. The *Typical* option installs the Client for Microsoft Networks, File and Print Sharing, the TCP/IP protocol, and automatic IP addressing.

10. Choose whether the computer is on a network. If so, enter the appropriate workgroup or domain name. If you select a domain name, you must enter a username and password with Administrator status.

11. Files are now copied to the hard disk. This may take several minutes.

12. The final phase of the Setup Wizard installs Start menu items, registers components, saves settings, and removes temporary files; this takes about five minutes.

13. The installation is now complete. Click *Finish* to restart the computer.

After the computer restarts, the Network Identification Wizard runs and prompts you for a default network username for the computer. You can also choose to automatically log on if the computer is not attached to a domain.

Upgrading to Windows 2000

The Windows 2000 installation program can upgrade systems running Windows 95/98/Me or Windows NT. To perform an upgrade, start SETUP.EXE (or WINNT32.EXE) from the existing operating system. The following sections discuss the upgrade process.

Checking hardware compatibility

The Windows 2000 setup program includes an option to test a computer for compatibility before an upgrade. Although these tests are also performed during an actual installation, you can use this option to find out whether an upgrade is likely to succeed. Use this command from the existing operating system to check compatibility:

```
winnt32 /checkupgradeonly
```

The setup program displays a report summarizing the compatibility of the computer's hardware. You can also create the same report without the Windows 2000 Professional CD-ROM with the CHKUPGRD.EXE utility, available for download from Microsoft at *http://www.microsoft.com/windows/downloads/default.asp*.

Upgrading from Windows 95/98/Me

You can start an upgrade installation from Windows 95, 98, or Me by running SETUP.EXE, which in turn runs WINNT32. If you start the installation in this manner, a Windows-based Setup Wizard replaces the text mode phase of installation.

Upgrading from Windows 95/98/Me saves most settings, but because of differences between operating systems, not all settings are kept in the upgrade. Also, some settings (such as security) are unique to Windows 2000 and must be set manually as with a new installation.

Upgrading from Windows NT

When you upgrade from Windows NT 3.51 or later to Windows 2000 Professional, the following settings are preserved:

- Control panel settings, including network configuration
- Registry settings
- Start menu contents and desktop layout
- Preferences for some Windows NT utilities
- Users, groups, and other security settings

IN THE REAL WORLD

Windows NT 3.51 and earlier supported HPFS (high-performance filesystem), which is not supported by NT 4.0 or Windows 2000. Systems running HPFS must be converted to NTFS before upgrading. The ACLCONV utility, available from Microsoft, can perform this conversion.

Unattended Installation

The Windows 2000 installation program supports the use of an unattended installation file, also called an *answer file*. This is an ASCII text file that includes the information that the installation program would normally prompt for during installation. An example answer file is included on the Windows NT CD-ROM as UNATTEND.TXT.

ON THE EXAM

Although the unattended installation answer file can have any valid filename, questions in the Windows 2000 Professional exam may refer to this file as UNATTEND.TXT.

The answer file includes sections corresponding to each portion of the installation process. You can create the answer file manually with a text editor, or you can use the Setup Manager utility, described in the next section. After you've created the answer file, use the WINNT or WINNT32 program to begin the installation:

```
WINNT32 /U:path\unattend.txt /S:path\I386
```

The /U option specifies the path to the answer file, and the /S option (required) specifies the path to the installation files.

Setup Manager

The Setup Manager utility provides an alternative to manually creating the answer file. This utility prompts you for various installation options and then creates an answer file that can be used for an automated installation.

The Setup Manager utility is located in the Deploy.cab archive in the \Support\ Tools directory of the Windows 2000 Professional CD-ROM. After extracting the files, run SETUPMGR.EXE to execute the utility.

The initial Setup Manager screen, shown in Figure 1-1, includes three options: creating a new answer file, creating an answer file that duplicates the current computer's configuration, or modifying an existing answer file.

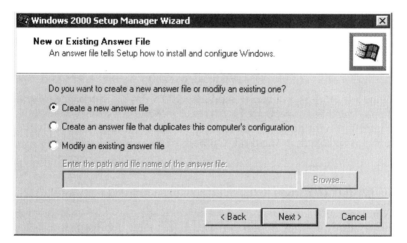

Figure 1-1: Setup Manager displays answer file options

ON THE EXAM

Along with unattended installation answer files, Setup Manager can create scripts for the System Preparation Tool and Remote Installation Services. Both of these features are discussed later in this section.

After choosing to create a new answer file, you can choose the level of user interaction for the automated installation. The following options are available:

Provide Defaults

Allows you to specify default choices for the installation options. Although these are selected by default, the user can still modify any options.

Fully Automated

No prompts are displayed to the user. For this option, you must provide answers for all installation options.

Hide Pages

Prompts the user only for options not specified by the answer file. The remaining dialogs are not displayed and use the choices in the file.

Read-Only

All installation dialogs are displayed, but the user cannot change the options selected by the answer file.

GUI Attended

The GUI portion of installation proceeds normally; only the text mode portion uses the answer file.

After selecting an option, you are prompted for the appropriate installation options. After selecting all options, you are prompted for a name and path for an answer file to be saved. You are also prompted for the location of the setup files, which are copied to a folder called WIN2000DIST for use by the automated installations.

Disk duplication

New to Windows 2000 is a disk duplication option, System Preparation Tool (SysPrep), which allows you to create a disk image from an existing installation and copy that image to other computers. This option can only be used when the computers are identical in configuration and can only be used for clean (non-upgrade) installations. Because a disk image is used, this option can also copy applications installed after the Windows 2000 installation.

IN THE REAL WORLD

Some hardware, such as sound and video cards, need not be identical between the computers; in particular, Plug and Play hardware can be detected on each system. The disk controllers and disk drive configurations must be identical, however.

You must use a third-party utility, such as PowerQuest DriveImage or Norton Ghost, to perform the actual disk imaging. Normally, disks copied from the same image may not work correctly with Windows 2000, because a unique security identifier is required for each computer. Windows 2000's System Preparation Tool corrects this potential problem.

The System Preparation Tool also creates a mini-Setup Wizard to prompt the user for information specific to the computer, such as username and computer name. This information can also be specified in a script created by Setup Manager, as discussed in the previous section.

You can install the System Preparation Tool from the Deploy.cab file in the \Support\ Tools directory of the Windows 2000 Professional CD-ROM. After installation, run SYSPREP.EXE to begin. After the preparation tool finishes, the computer is restarted.

ON THE EXAM

The System Preparation Tool modifies security and other settings on the computer to create a generic installation for distribution; thus, it should not be used on a production computer. You will usually need to reconfigure Windows 2000 Professional after running SYSPREP.

Remote Installation Services (RIS)

Remote Installation Services allows you to create a bootable image that can be used to start installations from any networked computer, using a central distribution of installation files. This works with a boot floppy or with computers that support remote boot with a boot ROM.

Windows 2000 Server is required to use Remote Installation Services. RIS requires the following services and configuration:

- A DNS server.

- A DHCP server.

- An Active Directory domain controller.

- A shared NTFS volume for the RIS files; this volume must not be the same volume on which Windows 2000 Server is installed.

ON THE EXAM

Remote Installation Services is included with Windows 2000 Server. You should understand the basics of RIS for the Windows 2000 Professional exam, but you do not need to know specific options.

Using Service Packs

Service packs are packages of fixes and enhancements to Windows 2000, periodically released by Microsoft after the release of the operating system. Each service pack includes a utility, UPGRADE.EXE, that installs the service pack.

New to Windows 2000 is a slipstreaming feature, which allows the corrections from service packs to be automatically included with installation. If you have a distribution of installation files on the network, you can use the upgrade.exe /slip command to modify the appropriate files using the service pack. After this is done, installing from that distribution will automatically include the updates provided by the service pack.

Configuring Windows 2000 Professional

Windows 2000 Professional includes a number of utilities that allow you to configure the operating system's features. Microsoft Management Console (MMC) and Task Scheduler are unique to Windows 2000; the other utilities are similar to those found in Windows NT 4.0. The following sections describe Windows 2000 Professional's key configuration utilities.

Microsoft Management Console (MMC)

Microsoft Management Console (MMC) is a generic utility for managing various aspects of Windows 2000. This extensible console can be used for tasks ranging from monitoring system performance to formatting disks. A typical MMC window is shown in Figure 1-2.

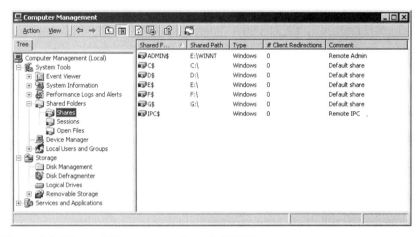

Figure 1-2: Microsoft Management Console (MMC)

You can access MMC by running MMC.EXE, by double-clicking the Administrative Tools control panel applet, or by running a shortcut to an MMC console. Many of the administrative tools included with Windows 2000 Professional are actually MMC snap-ins. MMC uses the following components:

Consoles
> A console is a configuration file that specifies the snap-ins that will be accessible to MMC. Different consoles can be loaded for different administrative tasks or configured for use by different administrators.

Snap-ins
> A snap-in provides a management interface for a particular feature in MMC. For example, Services, Shared Folders, and Local Users and Groups are available snap-ins.

Extensions

Extensions are snap-ins that can add functionality to existing snap-ins. For example, the Shared Folders snap-in has an optional extension called Send Console Message.

ON THE EXAM

MMC was first available as part of the Windows NT Option Pack for NT 4.0 and was used to configure IIS 4.0 features. Windows 2000 adds MMC consoles for typical workstation and server management tasks.

To manage the snap-ins included in a console, select Console → Add/Remove Snap-in. The Standalone tab allows you to add or remove standard snap-ins from the list, and the Extensions tab allows you to enable or disable extensions for the installed snap-ins.

Consoles are created in *author mode* by default. Several different modes can be selected by choosing Console → Options from the MMC menu:

Author mode

Allows users to modify and save the console file, and to add or remove snap-ins and extensions

User mode—full access

Allows users to add or remove snap-ins and access the full console tree

User mode—limited access, multiple window

Limits users to the snap-ins included in the console, but multiple windows can be used

User mode—limited access, single window

Limits users to the snap-ins included in the console and to a single window

---

ON THE EXAM

Some MMC snap-ins can also be used for administration of remote computers. Whether this is possible depends on whether the snap-in was written to support remote administration.

Task Scheduler

Task Scheduler allows applications to be scheduled for execution at specific times. The Scheduled Tasks window, shown in Figure 1-3, opens when you select the Scheduled Tasks applet in the Control Panel (described in the next section).

The Task Scheduler window displays any tasks currently scheduled. The Add Scheduled Task icon allows you to add a new task. This displays a wizard that allows you

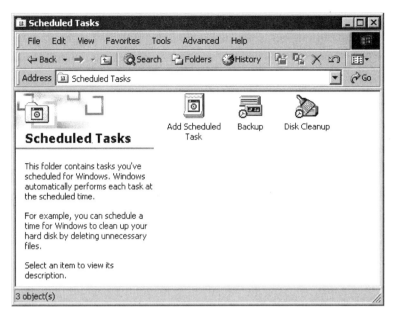

Figure 1-3: The Scheduled Tasks window

to select from a list of commonly used applications or select an executable file on disk. You are then prompted to choose one of the following scheduling options:

- Daily
- Weekly
- Monthly
- One time only
- When my computer starts
- When I log on

After selecting an option, you are prompted for further information: the specific time and date or day of the week to run the application. Next, you are prompted for a username and password; this user's access permissions are used when the task executes.

ON THE EXAM

For the Windows 2000 Professional MCSE exam, you should be experienced with creating tasks and modifying both basic and advanced task properties.

After a task is created, right-click on the icon and select *Properties* to display a tabbed dialog of options for the task, including the items you were prompted for by the wizard and a variety of advanced options.

Control Panel

Windows 2000 includes a Control Panel, similar to that found in Windows 95/98/ Me. This option is found in the Settings menu under the Start menu. The Control Panel window includes a number of separate dialogs, called *applets*, to configure various hardware devices and software services. A typical Control Panel display is shown in Figure 1-4. Note that, because some applications and services install additional Control Panel applets, your computer's list may vary.

Figure 1-4: The Windows 2000 Professional Control Panel

Many of the items found in the Control Panel can also be accessed in other ways; for example, the Network control panel is also the Properties dialog for the My Network Places icon. The applets available in Windows 2000 Professional include the following:

Accessibility Options
Allows you to enable a variety of options that may improve Windows 2000's usability for anyone unable to use the standard user interface options.

Add/Remove Programs
Allows you to add or remove software. This includes components of Windows 2000 as well as applications that support installation and uninstallation through the Control Panel.

Administrative Tools
Allows access to the MMC for computer management.

Date/Time
> Configures the computer's date, time, and time zone settings.

Display
> Includes settings relating to the display adapter and monitor. These include the appearance of the screen, screen savers and backgrounds, and video drivers.

Fax
> Includes settings for Windows 2000 Professional's fax features.

Folder Options
> Configures options for the display of folders, such as enabling and disabling HTML (web) content and the display of filename extensions and full paths.

Fonts
> Allows you to install and remove fonts. These are stored in the \WINNT\ FONTS directory.

Game Controllers
> Allows you to configure joysticks and other game-related devices.

Internet Options
> Opens Internet Explorer's options dialog.

Keyboard
> Allows you to configure the keyboard type, language, and speed settings.

Mouse
> Allows you to configure the mouse type, mouse pointers, and other settings.

Network and Dial-up Connections
> Configures network settings, as described later in this chapter, as well as dial-up networking features.

Phone and Modem
> Automatically detects or allows you to configure modems. Windows NT includes support for a wide variety of modems; some may require a driver provided with the modem.

Power Options
> Allows you to configure power management features of Windows 2000.

Printers
> Configures printers. Windows 2000 printing is described later in this chapter.

Regional Options
> Includes location-specific settings, such as currency and date formats.

Scheduled Tasks
> Schedules regular maintenance tasks, as discussed in the previous section.

Sounds and Multimedia
> Includes configuration settings for sound cards, video playback, MIDI controllers, and CD audio.

System
> Configures system settings, including the boot loader, hardware profiles, performance, and user profiles. The options available in this dialog are described in the next section.

Users and Passwords
> Displays a current list of users and allows you to grant or deny access to the computer and change passwords. The MMC snap-in, discussed later in this chapter, provides more sophisticated options.

ON THE EXAM

You should be familiar with each Control Panel applet and have experience using them for the Windows 2000 Professional MCSE exam.

The System Control Panel

The System applet of the Control Panel includes a variety of options. These include the following:

General
> Displays information about the computer and the Windows version.

Network Identification
> Includes settings for the computer's NetBIOS name and the workgroup or domain to which it is currently connected.

Hardware
> Allows you to create separate hardware profiles. Each profile includes the currently installed hardware and settings. This dialog also provides access to the Hardware Wizard, driver signing features, and the device manager.

User Profiles
> Allows you to create and modify user profiles (described later in this chapter).

Advanced
> Includes a variety of advanced options, described next.

The Advanced tab provides access to the following options:

Performance
> Allows you to specify whether performance is optimized for applications or background services. The *Change* button allows you to modify virtual memory settings.

Environment Variables
> Allows you to modify various system environment variables, such as temporary file directories.

Startup and Recovery
> Allows you to choose the default option and timeout for the boot menu; these values are stored in the BOOT.INI file, described earlier. The Recovery section of this dialog includes options for STOP errors and memory dumps.

The Registry

The Windows 2000 registry is a database of keys and values that are used to store the configuration of the hardware, user preferences, operating system settings, and settings for various applications. The Windows 2000 registry is very similar to the Windows NT 4.0 registry and similar, but not identical, to the registry used in Windows 95/98/Me.

The registry is organized in a hierarchical structure of keys and subkeys, each of which can hold one or more values. Values include a text identifier as well as a binary, string, word, or multiple string value. The registry has five main (root) subtrees. These include the following:

HKEY_CLASSES_ROOT
> This subtree stores file associations, which specify the programs to be run when files with particular extensions are used.

HKEY_CURRENT_USER
> This subtree stores information about the current Control Panel settings, loaded from the appropriate user profile at login. User profiles are explained later in this chapter.

HKEY_LOCAL_MACHINE
> This subtree stores hardware-specific data, such as drivers and interrupt settings, as well as software settings that do not change based on user profiles.

HKEY_USERS
> This subtree stores a default set of settings as well as settings for each separate user profile. The appropriate user's information is copied from here to the HKEY_CURRENT_USER subtree at login.

HKEY_CURRENT_CONFIG
> The keys in this subtree are used to store dynamic configuration information and temporary values used by some applications and device drivers.

HKEY_DYN_DATA
> This key stores dynamic hardware information, specifying the current settings for removable disk drives, PC cards, and other hardware that can be changed without rebooting.

ON THE EXAM

You should know these registry subtrees and their basic purposes for the Windows 2000 Professional exam. You should not need to know the function of specific registry keys within the subtrees.

Registry editors

Although most of the keys in the registry are set by the OS or based on your Control Panel settings, you can manually edit the registry. Because an incorrect setting can cause the system to be unusable, this should not be attempted without backing up the registry files.

There are two programs for editing the registry: REGEDIT and REGEDT32. Either of these can be run manually from a console prompt or the Run dialog. Both modify the same registry, but provide different feature sets:

- REGEDT32, shown in Figure 1-5, displays each subtree in a separate window, making some operations difficult, and does not support searching the entire registry. However, it allows access to security features. You can set permissions on registry keys, allowing them to be modified only by certain users or groups. REGEDT32 also includes a view-only feature, which is useful to prevent accidental changes. Additionally, REGEDT32 supports loading and unloading the registry keys of non-functioning operating system installations, which can be a valuable troubleshooting tool.

- REGEDIT is similar to the program of the same name in Windows 95/98/Me; it displays all of the subtrees in a tree structure. This program provides sophisticated search options and, additionally, allows you to export individual registry keys to text files and to import keys from text files, which is useful for backing up and restoring portions of the registry. REGEDIT does not support the security or read-only features of REGEDT32; thus, Microsoft does not recommend its use with Windows 2000.

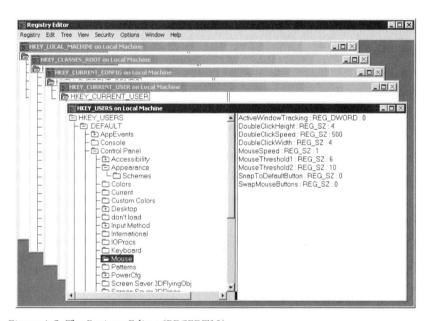

Figure 1-5: The Registry Editor (REGEDT32)

Configuring Mobile Systems

Although previous versions of Windows NT were not as suitable for mobile computers as Windows 98, Windows 2000 includes a number of features designed for use with mobile computers. These are described in the following sections.

Offline files and folders

Windows 2000 supports offline files and folders, which provide a local cache of files on a network server. You can use the files even while disconnected from the network, and they can be synchronized when a network connection is available.

To make a shared folder available offline, open its Properties dialog from Explorer. Select the Sharing tab, then click the *Caching* button. Check the *Allow caching of files in this shared folder* option. You can then select one of three caching settings:

Manual Caching for Documents
Allows users to specify particular files within the folder to be available offline

Automatic Caching for Documents
Automatically caches all documents the user accesses in the folder

Automatic Caching for Programs
Similar to the previous option, but intended for use with executable application files

To configure a mobile computer to use offline files, select the *Folder Options* command from the Tools menu in Explorer. The Offline Files tab includes the following options:

Enable Offline Files
Enables the offline files feature. The feature must also be enabled in the shared folder.

Synchronize all offline files before logging off
Synchronizes files when the user selects the Log Off option.

Enable reminders
Allows you to specify how often (in minutes) a reminder is displayed to synchronize files.

Place shortcut to Offline Files folder on the desktop
Creates a shortcut for the shared folder that supports offline files.

Amount of disk space to use for temporary offline files
Chooses the amount of disk space (in MB) for use as a cache.

Delete files
Deletes specified cache copies of offline files.

View files
Displays currently cached offline files.

Advanced
Allows you to set additional options, including switching to offline mode when a network connection is lost.

Synchronization Manager

The Synchronization Manager utility allows you to change synchronization settings and manually synchronize files. To access this utility, select *Synchronize* from the Tools menu in Explorer.

Within Synchronization Manager, use the *Synchronize* button to force synchronization of all cached files. The Logon/Logoff tab allows you to choose which files will
be synchronized at logon and logoff and, also, the network connection to use. The
On Idle tab lets you set synchronization to occur automatically when you are not
currently using the computer and it's connected to the specified network
connection.

Power management

Although useful for all computers, Windows 2000's power management features
are most commonly used with mobile computers. You can configure power
management options using the Power Options Control Panel applet. The applet
allows you to choose from a number of preset power management schemes, or
you can set custom options.

Windows 2000 supports the APM (Advanced Power Management) 1.2 specification, as well as the older ACPI standard. To enable APM features, choose the APM
tab in the Power Options dialog and select the *Enable Advanced Power Management Support* option.

Configuring Hardware

Windows 2000 supports the Plug and Play specification, unlike previous versions
of Windows NT. With compatible hardware, you can simply install a new device
while the computer is turned off, and Windows 2000 will recognize and install the
device during the boot process. With other hardware, you can use the Add New
Hardware applet in the Control Panel.

Device Manager

The Device Manager MMC snap-in allows you to manage the hardware devices
installed in your computer. To use this utility, right-click on the My Computer icon
on the desktop and select the *Manage* option.

Device Manager displays a list of devices currently installed. Highlight a device
and select *Properties* from the Action menu to display a dialog that allows you to
modify resource settings and display the device's current status.

System Information

The System Information utility is another snap-in that is useful in hardware troubleshooting. This utility can display IRQ, DMA, and other settings used by devices,
installed software, information about installed devices, and Internet Explorer
configuration.

The System Information snap-in is not included in the Administrative Tools MMC
console by default. You can add this snap-in to a custom console; see the discus-
sion of MMC earlier in this chapter.

Driver signing

Windows 2000 includes a driver signing feature to ensure the validity of device driver files. The files are signed with a digital signature by Microsoft or the device manufacturer.

By default, you are warned when unsigned driver files are in use. To change these options, open the System Control Panel applet, select the Hardware tab, and click the *Driver Signing* button. The Driver Signing Options dialog opens, which allows you to select whether unsigned driver files are ignored (allowed without warning), result in a warning, or are blocked from use.

The Signature Verification utility allows you to view detailed information from a file's digital signature. To run this utility, enter `sigverif` at the Run prompt or the command line.

Managing Disk Storage

Along with the standard partitioning scheme supported by DOS, Windows 3.x, Windows 95/98/Me, and Windows NT, Windows 2000 supports a new dynamic disk system that provides greater versatility in disk management. The following sections describe the basic and dynamic disk systems and explain basic disk administration tasks.

Basic Disks

Windows 2000 refers to disks using the partitioning schemes used in previous operating systems as *basic disks*. In this scheme, disks are divided into one or more partitions, each of which can contain volumes (units of storage accessible with a drive letter). The two basic partition types, primary and extended, are described in the sections that follow.

Primary partitions

A *primary partition* is a bootable partition on a disk. Each disk can contain only one active primary partition, although partitions can be marked inactive. A primary partition contains a single volume, which can be formatted with the NTFS, FAT, or FAT32 filesystems.

ON THE EXAM

In a typical single-drive installation, the primary partition uses all of the space on the disk drive and is formatted as a single volume, known as drive letter C:.

Extended partitions and logical drives

An *extended partition* can only be created after the primary partition and typically uses the disk space unallocated to the primary partition. An extended partition is divided into one or more *logical drives*, each of which can be formatted as a volume.

Logical drives are not bootable. The Windows 2000 system partition (the partition containing NTLDR and other boot files in the root directory) cannot be located on a logical drive, but the boot partition (the partition containing the operating system files in the \WINNT directory) can.

Dynamic Disks

New to Windows 2000 is a system of dynamic disks, which can be used instead of the basic scheme. The dynamic disk system treats the entire hard disk as a single partition. This partition can be further divided into one or more volumes. Three types of volumes are available; these are described in the sections that follow.

IN THE REAL WORLD

Dynamic disks are not compatible with most hardware RAID controllers, because they manage their own disk partitions. Use basic disks when using hardware RAID.

Simple volumes

A *simple volume* can use all or part of a single disk. Simple volumes are similar to volumes in the basic disk system, but can be resized dynamically without starting the computer. Simple volumes can be formatted with FAT, FAT32, or NTFS.

Spanned volumes

A *spanned volume* is a single volume that includes space on two or more physical disks. As many as 32 disks can be combined into a single volume. Windows 2000 writes data to the first disk in the spanned volume until it is full, then continues with the remaining disks. The loss of a single disk within a spanned volume will cause the loss of the entire volume. Spanned volumes may not be used for the system or boot partitions.

ON THE EXAM

Windows 2000 also supports a number of *fault-tolerant* disk configurations, which can combine multiple disks while providing for the failure of a single disk. These are included only with Windows 2000 Server; they are not covered on the Windows 2000 Professional MCSE exam.

Striped volumes

A *striped volume* combines several physical disks (2–32 disks) into a single volume, but makes a more efficient use of space. Data is stored in small sections (stripes) of each disk in turn, so that all disks maintain the same amount of free space.

The advantage of striping is speed; read or write requests can be distributed across several physical drives. However, as with a spanned volume, the loss of a single drive will cause the loss of all of the data on the volume. As with spanned volumes, striped volumes cannot be used for the system or boot partitions.

ON THE EXAM

Windows 2000 Server supports a fault-tolerant version of disk striping called *disk striping with parity*. This system uses the equivalent of one drive's storage space for parity information, divided between the drives.

Disk Management

The Disk Management snap-in is Windows 2000's main tool for disk administration. You can access this snap-in by adding it to a console or by accessing a console that already includes it, such as the Computer Management console. To access this console, select Programs → Administrative Tools → Computer Management → Storage → Disk Management from the Start menu.

The Computer Management console with the Disk Management snap-in selected is shown in Figure 1-6. The initial display shows a graphic representation of the disks in the system, each divided into its component partitions or volumes. Disks are labeled as basic or dynamic, and the system and boot partitions are labeled.

The following sections describe a number of basic disk management tasks using the Disk Management snap-in.

Partitioning

For basic disks, you can create a partition by right-clicking on the disk and selecting *Create Partition*. If a disk contains no partitions, you can also configure it as a dynamic disk. Right-click on a dynamic disk to create a volume.

After a basic partition or dynamic volume is created, right-click and select *Format* to configure it for a filesystem. This option is also available for existing volumes and will erase all data in the current volume.

For existing partitions, you can right-click on the partition and select *Properties* to display settings for the partition. This allows you to modify sharing, security, and quota options and provides access to troubleshooting tools.

Creating spanned volumes

To create a spanned volume, select an area of free disk space on a dynamic disk, right-click and select *Create Volume*. A spanned volume can also be extended with

---

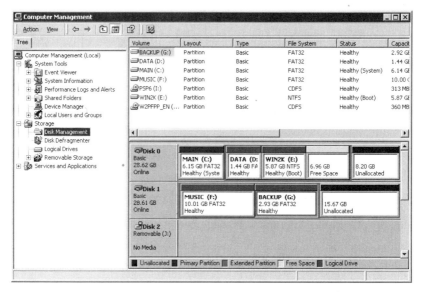

Figure 1-6: The Disk Management MMC snap-in

additional free space: select the volume and an area of free space, right-click, and select *Extend Volume*.

Creating striped volumes

To create a striped volume, select an area of free disk space on a dynamic disk, right-click, and select *Create Volume*. This requires a minimum of two areas of free space on separate dynamic disks. A striped volume cannot be extended.

Converting basic to dynamic storage

The Disk Management snap-in also provides a one-way method of converting basic disks to dynamic disks. To convert a disk, right-click the basic disk and select *Upgrade to Dynamic Disk*. This process preserves the data on the disk.

When a disk is upgraded, each primary partition or logical drive is converted to a simple volume on the dynamic disk; there is no longer any distinction between the partition types.

ON THE EXAM

Upgrading a disk to dynamic has the side effect of making the disk inaccessible to Windows NT 4.0 and earlier, Windows 98, and other operating systems; only Windows 2000 supports dynamic disks.

Volume sets and stripe sets, Windows NT 4.0's equivalent of spanned and striped volumes, can be included in the upgrade. Volume sets are converted to spanned volumes, and stripe sets are converted to striped volumes. These are no longer accessible to NT 4.0.

Defragmenting disks

As data is stored on disk, a file may be separated into one or more physical locations on the disk. For example, this happens when a volume has a number of small areas of free space and you write a large file to the disk. Although Windows 2000 has no trouble handling fragmented files, a large number of them can degrade performance.

The Disk Defragmenter snap-in, also included in the Computer Management console, allows you to analyze disk fragmentation and defragment disks as needed. Select a drive in the upper area of the window, then click *Analyze* to view a graph of the disk's fragments or *Defragment* to defragment the disk.

IN THE REAL WORLD

Windows NT 4.0 and earlier did not include the ability to defragment NTFS volumes. This is possible with the Windows 2000 Defragmenter. NTFS disks will require defragmentation less frequently than FAT or FAT32 volumes.

Disk Compression

Windows 2000 supports *disk compression* for specific files or folders on NTFS volumes. The files are stored in compressed form, but can be accessed like normal files; they are dynamically uncompressed automatically. This conserves disk storage, but requires more CPU time when files are being compressed or uncompressed.

Compressing files

To compress a file or folder, open its Properties dialog and click the *Advanced* button. The Advanced Attributes dialog includes a *Compress contents to save disk space* option; select this option to compress the file or folder. When you compress a folder, you are asked to choose whether to compress the folder only, or its contents, including files and subfolders.

Moving and copying files

File compression follows a set of inheritance rules when you move or copy files. The rules are as follows:

- When a file or folder is copied from an NTFS folder to another NTFS folder, it inherits the compression settings of the destination folder.

- When a file or folder is moved from an NTFS folder to another NTFS folder on the same volume, it keeps its current compression setting. If it is moved from one volume to another, it inherits the settings of the destination folder.

- When a compressed file or folder is moved or copied to a FAT partition, it is uncompressed, because FAT does not support compression.

ON THE EXAM

You may find it useful to have compressed files displayed in a distinct color in Explorer. To enable this option, select *Folder Options* from the Tools menu in Explorer. Select the View tab and check the *Display Compressed Files and Folders with Alternate Color* option.

Disk Quotas

Windows 2000 includes a disk quota feature, which can be used to limit the disk storage consumed by each user. To set quotas for a disk, right-click on the disk in My Computer or Disk Management and select *Properties*, then select the Quota tab, as shown in Figure 1-7. The following options are included:

Enable quota management
> If selected, quotas are enabled for the disk.

Deny disk space to users exceeding quota limit
> If selected, users will be unable to write to the disk after exceeding their quota. Otherwise, quotas will be used strictly for monitoring purposes.

Select the default quota limit
> Select the default disk quota for users or select *Do not limit disk usage* to disable quotas by default; you can still add quotas for individual users or groups. You can also set a lower warning level.

Select the quota logging options
> Select whether an event is logged when a user exceeds the quota or when a user exceeds the warning level.

The *Quota Entries* button at the bottom of the dialog displays a separate window listing all quota entries. Select Quota → New Quota Entry to add an entry for an individual user or group.

EFS (Encrypted Filesystem)

Encrypted Filesystem (EFS) is a new Windows 2000 feature that uses public-key encryption to encrypt and decrypt files in folders. To encrypt a folder's contents, select the General tab from the folder's Properties dialog, then click *Advanced.* Select the *Encrypt contents to secure data* option to encrypt the folder.

Encryption is transparent to the user; files are automatically decrypted when accessed, provided the user has permission to access the file. To decrypt a folder permanently, deselect the *Encrypt contents* option in the Advanced Properties dialog.

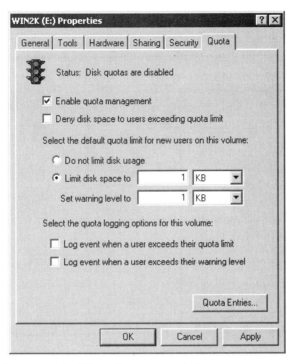

Figure 1-7: The Quota tab of the Disk Properties dialog

ON THE EXAM

Encrypted files are not accessible from operating systems other than Windows 2000. Also note that the encryption feature is not compatible with compression: a file can be compressed or encrypted, but not both.

Managing Backups

Windows 2000 includes a new backup program, Windows Backup. This utility is available from the Accessories → System Tools menu under the Start menu or by running the NTBACKUP.EXE program directly.

The main Backup screen includes options for the Backup Wizard, which prompts you for information to back up files; the Restore Wizard, which prompts you for information to restore files; and an option to create an emergency repair disk (ERD). The following sections describe the advanced features of the program.

Backing up files

Select the Backup tab to display a full set of backup options, as displayed in Figure 1-8. This dialog displays a hierarchical listing of the contents of the computer's disks. Select a drive, directory, or individual files to comprise the backup set.

You can also use Backup to back up the computer's registry and boot files. To enable this feature, check the *System State* option in the Backup tab.

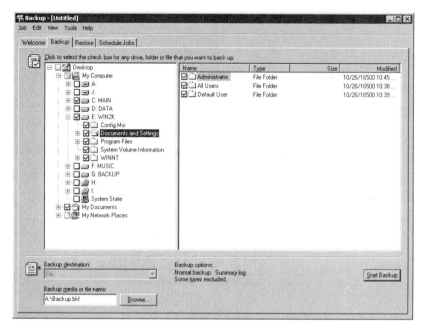

Figure 1-8: The Backup tab

The destination for the backup can be duplicate files (on another disk or removable media) or a tape if a tape device has been installed. To change the backup type, select *Options* from the Tools menu. The following types of backup are allowed:

Normal (full backup)
    Backs up all of the files on the volume regardless of when files were modified and clears the archive bits (file attributes that indicate whether a file has changed since the last backup)

Incremental backup
    Backs up all of the files that have been modified since the last backup and clears the archive bits

Differential backup
    Backs up all of the files changed since the last full backup but does not clear the archive bits, so each differential backup includes the same files as a previous one

Copy
    Similar to a full backup, but does not clear the archive bits

Daily copy
    Backs up all files modified on the current date

Restoring files

The Restore tab displays options for restoring files. A list of logged backups is displayed on the left, and you can select individual folders or files to be restored. Files can be restored to their original location, to a location you specify, or to a single flat folder.

Scheduling backups

The Schedule Jobs tab displays a calendar that displays currently scheduled backups. Use the *Add Job* button to add a backup job. A wizard prompts you for the files and folders to back up, the destination, and the backup type.

Managing Network Components

Windows 2000 is a versatile networking platform; Windows 2000 Professional is intended primarily as a network client. The following sections examine the key networking protocols and services included with Windows 2000 Professional, beginning with the complex and versatile TCP/IP protocol suite.

TCP/IP

TCP/IP (Transport Control Protocol/Internet Protocol) is a suite of protocols in widespread use on the Internet. These are also the protocols used with Unix systems. Windows 2000 installs TCP/IP support by default. This section describes TCP/IP and how to use Windows 2000 Professional as a TCP/IP client.

IP addressing

TCP/IP uses a system of *IP addresses* to distinguish between clients on the network. Each node has its own unique IP address. The IP address is a 32-bit number, expressed in dotted decimal format, such as 209.68.11.152. The four divisions of the IP address are referred to as *octets*.

A portion of the address is a network address, and a portion is a host address. The division between these components depends on the address class. In Class A addresses, the first octet is the network address and the remainder is the host. Class B networks use the first two octets as the network address, and Class C networks use the first three. Each class is also identified by a unique range for the first octet. Table 1-4 summarizes the IP address classes.

Table 1-4: IP Address Classes

Class	First Byte Range	Network/Host Octets	Number of Networks	Hosts per Network
A	1–126	1/3	126	16,777,214
B	128–191	2/2	16,382	65,534
C	192–223	3/1	2,097,150	254

Because most modern applications require a more versatile division, a technique called *subnet masking* is used to further subdivide the network and host addresses. A subnet mask is a 32-bit binary number with digits set to 1 representing the network address and digits set to 0 representing the host address. This allows a greater variety of possible numbers of hosts and networks.

Hosts on an IP network also have alphanumeric names corresponding to their IP addresses. These can be local names, such as server, or fully qualified names, such as server1.company.com. DNS (Domain Name Service) is used to translate between hostnames and addresses.

TCP/IP protocols and services

The TCP/IP suite includes a great many protocols and services. The following are some of the higher-level protocols and services typically used with Windows 2000 Professional:

ON THE EXAM

You should be familiar with all of the following protocols and services and their uses, but you don't need to know their technical specifics for the Windows 2000 Professional MCSE exam.

DHCP (Dynamic Host Configuration Protocol)
> Protocal that allows clients to be dynamically issued IP addresses from a pool of available addresses. Windows 2000 Professional can act as a DHCP client; Windows 2000 Server can act as a DHCP server. DHCP can also dynamically assign DNS and WINS server addresses and default gateway information.

DNS (Domain Name Service)
> An Internet standard protocol that translates hostnames into their corresponding IP addresses. This process is called *name resolution*. DNS can also translate IP addresses to hostnames (known as Reverse DNS.) Windows NT Workstation can act as a DNS client; Windows 2000 Server includes a DNS server implementation.

WINS (Windows Internet Name Service)
> Microsoft's alternative protocol for hostname resolution. WINS translates between IP addresses and NetBIOS names, described in Part 2. NetBIOS names can be resolved without a WINS server through the use of broadcasts or a local LMHOSTS file.

SLIP (Serial Line Internet Protocol)
> A protocol used for dial-up connections to servers. This is typically used by Internet service providers, but can also be used to dial in to Windows NT computers.

PPP (Point-to-Point Protocol)
> An alternative protocol for dial-up connections. PPP is newer and includes more sophisticated configuration and security features. In addition, although

---

SLIP supports TCP/IP connections only, PPP can support NetBEUI or IPX/SPX protocols.

HTTP (Hypertext Transfer Protocol)
> The protocol used for WWW (World Wide Web) servers. Windows NT Workstation includes Peer Web Services, a server for HTTP, FTP, and Gopher.

FTP (File Transfer Protocol)
> A protocol that allows for file transfers between computers and is commonly used on the Internet as well as on local TCP/IP networks.

Managing TCP/IP

You probably installed TCP/IP as part of the Windows 2000 Professional installation. If not, you can add it by using the *Install* button in the Local Area Connection Properties dialog. After TCP/IP is installed, highlight its entry and select *Properties* to display the following TCP/IP options:

General
> This is the only page displayed by default. It includes options for the IP address, which can be automatically or manually assigned, and for preferred and alternate DNS server addresses.

IP Settings
> This and the following pages of options are displayed by clicking the *Advanced* button from the General page. This page allows you to define multiple IP addresses and default gateway (router) addresses.

DNS
> This page allows you to specify multiple DNS server addresses. You can also specify default suffixes to be used for DNS.

WINS
> WINS is a service similar to DNS, but for NetBIOS computer names. This page includes options for the WINS client.

Options
> Displays a list of optional settings that can be configured with separate dialogs. These include IP security and TCP/IP filtering.

Other Protocols

Along with TCP/IP, Windows 2000 Professional supports a number of other network protocols. These include the following:

IPX/SPX
> IPX (Internetwork Packet Exchange) and SPX (Sequenced Packet Exchange) are routable protocols developed by Novell and are the default protocols for NetWare 4.11 and earlier networks, although NetWare does support other protocols. NWLink is Microsoft's implementation of the IPX/SPX protocols and is included with Windows 2000.

NetBEUI
> Microsoft's protocol built to support NetBIOS (described below) over networks. NetBEUI has a low overhead compared with other protocols and is

easy to configure, but is not routable. NetBEUI was installed by default with Windows NT 3.5 and earlier; Windows 2000 uses TCP/IP by default instead.

DLC

DLC (Data Link Control) is a non-routable protocol used for communication with IBM mainframes using the SNA architecture. It is also supported by some printers with network interfaces, such as Hewlett Packard's JetDirect interface. Unlike the other protocols listed here, DLC cannot be used to support file sharing between computers or other generic communication between hosts.

AppleTalk

A protocol developed by Apple and built into the Macintosh operating system. The AppleTalk protocol can be installed under Windows 2000 to allow connectivity with Macintosh networks.

IN THE REAL WORLD

Although DLC is supported by some printers and print servers, most of the newer models also support TCP/IP. TCP/IP is usually a much better choice, because it is easier to manage and configure.

Active Directory

One of the key new features of Windows 2000 is the Active Directory. This is a directory service that manages a database of users, groups, computers, and other network resources on the network in a single hierarchical Directory. Windows 2000 Professional acts as an Active Directory client.

ON THE EXAM

This section is a simple introduction to the concepts of Active Directory. You will learn more about Active Directory in Part 2 and subsequent parts. For the Windows 2000 Professional MCSE exam, you need to understand only the basic concepts.

Active Directory basics

Windows NT 4.0 and earlier used a system of trusts for communication between domains. Although Windows 2000 still supports domains, they are all organized as part of a unified Directory.

Active Directory supports the LDAP (lightweight directory access protocol) 1.2 and 1.3 standards. This allows a Windows 2000 network to share directory information with other services, such as Internet directories and networks using Novell's NDS.

Active Directory structure

Active Directory uses a hierarchical (tree) structure to organize network resources. At the lowest level, *objects* represent individual resources. These are organized into *domains*, which are in turn organized into *trees*. All of the domains within a tree share the same namespace (the standards for computer and other resource naming and the logical boundary within which a resource name must be unique) and a common schema (a definition of available object types and properties).

A Windows 2000 directory tree can be combined with other trees (with incompatible namespaces or schema) to form a *forest*.

Directory replication

Windows NT 4.0 and earlier use primary domain controllers (PDCs) and backup domain controllers (BDCs) to store information for a domain. The PDC is the primary source of information and security, and the BDCs maintain a copy of the database from the PDC.

In Windows 2000, there is only one type of domain controller. Domain controllers automatically replicate the user database for the domain, and they are interchangeable. Active Directory automatically organizes domain controllers into a logical ring, and data is replicated both ways around the ring.

Remote Access

Windows 2000 supports remote access, which allows users to connect to a Windows 2000 Professional or Server computer by modem or through another connection and act as network clients. The following sections describe Windows 2000's remote access features.

Remote access security

Windows 2000 includes support for the following basic security options, which are also supported by Windows NT 4.0:

PAP (Password Authentication Protocol)
An Internet standard for basic authentication. Passwords are sent as clear text, so this is not a secure protocol.

SPAP (Shiva PAP)
Shiva's improved version of PAP. Passwords are transmitted in encrypted form.

CHAP (Challenge Handshake Authentication Protocol)
A two-way protocol that sends encrypted tokens rather than passwords.

Microsoft-CHAP (Microsoft CHAP)
Microsoft's proprietary version of CHAP, supported only by Windows operating systems.

PPTP (Point-to-Point Tunneling Protocol)
A protocol used for VPNs (virtual private networks). Data is encrypted and encapsulated in packets, allowing the Internet or another public network to act as a transport for private networks.

In addition to these, Windows 2000 supports EAP (Extensible Authentication Protocol). EAP allows the use of additional security types, including smart cards, MD5 encryption, and digital certificates. Windows 2000 also supports RADIUS (Remote Access Dial-In User Service), a system for authentication and accounting of remote access.

ON THE EXAM

You should know the basic security options available for Windows 2000 remote access for the Windows 2000 Professional MCSE exam. EAP, RADIUS, and other Windows 2000 security features are explained in detail in Part 7, *Designing Security*.

Managing dial-out connections

To configure dial-out access to the Internet or a remote access server, select Settings → Network and Dial-up Connections from the Start menu. Select the *Make New Connection* option to display the Network Connection Wizard. Select one of these two options:

Dial-up to private network
Use to connect to a Remote Access server

Dial-up to the Internet
Use to connect to an Internet Service Provider (ISP)

You are then prompted for specific information, such as phone numbers and the security settings explained earlier in this section.

Managing dial-in connections

Windows 2000 also supports dial-in remote access. To enable this feature, select Settings → Network and Dial-up Connections from the Start menu. Select the *Make New Connection* option and then choose the *Accept incoming connections* option from the Network Connection Wizard dialog. You can then specify a list of users who are allowed to remotely access the computer.

Administration and Security

Windows 2000 includes several security features. This section explains the basics of Windows 2000 authentication and then examines users, groups, and security policies. This section also describes Windows 2000's printing and auditing features.

The Windows 2000 Logon Process

The first element of Windows 2000 security that a user encounters is the logon dialog. To provide security, Windows 2000 does not send passwords across the network during the logon process. The authentication process works as follows:

1. The user enters a username and password. The password is used to encrypt a string of numbers (the current time), and the resulting encrypted data is sent with the username to the domain controller or to the local computer's security subsystem when a domain is not in use.

2. The domain controller or security subsystem looks up the username and reads the encrypted token stored in the security database; if this matches the result sent with the logon request, access is granted.

3. An access token is sent to the client and used in subsequent network requests to continually verify the user's identity. The server uses this token to determine whether access is granted for files, folders, or other resources.

Users and Groups

Each person who accesses a Windows 2000 computer or network requires a *user account* that uniquely identifies the user. The user account and password are used at the logon dialog, and the user account's properties control the user's abilities on the network. Windows 2000 uses two kinds of user accounts:

Local users
> These are users of a particular computer that does not participate in a domain. These are the only type of users you can create in Windows 2000 Professional.

Domain users
> These are users of a domain; they can only be created on a Windows 2000 Server domain controller. Windows 2000 Professional users can log in to a domain using a domain user account.

Adding and modifying users

You can add or manage local users on a Windows 2000 Professional computer with the Computer Management MMC snap-in. To access this utility, select Programs → Administrative Tools → Computer Management from the Start menu. Open the Local Users and Groups object on the left side of the screen.

Highlight the *Users* option to display a list of users for the computer. After an installation, only Administrator and Guest (disabled) are included in this list. To add a user, right-click and select *New User*. To modify an existing user, double-click to display the Properties dialog.

The Properties dialog for a user is divided into three tabs:

General
Displays basic options. These include the user's full name and description, as well as options relating to passwords.

Member of
Lists the groups the user belongs to. Click *Add* to add a group to the list.

Profile
Specifies a user profile, which stores settings for the user, and an optional logon script.

Configuring groups

Groups allow you to combine similar users and assign them permissions or other functions. Windows 2000 uses two types of groups: *local groups*, used on stand-alone computers, and *global groups*, used in a domain. Windows 2000 Professional supports only local groups.

To manage local groups on a Windows 2000 Professional computer, select *Groups* under Local Users and Groups. The available groups are displayed. Right-click and select *New Group* to create a new group. Double-click on an existing group to modify its membership list.

ON THE EXAM

When granting access to a file or other resource, the best practice is to assign permissions to a group rather than individual users. This makes it easy to change permissions and to set up new users.

Default users and groups

The following user accounts are created by default when Windows 2000 Professional is installed:

Administrator
This is the default administration account. You are asked to specify a password for this account at installation. This account cannot be disabled or deleted and should be kept secure.

Guest

> This user cannot be renamed or deleted, but can be disabled. It has no password by default. Because this account is present on all systems and is a member of the Everyone group (explained later), it presents a significant security risk.

The following local groups are available by default:

Administrators

> The Administrator user is a member of this group. Members of this group are given full control to all resources of the computer.

Backup Operators

> Members of this group can access all files on the computer, regardless of file-system security. No users are members by default.

Guests

> The Guest user is a member of this group. This group has a simple set of rights by default.

Power Users

> Users in this group can perform some system tasks: for example, manage printers, install devices, shut down or restart the computer, or change the computer's date and time.

Replicator

> This is a special group used by the file replication system to duplicate files between computers.

Users

> This group includes a basic set of rights, such as the right to log on locally or over the network. All users are members of this group by default.

In addition to these, there are a number of system groups. These are groups that implicitly represent categories of users, but cannot be modified. The system groups include the following:

Everyone

> Includes all users of the computer or network

Authenticated Users

> Includes any user that has been authenticated with a valid user account

Creator Owner

> For a file or other resource, includes the user who created or owns the resource

Network

> Includes any users accessing the computer across the network (rather than locally)

Interactive

> Includes users accessing the computer via its own console

Anonymous logon

> Includes any user who has not been authenticated with a valid user account

Dialup

> Includes any user accessing the computer via a dial-up connection

Security Policies

Windows 2000 includes a number of security options you can set to customize local and network security. These are called security policies. To modify security policies, use the Security Settings MMC console. You can access this console by selecting *Local Security Policy* from the Administrative Tools Control Panel applet.

Account policies

Account policies include options that control the security of user accounts. The first category, Password Policy, includes the following options:

Enforce password history
> If this option is enabled, a number of the user's previous passwords will be logged. When a password is changed, the previous items cannot be used.

Minimum and maximum password age
> Specifies a minimum and maximum age before a password may be changed. The defaults are 0 days minimum and 42 days maximum.

Minimum password length
> Specifies a minimum length for passwords. There is no minimum by default.

Passwords must meet complexity requirements
> If this option is enabled, passwords must contain one or more capital letters, numerals, or punctuation marks and cannot contain the username or full name.

Store password using reversible encryption
> Stores a reversibly encrypted password for each user. This is only used with a domain and is used for certain security protocols.

The Account Policy section also includes an option for *Account Lockout Policy*. If this feature is enabled, accounts are locked out (disabled) after a specified number of invalid logon attempts. The following options are available:

Account lockout duration
> The duration of the lockout in minutes.

Account lockout threshold
> The number of invalid logon attempts before lockout. The default is 0, meaning the account lockout feature is disabled.

Reset account lockout counter after
> The number of minutes without an invalid logon attempt before the count of invalid attempts is reset to 0.

Security Options

The Security Options settings are listed under Local Policies. These include a large number of options to control various local security settings. The following are some important options:

Allow system to be shut down without having to log on
> If this option is enabled, a *Shut Down* button is displayed in the logon dialog and the computer can be shut down without a valid logon. This option is enabled by default.

Clear virtual memory pagefile when system shuts down
> If this option is enabled, the virtual memory (paging) file is cleared at shutdown. This option is disabled by default.

Disable Ctrl-Alt-Del requirement for logon
> If enabled, the Ctrl-Alt-Del keystroke is not required to display the logon dialog. This option is enabled by default in Windows 2000 Professional.

Do not display last username in logon screen
> If this option is enabled, the most recent username is not displayed in the logon screen. This option is disabled by default.

Audit Policy

Windows 2000 includes an auditing feature, which allows you to specify various events that will be logged for later examination. You can configure auditing from the Audit Policy item under Local Policies.

No auditing is enabled by default. To enable auditing for an event, double-click it. You can then choose whether the event's success or failure will be audited.

The results of auditing are displayed in the Event Viewer console, described in the "Optimization and Troubleshooting" section of this chapter.

NTFS Security

Windows 2000 supports a full range of security for NTFS partitions. FAT partitions do not support security. NTFS security treats files and directories as objects. Each file or directory has an ACL, and users or groups can be given permission to access it. The available NTFS permissions are described in Table 1-5.

Table 1-5: NTFS Permissions

Permission	Description
Read	View a directory's contents or open a file
Write	Write data to a file or create new files in a directory
Delete	Delete a file or directory
Change Permissions	Modify the permissions assigned to a file or directory
Execute	Execute a program file
Take Ownership	Modify the ownership of a file or directory

To modify permissions for a file or directory, right-click on it in Explorer. Select the Security tab, then click the *Permissions* button to display the Permissions dialog.

These permissions can be assigned individually or in preset combinations, such as Full Control, which includes all of the permissions. Another available permission, No Access, explicitly denies the user or group access to the resource, regardless of other permissions.

A user may have one set of permissions granted explicitly for a resource and one or more other permissions based on group membership. When this happens, the least restrictive permission becomes the effective permission, unless one of the permissions is No Access.

Inheritance is not automatic in NTFS security: permissions or restrictions given to a user for a directory are not applied to its subdirectories unless specified by selecting the *Replace Permissions on Subdirectories* option in the Permissions dialog. Permissions on files within a directory are not changed unless the *Replace Permissions on Existing Files* option is selected, but new files created in the directory inherit the directory's permissions.

The Everyone group is given Full Control access to NTFS volumes by default, effectively disabling NTFS security. This permission should be removed or restricted to secure the volume.

ON THE EXAM

Some MCSE exam questions ask you to determine a user's effective permissions for a file or directory. Be sure you know the various NTFS permissions and know what happens when user and group permissions are combined.

Copying and moving files

Files on NTFS partitions can be moved or copied in the same manner as local files, using Explorer (accessible from the My Computer icon on each computer) or over the network. Permissions are not always moved with the file, however:

- If the file is *moved*, the permissions of the original file are copied to the new location. Files can only be moved within a single NTFS volume. If you drag a file to a location on the same volume, a move operation is performed by default; for a copy, hold down the Ctrl key.

- If the file is *copied*, the copied file inherits the permissions of the new directory. Dragging a file to a location on a different volume always results in a copy operation.

Of course, if the destination folder is on a FAT or FAT32 partition, NTFS permissions are lost. If a file from a FAT or FAT32 partition is copied to an NTFS location, it inherits the permissions of the new parent directory.

File Sharing

As with other Windows versions, Windows 2000 supports file sharing. A folder can be shared using the Sharing tab of the folder properties dialog. Shared folders are listed by their share names when a user browses the My Network Places window, as described earlier in this chapter.

File sharing supports its own type of security, called *shared folder security.* Click the *Permissions* button in the Sharing tab to display the Share Permissions dialog.

Shares have a simple set of permissions that provide a lesser degree of security than that provided by NTFS, but can be used even with shared FAT or FAT32 volumes. The share permissions are described in Table 1-6.

Table 1-6: Share Permissions

Permission	Description
Full Control	Provides full access to files in the folder
Change	Allows the user to create, write, or delete files in the folder
Read	Allows Read access to files and directory listings

As with NTFS security, the Everyone group is given Full Control rights to shares by default. To provide security, this permission should be removed or restricted. For each user with permissions for a folder, you can specify Allow or Deny for each of the permissions listed in Table 1-6. Typically Allow is used to grant access. The Deny setting can be used to explicitly deny access when a user may have access via a group or via a permission setting for a higher directory.

ON THE EXAM

The Deny setting in Windows 2000 replaces the No Access permission in earlier versions of Windows NT.

As with NTFS security, a user may have permissions for a share assigned to the user as well as one or more groups. In this case, the least restrictive permission is used, unless one of the permissions is explicitly denied. If a user has both NTFS permissions and share permissions for a directory, the most restrictive permission is used.

Monitoring Users and Shares

Windows 2000 includes the Shared Folders snap-in, which enables you to monitor share use and the files currently opened by users. To access this utility, either add the Shared Folders snap-in to an MMC console or use the Computer Management snap-in. Shared Folders is located under System Tools.

Under Shared Folders, there are three options that allow monitoring and administration of shares:

Shares
> Lists the currently defined shares. For each share, the path the share represents and the number of users currently connected to the share are displayed.

Sessions
> Lists the users who are currently accessing one or more shares on the computer. Highlight a section and select *Disconnect Session* from the Action menu to disconnect a session.

Open Files
> Lists all shared files currently open. For each file, the current user, the open mode (Read or Write), and the number of locks on the file are displayed.

Managing Printers

Windows 2000 includes comprehensive support for printers. Printers installed on a computer are defined in the Printers folder, available from the Control Panel. Several components are involved in the printing process:

Printer
> The Windows 2000 object that corresponds with a hardware printer (print device) and stores jobs to be printed in a queue. Also called a logical printer.

Print device
> A physical printer. Remember that in Windows 2000 terms, printers are software and print devices are hardware.

Print job
> A document sent to the printer. Print jobs are stored in a queue until they are sent to the printer.

Print server
> The server that controls a printer. This is usually the machine the printer is attached to. Both Windows 2000 Professional and Windows 2000 Server can act as print servers; the Professional version is limited to 10 concurrent user connections to the printer.

Installing and configuring printers

Select *Add Printer* from the Printers folder to install a printer. A wizard prompts you for information about the printer. You can configure a local printer or configure local access to a shared printer on another machine or on the Internet. You are asked to specify the port the printer is attached to, the printer manufacturer and type, and whether the printer will be shared.

After a printer is installed, you can access its Properties dialog to configure it. This dialog includes the following tabs:

General
> Includes options for the printer's location and description and allows you to choose the printer driver.

Sharing
> Specifies whether the printer is shared and under what name. You can also install drivers for the printer for different operating systems from this dialog. Users running other systems (such as Windows 98) can then download a driver when they install a local icon for the shared printer.

Ports
> Specifies the ports the printer is connected to. You can also create a printer pool, described later, by selecting multiple ports. LPT (parallel), COM (serial), and UNC paths to shared printers can be used.

Advanced
> Specifies a time period when the printer is available. The priority for printer access is also set in this tab. When multiple logical printers are defined for one physical printer, documents are printed based on the priority. This allows you to give certain groups of users priority access to a printer.

Color Management

> Includes options for color management, which is used to ensure that colors remain accurate on different display and output devices.

Security

> Allows you to set permissions for access to the printer, similar to those used with NTFS directories. Permissions affect both local and remote users.

Device Settings

> Includes settings specific to the printer, defined by the printer driver software. Depending on the driver, one or more additional tabs may also be available.

Print pools

A logical printer can be assigned to two or more physical printers on different ports. This configuration is called a *print pool*. To create a pool, select the *Enable printer pooling* option in the Ports tab of the Printer Properties dialog and select two or more ports.

Print pools should be used with identical printers, or at least compatible printers. A document is sent to the first available printer in the pool.

Scheduling and priorities

In addition to configuring one printer to access multiple print devices (print pool), you can configure one print device with several printers. This technique is useful to assign several different users or groups permissions for a printer with different priorities or schedules.

To assign schedules and priorities, use the Advanced tab of the Printer Properties dialog. Configure a time period for the printer to be available if needed. Priority can be set between 1 and 99; 99 is the highest priority. Jobs from a higher priority printer are always sent to the print device first.

Managing print jobs

Open a printer within the Printers folder to display jobs currently printing or waiting to print. The options in the Document menu allow you to pause, resume, restart, or cancel the current document. Members of the Administrators or Print Operators groups can pause all printing or purge all print jobs from the Printer menu.

The print jobs list is managed by the print spooler service. Spool files are stored on the boot partition by default. If this partition has insufficient space, you can change the spool location by selecting *Server Properties* from the File menu of the Printers folder. Select the Advanced tab and specify a path to the new folder.

Optimization and Troubleshooting

Windows 2000 includes a variety of utilities for monitoring computer or network use and troubleshooting. This section examines methods of monitoring system performance, optimizing, and solving common problems.

Monitoring Performance

Windows 2000 includes the Performance Console for monitoring system performance and the Event Viewer for displaying error messages and audit results. These are described in the following sections.

Performance Console

The Performance Console snap-in displays a graph of the system's current performance and can optionally display a report or create a log. To start Performance Console, select *Performance* from the Administrative Tools Control Panel applet.

Performance Console monitors data items called *counters*; it includes a number of objects that contain counters for specific users. The following objects are commonly used:

Processor
    Includes counters related to the system processor (CPU). The Processor Time counter measures of the processor load.

Memory
    Includes counters that measure memory (RAM) performance.

PagingFile
    Includes counters that measure virtual memory performance.

LogicalDisk
    Includes counters related to logical disk drives (volumes). These counters are disabled by default.

Process
    Allows you to view information about a specific process. Useful for monitoring server processes.

ON THE EXAM

This is just a sampling of the objects included in Performance Console. The other categories available depend on the installed protocols and services. You should be familiar with the available objects for the Windows 2000 Professional MCSE exam.

Event Viewer

Event Viewer, similar to the utility of the same name in Windows NT 4.0, displays error messages and other information about past events. In Windows 2000, Event Viewer is an MMC snap-in. To access this snap-in, select *Event Viewer* from the Administrative Tools Control Panel applet.

Event Viewer displays three separate logs. For each log, events are displayed with their corresponding type, date, time, and source. Events are categorized by type, including information, warning, and error. The following logs are available:

Application log
> Includes events logged by applications, and such problems as application crashes.

Security log
> Includes messages relating to security. Security problems, such as incorrect logons, are included in this log if auditing is enabled. Security auditing is disabled by default.

System log
> Includes system error messages and status messages for system reboots and other events. If system events are selected for auditing, these are also included in this log.

Troubleshooting Boot Problems

If a Windows 2000 computer encounters a problem, it is often unable to boot correctly. The following sections describe some common problems with the Windows 2000 boot process.

Boot options

At the boot menu, you can press F8 to display a menu of boot options. These are useful for troubleshooting a computer that will not boot normally or that encounters problems during the boot process. The menu includes the following options:

Safe Mode
> This basic mode does not load network drivers, sets the display to VGA mode, and does not run applications set to run at startup. This often eliminates the cause of the boot failure and allows you to access the system to correct the problem.

Safe Mode with Networking
> This mode is identical to safe mode, but also loads network drivers.

Safe Mode with Command Prompt
> This mode is identical to safe mode, but displays a command prompt instead of the GUI. This mode does not include networking support.

Enable Boot Logging
> If this option is enabled, events related to the boot process are logged to the \winnt\ntbtlog.txt file.

Enable VGA Mode
> If this option is enabled, the system boots normally, but with the default VGA video driver.

Last Known Good Configuration
> If this option is selected, the system loads the control set from the Last Known Good control set, which is created after each successful boot. This often eliminates boot problems.

Directory Services Restore Mode
> This option is used to restore the Active Directory database and is available only on domain controllers running Windows 2000 Server.

Debugging Mode

Enables debugging features. This option is available only on Windows 2000 Server.

Boot Normally

Exits the Advanced options screen and boots normally.

ON THE EXAM

The Windows 2000 boot process is described in detail earlier in this chapter.

Emergency Repair Disk (ERD)

Windows 2000 supports the use of an emergency repair disk (ERD) to fix some problems with the registry or system files. You were prompted to create an ERD during installation.

To create an updated ERD, use the RDISK /S command at the command prompt. This disk should be updated frequently. Attempting to repair the system using an older disk can cause more problems than it solves.

To recover using the ERD, boot the Windows 2000 installation floppy or CD-ROM. When the installation program starts, press R to repair the current installation. Insert the disk and press D to recover using the disk.

Recovery Console

The Windows 2000 Recovery Console is available by pressing R after booting the Setup disks or CD-ROM. This loads a DOS-like command console that lets you perform basic file management tasks on FAT, FAT32, or NTFS volumes; this may be useful as a last resort to correct a problem that's preventing the computer from booting.

To start the recovery console, boot the Windows 2000 installation floppy or CD-ROM. When the installation program starts, press R to repair the current installation. Press C from the repair options to start the console.

At the console, type help for a list of available commands. The following are some of the most useful commands:

Cd/Chdir

Change directory (without options, displays current directory)

Copy

Copy a file

Del/Delete

Delete a file

Dir

Display a directory listing for the current directory

Disable
> Stop a system service

Enable
> Start a system service

Exit
> Exit the recovery console

Fdisk
> Manage disk partitions

Fixboot
> Fix a corrupt boot sector

Fixmbr
> Fix a corrupt MBR (master boot record)

Format
> Format a disk partition

Help
> Display available commands

Logon
> Log on to access secure Windows 2000 files

Map
> Display current drive mappings

Md
> Make a directory

More
> Display a text file, one page at a time

Rd/Rmdir
> Remove a directory

Ren/Rename
> Rename a file

Systemroot
> Switch to the system root directory (typically c:\windows)

ON THE EXAM

You should have a basic idea of the recovery console commands for the Windows 2000 Professional MCSE exam, but you should not need to know exact syntax.

Suggested Exercises

Because the Windows 2000 Professional MCSE exam is the first exam in the Windows 2000 track, it includes many questions about the basic operation of Windows 2000, its user interface and options, and its administrative utilities. You should have experience using and installing Windows 2000 Professional on a variety of systems for the exam.

Although it's possible to study for the exam using Windows 2000 Professional on a single computer, we recommend at least two networked computers so that you can practice networking, file sharing, and other features. Some of the exercises in this section require two computers on a network.

In addition to performing the exercises below, you should also have experience using each of Windows 2000 Professional's administrative tools described in the Study Guide section.

Installing Windows 2000 Professional

1. Install Windows 2000 Professional on a computer:

   a. Use the HCL and the hardware requirements listed in the Study Guide to determine whether the computer can run Windows 2000 Professional.

   b. Install a network card on the computer.

   c. Based on the hardware and the existing operating system, if any, determine the installation method to use.

   d. Perform the installation of Windows 2000 Professional, following the steps in the Study Guide. Install on an NTFS partition so that you'll be able to use the security features.

   e. If you have a second computer, install Windows 2000 on this computer, following steps a through d.

2. Install Windows NT or Windows 95/98 on a computer (or use an existing installation) and then upgrade the computer to Windows 2000 Professional. Note the settings that are preserved.

3. Use Setup Manager to create an answer file and use this file to perform an automated installation of Windows 2000 Professional.

4. Check Microsoft's web site for information about any Windows 2000 Professional service packs available. If available, download and install them.

Configuring Windows 2000 Professional

1. Run Microsoft Management Console (MMC) by typing MMC at the Run prompt. Add snap-ins to the console and verify that they work.

2. Try each of the items in the Administrative Tools menu. Note which of these are MMC consoles and the options they display.

3. Use Task Scheduler to schedule various programs at different times, and verify that they are executed.

4. Experiment with each of the applets in the Control Panel and note the options available.

5. Run REGEDT32 and browse through the registry keys, then look at the registry with REGEDIT and note the difference. Try editing and deleting keys (to avoid damaging the registry, log in as a new user and edit settings under that user's HKEY_USERS subkey).

Managing Disk Storage

1. Use the Disk Management snap-in to view the disks and partitions installed in your system.

2. If you have an empty disk drive available, create a basic disk partition (primary or extended) and format it with a filesystem.

3. Upgrade an existing basic disk with two or more partitions to a dynamic disk.

4. If you have two drives available, try creating a spanned volume, deleting it, and creating a striped volume.

5. Use the Disk Defragmenter snap-in to analyze and defragment an NTFS or FAT volume.

6. Set up disk quotas for all users. Log on as a non-Administrator user and save files until you reach the quota. As the Administrator, view the quota entries and note the user's status.

7. Encrypt a folder and verify that it can still be accessed. Decrypt it by disabling the Encryption option.

8. Use NTBACKUP to back up and restore files. Because backups can be made to a disk folder, you can use a folder on the same disk if you do not have a separate disk or tape drive.

Managing Network Components

1. Connect two or more computers to a network, then verify that one computer can access a shared file on the other computer.

2. Set both computers to use the same IP address and note the problems you have accessing shared files. Correct the problem.

3. If you have access to a network with an Active Directory domain, log on to the domain and browse its resources using the My Network Places window.

Administration and Security

1. Create an assortment of users on a Windows 2000 Professional computer and assign each to a number of groups.

2. Create a new group and assign several users as members.

3. Log on using the default Administrator and Guest accounts and note the differences in available resources. (You may need to enable the Guest account.)

4. Set various options in the Account Policy, Security Options, and Audit Policy snap-ins and verify that they are enforced.

5. Experiment with shared file and NTFS security settings by restricting a user's access to various folders. Log on as that user and verify that access is restricted.

6. Use the Shared Folders snap-in to monitor users and shares.

7. Install a printer (or just a printer driver if you have no printer) and share it. Verify that it can be accessed across the network. Send several print jobs to the printer, and open the printer's window to manage the jobs.

Optimization and Troubleshooting

1. Use the Performance Console snap-in to monitor a variety of counters.

2. View the system, application, and error logs in the Event Viewer snap-in and note the entries listed.

3. Press F8 to access the Boot Options menu while booting Windows 2000 Professional. Try each of the valid boot options. Especially note the system's behavior when in safe mode and its variations.

4. Load the Recovery Console using the setup boot disks. Type the HELP command to list the available commands, then experiment with some of these.

5. If you have two networked computers, try removing a network cable. Attempt to access shared files or browse the network from each computer and note the errors that occur.

Practice Tests

Comprehensive Test

1. Which of the following terms refers to an operating system's ability to run different portions of an application concurrently on the same processor?

   a. Multithreading

   b. Multitasking

   c. Multiprocessing

   d. Memory protection

2. You are installing Windows 2000 Professional on a computer with a Pentium 200 MHz processor, 1 GB of disk storage, 24 MB of memory, and a 16X speed CD-ROM drive. Which component will need upgrading before the installation?

   a. CD-ROM

   b. Memory

   c. CPU

   d. Disk

3. Which of the following is a list of hardware supported by Windows 2000 Professional?

   a. FAT

   b. HCL

   c. CHKUPGRD.EXE

   d. HAL

4. Which of the following filesystems is supported by Windows 2000 Professional but not by Windows NT 4.0?

    a.   NTFS

    b.   HPFS

    c.   FAT

    d.   FAT32

5. Which of the following filesystems can be used for a dual-boot system with Windows 2000 Professional and Windows 98? (Select all that apply.)

    a.   NTFS

    b.   HPFS

    c.   FAT

    d.   FAT32

6. Which of the following filesystems is not supported by Windows 2000 Professional?

    a.   NTFS

    b.   HPFS

    c.   FAT

    d.   FAT32

7. Which of the following filesystem conversions are possible using utilities included with Windows 2000 Professional? (Select all that apply.)

    a.   FAT to NTFS

    b.   FAT32 to NTFS

    c.   NTFS to FAT

    d.   NTFS to FAT32

8. Which of these operating systems cannot transfer any of its settings when upgrading to Windows 2000?

    a.   Windows NT 4.0

    b.   Windows NT 3.51

    c.   Windows 95

    d.   Windows 3.11

9. Which of the following can create an unattended installation answer file?

    a.   System Preparation Tool

    b.   Setup Manager

    c.   CHKUPGRD.EXE

    d.   UNATTEND.TXT

10. Which of the following tasks are performed by the System Preparation Tool? (Select all that apply.)

    a.   Create unattended installation answer file

    b.   Create a generic system for duplication

    c.   Create a disk image for duplication

    d.   Create a mini-Setup Wizard

11. Which command is used to install a Windows 2000 service pack during installation?

    a.   `winnt32 /slip`

    b.   `chkupgrade /slip`

    c.   `upgrade /slip`

    d.   `sysprep /slip`

12. MMC consoles can be used to perform which of the following tasks? (Select all that apply.)

    a.   Manage disks and partitions

    b.   Manage printers

    c.   View system information

    d.   View error and event logs

13. Which of the following utilities is used to schedule regular system backups?

    a.   Task Scheduler

    b.   NTBACKUP

    c.   AT.EXE

    d.   Job Scheduler

14. Which Windows 2000 Professional Control Panel applet is used to configure modems?

    a.   Modems

    b.   Phone and Modem

    c.   Ports

    d.   Telephony

15. Which of the following Control Panel applets is used to manage virtual memory settings?

    a.   System

    b.   Memory

    c.   Devices

    d.   Server

16. Which registry subtree stores file associations?

    a.   HKEY_CLASSES_ROOT

    b.   HKEY_LOCAL_MACHINE

    c.   HKEY_CURRENT_CONFIG

    d.   HKEY_DYN_DATA

17. Which registry subtree stores information loaded from a hardware profile?

    a.   HKEY_CLASSES_ROOT

    b.   HKEY_LOCAL_MACHINE

    c.   HKEY_CURRENT_CONFIG

    d.   HKEY_DYN_DATA

18. Which of the following is Microsoft's preferred registry editor for Windows 2000 Professional?

    a.   REGEDT32

    b.   REGEDIT

    c.   WINREG

    d.   HKEY_LOCAL_MACHINE

19. Which of the following is able to search the entire registry (all subtrees) at once for a value?

    a.   REGEDT32

    b.   REGEDIT

    c.   WINREG

    d.   HKEY_LOCAL_MACHINE

20. Which Windows 2000 disk system includes primary and extended partitions?

    a.   Basic disks

    b.   Dynamic disks

    c.   VFAT

    d.   NTFS

21. Which of the following disk conversions can be performed by Windows 2000? (Select all that apply.)

    a.   Basic to dynamic

    b.   Dynamic to basic

    c.   FAT to NTFS

    d.   NTFS to FAT

22. Which of the following can be bootable? (Select all that apply.)

    a.   Primary partitions

    b.   Extended partitions

    c.   Logical drives

    d.   Simple dynamic volumes

23. Which Windows 2000 partition contains the \WINNT directory?

    a.   Boot partition

    b.   System partition

    c.   Install partition

    d.   The C: drive

24. Which Windows 2000 partition contains the NTLDR boot loader?

    a.   Boot partition

    b.   System partition

    c.   Install partition

    d.   The C: drive

25. Which of the following disk configurations provides fault tolerance?

    a.   Simple volume

    b.   Spanned volume

    c.   Striped volume

    d.   None of the above

26. Which of the following disk configurations interleaves data between two or more physical disks?

    a.   Simple volume

    b.   Spanned volume

    c.   Striped volume

    d.   None of the above

27. Which of these volume types can be extended by adding an additional area of free space?

    a.   Simple volume

    b.   Spanned volume

    c.   Striped volume

    d.   Striped volume with parity

28. Which filesystems can be defragmented using the Disk Defragmenter snap-in? (Select all that apply.)

    a.   FAT

    b.   FAT32

    c.   NTFS

    d.   CDFS

29. Which backup types clear the archive bits? (Select all that apply.)

    a.   Normal

    b.   Differential

    c.   Incremental

    d.   Copy

30. Which of the following is not a valid TCP/IP address?

    a.   128.60.22.2

    b.   192.168.0.1

    c.   0.238.62.2

    d.   216.92.49.99

31. DNS performs which of the following functions?

    a.   Resolves IP hostnames to IP addresses

    b.   Resolves NetBIOS names to IP addresses

    c.   Assigns names to IP addresses

    d.   Translates IP addresses to MAC addresses

32. Which of the following protocols automatically assigns IP addresses?

    a.   TCP

    b.   DHCP

    c.   WINS

    d.   FTP

33. Which of the following are dial-up protocols? (Select all that apply.)

    a.   SLIP

    b.   DHCP

    c.   PPP

    d.   HTTP

34. Which of the following transport protocols is used chiefly by NetWare networks?

    a.   TCP/IP

    b.   IPX/SPX

    c.   NetBEUI

    d.   DLC

35. Which of these transport protocols is used by mainframe computers and printers?

    a.   TCP/IP

    b.   IPX/SPX

    c.   NetBEUI

    d.   DLC

36. In Active Directory, which term represents an individual resource, such as a user or printer?

    a.   Tree

    b.   Forest

    c.   Organizational Unit

    d.   Object

37. Which type of user account can be used only in a network with at least one Windows 2000 Server computer?

    a.   Local user account

    b.   Domain user account

    c.   Local guest account

    d.   Local administrator

38. Which of the following user accounts is disabled by default?

    a.   Administrator

    b.   Guest

    c.   Everyone

    d.   Backup

39. Account lockouts happen when there is an excess of:

    a.   Concurrent users

    b.   Logons per day

    c.   Invalid logon attempts

    d.   Password changes

40. Where can you set a maximum age before a password is required to be changed?

    a.   Account Policy

    b.   Security Options

c. Audit Policy

d. User Profile

41. Which set of options can be used to eliminate the requirement for the Ctrl-Alt-Del keystroke at logon?

a. Account Policy

b. Security Options

c. Audit Policy

d. User Profile

42. In Windows 2000 printing, which of the following refers to a hardware printer?

a. Printer

b. Print device

c. Print spooler

d. Printer driver

43. Which utility can display a graph of CPU usage over time?

a. System Monitor

b. Performance Console

c. Event Viewer

d. Performance Monitor

44. You are troubleshooting a computer that is unable to boot properly. The boot process aborts during the real mode portion of the boot process. Which of the following boot options may allow you to complete a boot and correct the problem?

a. Safe mode

b. VGA mode

c. Recovery Console

d. Reinstall Windows 2000

Case Study

Text Formatting Key:

Describes requirements

Conflicts with requirement

Irrelevant background information

You are the network administrator for FSC Software company. The company's current network consists of **ten computers running Windows 98, four computers** running Windows NT Workstation 4.0, and a Macintosh machine in the graphics department. All of the **Windows 98** machines have **16 MB of RAM**. Two of the **Windows NT** computers have *16 MB*, and the other two have **64 MB**.

You are **adding four** new **Pentium III 600 MHz** PCs **to the network**. They have **10 GB hard disks, floppy drives, network cards**, and **32 MB of RAM**. They currently *do not have CD-ROM drives*. You would like to **install Windows 2000 Professional** on the new machines. You also plan to **upgrade the NT 4.0 machines to Windows 2000 Professional**, *preferably without spending* any extra *money.*

Multiple Choice

1. Which of the following additional hardware will the new machines require before installing Windows 2000 Professional?

    a.   Larger hard disks

    b.   Additional RAM

    c.   CD-ROM drives

    d.   None of the above

2. How many of the Windows NT machines can be upgraded to Windows 2000 professional without a hardware upgrade?

    a.   One

    b.   Two

    c.   Four

    d.   None

Create a Tree

1. You are considering a number of other upgrades to the network. Place each of the following under the correct heading: *Possible with Windows 2000 Professional* or *Requires Windows 2000 Server*.

    a.   Upgrade from a workgroup-based to a domain-based network.

    b.   Use AppleTalk to access shared files on the Windows network from the Macintosh.

    c.   Use NTFS security to control access to files.

    d.   Install a public web server.

    e.   Use shared folders to share data across the network.

2. Place each of the following filesystems under one of these headings: *Windows 2000/Windows 98*, *Windows 2000/NT*, or *Windows 2000/98/NT*.

    a.   FAT

    b.   FAT32

    c.   NTFS

Answers

Comprehensive Test

1. a. Multithreading is the ability to run different portions of an application (threads) at the same time.

2. b. Only the memory would require an upgrade (to 32 MB or preferably more) before installation.

3. b. The HCL (Hardware Compatibility List) is a list of hardware supported by Windows 2000 Professional.

4. d. FAT32 is supported by Windows 2000 Professional and by Windows 98, but not by Windows NT 4.0.

5. c, d. FAT or FAT32 could be used for a dual-boot system with Windows 2000 Professional and Windows 98.

6. b. The HPFS filesystem is supported only by Windows NT 3.51 and earlier and by OS/2.

7. a, b. Windows 2000 Professional can convert FAT or FAT32 to NTFS. NTFS partitions cannot be converted to other formats.

8. d. Windows 3.11 cannot be upgraded to Windows 2000 Professional; a clean installation of Windows 2000 Professional would be required.

9. b. Setup Manager can create an unattended installation file. UNATTEND.TXT (choice d) is a typical name for the unattended installation file.

10. b, d. The System Preparation Tool creates a generic system for duplication; it does not perform the actual duplication. It also creates a mini-Setup Wizard to personalize each system.

11. c. The `upgrade.exe /slip` command integrates a service pack into the installation files for use during installation.

12. a, c, d. MMC consoles can be used to manage disks, view system information, and view error and event logs; printers (choice b) are managed using the Printers Control Panel.

13. b. NTBACKUP can schedule regular backup jobs. Task Scheduler (choice a) schedules applications, but is not intended for backups.

14. b. Modems are configured using the Phone and Modem Control Panel applet.

15. a. Virtual memory is managed using the System Control Panel applet.

16. a. The HKEY_CLASSES_ROOT registry subtree stores file associations.

17. b. The HKEY_LOCAL_MACHINE registry subtree stores information loaded from a hardware profile.

18. a. REGEDT32 is Microsoft's preferred registry editor.

19. b. REGEDIT is able to search the entire registry for a value.

20. a. Basic disks include primary and extended partitions.

21. a, c. Windows 2000 can convert basic to dynamic disks. Dynamic disks cannot be converted to basic (choice b) without repartitioning. Windows 2000 can also convert FAT partitions to NTFS partitions. NTFS partitions cannot be converted to FAT without reformatting.

22. a, d. Primary partitions on basic disks and simple volumes on dynamic disks can be bootable.

23. a. The boot partition contains the \WINNT folder.

24. b. The system partition contains the NTLDR boot loader.

25. d. None of these volumes provide fault tolerance. Fault-tolerant disk configurations, such as mirrored volumes and disk striping with parity, are supported by Windows 2000 Server.

26. c. A striped volume interleaves data between two or more physical disks.

27. b. A spanned volume can be extended. A striped volume (choice c) cannot be extended.

28. a, b, c. FAT, FAT32, and NTFS volumes can be defragmented with the Disk Defragmenter snap-in.

29. a, c. Normal and incremental backups clear the archive bits; differential and copy backups (choices b and d) do not.

30. c. Zero cannot be used in the first or last octets, so this is an invalid address.

31. a. DNS (Domain Name Service) resolves IP hostnames to IP addresses.

32. b. DHCP (Dynamic Host Configuration Protocol) dynamically assigns IP addresses to clients.

33. a, c. SLIP (Serial Line Internet Protocol) and PPP (Point-to-Point Protocol) are dial-up protocols.

34. b. IPX/SPX is used chiefly by NetWare networks.

35. d. The DLC protocol is used by IBM mainframe computers and by some network printers.

36. d. An object represents an individual user or other network resource in Active Directory.

37. b. Domain user accounts can be used only in Windows 2000 Server.

38. b. The Guest account is disabled by default.

39. c. Accounts are locked out when there is an excessive number of invalid logon attempts.

40. a. The maximum password age can be set in Account Policy.

41. b. Security Options includes an option to eliminate the requirement for the Ctrl-Alt-Del keystroke.

42. b. Print Device refers to a hardware printer.

43. b. Performance Console can display a graph of CPU usage over time.

44. a. Safe mode may allow you to boot and correct the problem. VGA mode (choice b) would not be effective because the problem happens in the real mode boot phase, and therefore probably does not involve the video card or drivers.

Case Study: Multiple Choice

1. d. None of the above. The machines have sufficient RAM and disk storage. Although they do not have CD-ROM drives, you can install from a shared directory on the network or a local copy of the \I386 directory.

2. b. The two machines with 16 MB of RAM will require a memory upgrade before installing Windows 2000 Professional.

Case Study: Create a Tree

Create a Tree Answer # 1

Possible with Windows 2000 Professional	Requires Windows 2000 Server
Use NTFS security to control access to files	Upgrade from a workgroup-based to a domain-based network.
Use shared folders to share data across the network	Use AppleTalk to access shared files on the Windows network from the Macintosh.
	Install a public web server.

Create a Tree Answer # 2

Windows 2000/Windows 98	Windows 2000/NT	Windows 2000/98/NT
FAT32	NTFS	FAT

Highlighter's Index

Windows 2000 Basics

Operating System Characteristics

Operating System	RAM	Disk Storage Required	Multi-tasking?	Multi-processing?	Plug and Play?
DOS	256K	None	No	No	No
Windows 3.1x	2 MB	10 MB	Cooperative	No	No
Windows 95	4 MB	40 MB	Preemptive	No	Yes
Windows 98	16 MB	175 MB	Preemptive	No	Yes
Windows NT Workstation 4.0	12 MB	117 MB	Preemptive (protected)	Yes (two processors)	No
Windows NT Server 4.0	16 MB	124 MB	Preemptive (protected)	Yes	No
Windows 2000 Professional	32 MB	650 MB	Preemptive (protected)	Yes	Yes
Windows 2000 Server	64 MB	671 MB	Preemptive (protected)	Yes	Yes

Windows 2000

New version of Windows NT (after NT 4.0)

Two versions: Professional and Server (also Advanced Server and Datacenter)

New features: Active Directory, dynamic disks, MMC, user interface enhancements, hardware support, VPN support, IPP (Internet printing)

Network Types

Peer-to-peer (workgroup)
> Each machine acts as both client and server; no dedicated servers; best for 10 workstations or less; supported by Windows 95, 98, and 2000 Professional

Client/server (domain)
> Uses one or more dedicated servers (domain controllers); centralized security and administration; best for 10 workstations or more or when security is important; supported by Windows NT Server and 2000 Server

Computer Types

Domain controllers
> Run Windows 2000 Server; each maintains a copy of user account database (Active Directory); multiple controllers synchronize periodically

Member servers
> Run Windows 2000 Server, but not configured as domain controllers; each relies on domain controllers for security; do not maintain a copy of the Directory database

Clients
> Typically run Windows 2000 Professional, Windows 95/98, and others; can log in to the domain and access its resources

Boot and System Partitions

System partition
> NTBOOTDD.SYS, NTLDR, BOOT.INI, BOOTSECT.DOS, NTDETECT.COM

Boot partition
> NTOSKRNL.EXE, HAL.DLL, \WINNT files

BOOT.INI

ARC entries:

> `adapter(x)disk(x)rdisk(x)partition(x)\directory = description`

BOOT.INI options:

/basevideo
> Use VGA mode instead of defined video driver

/fastdetect=ports
> Disable scanning for a serial mouse on the COM ports specified

---

Installing Windows 2000 Professional

Hardware Requirements

Item	Minimum	Recommended
CPU	Pentium 133 MHz	Pentium 200 MHz or faster

Item	Minimum	Recommended
RAM	32 MB	64 MB or more
Display	VGA	Super VGA, or better
Hard disk	SCSI or IDE; 650 MB of space required for OS	2 GB or more
CD-ROM	SCSI or IDE (not required for network installations)	12X speed or faster
Network interface card	Not required	Any supported by NT; only required for network access

Filesystems

FAT (file allocation table)

Originally implemented by DOS; limited to 8-character file names with 3-character extensions; partitions up to 2 GB

FAT32

Implemented by Windows 95 (OSR2 and later) and Windows 98; provides for more reliable storage and more efficient use of space; partitions up to 4 TB (terabytes)

NTFS (NT filesystem)

Supported only by Windows NT 4.0 and Windows 2000; supports long filenames; partitions up to 16 EB (exabytes); fault tolerance, security, encryption (in Windows 2000), and compression

Upgrading to Windows 2000

Hardware compatibility check:

```
winnt32 /checkupgradeonly
```

From Windows 95/98: Preserves some settings
From Windows NT: Preserves Control Panel settings, network configuration, registry settings, Start menu contents, desktop layout, preferences for some utilities, security settings

Unattended Installation

Answer file: Specifies options for installation
Setup Manager: Creates answer files, SYSPREP files, remote installation scripts
Disk Duplication: System Preparation Tool (SYSPREP) creates generic system; may require reinstall; drive imaging requires third-party software
Remote Installation Services (RIS): Install remotely with floppy or boot image from central distribution

Service Packs

Upgrade.exe installs service pack
Slipstreaming: `Upgrade.exe /slip` adds service pack changes to installation files for use during install

Configuring Windows 2000 Professional

Microsoft Management Console (MMC)

Uses consoles, snap-ins, extensions
Save consoles in author mode or user mode with full or limited access
Used for most Windows 2000 management functions

Task Scheduler

Schedules tasks daily, weekly, monthly, at specified times
Requires username and password

Registry Subtrees

HKEY_CLASSES_ROOT
Stores file associations

HKEY_CURRENT_USER
Stores Control Panel settings; loaded from user profile at logon

HKEY_LOCAL_MACHINE
Stores hardware-specific data

HKEY_USERS
Stores default user settings and settings for each user profile

HKEY_CURRENT_CONFIG
Stores dynamic configuration information and temporary values

HKEY_DYN_DATA
Stores dynamic hardware information

Registry Editors

REGEDT32
Uses separate windows for subtrees; supports security, view-only option; recommended by Microsoft

REGEDIT
Uses single window; can search entire registry; does not support security

Managing Disk Storage

Basic Disks

Disks are divided into partitions.
Primary partition: One active per disk; bootable; one drive letter.
Extended partition: Uses space not used by primary; one per disk; divided into logical drives; not bootable.

Dynamic Disks

Each disk is a single partition; contains one or more volumes.

Simple volumes: FAT, FAT32, or NTFS; can be resized dynamically.
Spanned volumes: Treat 2-32 disks as single volume; data stored sequentially; not fault tolerant.
Striped volumes: Treat 2-32 disks as single volume; data is interleaved between disks; not fault tolerant; faster speed.

Disk Quotas

Can be set for all users or individual users
Set from Quota tab of Disk Properties
Quota Entries window displays quotas; monitors users

EFS (Encrypted Filesystem)

Dynamically encrypts files with public-key encryption.
Files are decrypted dynamically when accessed by valid user.
Set for folders in General tab of Properties.
Decrypt by turning off encryption option.

Backup Types

Normal (full backup)

Backs up all of the files on the volume, regardless of when files were modified, and clears the archive bits

Incremental backup

Backs up all of the files that have been modified since the last backup and clears the archive bits

Differential backup

Backs up all of the files changed since the last full backup; does not clear the archive bits

Copy

Similar to a full backup, but does not clear the archive bits

Daily copy

Backs up all files modified on the current date; does not modify archive bits

Managing Network Components

Protocol Suites

Protocol	Routable	Typical Application
TCP/IP	Yes	Unix; Windows NT; Windows 2000
NetBEUI	No	Small networks; Windows 95/98; Windows for Workgroups
IPX/SPX	Yes	NetWare compatibility
AppleTalk	Yes	Macintosh compatibility
DLC	No	IBM mainframes; some printers and print servers

IP Address Classes

Class	First Byte Range	Network/Host Octets	Number of Networks	Hosts per Network
A	1–126	1/3	126	16,777,214
B	128–191	2/2	16,382	65,534
C	192–223	3/1	2,097,150	254

Administration and Security

Users and Groups

Local users: For one computer; Windows 2000 Professional
Domain users: For domain; Windows 2000 Server domain controllers
Local groups: For one computer; Windows 2000 Professional only
Global groups: For domain; Windows 2000 Server only

NTFS Permissions

Permission	Description
Read	View a directory's contents or open a file
Write	Write data to a file or create new files in a directory
Delete	Delete a file or directory
Change Permissions	Modify the permissions assigned to the file or directory
Execute	Execute a program file
Take Ownership	Modify the ownership of a file or directory

File Sharing Permissions

Permission	Description
Full Control	Provides full access to files in the folder
Change	Allows the user to create, write, or delete files in the folder
Read	Allows Read access to files and directory listings

Optimization and Troubleshooting

Monitoring Performance

Performance console: Monitors counters; can chart, log, and alert
Event Viewer: Views system, application, and security logs

Troubleshooting Boot Problems

Press F8 for boot menu.
Last Known Good: Loads control set from last successful boot
Recovery Console: Loads from setup boot disks; DOS-like command interface

PART 2

Windows 2000 Server

Exam Overview

Microsoft Windows 2000 Server is one of four Windows 2000 operating systems. Windows 2000 Professional, covered in Part 1, is a client operating system that replaces Windows NT Workstation. Windows 2000 Advanced Server and Datacenter Server are scaled-up versions of Windows 2000 Server.

Microsoft's MCP Exam 70-215, *Installing, Configuring, and Administering Microsoft Windows 2000 Server*, will measure your ability to administer Windows 2000 Server primarily as a member server in an Active Directory environment. You will also need to be familiar with using Windows 2000 Server as a file, application, print, and web server.

Windows 2000 is often used a client/server environment. It is much easier to understand a server's functions if you are familiar with the client's needs. I would recommend that you read Part 1, *Windows 2000 Professional*, before reading this chapter. We have arranged the parts of this book in the order that we would recommend you take the tests.

Objectives

Need to Know	Reference
How to upgrade from NT 4.0	"Installing Windows 2000 Server" on page 102
How to create unattended answer files using Setup Manager	"Unattended installation" on page 105
How to deploy service packs	"Installing service packs" on page 106
How to troubleshoot failed installations	"Understanding failed installations" on page 106
How to control access to printers	"Print Server Administration" on page 125

Need to Know	*Reference*
How to create and manage user profiles	"User profiles" on page 123
How to create and manage policies	"Managing Group Policies" on page 125
How to manage network protocols and services	"Managing Network Components" on page 119
How to create and manage a virtual private network (VPN)	"Virtual private networks" on page 122
How to manage processes	"Task Manager" on page 128
How to recover from a disk failure	"Disk Tools" on page 129
How to use safe mode	"Safe Mode" on page 130

Need to Apply	*Reference*
Install Windows 2000 Server (attended and unattended)	"Unattended installation" on page 105
Create and manage Distributed Filesystems (standalone and domain)	"The Distributed Filesystem" on page 111
Update, sign, and manage device drivers	"Device Drivers" on page 126
IIS permissions	"WebDAV permissions" on page 120
Install and manage Terminal Services	"Remote administration mode" on page 121
Use Terminal Services for remote administration	"Remote administration mode" on page 121
Share applications with Terminal Services	"Application sharing mode" on page 121
Use the Encrypted Filesystem (EFS)	"The Encrypted Filesystem (EFS)" on page 112
Assign disk quotas	"Disk quotas" on page 109
Use Data Compression	"Data Compression" on page 114
Manage and configure remote access	"Remote Access" on page 122
Audit events	"Auditing" on page 127
Use the Security Configuration and Analysis snap-in	"Security Configuration and Analysis" on page 127
Use the Performance Console	"Performance Console" on page 128
Use the Recovery Console	"Recovery Console" on page 130
Use Windows Backup	"Backup and Restore" on page 116
Hardware configuration and troubleshooting	"Hardware Issues" on page 130

Study Guide

This chapter includes the following sections, which address various topics covered on the Windows 2000 Server MCSE exam:

Window 2000 Server Basics

Describes the editions of Windows 2000 Server, including Advanced and Datacenter Server. Covers Windows 2000 architecture, including user and kernel modes, the Hardware Abstraction layer, and networking basics.

Installing Windows 2000 Server

Describes the hardware requirements and installation options for Windows 2000. Covers the installation steps, including pre-copy, text mode, and GUI mode. Covers unattended installation options and failed installations. Also covers NT domains and Active Directory.

Managing Disk Storage

Covers NTFS Version 5, including disk quotas, reparse points, and Native Structured Storage. Also covers link tracking, sparse files, the Distributed File-system, and the Encrypted Filesystem.

Windows 2000 Active Directory

Covers Active Directory basics, installation, and management of Active Directory. Also gives definitions of common Active Directory terminology.

Managing Network Components

Describes Internet Information Server 5, Telnet and FTP services, Terminal Services, and remote access.

Administration and Security

Describes users, user profiles, groups, group nesting, and managing Group Policies. Also covers printing, device drivers, auditing, and Kerberos.

Optimization and Troubleshooting

Describes the Task Manager, *Performance Console*, Network Monitor, SNMP, and disk tools. Also covers hardware issues, safe mode, and the recovery console.

Windows 2000 Server Basics

Windows 2000 is a group of operating systems that support both the client/server and peer-to-peer networking models. It is Microsoft's successor to the Windows NT platform. Windows 2000 Professional, covered in Part 1, replaces Windows NT Workstation. Windows NT Server and Enterprise Server are replaced by three versions of the Windows 2000 Server platform. This chapter will help you to prepare for MCP Exam 70-215, *Installing, Configuring, and Administering Microsoft Windows 2000 Server.*

Windows 2000 Server Editions

Windows 2000 Server is available in three editions: Server, Advanced Server, and Datacenter Server. Windows 2000 Advanced Server and Datacenter Server are not emphasized on the Windows 2000 Server exam, but you should be familiar with their roles within the Windows 2000 family of operating systems.

Windows 2000 Server

Windows 2000 Server is the least expensive of the three new server operating systems. It includes application, file, print, web, and FTP servers. The most significant change, compared to Microsoft NT Server Version 4, is the addition of Active Directory, which unifies administration of users, groups, computers, printers, applications, files, and security into a single, hierarchical structure. Active Directory replaces the older Windows NT Domain structure. Windows 2000 Server would be a good choice for small- to medium-sized networks.

Windows 2000 Advanced Server

Windows 2000 Advanced Server includes all the features of Windows 2000 Server and adds greater scalability features, including clustering and support for eight CPU symmetric multiprocessing, compared to four in Windows 2000 Server. Windows 2000 Advanced Server would be a good choice for medium- to large-sized networks.

Windows 2000 Datacenter Server

Windows 2000 Datacenter Server provides many advanced features, such as support for 16 CPUs (as many as 32 in some custom OEM setups) and 4-way clustering with built-in load balancing. Datacenter Server is meant to handle the demands of large e-commerce web sites and other large-scale projects. Many Datacenter installations will run on custom hardware designed to handle the specific needs of the particular project.

Windows 2000 Architecture

Windows 2000, like Windows NT, is a modular operating system. It consists of many separate components that all work together in a structured way. These components reside in one of two layers, *user mode* and *kernel mode*. These layers are further divided into subsystems. The core of the operating system runs in kernel mode. Applications run in user mode.

User mode

The user mode contains two types of subsystems:

Integral subsystem
Consists of the workstation, server, and security services

Environment subsystem
Includes support for both Win32 and POSIX applications

IN THE REAL WORLD

The user mode also includes the Windows On Windows (WOW), Virtual DOS Machine (VDM), and OS/2 subsystems. Some specialized programs, such as proprietary accounting or insurance programs, may still run only in DOS mode. The VDM feature will help these programs to be less likely to crash the entire system in the event of a failure.

Kernel mode

The kernel mode contains the Hardware Abstraction Layer (HAL), kernel mode drivers, and the Windows 2000 Executive. The kernel mode provides low-level services to the user mode components. Kernel mode components have priority access to the computer's resources, such as RAM and CPU. The executive deals with Input/Output, device drivers, and the Virtual Memory Manager (VMM), among other duties.

Hardware Abstraction Layer (HAL)

The Hardware Abstraction Layer makes it easier for Windows 2000 to run on a variety of hardware architectures. By acting as a translator between software requests and the actual hardware implementation of the request, HAL allows Windows 2000 to provide a uniform interface between hardware and software.

Networking Basics

Windows 2000 supports both the client/server (domain) and peer-to-peer (workgroup) networking models. Microsoft recommends the workgroup model for networks consisting of 10 or fewer computers when neither security nor centralized administration is required. In every other case, the domain model is preferred. Share level security is possible in a Windows 2000 based workgroup, but it quickly becomes inconvenient as the number of shared resources increases.

The Active Directory model

Windows 2000 introduces a major improvement to the Windows domain networking model, called Active Directory Services. The traditional Windows NT

> **ON THE EXAM**
>
> Generally, when Microsoft refers to security in a question, it means user-level security with a centralized security database. Both of these require the domain model.

domain and workgroup models are still supported in Windows 2000. However, these are being replaced by a much more efficient networking model that is similar to Novell's Netware Directory Services (NDS). Active Directory provides centralized administration of all network components, including users, groups, files, and printers, across the entire network. Active Directory is covered in more detail in the "Windows 2000 Active Directory" section of this chapter.

Installing Windows 2000 Server

Windows 2000 can be installed using one of three executable files: setup.exe, winnt.exe, or winnt32.exe. If you choose to run setup.exe, it will determine whether to run winnt.exe or winnt32.exe based on the computer's current operating system. For Windows 9x, Windows NT 3.51, and Windows NT 4.0, winnt32.exe is used. For MS-DOS and Windows 3.1x, winnt.exe is used.

Both winnt32.exe and winnt.exe have several switches that can be used to give the installation program optional information. You won't ever need to know or use most of the available switches, but I've summarized a few of the common switches in Table 2-1 and Table 2-2.

Table 2-1: Common winnt.exe Switches

Switch	Description
/u:answerfile	Unattended installation using the specified answer file
/udf:id,UDFfile	Allows an ID to specify modifications to the answer file based on the contents of the UDFfile
/s:path	Allows the path of the installation files to be specified

Table 2-2: Common winnt32.exe Switches

Switch	Description
/s:path	Allows the path of the installation files to be specified
/udf:id,UDFfile	Allows an ID to specify modifications to the answer file based on the contents of the UDFfile
/debugX:file- name	Allows either errors (debug1), warnings (debug2), information (debug3), or detailed information (debug4) to be copied into the file specified
/checkupgrade- only	Allows you to check the Windows 9x or NT computer for Windows 2000 upgrade compliance

Planning the Installation

The first consideration when installing Windows 2000 Server is to make sure your computer meets the minimum hardware requirements. These minimum requirements are important to remember for the test. When you are actually planning a Windows 2000 network, you should make sure your server's hardware will meet the performance goals that your users expect. The minimum RAM and CPU requirements listed here would not be suitable for even the smallest of networks.

Hardware requirements

The minimum and recommended hardware requirements for Windows 2000 Server have changed significantly compared to Windows NT Server 4, as shown in Table 2-3.

Table 2-3: Windows 2000 Server Hardware Requirements

Item	Minimum	Recommended
CPU	133 MHz Pentium or equivalent	Faster
RAM	64 MB	128 MB
Disk Storage	671 MB	2 GB
Display	640 x 480 VGA	1024 x 768 SVGA

In addition to these items, I recommend that each computer have a Windows 2000 compatible network card. Otherwise, the computer will not be able to communicate and share resources with the rest of the network. An optional CD-ROM and floppy drive provide greater flexibility, especially for installation.

ON THE EXAM

Although 64 MB is the minimum required RAM, on networks that contain more than five computers, Microsoft recommends a minimum of 128 MB of RAM for the server that has more than five clients.

Windows 9x computers won't be able to see an NTFS partition. If you are dual booting a Windows 9x/Windows 2000 machine, you may want to avoid using NTFS. Keep in mind that FAT and FAT32 partitions don't offer the same level of security as NTFS.

CD and network installation

There are two main ways to install Windows 2000 on your network. One way is to install directly from the CD-ROM on each computer, the other way is to copy the installation files to a network share and install over the network. You can only perform an over-the-network installation if the target computers are already on a working network and can read files from a shared network drive.

The installation process

The Windows 2000 Server installation is divided into three phases: pre-copy, text mode, and GUI mode. You can make boot disks for non-Windows NT computers by running the makeboot program. For a Windows NT machine, use the makebt32 program. Both of these programs are located in the bootdisk directory of the Windows 2000 Server installation CD-ROM. You can type makebt32 a: to make a boot disk from a blank floppy in the A: drive.

Pre-copy

1. Run setup.exe from a network share or reboot the computer with either the first boot floppy or the installation CD-ROM, if supported.

2. The HAL, some fonts, drivers, and Windows setup files are loaded into RAM.

Text mode

1. The Welcome To Setup screen appears. Press *Enter.*

2. The license agreement is displayed. If you agree to the terms of the license, press F8 to continue.

3. A listing of all the available disk partitions and free space is shown. Select a partition to use for the installation.

4. Choose to format the partition using the NTFS or FAT filesystem. Windows 2000 domain controllers must use NTFS.

5. The computer will reboot.

GUI mode

1. A Windows Setup Wizard screen appears. Your mouse should now work. Click the *Next* button to move to the next step throughout the rest of the installation.

2. The installation program will copy and load files for a few minutes.

3. The Regional Settings screen appears. Be sure to choose the correct time zone and keyboard layout.

4. The Personalize Your Software screen appears. If you type in your name or organization, Windows 2000 will share this data with compatible programs that are subsequently installed on this machine.

5. The Your Product Key screen appears. Enter the product key.

6. The Licensing Mode screen appears, as shown in Figure 2-1. Choose either *Per Server* or *Per Seat.*

7. The Computer Name and Administrator Password screen appears. Fill in the appropriate fields.

8. The Windows 2000 Server Components screen will appear. Choose which components you need.

9. The Date and Time screen appears. Set the date and time.

10. The Network Settings screen appears. You can choose to join either a work-group or a domain.

11. The setup program copies files and saves your configuration. Click the *Finish* button to reboot the computer.

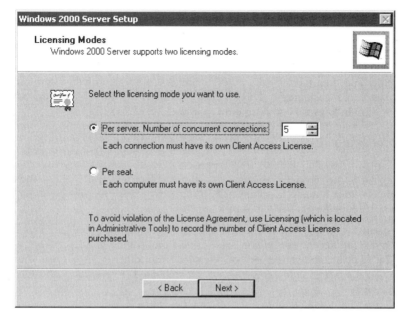

Figure 2-1: Choose a licensing mode for Windows 2000 Server

After the computer reboots, you will log in normally by pressing the Ctrl-Alt-Del keys. Windows 2000 will try to detect any new hardware, and the Windows 2000 Configure Your Server dialog box appears. You can either configure the server now or choose to do it later.

Unattended installation

To perform an unattended installation of Windows 2000 Server, you must use an answer file. This is a script that will automatically answer questions you would have had to manually respond to during the installation. Unattend.txt is an example of an answer file, which you can find on the Windows 2000 Server installation disk in the \i386 directory. This file can be modified to suit your needs.

There are other resources available in compressed format in the file Deploy.cab, which is in the \Support\Tools directory of the installation disk. You can decompress the .cab file using Windows Explorer. After you decompress the file, you can read the Unattend.doc file for detailed descriptions of each of the answer file's components, which are called keys.

A program called Setup Manager is also contained in the Deploy.cab file. This program can help you to create your own answer file. If you'd rather make the answer file manually, you can use a word processor and just modify the existing

Unattend.txt file. Be sure you save the new answer file as a plain text document. The setup manager is described in detail in Part 1.

Two tools you should be familiar with when performing unattended installations are syspart and sysprep. Sysprep, which is covered in Part 1, is used to help create a disk image to be copied on similar, if not identical, computers. It's best if you only use identical installation images on identical computers, otherwise you risk having incompatible settings copied.

Syspart is used when the computers aren't similar enough to risk using sysprep. Syspart allows the file copy phase of the installation to be completed on one computer and then used by the other computers, even if the rest of the installation has to be customized. This can save a huge amount of time if you are deploying Windows 2000 to a large number of dissimilar computers.

Distribution folders

If you plan to install Windows 2000 Server on multiple computers, you can create a template of the directory structure you want to be copied. All of the destination computers must already be connected to the network and be able to copy files from a shared network drive.

There can be as many as eight different distribution folder configurations used during the automated installation. These folders can include Windows 2000 system files and specific hardware device drivers, along with other types of files. A master copy of the distribution folders can be modified to quickly update new installations.

Installing service packs

A service pack is an update to the operating system that usually fixes a reliability or security issue. Microsoft has made a few changes to the process of installing and maintaining service packs.

The first major change is that a service pack can be applied during the installation of Windows 2000. You can create a master installation directory on a network share that contains both the Windows 2000 operating system installation files and all available service packs. If you install Windows 2000 from this folder, all of the appropriate operating system and service pack files are installed automatically. Microsoft calls this process *service-pack slipstreaming.*

If Windows 2000 is already installed and you need to apply a service pack, run Update.exe /slip to install the necessary files from the service pack. You do not need to reapply the service pack if you've added or removed services from the system.

Understanding failed installations

There are many reasons why Windows 2000 Server can fail to complete its installation successfully. Your best strategy is to take a systematic approach to figure out what went wrong. First, make sure your computer meets the minimum hardware requirements. Also, be sure you are using the latest disk controller drivers.

Many potential problems can occur while trying get the data from the installation media to the target computer's hard drive. If you are going to perform a network installation, be sure that your target computer can connect to and read files from the shared source directory. A network failure or a lack of permissions will prevent you from accessing the installation files.

Even if you are installing from a local CD-ROM, a network failure, such as a broken wire or faulty hub, will prevent you from connecting to the domain controller. If you can't connect to the domain controller, continue the installation as a member of a workgroup and attempt to connect after you finish the installation.

If you are installing directly from a local CD-ROM drive, be sure that your drive is supported by Windows 2000. If Windows 2000 doesn't recognize the CD-ROM drive, you'll have to replace it with a supported drive. You can find the most current list of supported hardware on Microsoft's web site by searching for the Windows 2000 Hardware Compatibility List (HCL).

IN THE REAL WORLD

If you install a supported CD-ROM drive and still receive errors, the installation CD itself may be corrupt and Microsoft will replace it. This is very rare, so try to check the CD in a different computer before asking for a replacement.

You may get an error message stating that a dependency service failed to start. This is probably caused by improper network settings. Be sure that the network adapter is compatible with Windows 2000 and that the installed protocols are supported on your network.

Upgrading a Windows NT Domain

Because most Windows 2000 Server installations involve the upgrading of an existing Windows NT domain, the exam tests your knowledge of the issues involved with the migration from Windows NT to Windows 2000. With the introduction of Active Directory in Windows 2000, there are many significant changes you'll need to become familiar with, even if you have experience administering a Windows NT domain.

When upgrading a Windows NT network to Windows 2000, you must upgrade the primary domain controller (PDC) first. In a Windows 2000 network, there are no backup domain controllers (BDC); there are only domain controllers, standalone servers, and member servers. A Windows 2000 domain controller must use the NTFS.

Upgrading the primary domain controller

If the PDC is running WINS or DHCP services, you must stop them before beginning the installation of Windows 2000 Server. Failing to do so will prevent the installation program from converting those databases properly. You can stop both of these services using the Services applet in the Control Panel.

To explain the process of upgrading to Windows 2000, we need to use a few terms that have to do with the Active Directory model. These terms and other Active Directory topics are covered in the "Windows 2000 Active Directory" section of this chapter.

One of the great features of Windows 2000 is that, after you've upgraded the PDC, it will perform like a Windows 2000 Server to Windows 2000 clients, while simultaneously behaving like a Windows NT 4 PDC to other clients and servers. This means that, during the transition period, the network should continue to function normally and slowly improve as you add more Windows 2000 clients.

When upgrading the PDC, you'll have the choice of creating a *new domain* or a *child domain*. There will also be a choice of creating a *domain tree* in an *existing forest* or creating a *new forest*. All of these options will be explained later.

The Security Accounts Manager (SAM) file needs to be upgraded to the new Windows 2000 format. You can store the Windows 2000 version of this file on any type of partition. There are two other files you'll need to store during the upgrade: the log file and the system volume file (SYSVOL). The log file can be stored on any type of partition, but the system volume file must be stored on an NTFS partition.

After you've finished upgrading the PDC, you should verify that the server is functioning properly before upgrading any other computers on the network. This is very important, because the new Windows 2000 domain controller's configuration will be copied and used for all of the Windows NT backup domain controllers destined to become Windows 2000 domain controllers.

Upgrading backup domain controllers

You should upgrade the backup domain controllers next. Even though you've thoroughly tested the new Windows 2000 domain controller and each BDC will use that configuration information, you should still test each upgraded BDC before moving on to the next. Upgrade them one at a time until all of the former BDCs are running well under Windows 2000. You can then move on to the member servers.

Upgrading a member server

There are no special requirements when choosing which member server to upgrade first. You may want to verify that each is functioning properly before moving on to the next one.

The transition period

After the PDC has been upgraded to Windows 2000, the network is running in *mixed mode*. This means that to Windows 2000 clients the domain controller will behave like a Windows 2000 domain controller, and to other clients it will behave like a Windows NT PDC. The main differences are that only Windows 2000 clients can take advantage of transitive trust relationships and group nesting, both of which are explained later in this chapter.

After the PDC and all of the BDCs are upgraded to Windows 2000 domain controllers, you can make a one-time only, one-way switch from mixed mode to native mode. After this is done, all clients can take advantage of transitive trust relationships and group nesting, both of which make access to resources more efficient. Prior to the switch, only Windows 2000 clients had access to these features.

Managing Disk Storage

There are some significant differences between Windows NT 4 and Windows 2000 involving file management and disk storage. Many of the basic disk management topics, such as FAT versus NTFS, RAID levels, and basic file permissions, are covered in Part 1.

Windows 2000 supports both *basic disks* and *dynamic disks*. Basic disks can contain primary and extended partitions, and logical drives can be added within the extended partition. This is the familiar setup in DOS- and Windows-based computers. Dynamic disks are an optional new feature included with Windows 2000, but you may not want to upgrade your basic disks to dynamic disks.

- Dynamic disk advantages
  - Can resize a dynamic disk without rebooting.
  - A single dynamic disk can span multiple physical disks and can support RAID 0, 1, and 5.
- Dynamic disk disadvantages
  - Can only be accessed by Windows 2000 computers
  - Less fault tolerant than basic disks

Changes to NTFS in Windows 2000

Windows 2000 comes standard with a new version of its secure filesystem, NTFS5. Version 5 of NTFS has a few new features, such as reparse points and Native Structured Storage, both of which are covered later in this section.

Windows 2000 domain controllers must use NTFS. Microsoft recommends that all Windows 2000 clients also use NTFS, unless they are used as multi-boot machines. The reason for this exception is that most operating systems cannot read an NTFS volume.

Disk quotas

Windows 2000 allows an administrator to limit and monitor the amount of disk storage used by every user on an NTFS volume. Disk quotas do not apply to non-NTFS volumes. The quota data is calculated by determining ownership of files and folders. If a user owns a file, that file will be charged against their quota. Compressed files are charged against the quota at their uncompressed file size.

Reparse points

Reparse points allow additional functionality to be layered on top of the normal NTFS functionality. User-defined functions can be executed when a file or folder that contains a *reparse attribute* is opened. You may be familiar with a different definition of parsing from the programming world. In this case, parsing refers to the actual way the identifying name of a file or folder is used by the operating system to determine what to do next.

In standard NTFS, if a file is double-clicked on and the user has permission to open the file, the operating system would proceed to open the file. If that file has a reparse attribute, when the operating system attempts to parse the file name, functionality is turned over to a user-defined process, and instead of directly opening the file, it might perform some other task first. A good example of this is described below.

Native Structured Storage

One new feature that takes advantage of reparse points is Native Structured Storage (NSS). This allows files that contain embedded ActiveX components to be stored separately from the ActiveX component itself. When the file is opened, a reparse point is read in the filename, which causes both the ActiveX component and the document to be opened and the application to behave as if the two files were stored together in the same file. This procedure provides a more efficient way to store ActiveX embedded files on Windows 2000 NTFS volumes.

Link tracking

Windows 2000 has a domain-wide shortcut tracking system that will make sure that all of your shortcuts continue to point to the correct targets even if changes have been made to the path that the shortcut refers to. If the client computer is subscribed to the *link tracking service*, all shortcuts will be automatically updated even if the file location, volume location, computer name, or share name that the targeted resource resides on changes. This feature is only available through NTFS and only within the Windows 2000 domain that the client resides in.

Sparse files

In some specialized applications, such as a large database, certain areas of the data file may contain large areas of filler data (all binary zeros). Instead of storing each individual zero bit, the location of a range of zero bits can be stored and the disk space that would have been used by the complete file can be reassigned as free space. When the file is opened, the actual data is read normally and the range of zeros is dynamically restored. This feature is only available with Windows 2000 and NTFS.

The Change Journal

The *Change Journal* is used to keep track of changes that occur on an NTFS volume. This data is stored as a stream with a time limit, so that the log file automatically deletes older data while making room for more current data.

A *unique sequence number* is assigned to all changes on a volume. This information is useful for many tasks, including incremental backups and directory replication.

The Unique Sequence Number Journal

To keep track of individual changes to a volume, every change is assigned a unique sequence number, and that number and the type of change made are stored in the *Unique Sequence Number Journal*. This data is especially useful for backing up data and for directory replication.

The Distributed Filesystem

Windows 2000 allows users to view files and folders that are physically distributed on multiple computers throughout the domain inside a single folder. A *Distributed Filesystem* (Dfs) folder on the server will automatically link the user to the correct location of the resource. A *Dfs root* is the main folder that contains the *Dfs links*, which are subfolders that are mapped to resources throughout the Windows 2000 domain. Dfs is covered in detail in both Part 3 and Part 4.

If a file server crashes, a system administrator can point the Dfs link to an alternate location, and users will automatically connect to the new location without noticing a change. Dfs does not affect the permissions of the resources it links to. A user must have permissions for the remote resource to gain access to it through the Dfs link.

Standalone Dfs roots versus domain Dfs roots

A *standalone Dfs root* is a folder that is physically located on only one server. If you are using Active Directory, you can create a *domain Dfs root* instead, which will be replicated across multiple servers, providing greater fault tolerance. You can create both standalone and domain Dfs roots using the Dfs snap-in.

Dfs links

After you've created the Dfs root folder, you can create Dfs links by choosing the *Action → New Dfs Link* from the Dfs snap-in. With a domain Dfs root, each Dfs link can point to multiple identical shared resources, and the server will automatically distribute traffic between the copies of the shared resource.

In addition to the fault tolerance provided by using a domain Dfs, you can configure the server to automatically replicate the Dfs data. Dfs replication is disabled by default, but you can enable it by changing the replication policy in the Dfs snap-in. A quick way to do this is by right-clicking on the Dfs folder and choosing *Replication Policy*. You'll see a list of servers; choose the ones you want to participate and then press the *Enable* button.

File Replication Service (FRS)

The *File Replication Service* automatically copies and synchronizes files throughout the domain. It uses unique sequence numbers, covered earlier in this chapter, to make sure the most recent changes are applied. FRS is included as a standard feature of Windows 2000 Server and runs automatically on all domain controllers.

One of FRS's main responsibilities is that it automatically replicates the Windows 2000 system volume among all the domain controllers. Because there is no PDC, all domain controllers have equal status in the network.

FRS uses a reversible virtual ring topology among the FRS-enabled servers to define the order of replication among the participants. During replication, if the next DC in line is unavailable, another DC is automatically contacted to continue the replication process seamlessly.

For replication purposes, the domain model is temporarily superceded by a logical structure called a site. The main requirement for a site is that subnets within a site are connected by at least a 512 Kbps connection. Other than that one stipulation, a site may contain multiple domains, or a single domain can contain multiple sites. Data can be replicated within a site or between sites. There are two main types of replication: *intrasite* and *intersite*.

Intrasite replication

Intrasite replication passes data between domain controllers within the same site. It is configured automatically and runs every five minutes by default; however, replication is *trigger-based*, meaning if a replicating server has any changes, it will notify its replication partner. The data that passes between the replicating partners is not compressed.

Intersite replication

Intersite replication passes data between domain controllers in separate sites. The default synchronization interval is three hours, but you can configure it manually. The data passed between domain controllers on different sites is compressed up to 90 percent.

Knowledge Consistency Checker (KCC)

For domain controllers that are both in the same domain and the same site, the *Knowledge Consistency Checker* monitors and optimizes the virtual ring topology used to determine the order of replication. This is especially important if a DC is added to or removed from the site.

The Encrypted Filesystem (EFS)

The *Encrypted Filesystem* is part of the new NTFS included with Windows 2000 Server. The Encrypted Filesystem uses a set of four keys: a public key, a private key, a random file encryption key (FEK), and a recovery key. The Windows 2000 EFS uses the Data Encryption Standard X (DESX). Encryption and keys are covered in greater detail in the security chapter.

A *public key* is used to encrypt files that can later be decrypted by applying either the matching *private key* or by using the *recovery key*, which was automatically generated at the time of encryption. In North America a 128-bit FEK is used. Otherwise, a 40-bit FEK is used.

The U.S. government has relaxed some of its restrictions on American companies, such as Microsoft, from exporting strong encryption technology. You can now get versions of software that use 128-bit encryption on a wider scale throughout the world.

The more bits in the encryption key, the stronger the encryption. However, using the Windows 2000 EFS doesn't necessarily mean your data is completely private. A system administrator with the appropriate permissions can use a special recovery key to decrypt data without the use of the user's private key.

ON THE EXAM

The EFS service only encrypts the data while it is stored on an NTFS volume, not during transport over the network. Most packet sniffing programs will be able to intercept and reassemble the data it captures as it's transported across the network in a decrypted state.

A system administrator can create a domain-wide policy to determine which accounts will have permission to decrypt files using recovery keys. This policy will apply to all computers that are members of the domain. If you are using a stand-alone machine that is not a member of a Windows 2000 domain, the local administrator account will have permission to use recovery keys. This policy is called the *Encrypted Data Recovery Policy* (EDRP).

ON THE EXAM

Encrypted data can be backed up by members of the Backup Operators group without the use of any keys. The data is sent to and from the backup media in an *opaque stream* without ever decrypting it.

Encryption can be used on individual files or entire folders. After a file is encrypted, the subsequent decryption and re-encryption are done automatically as the file is opened, modified, and saved. If a failure occurs during the encryption process, the entire file remains unencrypted. It is not possible for a file to become partially encrypted. You may have to reboot the system to have the file restored to a useable state if a serious error occurs during the encryption process.

To encrypt all the data in a folder, right-click on the folder and choose *Advanced* from the *Properties* menu. Choose *Encrypt Contents to Secure Data* and click *OK*. The Confirm Attribute Changes dialog box will appear. Choose *Apply Changes To This Folder, Subfolders, and Files* to automatically encrypt the existing contents of the folder. From then on, the process of encrypting and decrypting files in that folder or any of its subfolders will be automatic.

You can also encrypt files or folders from the command line using the `cipher` command. The `cipher` command has many parameters that perform specific operations. Parameters are separated from the `cipher` command and each other by a single space. Some parameters can be used in combination with others. They are listed in Table 2-4.

Table 2-4: The cipher Command

Parameter	Function
/a *filenames*	When used with /e or /d, the /e or /d will apply to all filenames that match those specified.
/d	Decrypt.
/e	Encrypt.
/f	When used with /e or /d, it forces encryption or decryption on all specified files and folders, even if they are already in the specified encryption state.
/h	Displays hidden files, including system files.
/I	Ignores errors.
/k	Creates a new file encryption certificate.
/q	Limits the message output to only the essential data needed to run `cipher`.
/s:dir	Specifies the folder (automatically including all subfolders) that the `cipher` command will apply to.
pathname	Allows you to specify multiple filenames or folders and allows the use of wildcards.

Data Compression

Windows 2000 NTFS includes a built-in *data compression* feature. This allows files and folders to occupy less space. If a file is compressed, NTFS will automatically uncompress it when it is opened and re-compress it when it is closed or saved. You can view or change compression settings for a file from the Advanced Attributes dialog, as shown in Figure 2-2. You can also set compressed files and folders to have a different color by selecting Tools → Folder Options → View, then selecting *Display Compressed Files and Folders with Alternate Color.*

When you copy or move compressed files (as shown in Table 2-5), you may notice that the performance is slower than with uncompressed files. If a user requests that EFS compress a previously compressed file (such as a WinZip

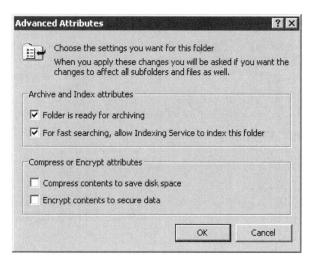

Figure 2-2: The Advanced Attributes dialog

archive), if the file cannot be made any smaller, the archive bit is changed to indicate it's compressed and the file is otherwise left as is.

Table 2-5: Moving Compressed Data

Situation	Result
Copying a file within an NTFS volume	The file inherits the state of the destination folder.
Moving a file within an NTFS volume	The compression state remains unchanged.
Copying a folder within an NTFS volume	The folder inherits the state of the destination folder.
Moving a folder within an NTFS volume	The compression state remains unchanged.
Copying a file between NTFS volumes	The file inherits the state of the destination folder.
Moving a file between NTFS volumes	The file inherits the state of the destination folder.
Copying a folder between NTFS volumes	The folder inherits the state of the destination directory.
Moving a folder between NTFS volumes	The folder inherits the state of the destination directory.
Copying a file from NTFS to FAT	Everything is uncompressed.
Moving a file from NTFS to FAT	Everything is uncompressed.
Copying a folder from NTFS to FAT	Everything is uncompressed.
Moving a folder from NTFS to FAT	Everything is uncompressed.
Copying or moving to a floppy disk	Everything is uncompressed.

Windows 2000 NTFS will not allow you to copy a compressed file to an NTFS volume unless there is enough room for the file in its uncompressed state. This is because the space calculated for a compressed file is based on its uncompressed size, rather than its current size.

Backup and Restore

Windows 2000 Server comes with a built-in backup program called Windows Backup. You can use this utility to back up files manually or to schedule automatic backups. Windows Backup is permission based, and only those users with the proper file access permissions can back up or restore files. You can back up a single file, the whole network, or anything in between (see Table 2-6).

All files can be backed up by anyone in the Administrators, Backup Operators, or System Operators group. Otherwise, the user will need to have at least Read permission to perform a backup and Write permission to perform a restore. Windows Backup can be run from a command line by executing ntbackup.exe.

Table 2-6: Windows Backup Types

Type	Description	Archive Bit
Full	Backs up all the selected files and folders	Cleared
Copy	Backs up all the selected files and folders	Unchanged
Incremental	Backs up only selected files and folders with an archive bit	Cleared
Differential	Backs up only selected files and folders with an archive bit	Unchanged
Daily	Backs up all the files and folders that have been modified that day	Unchanged

With the number of choices available for backup, you should be able to find a backup strategy to fit your needs. Following is a list of the available built-in backup types and when they might be most useful:

Full

> This is the simplest type of backup. All you have to do is choose the files and folders you want to back up, and they'll be copied. To let the other backup methods know a file has been backed up already, the archive bit is cleared when a file is copied by this method.

Copy

> This method is especially useful to make an extra copy of a file without changing the file's archive bit attribute. Because other methods, like incremental and differential, look for a file's archive bit, a copy backup won't interfere with these types because it leaves the archive bit unchanged.

Incremental

An incremental strategy is a good choice to save disk space while retaining automation. It will only back up the selected files that have the archive bit and, because it clears the archive bits for files it has backed up, it won't back up the same file needlessly.

Differential

This method will also save disk space compared to a full backup, but it leaves the archive bit unchanged and can potentially back up an unchanged file multiple times. Although it backs up only files with archive bits set, it doesn't clear the archive bits on files it has backed up.

Daily

This method is most useful for the traditional automated late night backup. It doesn't use the archive bits, it uses the last modified timestamp of a file to determine whether or not it should back it up. Daily backup doesn't modify the archive bits of files it backs up.

Windows 2000 Active Directory

Windows 2000 Active Directory is such a fundamental change to the Windows networking philosophy that it is the main focus of two of the seven core exams. Although the Server exam refers to a few Active Directory concepts, you won't need the type of in-depth knowledge for it that is required for the two Active Directory exams.

Active Directory Basics

A Windows 2000 domain has a few differences from a Windows NT domain. A Windows 2000 domain uses DNS domain names rather than NetBIOS names. DNS is the hierarchical naming scheme commonly used on the Internet. This method of organizing is sometimes called a *namespace*.

The first Windows 2000 Server in a domain can be assigned a DNS domain name, like mycompany.com. This computer would be called the root server. Unless you specifically join an existing forest, a new forest will be automatically created with mycompany.com as the *forest root domain*. As more child domains get added to the domain tree, their names are added to the root domain name.

Each department with its own domain would add its unique name in front of the root domain, like sales.mycompany.com or service.mycompany.com. If the sales force is divided into inside and outside sales, these child domains would also add their unique name to the front of their respective parent domains, like inside.sales.mycompany.com and outside.sales.mycompany.com.

If mycompany.com merges with yourcompany.com and we both have Windows 2000 domains, the yourcompany.com domain tree can become a member of the mycompany.com forest or vice-versa. Forests allow transitive trusts. This means that if computer A trusts computer B and computer B trusts computer C, then computer A automatically trusts computer C without having a separate trust relationship established. This works automatically throughout the entire forest, regardless of the domain.

Planning and Implementing Active Directory

Planning your naming scheme is one of the first considerations. You can choose to register a single domain name for use inside and outside a firewall, or you can register two separate domain names. There are advantages and disadvantages to both methods.

If you choose to use the same domain inside your network as you use for your Internet presence, you have to be very careful not to allow access to private data on the public Internet. Because of the additional security concerns, it is generally more complex to successfully manage a domain using this naming scheme.

If you choose to use a different domain name inside your network than you use for your Internet presence, it is much easier to figure out whether a resource is public or private. This makes the security a bit easier to manage.

Installing Active Directory Services

If you've just finished installing Windows 2000 Server on the first computer in the domain and the Configure Your Server window is being displayed, choose the *Active Directory Installation Wizard*. Otherwise, you can open the Configure Your Server window by choosing it from the Start → Programs → Administrative Tools menu.

IN THE REAL WORLD

A Windows 2000 standalone server can be promoted to a domain controller. This is especially useful for load balancing, because all Windows 2000 domain controllers are peers and can share the processing and storage loads as they grow with your network. You can use the DCPRO-MO.EXE program to upgrade existing standalone servers to domain controllers.

Managing an Active Directory Network

In the Active Directory system, all network resources are called *objects*. Common objects include users, groups, computers, and printers. You can organize these objects into manageable groups, called *Organizational Units* (OU). You can then add, move, or remove objects in an OU using the Active Directory Users and Computers snap-in, which can found under the Start → Programs → Administrative Tools menu.

You can make the organizational units reflect the actual structure of your company or group objects with similar functions. Because it is easy to move objects from one OU to another, you can be flexible and creative in dividing your network's resources without much worry of having to get it absolutely perfect the first time.

An additional administrative aid is that you can assign permissions to an entire OU at once or to any individual objects within the OU.

You might consider putting all of the file servers or printers in an OU and assigning their administration to a junior system administrator. This can be accomplished using the Delegation of Control Wizard (see Figure 2-3), which can be accessed from the Active Directory Users and Computers snap-in. The wizard will walk you step by step through the delegation process. This is a great low-risk way to give junior administrators some additional responsibility.

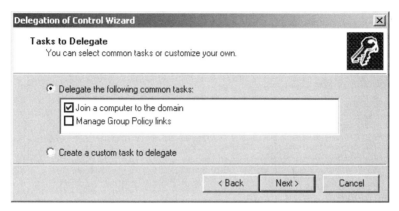

Figure 2-3: The Delegation of Control Wizard

Managing Network Components

Windows 2000 Server has many new networking applications. Three new additions to Windows 2000 Server are Internet Information Server 5 (IIS), Telnet, and Terminal Services. All of your networking services rely on standard network protocols, the most important of which is TCP/IP. You should read the "Managing Network Components" section of Part 1 if you're not familiar with TCP/IP and other basic network protocols.

Internet Information Server 5.0 (IIS)

Internet Information Server allows Windows 2000 to publish and share files within the intranet, across the Internet, or both. In addition to the web server and File Transfer Protocol (FTP) server, Windows 2000 also includes Telnet server and a Windows terminal server.

The web server

A web server allows you to publish documents viewable in a variety of web browser clients. This web server supports both standard HTML and Active Server Pages (ASP). When you install IIS, a default web site is created to act as a template as you modify the properties of your web server. These properties are collectively called the *web environment*. IIS 5 includes a new feature to help you manage your web environment, called WebDAV.

You can create a virtual directory named WebDAV and store your web site files in it. You can then add, remove, modify, search, and lock files in the WebDAV directory remotely by using a Microsoft client, such as Internet Explorer 5 or any Microsoft Office 2000 application. Access to all web directories, including WebDAV, is permissions based.

WebDAV permissions

You can set permissions for the WebDAV folder to control access to the data available through the IIS server. The basic permissions are Read, Write, and Directory Browsing.

The Read permission gives users the ability to view and copy files stored in the WebDAV directory. The Write permission allows users to save files into the WebDAV directory. The Directory Browsing permission allows the user to see all the files in the WebDAV folder.

ON THE EXAM

WebDAV permissions are very similar to standard Windows 2000 permissions. You should be familiar with basic permissions, such as Read, Write, Execute, and No Access, covered in the "Administration and Security" section in Part 1.

The File Transfer Protocol (FTP) server

An FTP server allows you to send and receive files between computers. The IIS FTP server will accept connections from any compatible FTP client, as long as the user has the proper permissions to access the site. One new feature of IIS 5 is that it supports *FTP restart*. If the FTP client also supports FTP restart, a broken connection can be automatically restarted where it left off, rather than starting over again from the beginning.

The Telnet server

Telnet allows you to log in to a computer and remotely execute programs. Telnet has been a part of Unix systems and the Internet in general for quite a long time.

IN THE REAL WORLD

Including a Telnet server is just one of the many signs that Microsoft has a more mature and cooperative approach to including standard Internet technology in Windows 2000. Another significant change is the shift from NetBIOS to DNS.

Windows 2000 Server includes a license that only allows two simultaneous Telnet clients to connect, which nearly negates the fact that they included it at all. You can buy more licenses to allow a reasonable amount of simultaneous connections.

Terminal Services

Windows 2000 Terminal Services is somewhat like a graphical Telnet session. The application and the data actually reside on a remote server, but the user sees the output of the program on their screen as if they were running the program locally. This is accomplished by the Terminal Services client's transmitting keyboard and mouse data to the terminal server, which then passes the information along to the application.

Terminal Services allows great flexibility in the client hardware, because all of the actual computing is being done remotely on the server. It also allows an administrator to upgrade only a single copy of the program (on the server) and, the next time clients start the program, that will be the new version. In large organizations this can save hundreds of hours of installing applications on individual workstations.

The one major drawback of using Terminal Services to share applications is that because the terminal server is doing all the computing work for several clients, it needs to be a very fast computer with a huge amount of RAM.

Terminal Services runs in one of two modes, *remote administration mode* or *application server mode*. Both of these modes are explained a little later in this section. You have to choose which mode to use when you install Terminal Services.

Installation and configuration

If Terminal Services is not already installed, you can install it with the Add/ Remove Programs applet in the Control Panel. Select *Terminal Services* from the Add/Remove Windows Components section. The files will be copied from the Windows 2000 Server installation media.

Remote administration mode

Remote administration mode allows an administrator to control the server as if they were actually logged in locally to the server. This doesn't require much computing power compared to running application sharing, so it shouldn't be a major performance drain on the server.

The administrator can connect to the server over any TCP/IP connection. The standard Windows 2000 Server license allows two simultaneous remote administration connections.

Application sharing mode

Terminal Services allows applications to be stored remotely on a server or servers, and clients can run applications remotely. The performance depends on both the speed of the server and the speed of the connection between the client and the server.

Microsoft requires both a Windows 2000 Client Access license and a Terminal Services Client Access license for each client that connects to the terminal server for application sharing.

ON THE EXAM

When you choose to install Terminal Services in remote administration mode, the files needed for application sharing are not installed. If you later want to convert to application sharing mode instead, you'll need to reinstall Terminal Services.

Remote Access

Windows 2000 Server's standard Routing and Remote Access Service (RRAS) is an expanded and improved version of Windows NT RAS. Its major features include a RADIUS server, support for OSPF and RIP for IP routing, IPX routing, demand-dial routing, a multiprotocol router, a virtual private network (VPN) server, and a standard RAS server.

Remote Access Service (RAS)

The Remote Access Service part of RRAS should be familiar to anyone who is familiar with RAS for NT. RAS provides support for standard dialup connections or a VPN connection using Point-to-Point Tunneling Protocol (PPTP). Windows 2000 RAS also supports ISDN, DSL, X.25, T-Carrier, and ATM connections through either a modem or an Ethernet interface.

Windows 2000 can provide Internet service using either Internet Connection Sharing (ICS) or Network Address Translation (NAT). However, if you are using the Internet Key Exchange (IKE), you won't be able to use NAT. IKE is explained in more detail in Part 7, "Planning IP Security."

ON THE EXAM

You won't need to know the details of how all the connection protocols or routing methods work, but you should be aware of which technologies are supported by Windows 2000 RRAS.

Virtual private networks

In the past, when two remote computers needed to transfer data securely, a dedicated connection was used. A common method was leasing a T1 line over which only the private data was sent between the remote computers. This wasn't very practical or economical.

With the explosive growth of the Internet, virtually every place can be connected to every other place without having a dedicated line connecting the remote sites. The drawback is security. If you're sharing a connection with dozens, hundreds, or thousands of other people and using several communications carriers, you can't be sure your data isn't being viewed by someone during its journey.

If you can encrypt, or scramble, the data and then send it over the public Internet, you can achieve a virtually private, secure connection without a dedicated line. Instead of using standard PPP, a VPN uses a more secure protocol, such as Point-to-Point Tunneling Protocol (PPTP), Layer 2 Tunneling Protocol (L2TP), or IPSec. All of these protocols are supported by Windows 2000 Server.

Administration and Security

A system administrator has to make sure that people who are authorized to have access to a network resource get it quickly and easily, but make sure that people who aren't authorized cannot gain access, no matter how hard they try. This balancing act is made a little easier with the new Active Directory structure of Windows 2000.

Managing Users and Groups

The *Microsoft Management Console* (MMC), also discussed in Part 1, is the primary way to manage accounts and resources in Windows 2000. The MMC itself is only a framework, but there are several components, called snap-ins, that provide the functionality needed to perform almost any administration task. The MMC is customized to include all the snap-ins that have been added to it.

User profiles

There are three types of user profiles supported in Windows 2000: local, roaming, and mandatory. A *local user profile* is established automatically the first time a user logs in to a Windows 2000 computer. Whatever changes the user makes are stored in the local profile, so the next time they log in to that computer, the configuration will be the same as when they last logged out.

Roaming user profiles (RUP) allow a user to log in to any computer in the domain and be presented their personal settings. An administrator can store profile information on a server, rather than on a local machine, so when a user logs in, the configuration information is transferred to that computer. If the user makes changes to their profile, those changes are sent back to the server so that the profile remains synchronized.

There may be cases when you don't want a user to be able to change their profile. Because a profile can be used to grant and restrict access to certain applications, this is a useful administrative tool. A *mandatory profile* is a roaming user profile that cannot be modified by the user. You can designate a roaming user profile as a mandatory user profile by renaming the user's Ntuser.dat file to Ntuser.man.

Groups

Although you can manage individual users with user profiles, sometimes it's easier to take a wider view and put users who have similar requirements in groups. Groups allow you to make changes (especially those having to do with security) apply to all the members of the group at once.

The two main types of groups in Windows 2000 are distribution groups and security groups. Distribution groups cannot be assigned permissions and are only used by standalone applications that support Active Directory, not by Windows 2000 itself. These applications will be able to use these informal distribution groups as an easy way to deliver information, such as email messages or memos, to a group of users.

A security group includes all the functionality of a distribution group and allows permissions to be assigned. The three main types of security groups, domain local, global, and universal, are described in Table 2-7.

Table 2-7: Windows 2000 Security Groups

Type	Function	Members
Domain Local	Provides access to only those resources located in the domain that the group was created in	Any members of any trusted domains, including global groups
Global	Provides access to any resources in any trusted domain	Only members of the domain that the global group was created in
Universal	Provides access to any resources in any trusted domain	Any members of any trusted domains

Group nesting

In some cases it is possible to make one group a member of another group. This is referred to as *group nesting*. However, doing this reduces your flexibility in assigning permissions, because permissions of the parent group apply to the child groups. This can quickly become an administration nightmare, because users who previously had access to a resource can no longer connect and you have to untangle the nested permissions.

ON THE EXAM

Universal groups can be used only if all of the trusted domains are running in Windows 2000 native mode. Global groups can also contain other global groups of the same domain while running in native mode. Native mode and mixed mode are discussed earlier in this chapter in "The transition period."

Managing Group Policies

Active Directory provides a hierarchical structure to manage all aspects of the network. This structure also applies to policies. Windows NT system policies, which included local and computer policies, have been superceded by a new approach called *Group Policy Objects* (GPO).

Group Policies can be used to manage settings for users in a particular OU, a group, or a domain. These settings include providing shortcuts, adding programs to the start menu, redirecting a folder's path, and running login scripts. Because GPOs can be nested, a single user may be affected by multiple GPOs. There are a few group policy terms you should be familiar with:

Group Policy Object (GPO)
  The actual settings that apply to the OU, group, or domain.

Group Policy Container (GPC)
  The Active Directory object that contains a GPO itself, the GPO's state (enabled/disabled), a version number for tracking, and additional user and Group Policy information.

Group Policy Template (GPT)
  A GPT is created whenever a GPO is created. The GPT contains application settings information, security, and script files.

Print Server Administration

Although more and more information is being passed electronically through web sites and email, managing printed material is still a priority for network administrators. There are a couple of Windows 2000 printing terms that you'll have to be familiar with:

Printer
  A logical object that can include one or more print devices

Print device
  The actual piece of hardware that prints documents

Print server
  The computer that controls the print spool

Print spool
  The list of the items, called *print jobs*, that are waiting to get printed

Network printers

If a print device is attached to a computer directly and that computer stores the print jobs locally, the print device is called a *local printer*. If a print device can accept print jobs that were sent over a network, the print device is called a *network printer*. You can add both a local and a network printer using the Add Printer wizard in the Control Panel.

Managing print jobs

When you plan how to set up printing on your network, you'll have to figure out how many print devices you'll need to meet the printing demand. You can then create logical printers and configure them to use one or more print devices. If several print devices have very similar capabilities or, better yet, are the exact same model, you can distribute jobs among them in a structure called a print pool. The user only sees one printer, but the actual print device that performs the print job may vary.

You can also make one print device represent multiple printers. You can then assign a higher priority to a certain printer and give a group access to that printer. This will allow prioritization with only one print device available.

Printers can be managed through permissions and can be configured remotely through a web browser. An administrator can prioritize, cancel, pause, or resume print jobs.

Device Drivers

Device drivers are a kind of software that helps Windows communicate with a particular piece of hardware, like a video card or a modem. You can check which drivers are being used for a particular device using the Device Manager snap-in. If a device driver is not functioning properly, Windows may not be able to use the device. In the worst cases, the faulty driver could cause a system crash. The odds of having a faulty driver make its way into a Windows 2000 system have been greatly reduced with the addition of a driver certification process called *driver signing*.

Driver signing

Microsoft has thoroughly tested many drivers in various hardware configurations running under Windows 2000. If the driver passes all of Microsoft's tests, an encrypted digital signature is added to the device driver. Windows 2000 is set up to warn you if you are installing an unsigned device driver. You can also configure Windows 2000 to stop warning you or to prevent all unsigned device drivers from being installed.

Auditing

If you need to maintain a secure network, you should keep track of attempted accesses to network resources. *Auditing* is the process of keeping a record of events that happened on your network. Suppose you need to make sure a certain file isn't being viewed by any unauthorized users. You can audit file access by monitoring who tried to access a file, when the attempt was made, and whether it was successful or not.

You can set up auditing as part of an *audit policy*. If the computer you want to monitor is a domain controller, the audit policy will apply to all the domain controllers. Otherwise, the audit policy applies only to the local computer. You can configure audit policies using the Group Policy snap-in.

Security Configuration and Analysis

There are three security snap-ins available for the MMC. The Group Policy snap-in, covered earlier in this chapter; the Security Configuration and Analysis snap-in; and the Security Templates snap-in. Each snap-in provides tools that handle specific security needs.

The Security Configuration and Analysis snap-in allows you to set up security policies by importing *security templates* and applying these to Group Policy Objects. It also allows you to view the current security status in great detail. In addition to allowing you to view the security settings, this snap-in will also suggest changes that it thinks you should make to the current security policy.

Kerberos

Windows 2000 has upgraded its logon security by using a security protocol called *Kerberos*. In Windows NT, only the user was authenticated. In Windows 2000, both the user and the server that the user is logging in to are authenticated by the Kerberos service that is running on a Windows 2000 domain controller. Kerberos has a lot of new terminology associated with it:

Authenticator
> Used to verify that the user making the login request is who she says she is.

Principals
> The user that is trying to log in and the server that may allow the connection.

Secret key
> The encrypted password that is passed between principals and the Kerberos server.

Session key
> An encrypted password valid only for the current login session between the principals.

Kerberos realm
> The complete group of computers that the Kerberos server provides authentication for. In Windows 2000, it is the whole domain.

Optimization and Troubleshooting

No matter how well your network is running, it can always be improved. Windows 2000 Server includes a lot of monitoring tools. The most common tools include the Task Manager, the Performance Console, and the Network Monitor. After all the hardware is installed and the network is up and running, a good portion of a network administrator's job is looking for ways to improve performance and addressing potential problems before they get out of hand. You'll probably become very familiar with all the tools described in this section.

Task Manager

The Windows 2000 Task Manager allows you to monitor the status of individual applications, processes, and both CPU and RAM usage. You can start the Task Manager by right-clicking on the task bar and choosing Task Manager or by pressing Ctrl-Alt-Del while Windows 2000 is running.

Under the Application tab, you can start and stop entire programs. Under the Processes tab, you can view the status of individual processes. The process data shown includes a process ID, the percentage of CPU time being used, and the amount of RAM being used. You can also stop a process from this screen. The performance tab allows you to monitor the CPU and RAM usage for the local computer.

Performance Console

The Performance Console is a container for two snap-ins: the System Monitor snap-in and the Performance Logs and Alerts snap-in. You can monitor both the local computer and remote computers on the network with the System Monitor and the Performance Logs and Alerts snap-in.

The System Monitor can be used for live monitoring, or it can store data to be later presented in graphs, charts, or reports. You should run the System Monitor as soon as your Windows 2000 network is set up properly and users are accessing the network resources without any trouble. This original performance data is called a *baseline*. Later on, you can compare the current performance to the baseline data to measure changes in the network. This will help take the guesswork out of determining how best to improve and expand your network in the future.

The Performance Logs and Alerts snap-in is a Windows 2000 service that can run and collect data for later analysis in the System Monitor. It can collect data from both local and remote computers. You can run more than one copy of the Performance Logs and Alerts service simultaneously.

Network Monitor

The Windows 2000 Server Network Monitor can monitor, capture, or store data that is being transmitted on the local subnet. The sheer volume of data usually prevents an administrator from wanting to capture all of the data that is passing over the subnet.

You can filter the type of data you'd like Network Monitor to capture. For example, you can monitor all the data passed between two IP addresses or all the data transmitted using a particular protocol. You can also create a set of filtering rules using common logical operators such as AND, OR, and NOT.

Network Monitor can display the data for your analysis or allow you to save it in a log file that can be sent to someone who specializes in analyzing network traffic.

SNMP

Simple Network Management Protocol (SNMP) is a common protocol used to monitor and troubleshoot TCP/IP. SNMP distributes the work among three main components, the *Network Management Station* (NMS), the *agent*, and the *Management Information Base* (MIB):

* The NMS receives data that was stored in the MIB by the agent.

* The agent collects data from the monitored hardware and stores it in the MIB.

* The MIB is a database of stored information collected by the agent meant for analysis after it is transferred to the NMS.

To provide limited security, computers that will be using SNMP can use a community password shared by all the agents and network management stations. This password is called the *SNMP community name.*

There are several third-party programs that provide a user-friendly way of managing the monitoring of a Windows 2000 network through the use of SNMP. Some of these programs can be set up to email or page system administrators when problems occur.

Disk Tools

Windows 2000 Server includes two disk troubleshooting tools, *Check Disk* and *Disk Defragmenter.* Microsoft has almost always included both a check disk and disk defragmenter program with all their operating systems, with one notable exception: Windows NT did not come with its own built-in disk defragmenter.

Windows 2000 includes the Disk Defragmenter snap-in. Windows 2000 Server does not automatically optimize where data is stored on a disk. As files are added, modified, or deleted, the fragmentation of data increases. This results in a performance decline. It is usually quite gradual, so be sure to set up a regular schedule for defragmenting the disks on your network. Be sure you run Disk Defragmenter only when the server isn't doing much disk I/O to avoid major performance penalties.

Check Disk is a simple tool used to check for both filesystem errors and bad sectors on the hard drive. You should try to close as many applications as possible before running the Check Disk program.

Hardware Issues

Microsoft publishes a Hardware Compatibility List (HCL). There is a copy of this list on the Windows 2000 Server installation media and an updated copy on Microsoft's web site. The hardware on the HCL has been specifically tested and approved for the Windows 2000 platform. Windows 2000 may run perfectly well on hardware that is not on the HCL, but the HCL gives you an opportunity to let someone else do the testing for you. You may have a more difficult time getting Microsoft to help you with hardware that is not on the HCL.

Safe Mode

Windows 2000 Server can be started with the bare minimum of device drivers and services running to help you troubleshoot a problem. This is particularly useful if you installed a faulty driver or made a severe configuration error. After you've fixed the problem, you can restart Windows 2000 normally.

Safe mode allows you to gradually increase the number of drivers and services that are running until you've solved the problem. Safe mode can be used with or without networking and in VGA mode. You can also use the Last Known Good Configuration, send debugging information to another computer through a serial cable, or store data locally to a log file during the boot process.

If none of these techniques works, you may have to use the emergency repair disk (ERD) or reinstall Windows 2000. You can create an emergency repair disk by choosing Start → Run, typing RDISK, and clicking OK. Be sure to have a blank floppy ready and follow the on-screen instructions.

Recovery Console

The recovery console is a command-line interface used for troubleshooting a damaged Windows 2000 computer. You can run the recovery console by booting the damaged server using either the Windows 2000 installation floppies or, if possible, by booting from the installation CD-ROM. The recovery console allows an administrator to start and stop services as well as providing access to most areas of the local hard drives. You need to log in with the local administrator's password to use recovery console.

To install the recovery console, you'll need to run the winnt32 program with the switch /cmdcons, which will then prompt you to authorize the change; from then on, when you boot, another line reading Microsoft Windows 2000 Command Console will be available. You need a local administrator account to use the recovery console.

Suggested Exercises

The Windows 2000 Server exam requires you to be familiar with both the Windows 2000 operating system and how it can be used to manage a network environment. Previous experience managing a Windows NT network will be helpful, as will spending as much time as possible using the new features of Windows 2000 itself.

Hands-on experience is always the best way to really get to know an operating system well, and following these exercises will give you a structured approach as you get to know Windows 2000.

Installing Windows 2000 Server

1. Install Windows 2000 Server using the installation CD on a single machine with a blank hard drive.

2. Upgrade a Windows NT Server with Windows 2000. Verify which configurations remained in place.

3. Perform an unattended installation using an answer file. Try to use either sysprep or syspart.

4. Install Windows 2000 Server from a network share.

Creating User Accounts and Groups

1. Create an alternate Administrator account and several user accounts.

2. Put some users in predefined groups and verify that group permissions apply to the user accounts based on their group.

3. Create your own groups and assign permissions to the groups. Add user accounts to the new groups and make sure permissions are working properly.

4. Nest your groups and see if permissions are being transferred properly to the users in the nested groups.

Creating a Group Policy and User Profiles

1. Create a Group Policy for one of your groups and test it.

2. Create a user profile and see how it interacts with the Group Policy.

3. Create a roaming profile and test it. Change it into a mandatory profile and try to circumvent it.

Creating a Dynamic Disk

1. Create a dynamic disk and then resize it. Check to see if everything is working properly. Try to resize it below the minimum size needed to contain all your files.

2. Create a dynamic disk that includes RAID 5. If you have hot-swappable disks, pull one out and see what happens. Put it back and resize the dynamic disk without rebooting.

Using the Task Manager

1. Open the Task Manager and look at the application and processes lists. Close all unnecessary applications and see which processes remain. Sort by CPU and RAM usage.

2. Open a program and force-quit it by using the Task Manager.

3. Create performance graphs while opening and closing applications.

Practice Tests

Test Questions

1. What is the maximum number of processors Windows 2000 Server can support?

    a. 2

    b. 4

    c. 8

    d. 16

2. Which components are part of the Windows 2000 kernel mode? (Select all that apply.)

    a. The integral subsystem

    b. The Hardware Abstraction layer

    c. The Windows 2000 Executive

    d. The environment subsystem

3. You have been asked to create a temporary network for the billing department to use during an upgrade to a new billing system. There will be a maximum of seven employees using the network at a given time. You are required to provide the most efficient solution possible.

    Required Result: Users must be able to share password-protected files between computers on the billing network.

    Optional Result: Users can share a single printer.

Optional Result: Users can log in to the billing network and gain access to shared folders on every billing computer without having to type in a password again.

Solution: Create a workgroup environment and attach a printer to one of the workstations. Share the printer and provide the billing department employees with the printer's password.

    a.   The solution meets the required result and both of the optional results.

    b.   The solution meets the required result and only one of the optional results.

    c.   The solution meets the required result only.

    d.   The solution does not meet the required result.

4. Which programs can be used to install Windows 2000 Server? (Select all that apply.)

    a.   setup.exe

    b.   install.exe

    c.   winnt32.exe

    d.   win2k.exe

5. You plan on installing Windows 2000 Server on a computer that is already running Windows 98 Second Edition. Which installation file(s) could you use? (Select all that apply.)

    a.   winnt.exe

    b.   winnt32.exe

    c.   setup.exe

    d.   upgrade.exe

6. You are planning to install Windows 2000 Server on a Pentium III computer with 30 gigabytes of free hard drive space and a 21-inch monitor. What is the minimum amount of RAM you'll need to install Windows 2000?

    a.   32 MB

    b.   64 MB

    c.   96 MB

    d.   128 MB

7. Which files are required to perform an unattended installation of Windows 2000 Server?

    a.   Answer file

    b.   Difference file

    c.   Slipstreaming file

    d.   Automation file

8. When can you install service packs for Windows 2000 Server?

    a.   Only after the installation is complete

    b.   During the installation

    c.   Only while running in native mode

    d.   None of the above

9. You are upgrading a Windows NT network to run Windows 2000.

Required Result: Allow Windows NT clients to continue to access network resources normally and allow Windows 2000 clients to take advantage of the Windows 2000 Server's advanced capabilities.

Optional Result: Maintain security on the network during the transition period.

Optional Result: Allow users to use the same account information on the new server.

Solution: Upgrade the PDC to Windows 2000 Server and verify that everything is running properly. Then upgrade each BDC separately, making sure each is running properly before moving on to the next. Upgrade member servers and standalone servers in alphabetical order, based on their computer names.

    a.   The solution meets the required result and both of the optional results.

    b.   The solution meets the required result and only one of the optional results.

    c.   The solution meets the required result only.

    d.   The solution does not meet the required result.

10. You are the administrator for a Windows NT network consisting of 1 PDC, 15 BDCs, and 235 member servers. All the member servers are running Windows NT Workstation. As soon as you upgrade the PDC to Windows 2000 Server, which mode(s) can you run in? (Select all that apply.)

    a.   Native mode

    b.   Transitive mode

    c.   Mixed mode

    d.   a or c

11. When can Windows 2000 have transitive trust relationships?

    a.   In native mode only

    b.   In both native and mixed mode

    c.   In mixed mode only

    d.   Never

12. You are installing a Windows 2000 Server as a domain controller. Which file-system(s) can you use? (Select all that apply.)

    a.   FAT

    b.   FAT32

    c.   NTFS

    d.   HPFS

    e.   VFAT

13. You have been assigned a disk quota of 50 MB. You are already using 42 MB and you'd like to store a 9 MB text file in your folder. You use file compression to shrink the text file to 6 MB, but when you try to copy it into your folder, you can't. What is the most likely cause of the failure?

    a.   The file has been corrupted during the compression process.

    b.   There has been a disk failure on the file server.

    c.   You have exceeded your 50 MB quota.

    d.   You have renamed the file after it is compressed.

14. What can the link tracking service be used for under Windows 2000?

    a.   Web site traffic analysis for IIS

    b.   Windows shortcut management

    c.   Web site traffic analysis for a Windows 2000 proxy server

    d.   Transitive trust relationship management

15. A backup program can gather information on changes that have occurred on a Windows 2000 file server using which technology?

    a.   Sparse files

    b.   The System Journal

    c.   The Change Journal

    d.   Mod files

16. File Replication Service uses which logical networking topology?

    a.   Bus

    b.   Mesh

    c.   Ring

    d.   Star

17. Which types of keys are used in the Windows 2000 Encrypting Filesystem? (Select all that apply.)

    a.   Encryption key

    b.   Private key

c. Public key

d. Recovery key

18. Which Windows 2000 Servers can use the Encrypting Filesystem?

a. A standalone server running the FAT32 filesystem

b. A standalone server running the NTFS filesystem

c. Any Windows 2000 Server, regardless of filesystem

d. Domain controllers only

19. A member of the backup operators group is trying to back up an encrypted file owned by a system administrator to a tape backup device. Is this possible?

a. No, only a user logged in with a system administrator account may back up files owned by an administrator account.

b. Yes, members of the backup operators group can back up encrypted files regardless of ownership.

c. No, encrypted files cannot be backed up to tape drives. They can only be backed up to NTFS formatted disks.

d. Yes, as long as the administrator gives the backup operators group Read permissions for the encrypted file.

20. A user has a disk quota of 15 MB. They are already using 12 MB and decide to compress their files to make room for more. After compressing the files, the user realizes one of their documents is an important sales proposal. He decides to encrypt the file without success. What is the most likely cause?

a. Compression has no effect on disk quota.

b. Only a system administrator can encrypt files.

c. You can't encrypt a compressed file.

d. You have to encrypt the file before compressing it.

21. What is the name of the command-line encryption utility in Windows 2000?

a. `encrypt`

b. `cipher`

c. `opaque`

d. `secure`

22. What happens to a compressed file when it is moved to a floppy disk under Windows 2000?

a. It is uncompressed.

b. It remains compressed.

c. You are given a choice of whether or not you want compression preserved on the floppy.

d. You have to reformat the floppy with a Windows 2000 machine first, then you can store compressed files on it.

23. You move a compressed file from one NTFS volume to another NTFS volume. The destination folder is not compressed. Which choice best describes what will happen to the file and why?

   a. Because both folders are on NTFS volumes, the compression state will remain the same.

   b. Under NTFS, files inherit the compression state of the destination folder, so the file will be uncompressed.

   c. Under NTFS, compression states are only maintained within the same NTFS volume, so the file will be uncompressed.

   d. Because the file is compressed, it must be uncompressed before it can be moved to another volume, regardless of whether that volume is FAT or NTFS.

24. When you use Windows Backup to perform a differential backup, what happens to the archive bits?

   a. They are updated.

   b. They remain the same.

   c. Under NTFS the archive bits are updated, under FAT they remain the same.

   d. Under NTFS the archive bits remain the same, under FAT they are updated.

25. Which type of computer names does Windows 2000 Active Directory use?

   a. NetBIOS

   b. NetBEUI

   c. TCP/IP

   d. DNS

26. You decide to host an Internet web site on your Windows 2000 Server. What is the name of the folder you should store your web files in for maximum convenience and security?

   a. WebDEV

   b. WebDAV

   c. WebSITE

   d. WebPAGE

27. What can happen when a prematurely broken FTP session is reestablished with an IIS 5 FTP server?

    a.   The file being transferred during the break will need to be transferred from the beginning.

    b.   All files will need to start their transfer session from the beginning.

    c.   It resumes the session where it left off, as long as the FTP client is capable of doing so.

    d.   It resumes the session where it left off, regardless of the FTP client.

28. A user on your Windows 2000 network would like to telnet into the Windows 2000 Server and run an application remotely. Which operating systems can they use to perform this task, assuming they have a Telnet program installed and NTLM authentication has been turned off in the Telnet server's configuration?

    a.   Windows 2000

    b.   Linux

    c.   Solaris

    d.   Windows NT

    e.   a and d

    f.   All of the above

29. Which modes can Terminal Services be installed in? (Select all that apply.)

    a.   Application sharing

    b.   Remote sharing

    c.   Remote administration

    d.   Application tuning

30. You install Terminal Services in application sharing mode. You plan on sharing a large database application with 500 computers. To ensure maximum performance, which two upgrades should you perform? (Select all that apply.)

    a.   Add RAM to the server

    b.   Add RAM to the clients

    c.   Install a fast SCSI hard drive in the server

    d.   Install a fast SCSI hard drive in the clients

31. Which connection type can be used with a virtual private network using two Windows 2000 computers?

    a.   Ethernet

    b.   56K modem

c.   ISDN

d.   All of the above

32. What is the name of the file that stores a mandatory profile in Windows 2000?

    a.   ntprofile.dat

    b.   ntprofile.man

    c.   ntuser.dat

    d.   ntuser.man

33. You would like to create a universal group on your Windows 2000 network. What requirements have to be met before you can do this?

    a.   You need at least one Windows 2000 Server on the network.

    b.   You need at least two Windows 2000 Servers on the network.

    c.   You must be running in mixed mode.

    d.   You must be running in native mode.

34. Which of the following statements, in regard to printing in a Windows 2000 environment, is incorrect?

    a.   A print device can refer to more than one logical printer.

    b.   A logical printer can refer to more than one print device.

    c.   A print pool can contain more than one print device.

    d.   Print devices can be assigned permissions.

35. You are planning on installing new video cards in all the web design computers. All of the web designers use identical computers, so you take one to test the new video card in before ordering the rest of the cards. It functions perfectly. Now that you know the card and its driver work well, you don't want to get any more warnings about the device driver being unsigned. You decide to sign the device driver and register the certificate throughout the domain. Is this possible?

    a.   Yes, as long as all the web design computers are in that domain.

    b.   No, only Microsoft can sign device drivers.

    c.   Yes, as long as the video card is on the HCL.

    d.   No, each copy of the device driver must be signed on the computer it is installed on.

36. You want to keep track of all the users that are trying to access the payroll file. What should you do?

    a.   Run the network monitor to capture all network data on the subnet.

    b.   Take ownership of the payroll file and set the security to no access.

c. Create an audit policy to monitor both successful and failed access to the payroll file.

d. Move the payroll file to a local folder on your workstation.

37. What is the name of the area that a Kerberos server provides authentication services for?

   a. Domain

   b. Zone

   c. Realm

   d. Scope

38. What does Kerberos provide authentication for? (Select all that apply.)

   a. The user trying to log into the server

   b. The server that the user is trying to log into

   c. The domain controller for the network the user is logging into

   d. Only the user trying to log in

39. Which parameters can Task Manager be used to monitor?

   a. RAM

   b. Disk

   c. CPU

   d. a and c

   e. All of the above

40. When you first get your network running properly, you decide to use the System Monitor to store some current performance information so you can compare it to the performance as more clients are added to the network. What is this original data called?

   a. Primary traffic

   b. Default traffic

   c. Baseline

   d. Timeline

41. What is an SNMP community?

   a. A group of computers participating in SNMP monitoring

   b. The domain where an SNMP Network Management Station resides

   c. A password

   d. A type of global group

42. You are trying to log on using the recovery console by booting the computer from the Windows 2000 setup disks. What type of logon account do you need?

    a.   A valid user account on the domain

    b.   A valid user account on that computer

    c.   A backup operator's account on the domain

    d.   A local administrator's account for that computer

Case Study

Text Formatting Key:

- **Describes requirements**
- *Conflicts with requirement*
- Irrelevant background information

Brennan Robotics has hired you to plan the **upgrade** of their **Windows NT 4 domain** to a **Windows 2000 Active Directory domain**. They currently have a **primary domain controller** running on a **dual Pentium 500 MHz** system. They also have **three backup domain controllers**, two running on **single Pentium 133 MHz** system, the other on a **Pentium 100 MHz**. The have a few dozen Windows NT Workstation 4.0 and Windows 98 desktop systems. The **Windows NT Workstations** are running on **Pentium 133 MHz** systems and the **Windows 98** machines are running **Pentium 100 MHz** processors. They'd like to *upgrade all* PDC and *BDC systems* to *Windows 2000 domain controllers*, using their existing hardware. Once you've gotten as many servers running Windows 2000 as possible, they'd like you to *upgrade all* the Windows NT and *Windows 98 systems* to Windows 2000 Professional so the domain can be run in Windows 2000 native mode. This should be done *without any* further *hardware expenditure.* If you can't upgrade the Windows 98 machines and therefore **can't run in Windows 2000 native mode** without a hardware upgrade, you should at least *set up a domain dfs root,* so the Windows 98 machines can take advantage of the mixed mode Active Directory capabilities of Windows 2000.

Multiple Choice

1. How many backup domain controllers should be upgraded to Windows 2000 Server before the primary domain controller?

    a.   One

    b.   Two

    c.   Three

    d.   None

2. How many backup domain controllers should be upgraded to Windows 2000 Server before the Windows NT Workstations are upgraded to Windows 2000 Professional, assuming no hardware changes are made?

    a.   One

    b.   Two

    c.   Three

    d.   None

Create a Tree

1. Put the following backup types under the headings *Clears Archive Bit* and *Unchanged Archive Bit*:

   Differential   Incremental   Copy   Full   Daily

2. Given the following user and group account information, put each user or group into a new group, leaving no group unfilled. The new groups are: *domain local, global,* and *universal.*

Name	Description
Andy	Local domain user account
Marie	Network Admin from a trusted domain
Programmers	Global group of database programmers from a trusted domain

Answers

Comprehensive Test

1. b. Windows 2000 Server supports up to 4 processors, Advanced Server supports up to 8, and Datacenter Server supports up to 16, with special OEM versions supporting up to 32.

2. b, c. The Hardware Abstraction Layer (HAL) and the Windows 2000 Executive are part of the kernel mode. The integral and environment subsystems are part of the user mode.

3. b. The solution meets the required result and the first optional result. A workgroup environment allows users to share files and a printer, but each shared folder will require a password for access.

4. a, c. Setup.exe and winnt32.exe are both Windows 2000 installation programs, along with winnt.exe. Install.exe is a common DOS-based installation file, and win2k.exe is not a Windows 2000 installation program.

5. b, c. Windows 98 can use either winnt32.exe or setup.exe. Winnt.exe is used for 16-bit operating systems, and upgrade.exe is not a Windows 2000 installation program.

6. b. The minimum required for installing Windows 2000 Server is 64 MB. If you are going to support more than 5 computers on the network, you should have a minimum of 128 MB.

7. a. The answer file is the only file that is required to perform an unattended installation of Windows 2000 Server.

8. b. You can install service packs during the installation of Windows 2000 Server using a process known as *service-pack slipstreaming*.

9. a. You should upgrade and test the PDC first, followed by each BDC, one at a time. After you're done with the PDC and BDC computers, it doesn't matter in which order member servers and standalone servers are upgraded.

10. c. Once all of the BDCs and member servers are upgraded to Windows 2000, you can make a one time only, one-way switch from mixed mode to native mode. Until then, you can only run in mixed mode.

11. a. Only a native mode Windows 2000 network can have transitive trusts.

12. c. Windows 2000 domain controllers can only use NTFS.

13. c. Windows 2000 charges you for the uncompressed file size even if the file is compressed.

14. b. The link tracking service is used to maintain shortcuts even if the file or folder has been modified or moved.

15. c. The Change Journal, along with the Unique Sequence Number Journal, are useful to backup programs. Sparse files would be of no help in tracking changes, and mod files are fictitious.

16. c. File Replication Service uses a logical ring topology.

17. a, b, c, d. The Encrypting Filesystem uses encryption, private, public, and recovery keys.

18. b. The Encrypted Filesystem can only be used on NTFS volumes.

19. b. Encrypted data can be backed up by members of the backup group. A more likely solution is that either the tape is full or there is a problem with the tape backup device.

20. c. A file may be encrypted or compressed, but never both.

21. b. `cipher` is the name of the Windows 2000 command-line encryption program.

22. a. Whenever a compressed file is moved to a floppy disk it is uncompressed automatically.

23. b. When you move a file from one NTFS volume to another, the file inherits the compression state of its destination folder.

24. b. A differential backup leaves the archive bits unchanged.

25. d. Windows 2000 Active Directory uses DNS names rather than NetBIOS names.

26. b. Storing your web files in the WebDAV folder makes web site administration easier.

27. c. The FTP server included with IIS 5 is capable of resuming a broken session as long as the FTP client also supports this feature.

28. f. The Windows 2000 Telnet server will allow connections with any compatible Telnet client, regardless of the operating system the Telnet client is running on.

29. a and c. You can install Terminal Services in application sharing mode or remote administration mode.

30. a, c. When you are using Terminal Services to share applications, the server is doing all the hard work. You should upgrade the server rather than the clients.

31. d. Windows 2000 can create a VPN using dialup or dedicated connections.

32. d. Ntuser.man is the name of a mandatory profile. To make a roaming profile a mandatory profile, you'd rename ntuser.dat to ntuser.man.

33. d. Universal groups can only exist when Windows 2000 is running in native mode.

34. d. A print device is the physical machine that prints. A logical printer that represents the device can be assigned permissions, but the device itself cannot.

35. b. Microsoft digitally signs device drivers after they test them. You cannot sign your own device drivers.

36. c. An audit policy is the best solution. Moving or changing permissions on the file would cause the authorized users to have trouble accessing the file. Monitoring network traffic isn't an efficient way to keep track of file access.

37. c. A realm is the area covered by a Kerberos authentication server.

38. a, b. Kerberos provides authentication for both the user and the server they are logging into. Kerberos doesn't authenticate the domain controller unless the user is logging into that machine. Because both a and b are correct, d isn't.

39. d. Task Manager is used to monitor RAM and CPU usage, not disk performance.

40. c. Initial performance tests are called baselines. A, b, and d have nothing to do with performance testing a computer.

41. c. An SNMP community is a shared password between computers running SNMP monitoring.

42. d. You need a local administrator's password regardless of how the recovery console program was started.

Case Study: Multiple Choice

1. d. You have to upgrade the PDC first. Then you should upgrade the BDCs and standalone servers, followed by the client computers.

2. b. Two of the three BDCs are running Pentium 133 MHz chips, the minimum required for Windows 2000 Server. The other BDC, which is running a 100 MHz Pentium, must be upgraded before it can run Windows 2000 Server.

Case Study: Create a Tree

Create a Tree Answer # 1

Clears Archive Bit	Unchanged Archive Bit
Normal	Copy
Incremental	Daily
	Differential

Create a Tree Answer # 2

Domain Local	Programmers
Global	Andy
Universal	Marie

Highlighter's Index

Windows 2000 Editions

Version	CPUs Supported
Professional	2
Server	4
Advanced Server	8
Datacenter Server	16 (up to 32 in some OEM editions)

Windows 2000 Architecture

User Mode	Kernel Mode
Integral subsystem: workstation, server, and security services	Hardware Abstraction Layer (HAL)
Environment subsystem: Win32 and POSIX support	Kernel mode drivers and Windows 2000 Executive

Windows 2000 Installation Files

File	Supported Operating Systems
Setup.exe	MS-DOS, 16- and 32-bit Windows operating systems
Winnt.exe	MS-DOS and 16-bit Windows operating systems
Winnt32.exe	32-bit Windows operating systems

Windows 2000 Server Hardware Requirements

Item	Minimum	Recommended
CPU	133 MHz Pentium or equivalent	Faster
RAM	64 MB	128 MB
Disk Storage	671 MB	2 GB
Display	640 x 480 VGA	1024 x 768 SVGA

Windows NT Upgrade Order

1. Windows NT primary domain controller
2. Windows NT backup domain controllers
3. Standalone and member servers

Encrypting Filesystem Keys

1. Public key
2. Private key
3. Encryption key
4. Recovery key

Windows Backup Types

Type	Description	Archive Bit
Full	Backs up all the selected files and folders	Cleared
Copy	Backs up all the selected files and folders	Unchanged
Incremental	Backs up only selected files and folders with an archive bit	Cleared
Differential	Backs up only selected files and folders with an archive bit	Unchanged
Daily	Backs up all the files and folders that have been modified that day	Unchanged

Windows 2000 Security Groups

Type	Function	Members
Domain local	Provides access to only those resources located in the domain that the group was created in	Any members of any trusted domains, including global groups

Type	Function	Members
Global	Provides access to any resources in any trusted domain	Only members of the domain that the global group was created in
Universal	Provides access to any resources in any trusted domain	Any members of any trusted domains

Kerberos Terms

- An *authenticator* is used to verify that the user making the login request is who they say they are.

- The user that is trying to log in and the server that may allow the connection are both called *principals*.

- The *secret key* is the encrypted password that is passed between principals and the Kerberos server.

- The *session key* is an encrypted password valid only for the current login session between the principals.

- A Kerberos *realm* is the complete group of computers that the Kerberos server provides authentication for. In Windows 2000, it is the whole domain.

SNMP Tools

- The Network Management Station (NMS) receives data that was stored in the Management Information Base (MIB) by the agent.

- The agent collects data from the monitored hardware and stores it in the MIB.

- The MIB is a database of stored information collected by the agent and meant for analysis after it is transferred to the NMS.

PART 3

Active Directory

Exam Overview

Compared to Windows NT Version 4, Windows 2000 includes many incremental improvements to both its internal architecture and its user interface. Where the two operating systems really stand apart is in their directory structure. Windows NT scatters network resources among many domains, each with its own one-way trust relationship. Windows 2000 simplifies the management of network resources across multiple domains with the introduction of Active Directory.

Active Directory creates a hierarchical structure for every resource in the enterprise. Administration of user accounts, files, and printers from all your domains can be easily managed from a single, all-encompassing directory of network resources.

MCSE exam 70-217, *Implementing and Administering a Microsoft Windows 2000 Directory Services Infrastructure*, will test your knowledge of how to install, configure, and secure an Active Directory environment. Once you get familiar with the Active Directory approach, you'll find it's a more intuitive way to manage network resources. Here's a list of Microsoft's exam objectives and where they are covered in this chapter.

Objectives

Need to Know	Reference
How to create sites and subnets	"Creating Active Directory Components" on page 162
How to create site links and site link bridges	"Creating Active Directory Components" on page 162
How to create connection objects	"Creating Active Directory Components" on page 162
How to create global catalog servers	"Creating Active Directory Components" on page 162

Need to Know	Reference
How to configure and manage DNS zones	"DNS for Active Directory" on page 178
How to create and manage Group Policy Objects	"Group Policies" on page 175
How to create accounts both manually and with scripting	"Creating accounts" on page 170
How to delegate administrative control	"Delegating administrative control" on page 175
How to move and locate Active Directory objects	"Managing Active Directory Objects" on page 169
How to publish and secure Active Directory objects	"Publishing Resources" on page 173; "Securing Resources" on page 173
How to manage Active Directory performance	"Optimizing Performance" on page 195
How to manage domain controller performance	"Troubleshooting Active Directory" on page 196
How to use Administrative Templates	"Administrative Templates" on page 177
How to use Security Templates	"Security Templates" on page 190
How to create an audit policy	"Audit Policies" on page 192

Need to Apply	Reference
Install Active Directory and verify the installation	"Installing Active Directory" on page 158
Move objects between sites and transfer operations master roles	"Moving Server Objects Between Sites" on page 181; "Transferring operations master roles" on page 185
Install and configure DNS for Active Directory	"Installing and Configuring DNS" on page 179
Install Windows 2000 with Remote Installation Services (RIS)	"Remote Installation Service (RIS)" on page 187
Configure RIS Security	"Remote Installation Service (RIS)" on page 187
Perform both intersite and intrasite replication	"Creating Active Directory Components" on page 162
Pre-stage RIS clients	"Pre-Staging RIS Clients" on page 189
Authorize a RIS server and grant account creation rights	"RIS Account Creation" on page 190
Restore Active Directory	"Restoring Active Directory" on page 194
Recover from a system failure	"Troubleshooting Active Directory" on page 196
Troubleshoot Active Directory Components	"Troubleshooting Active Directory" on page 196

Need to Apply	Reference
Troubleshoot DNS for Active Directory	"Troubleshooting Active Directory" on page 196
Troubleshoot Group Policies	"Troubleshooting Active Directory" on page 196
Troubleshoot software deployment	"Troubleshooting Active Directory" on page 196

Study Guide

This chapter includes the following sections, which address various topics covered on the *Implementing and Administering a Microsoft Windows 2000 Directory Services Infrastructure* MCSE exam:

Introduction to Active Directory
> Introduces the vocabulary and concepts needed to understand the Windows 2000 Active Directory architecture.

Installing Active Directory
> Discusses the steps necessary to plan for and install Active Directory. It also describes how to verify that the installation was successfully completed.

Configuring Active Directory
> Describes how to set up the Organizational Unit (OU) structure and discusses the creation and management of Active Directory components.

Active Directory Objects
> Describes the building blocks of Active Directory objects. Discusses how to create, manage, and move objects through the use of Group Policies, administrative templates, and software policies.

DNS for Active Directory
> Describes the creation and integration of DNS zones. Includes dynamic updates, DNS monitoring, and replication.

Directory Maintenance and Replication
> Describes both intersite and intrasite replication.

Remote Installation Service (RIS)
> Describes the steps necessary to automatically deploy Windows 2000, including disk images, security, and troubleshooting Remote Installation Service.

Active Directory Security
> Discusses issues related to Directory Services infrastructure and Group Policy security. Describes security templates, audit policies, and security events.

Active Directory Maintenance
> Describes techniques for managing accounts and backing up and restoring Active Directory. Discusses how to optimize the performance of both Active Directory and the domain controllers that support it.

Troubleshooting Active Directory
> Discusses how to troubleshoot problems with DNS, Group Policies, Active Directory components, and software deployment. Describes how to recover from a system failure.

Introduction to Active Directory

Active Directory replaces the Windows NT domain model. It is designed to simplify access to network resources by providing network administrators with the ability to add, modify, and remove both users and resources from a single, hierarchical database. There are many new concepts to learn, but if you keep in mind that its two main functions are to keep track of all the available network resources and to provide access only to authorized users, you'll have no trouble getting up to speed with Active Directory.

Active Directory is stored on Windows 2000 domain controllers. Only Windows 2000 Servers can be Windows 2000 domain controllers. One major change between Windows NT and Windows 2000 is that there are no primary or backup domain controllers on a Windows 2000 network. All Windows 2000 domain controllers are equal and replicate the Active Directory database using a virtual ring topology.

Terminology

The following terms relating to Microsoft Active Directory will be useful in understanding how Active Directory works. A solid understanding of the vocabulary will help make an abstract concept like Active Directory a lot easier to grasp:

Domain
> A network of computers and related hardware that share a user database. This user database is replicated among all the domain controllers. The main benefits of a domain are centralized administration of network resources and a single user logon to access those resources, regardless of where the resources are physically located in the domain.

Organizational Unit (OU)
> A tool for dividing domain resources into groups that match the actual structure of your business. For example, the Accounting Organizational Unit can contain the user accounts of employees in the accounting department, the folders that store financial data, the printers used for invoices, and the billing software. Permissions can then be granted to the OU as a whole.

Tree

A collection of Windows 2000 domains with two-way trust relationships. These domains share a common root domain, such as oreilly.com. Subdomains of the root domain are named in DNS dotted format, to the left of the root domain. Two examples of this naming scheme would be linux.oreilly.com and windows.oreilly.com.

Forest

A collection of two or more trees, each with its own root domain name. The trees in the forest automatically have transitive trust relationships. This means that if tree A trusts tree B and tree B trusts tree C, tree A automatically trusts tree C and vice-versa, without any separate trust relationships between A and C.

Site

A section of the network that has a fast enough TCP/IP connection to allow for efficient replication of files. Microsoft recommends a minimum of 512 Kbps for efficient replication. Because the main requirement is speed, a single site can span multiple domains or a domain can have multiple sites, depending on the network bandwidth available.

Object

Any individual component on the network, including files, folders, scanners, printers, tape backup devices, and even user accounts.

Container

An object that contains other objects is called a container. A folder that contains files would be a container because the folder is an object and its files are also objects.

Attribute

An object is described by its attributes. A file's attributes would include its name, size, location, and permissions.

Class

A way to describe objects within the Active Directory schema. A class is just the list of attributes that describe an object. Basically, the file object is the physical file itself. The file class is the logical definition of the file's properties, such as name, size, and location.

Schema

A list of what types of objects can be managed in the Active Directory database. The schema is made up of classes (definitions of objects) and attributes (containers for the descriptions of objects). The schema can theoretically be modified by a qualified programmer to customize and extend Active Directory to meet their individual needs.

Installing Active Directory

After you have at least one Windows 2000 Server up and running, you can get started with Active Directory. You'll need to do a bit of planning first. The best way to get started is to take an inventory of all the hardware and map out the physical network connections.

If all the network administration tasks are handled from one location, this process can be relatively simple. If you are configuring an Active Directory that spans multiple physical locations across WAN links, it will get quite complex.

IN THE REAL WORLD

When planning a network, you should always take a methodical approach and document everything you've done. There will come a day when another administrator will have to figure out what you've done after you've gone on to bigger and better things. Just remember . . . some day that other administrator will be you.

Planning

Every Windows 2000 domain and its Active Directory can consist of millions of objects. Instead of adding new domains for each location, you should consider breaking down a single large domain into Organizational Units (OU), which are covered in detail later in this chapter.

There are a few cases where multiple domains would be a better solution. If two locations have different Internet domain names, they'll probably want to keep their identities separate on the private portions of their networks, too.

If you have slow WAN connections between physical locations or very strict security requirements in a certain location, you probably want to use separate domains to reduce replication and authentication traffic across those links. Otherwise, keep it as simple as possible by using one domain.

Microsoft recommends that you register at least one domain name for your network from an official naming organization, like Network Solutions. You can choose to register a single domain name for use inside and outside a firewall, or you can register two separate domain names. There are advantages and disadvantages to both methods.

If you choose to use the same domain for the private portion of your network as you do for your Internet presence, you have to be very careful not to allow access to your private data from the public Internet. With the sheer number of security holes in all network operating systems, including Windows 2000, this can be a serious issue. Because of the additional security concerns, it is generally more complex to successfully manage a domain using this naming scheme.

If you choose to use a different domain name inside your network than you use for your Internet presence, it is much easier to figure out whether a resource is public or private. This makes the security a bit easier to manage.

Installation

If you've just finished installing Windows 2000 Server on the first computer in the domain and the Configure Your Server window is displayed, choose the Active Directory Installation Wizard. Otherwise, you can open the Configure Your Server window by choosing it from the Start → Programs → Administrative Tools menu.

When you begin the installation with the Active Directory Installation Wizard, you'll have the choice of creating a new domain controller for a new domain or adding a domain controller to an existing domain.

If you choose to create a new domain controller, you'll have the choice of either starting a new tree or joining an existing tree as a subdomain. Active Directory requires a DNS server to function properly. The Active Directory Installation Wizard allows you to make the current computer the DNS server during the installation process. Following is a description of the steps involved in running the wizard:

1. Start the Active Directory Installation Wizard from the Configure Your Server dialog box. During the install, you'll have to click the *Next* button to move between screens.

2. You'll see the Domain Controller Type screen. Here's where you'll have to choose to either create a domain controller for a new domain or add a domain controller to an existing domain. I'll assume you're starting from scratch and want to create a new domain.

3. You'll see the Create Tree or Child Domain screen. Create a new tree.

4. You'll see the Create or Join Forest screen. Create a new forest.

5. You'll see the New Domain Name screen. Type your registered domain name in the Full DNS Name for New Domain box.

6. For some reason, Microsoft didn't kill off NetBIOS completely, so the next screen you'll see will show you the shortened DNS domain name as a Domain NetBIOS name.

7. You'll see the Database and Log Locations screen. You should see the path WINNT\NTDS.

8. You'll see the Shared System Volume screen. You should see the path WINNT\SYSVOL.

9. You'll get a warning screen about the need for a DNS server. Click *OK*, and the Configure DNS Wizard will start.

10. Choose *Install and Configure DNS on This Computer.*

11. You'll see the Permissions screen. Choose *Permissions Compatible Only with Windows 2000 Servers.*

12. You'll see the Directory Services Restore Mode Administrative Password screen. Type in the password that will be required if you ever have to restore Active Directory.

13. You'll see a report of all the choices you've made so far.

14. After you've accepted the configuration, the wizard will actually start the configuration process. You'll see a progress bar, and it could take a few minutes to finish.

15. You'll see the Completing the Active Directory Installation Wizard screen. Click *Finish*, then click *Restart*. When the computer reboots, you should be all set.

Verifying the Active Directory installation

There are a couple of quick tests to be sure that Active Directory and DNS are working. Look for the new domain you created in My Network Places. If you see your domain name, you should be okay. You can also look for your domain using the Active Directory Users and Computers MMC snap-in:

1. Choose Start → Programs → Administrative Tools → Active Directory Users and Computers. The Users and Computers MMC snap-in is displayed, as shown in Figure 3-1.

2. There should be a directory tree with your domain name listed; double-click it and it should expand.

3. Double-click on *Domain Controllers* and be sure the name of the server you installed AD on is listed.

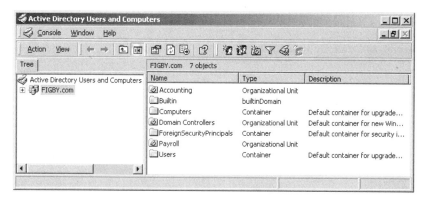

Figure 3-1: The Active Directory Users and Computers snap-in

If both of these tests work out well, your last step is to make sure DNS is set up properly. Windows 2000 has a built-in testing utility to make sure DNS is working. You should definitely try this before moving on:

1. Choose Start → Programs → Administrative Tools → DNS.

2. You should see the name of your server listed. Right-click and choose *Properties*, then choose the Monitoring tab.

3. Click in the *A Simple Query Against This DNS Server* check-box. If you already have the server connected to other DNS servers, you can also choose the *A Recursive Query to Other DNS Servers* checkbox.

4. Click on the *Test Now* button. In the results, you should see that the server passed the test or tests.

Configuring Active Directory

Managing Active Directory is usually handled through the Microsoft Management Console (MMC) and its snap-ins. You can pretty much right-click on any object to configure its properties. It's a good idea to wander around and explore all the snap-ins and the objects they manage.

Creating new objects is almost as easy. Most objects can be created using the pull-down menus in the MMC or through right-clicking on a container or parent object. If you follow along with all the step-by-step instructions in this chapter, you'll have a good idea of what day-to-day administration of Active Directory is like.

Creating Active Directory Components

Because every component in Active Directory is an object and most objects are managed through the MMC, you'll be using this tool several times a day, every day, if you manage an Active Directory environment.

As you add more and more objects to the Active Directory database, efficient replication of information on the network becomes more important. The best replication strategy is often divide and conquer.

Managing intersite replication

There are two main types of replication in Windows 2000, intrasite and intersite:

Intrasite replication
   The replication of data within a single site

Intersite replication
   The replication of data between two or more sites

Sites

Domain controllers need to pass information back and forth to keep network information up-to-date. Sites are used to maximize replication speed among domain controllers. You can have many sites in a single domain, or a single site can span multiple domains. The main requirement for a site is that the domain controllers have fast network connections to each other.

Sites replicate by informing their replication partners that they have a change. Because speed is the main consideration in setting up a site, this replication occurs whenever it is necessary and not after a default interval. If site replication traffic is bogging down your network, consider reconfiguring the sites or installing faster network connections.

IN THE REAL WORLD

Microsoft recommends at least a 512-Kbps connection between domain controllers in a site. Most LANs run at 10 or 100 Mbps. It's usually when you cross WAN links for replication that you'll have to be concerned with speed. Don't forget that you're sharing the WAN connection with a lot of other traffic.

After you've drawn a network map of all your domain controllers and determined the interconnectivity speeds, you can start adding replication sites. Use the following steps to add a new site:

1. Choose Start → Programs → Administrative Tools → Active Directory Sites and Services. The Sites and Services Console is now displayed, as shown in Figure 3-2.

2. Right-click on the *Sites* folder and choose *New Site*.

3. You'll see the New Object—Site screen. Type in a name for the site.

4. Choose a site link object from the list (which may contain only one choice) and click the *OK* button.

5. Repeat the relevant steps until you've created site links for your entire network.

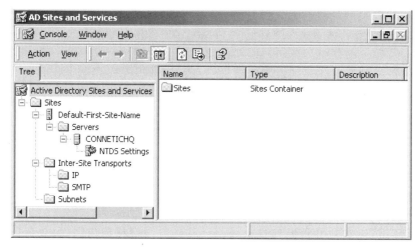

Figure 3-2: The Active Directory Sites and Services console

Subnets

TCP/IP networks are divided into smaller networks, called *subnets*, for easier management. Usually domain controllers on the same subnet or bordering subnets are part of the same site.

If you're already familiar with TCP/IP addressing, you can create your own subnets and start associating sites with your new subnets. You can create your own subnet using the following steps:

1. Choose Start → Programs → Administrative Tools → Active Directory Sites and Services.

2. Double-click on the *Sites* folder.

3. Right-click on the *Subnets* folder and choose *New Subnet*.

4. You'll see the New Object—Subnet screen.

5. Type in the IP address for the new subnet and the subnet mask, which will determine how many addresses are included in the subnet.

6. You'll see a list of the existing sites; choose the site you want to associate with the new subnet.

Site links

Before two or more sites can begin to replicate data, you have to establish a *site link* between them. After you've created at least two sites, you can set up a site link between them. If you need to, you can also add another DC to an existing site by adding another link to the site. Use the following steps to create a site link:

1. Choose Start → Programs → Administrative Tools → Active Directory Sites and Services.

2. Double-click on the *Inter-Site Transports* folder. Right-click on the *TCP/IP* folder and choose *New Site Link*.

3. You'll see the New Object—Site Link screen. Type a name for your new site link.

4. Choose at least two sites and click the *OK* button.

IN THE REAL WORLD

If your domain doesn't have a dedicated connection to the Internet, you can choose SMTP instead of TCP/IP for the site link replication protocol. If you'd like to do this, you'll need an Enterprise CA, which is described in Part 7, *Designing Security*, and you'll have to run SMTP on all the domain controllers that connect to the site.

After you've created a site link, it's easy to add a new site to the existing link or remove a site from the link. Use the following steps to perform either function:

1. Choose Start → Programs → Administrative Tools → Active Directory Sites and Services.

2. Double-click on the *Inter-Site Transports* folder. Right-click on the *TCP/IP* folder and choose *Properties*.

3. Under the General tab, look inside the *Sites Not in This Site Link* box for the site you want to add to the site link.

4. Choose the site you want to add, press the *Add* button, and then press *OK*.

If you have the opportunity to have multiple connectivity options between domain controllers in a site, such as an Ethernet connection and a RAS connection, you can set up a redundant site link.

In the case of an RAS and an Ethernet connection, the Ethernet connection would be much faster under almost any circumstances. You can assign a value to each connection, called a *site link cost*. Of the available site links, Windows 2000 will automatically use whichever link is cheapest. You can configure a site link cost by using the following steps:

1. Choose Start → Programs → Administrative Tools → Active Directory Sites and Services.

2. Double-click on the *Inter-Site Transports* folder.

3. Double-click on the *TCP/IP* folder.

4. Right-click on the proper site link and choose *Properties*.

5. You'll see the Site Link Properties screen.

6. The default cost for all links is 100. Type in a new cost in the Cost box to reflect the priority of the link. The lower the cost, the higher the priority.

IN THE REAL WORLD

You can configure a set interval when sites should check for updates in the same place as you set the cost of the link. However, you'll have faster replication if the *Ignore Schedules* property is selected in the Inter-Site transport properties. Right-click on the *Inter-Site Transports* folder, choose *Properties* and make sure *Ignore Schedules* is selected.

Link bridges

If you add more than two sites to a site link, the costs of the individual connections are *bridged*. The entire site link is considered one connection, and the individual sites will automatically find each other for replication purposes. This assumes all the sites in a site link are using the same protocol (TCP/IP).

If you're using more than one connection protocol between sites in a site link or if the sites in a site link can't reach each other across the TCP/IP network because of a routing issue, you can manually create a bridge between sites.

If sites are all able to see each other, the site link is *transitive*. This should be the case unless you have very specific reasons for not configuring your network this way. If they need a site link bridge set up so they can replicate, the site link is referred to as *intransitive*.

You can set up a site link bridge by using the following steps:

1. Choose Start → Programs → Administrative Tools → Active Directory Sites and Services.

2. Double-click on the *Inter-Site Transports* folder.

3. Right-click on either the *TCP/IP* or *SMTP* folder and choose *New Site Link Bridge*.

4. You'll see the New Object—Site Link Bridge screen. Type in a name for the new site link bridge.

5. Choose at least two sites to add to the site link bridge and click the *OK* button.

If you have many intransitive sites and you don't want to manually configure site link bridges for them, you can select *Bridge All Site Links* from
either the TCP/IP or SMTP properties in the Inter-Site Transports folder.

Bridgehead servers

Any domain controller can be used for intersite replication. If you have some
domain controllers with particularly fast network connections, you can give them
priority in the replication process. The server that will have the highest priority is
called a *bridgehead server.*

If your network has a firewall between replicating sites, you'll have to specify a
preferred bridgehead server to ensure replication is successful. The firewall proxy
server can receive replication data and pass it to domain controllers inside the
firewall.

You can have more than one bridgehead server for a site, but only one at a time
will be considered the *preferred bridgehead server.* You can configure a preferred
bridgehead server by using the following steps:

1. Choose Start → Programs → Administrative Tools → Active Directory Sites and
   Services.

2. Right-click on the domain controller you want to make the preferred bridgehead server and choose *Properties.*

3. You'll see the Domain Controller Properties screen. Look for the *Transports
   Available for Inter-Site Data Transfer* box.

4. Choose the intersite transport or transports on the list that the DC will be a
   preferred bridgehead server for.

5. Click the *Add* button and click *OK.*

Managing intrasite replication

Replicating data between domain controllers within the same site is called intrasite replication. Active Directory automatically creates a *virtual ring* topology to
handle intrasite replication. A virtual ring isn't necessarily physically wired in the
ring topology, but data is passed from one computer to the next in a set order.

Replication data is passed between the participating domain controllers in the
same direction around the ring until a failure occurs. If a domain controller is
unable to participate in the replication process, traffic is automatically routed
around it and continues with the next available domain controller.

Active Directory will recognize if a domain controller is added to or removed from
a site and automatically adjust the ring's topology. To ensure the best performance, Active Directory will periodically look for a more efficient way to pass data
among the domain controllers in a site. If it finds one, the replication path is automatically updated.

Global catalog servers

The global catalog is a database of object attributes for the entire Active Directory forest. The global catalog is automatically initialized on the first domain controller in a forest. This computer is called the *global catalog server.*

The global catalog will contain all the attributes for every object in its own domain. For other domains in its tree and forest, it contains a partial list of the most frequently used attributes of the rest of the objects in the forest.

The two main purposes for the global catalog are to respond to requests for object information and to provide domain controllers with authentication information. When a program wants to open a file and the relevant information isn't provided by the local domain controller, that DC asks the global catalog server what the file's attributes are, such as: name, size, location, and permissions. Based on the results, the program can determine what to do next.

Users can log on from any computer in the forest, regardless of physical location. This is made possible because the global catalog server provides logon information to the local domain controller attempting to log the user on. If the global catalog server is down, users can only log on locally to computers for which they have the required permissions.

ON THE EXAM

Members of the Domain Admins group can log on to the network regardless of whether or not the global catalog server is down.

Global catalog servers can generate a lot of network traffic because they have to constantly deliver information about every object in the forest whenever it's requested. Although it's a good idea to have multiple global catalog servers for both reliability and load balancing, be sure the server has a high-bandwidth connection.

Organizational Unit Structure

The best way to break down a Windows 2000 domain into manageable sections is through the Organizational Unit (OU) structure. Each unit can reflect the actual departmental breakdowns inside your organization. You can assign user accounts, folders, physical equipment, and any other object to a specific OU. You can then assign permissions to the OU. If a user switches departments, you can move them to the new OU and they will inherit the new OU's permissions.

Organizational Units are arranged in a hierarchy. This can start as a simple geographic breakdown and layer down into departments within each location. You can have as many layers as you'd like, but fewer layers make managing the OU proportionally easier.

Creating Organizational Units

You can create a different OU structure for every domain in the forest. The most logical way to design your OU structure is to match the real departments and jobs in your organization to each OU.

Because the OU structure is hierarchical, you can create a flowchart of the departments and use it as a map when creating an OU hierarchy. To create a new OU, use the following steps:

1. Be sure you're logged on as an administrator. Choose Start → Programs → Administrative Tools → Active Directory Users and Computers.

2. Choose to create either a new OU in the domain or a sub-unit of an existing OU.

3. Choose Action → New → Organizational Unit.

4. You'll see the New Object—Organizational Unit screen. Type a name for the OU and click on the *OK* button.

5. Repeat the relevant steps until you've created a complete OU structure for your organization.

IN THE REAL WORLD

You can modify your OU structure at any time. However, it would be more efficient to take the time to map out which user accounts, folders, and equipment are needed for every department and create the OU structure all at once. If the framework is in place, the assignment of permissions becomes a lot easier.

Configuring Organizational Units

After you've taken the time to simulate the actual structure of your organization with an OU hierarchy, you can begin to customize each OU to fit the security and accessibility needs of your users. You can configure an OU by using the following steps:

1. Choose Start → Programs → Administrative Tools → Active Directory Users and Computers.

2. Click the plus sign next to the proper domain name to see which Organizational Units are available.

3. Right-click on the OU and choose *Properties*.

4. Choose one of the three configuration tabs (*General*, *Managed By*, or *Group Policy*). These tabs are described in more detail in Table 3-1.

5. Configure the OU and click the *OK* button when you're finished.

Table 3-1: Organizational Unit Properties

Tab	Available Properties and Their Uses
General	Contains a general description and geographical location. Filling in these properties accurately is useful when doing a keyword search for Organizational Units.
Managed By	Contains the contact information for the department head of the OU. Keeping these properties up-to-date will make contacting a user easier if there is a security or maintenance problem with his or her account.
Group Policy	Contains information about the Group Policies assigned to the OU. This information will make the future assignment of policies to similar Organizational Units easier.

Managing Active Directory Objects

Because Active Directory can hold millions of objects, the task of managing all of them can become quite daunting. The best way to deal with all the objects is to name them consistently, store them in Organizational Units, and assign policies and permissions to groups of objects, rather than individually.

Active Directory object naming conventions

Every object in the Active Directory database has at least one unique name to separate it from every other object. To manage all the different types and locations of objects, a few related naming schemes are used in Active Directory. They're all fairly straightforward, so you should have no trouble using them.

Underneath all the descriptive names an object may have, a unique 128-bit number, called a *globally unique identifier* (GUID), is permanently associated with every object. This number remains constant for the life of the object, regardless of other changes to the object's name or location.

DNS allows people to assign memorable names to computers that are really identified by unique 32-bit IP addresses. The same is true for Active Directory, which allows a user-friendly *distinguished name* (DN) to be mapped to the GUID. It would be difficult to remember a long GUID like the above sample, but it's easier to remember an account name like kirtb or a folder called payroll.

A distinguished name includes not only the user-friendly name of the individual object, called a *common name* (CN), but its entire path in the directory. This path can consist of a *domain component* (DC) (like oreilly.com), several hierarchical

Organizational Unit (OU) names (like employees and its subdivision, editors), and, finally, by the user-friendly portion of the distinguished name. So, the entire DN might look like: oreilly.com/employees/editors/katie. If Katie decided to work in the production department for a few months, her account's DN would change, but the underlying GUID would remain the same.

If two objects have the same common name, it's not a problem so long as they're in different Organizational Units. Their distinguished names would be different because the OU portion of their paths wouldn't be the same.

There is one other type of name, called a *user principal name* (UPN). It's a user-friendly name, usually comprised of part or all of a user's real name. This type of naming scheme is often used for email addresses. These must be unique to the domain to avoid confusion.

Creating accounts

There are two major types of user accounts in a Windows 2000 network, local user accounts and domain user accounts. Both types of accounts are objects in the Active Directory environment:

Local user account
Grants access to resources that are on the local computer where the account was created

Domain user account
Grants access to resources throughout the entire network, as long as trust relationships exist between domains

You can set up local user accounts on computers that aren't yet connected to the rest of the network or on mobile systems, which are often used without a network connection, yet still need some form of security. When you create a local user account, the password is stored only on the local computer.

Most of the time, the best solution is to create a domain user account. This will allow the greatest flexibility in accessing resources. To take full advantage of domain user accounts in Active Directory, you should store user accounts within an OU. As long as you are logged in as an administrator for the local machine, you can create a new local user account by using the following steps:

1. Choose Start → Programs → Administrative Tools → Computer Management. This opens the MMC snap-in shown in Figure 3-3.

2. Click the plus sign next to the Local Users and Groups snap-in.

3. Right-click on *Users* and select *New User.*

4. You'll see the New User screen. Configure the account with a username, password, and whatever other details you need.

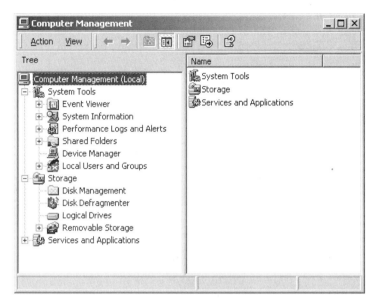

Figure 3-3: The Computer Management MMC snap-in

As long as you are logged in as an administrator for the domain, you can add a new domain user account by using the following steps:

1. Choose Start → Programs → Administrative Tools → Active Directory Users and Computers.

2. Double-click on the correct domain and right-click on *Users.*

3. Choose *New* and then choose *User.*

4. You'll see the New Object—User screen. Be sure to fill in both the *User Logon* and *User Logon Name* (pre-Windows 2000), if the user will be logging into the domain from any version of Windows other than 2000.

5. Click the *Next* button and configure the password and password options.

6. Click the *Finish* button.

Locating objects

All objects have descriptive properties, called *attributes*. When you search for an object, you'll really be searching for one or more of the object's attributes that make it unique in the network. Some common attributes are: Name, Organizational Unit, and Description.

There is a tool called Find to help you search for objects in the Active Directory. If you've used an Internet search engine, you'll be prepared for using the Find program. You can start Find by using the following steps:

1. Choose Start → Programs → Administrative Tools → Active Directory Users and Computers.

2. Right-click on the smallest container you think might contain your object and choose *Find.*

3. You'll see the Find Users, Contacts and Groups screen. Fill in whatever you know about the object and click the *Find Now* button.

Moving objects

You can either move objects within a domain or between domains. There are different rules that apply to each type of move. Moving objects within a domain is far less complex and error prone. You can move an object within a domain by using the following steps:

1. Choose Start → Programs → Administrative Tools → Active Directory Users and Computers.

2. Highlight the object you want to move and choose Action → Move.

3. Choose the destination OU and click the *OK* button.

There are only a few simple rules for moving an object within a domain:

- You can move more than one object at a time.

- Objects lose permissions that they inherited from their former OU and inherit permissions from their new OU.

- Permissions directly applied to the object itself remain unchanged.

You can also move objects between domains. The best way to do this is by using the MOVETREE program, which is included on the Windows 2000 installation media. It can be used to move just about any object, with a few notable exceptions, like system objects and domain controllers. Common objects, like users, groups, files, and folders can be moved easily between domains. MOVETREE is a command-line program with many options, which are described in Table 3-2.

Table 3-2: MOVETREE Command Options

Option	Description
/?	Brings up the MOVETREE help file
/check	A trial run that tests the move without actually moving the objects
/continue	Continues a paused or stopped MOVETREE operation
/start	Runs a check operation and then actually performs the move
/startnocheck	Executes the move operation without performing a check
/verbose	Reports progress during the move operation (useful for both troubleshooting and learning about what's happening)

Publishing Resources

Users will look in the Active Directory for all the resources that are available to them on the network. Some items, such as a Windows 2000 network printer, are visible in the directory automatically, just by physically installing them on the network. Other items, like shared folders and user accounts, have to be *published* by a network administrator to be seen in the Active Directory.

Different types of objects are published in different ways. Most common items, such as user accounts, shared folders, and legacy NT printers, are published using the Active Directory Users and Computers snap-in. The most common item you'll probably have to publish is a shared folder. Use the following steps to publish a shared folder in the Active Directory:

1. Choose Start → Programs → Administrative Tools → Active Directory Users and Computers.
2. Choose the domain you want the shared folder to be in.
3. Right-click on the container you want to hold the folder.
4. Choose New → Shared Folder.
5. You'll see the New Object—Shared Folder screen. Fill in a name for the folder and type the UNC path that you want the shared folder to point to.

Securing Resources

The most flexible way to secure resources in a Windows 2000 network is through permissions. Permissions describe which actions are available to a user or group. There are several types of permissions that can be assigned. The five most common permissions are described in Table 3-3.

Table 3-3: Windows 2000 Permissions

Permission	Function
Read	View an object and its properties, such as its owner and permissions, without changing them
Write	Modify an object without changing its owner or permissions
Full Control	Includes Read and Write permissions and adds the ability to modify, delete, take ownership, and change permissions
Create All Child Objects	Add any object to an Organizational Unit
Delete All Child Objects	Remove any object from an Organizational Unit

Windows 2000 stores permission information for every object in a file called the *Access Control List* (ACL). This ACL is the same file that is used to store NTFS permissions. Active Directory will automatically recognize NTFS permissions and use the Windows 2000 equivalents.

It is easier to assign permissions to groups of users, rather than to each individual user. A user's permissions will be a combination of their individual permissions plus any permissions assigned to any group the user belongs to. Permissions can be either granted or denied on an object-by-object basis.

IN THE REAL WORLD

A user can belong to many groups. The denial of a permission in any of the user's groups will deny the user permission regardless of other permissions, including Full Control.

Because Active Directory lists all the objects in one hierarchical directory and permissions can be inherited, assigning permissions is a straightforward process in Windows 2000. Most permissions can be assigned by using the following steps:

1. Choose Start → Programs → Administrative Tools → Active Directory Users and Computers.

2. Choose View and make sure *Advanced Features* is selected.

3. Click once on the object you want to assign permissions for.

4. Choose Action → Properties, then choose the Security tab.

5. Click on the *Add* button, choose the group you're assigning permissions for, and then place checkmarks in either the *Allow* or *Deny* boxes for the desired permission.

The five permissions discussed in Table 3-3 are called *standard permissions*. These are used most often. If you need to control access in a more specific way, there are many more permissions available, called *special permissions*. If you'd like to see the special permissions for an object, follow the first four steps listed earlier and continue on with the following steps:

1. In the Security tab, click the *Advanced* button.

2. You'll see the Access Control Settings screen. Choose the object you want to modify and click the *View/Edit* button.

3. Add or remove checkmarks for the appropriate special permissions.

IN THE REAL WORLD

When you assign permissions, you can choose to make any child object of the existing object automatically inherit its parent's permissions. This can greatly reduce the amount of work needed to secure a directory structure.

Delegating administrative control

An efficient Active Directory Organizational Unit structure will closely mirror the company's departmental structure. To ensure security throughout the network, many tasks, such as backing up or deleting files, can only be performed with the administrator's account. To make an OU run more efficiently, permissions usually assigned only to an administrator can be *delegated* to a departmental manager.

This will allow departments to work much more independently and quickly, without a major change to the level of security. As long as each manager can be trusted and protects their account, there is no downside to shifting some administrative control to local managers.

Windows 2000 allows you to individually assign permissions to each object in the Active Directory. However, it is often easier to manage permissions if they are assigned to an OU, rather than an individual, or to a folder, rather than a file. You can distribute control by using the Delegation of Control Wizard.

The wizard will walk you through giving a user or group of users permission to perform tasks or control objects that they wouldn't normally have access to. You can start the wizard by choosing Start → Programs → Administrative Tools → Active Directory Users and Computers. Select the object you want to delegate control for and choose Action → Delegate Control.

IN THE REAL WORLD

You may want to delegate control of such objects as a printer or database server to a competent manager who may need to perform mundane, but time-constrained, operations to it without the intervention of a system administrator.

Group Policies

Most companies have several departments, and each department requires its users to use a specific group of programs. The accounting department will use billing software, and technical support will use a database to keep track of service requests. You can customize each department's Windows desktop to reflect their individual needs by assigning Group Policies.

Implementing a Group Policy

Group Policies are used for both convenience and security. Before you actually start creating Group Policies, you should take an inventory of which programs each department or OU will need to have available and any other settings they'll need.

Creating a Group Policy Object (GPO). A Group Policy Object is the container that stores the Group Policy settings. There are two types of Group Policy Objects, *local* and *non-local:*

Local GPO
 Every Windows 2000 computer has one local GPO to store its default settings, regardless of whether or not it is connected to a Windows 2000 network.

Non-local GPO
 These are applied to either users or computers and take precedence over a computer's local GPO. Non-local GPOs can control settings on a domain, OU, or site level. Permissions are cumulative.

There is a Group Policy snap-in for the Microsoft Management Console. You can access the snap-in in several different ways, depending on which type of GPO you want to configure. Use the information in Table 3-4 to determine the best way to open the Group Policy snap-in.

Table 3-4: Group Policy Snap-In

Type of GPO	How to Open the Snap-In
Local GPO for the current computer	In the MMC, choose *Console → Add/Remove Snap-In.* Click on the Standalone tab, and press *Add.* Then click on *Group Policy, Add* and be sure the local computer is visible. Click *Finish, Close, OK.*
Local GPO for a remote computer	Same as above, except instead of looking for the local computer, browse the network for the remote computer.
Non-local GPO for an OU or a domain	Choose Start → Programs → Administrative Tools → Active Directory Users and Computers. Right-click on the OU or domain, choose *Properties,* and click on the Group Policy tab. Choose either *New* for a new GPO or *Edit* to modify an existing GPO.
Non-local GPO for a site	Choose Start → Programs → Administrative Tools → Active Directory Sites and Services. Right-click on the site, choose *Properties,* and click on the Group Policy tab. Choose either *New* for a new GPO or *Edit* to modify an existing GPO.

Group Policies apply to either a computer's settings or a user's settings. *Computer configuration settings* apply to the physical machine regardless of which user is logged in to it. *User configuration settings* apply to the user and roam with the user to any computer they log in to on the network. There are three main types of settings that can apply to either computer or user configuration settings: *Administrative Templates, Software Settings,* and *Windows Settings.*

Administrative Templates. Administrative Templates contain policy settings for network configuration, logon and logoff settings, and several Windows programs, such as Internet Explorer, MMC, and the task scheduler. These can apply to both the user and the computer.

Some settings will apply to only the computer or only the user. Settings that apply only to the computer include: disk quotas, DNS settings, and printers. Settings that apply only to the user include modifications to the Control Panel, desktop, Start menu, and taskbar. There are more than 400 settings that are controlled by Administrative Templates.

Software Settings. Software Settings control how software is installed. These settings can provide a framework for third-party vendors to determine how their software is installed in Windows 2000. By default, Software Settings only control software installation issues; after software is installed, it can be controlled by other Group Policies that apply to a domain, an OU, or a site.

There are two ways to manage applications after they are installed in an Active Directory environment. A program can be assigned to a computer or published to a group of users:

Assigning a program
   A program can be assigned to a particular computer or group of computers. This will allow users with access to the computer(s) to run the program.

Publishing a program
   A program can be published to a user or group of users. These users will have access to the program.

Windows Settings. Windows Settings are divided into two groups, scripts and security. These settings apply to both user and computer settings. There are two types of scripts, logon/logoff and startup/shutdown:

Startup/shutdown
   Run when the computer is booting up or shutting down

Logon/logoff
   Run when a user is logging on or off of the computer

The security settings portion of the Group Policy Windows Settings can be used as an alternative to using an Administrative Template. These settings can be applied to local and non-local GPOs. Windows Settings that apply only to users include policy settings for folder redirection, Internet Explorer maintenance, and Remote Installation Services.

A computer can have multiple scripts that need to execute. There is a default time limit of 10 minutes for all scripts to finish executing. This can cause problems if either the logoff or shutdown script doesn't have time to finish. You can increase the timeout with a software policy.

Modifying Group Policy inheritance. In Active Directory, there is a hierarchical structure for all objects. A parent container, such as a folder, can have child containers, such as subfolders. Group Policies are inherited by default, but there are a few exceptions. A setting specifically applied to a child object overrides only that particular inherited setting. Other settings that were inherited remain in place. Different types of objects can have different types of settings, so only mutual categories of settings can be inherited.

Filtering Group Policy settings with security groups. Multiple Group Policies can be assigned to a particular domain, OU, or site. Security settings are cumulative, so by applying the correct permissions to security groups, you can control access in a layered fashion.

DNS for Active Directory

Domain Name Service (DNS) is the naming scheme used on the Internet. Windows 2000 abandons the NetBIOS naming scheme used in previous versions of Windows, replacing it with the standard DNS system. You're probably already familiar with the DNS dotted name format. An example would be www.oreilly.com.

The *top-level domain* in this address is "com," meaning it is a commercial enterprise. Top-level domain names like com, gov, edu, and org are shared by many domains. The *second-level domain* is the unique descriptive name, "oreilly." The final part of this *fully qualified domain name* (FQDN) is the *hostname,* "www."

Since the early days of the Internet, people have named their computers by the method that they could use to exchange information. If the computer at oreilly.com was a File Transfer Protocol (FTP) server, it would be named ftp.oreilly.com. If the computer was a web server, it would be named www.oreilly.com. Current computers are powerful enough to host multiple servers and can accommodate multiple names and IP addresses on a single machine.

The FQDN can also accommodate extra names if a subdomain is involved. If there were a computer named "elephant" in the animals subdomain of the oreilly.com root domain, the FQDN of the elephant computer would be elephant.animals.oreilly.com.

The naming scheme for DNS is called a *namespace*. There are two types of DNS namespaces, *contiguous* and *disjointed*. All the names in a contiguous namespace share the same name for at least one level of the FQDN. An example of a contiguous namespace is an Active Directory tree and its subdomains. The oreilly.com tree has subdomains of linux.oreilly.com and windows.oreilly.com.

Domains in a disjointed namespace, such as an Active Directory forest, are part of the same network, but have different domain names. A theoretical example would be the Ford Motor Company forest. Both Jaguar and Volvo are distinct parts of the Ford Motor Company. Computers in various locations of the forest may have totally different names.

Within the disjointed namespace, there could some be contiguous namespaces for local dealerships, like dallas.ford.com and austin.ford.com. There could also be disjointed namespaces like sales.jaguar.com, service.volvo.com, and www.ford.com. All of these computers are still part of the same forest and can have two-way transitive trust relationships, but because at least some part of the namespace is disjointed, the forest itself is a disjointed namespace.

IN THE REAL WORLD

When you attempt to connect to a computer via Telnet or FTP, unless you know the computer's Internet Protocol (IP) address, you'll probably have to use the FQDN. If you frequently connect to computers in a few domains and don't want to type the FQDN, you can add these domains to the *Append these DNS suffixes* list in your network configuration, and Windows 2000 will attempt to find the hostname in each of the listed domains. Typing `ping books` a few times a day is easier than having to type `ping books.oreilly.com`.

Installing and Configuring DNS

A computer that stores the database of domain names and their Internet Protocol (IP) addresses is called a *name server*. Active Directory requires at least one name server, but having multiple name servers will improve both reliability and speed of finding resources on the network.

Another way of improving your DNS system is to divide your namespace into *zones*. Each zone, or subdivision, would have its own name server. This can help distribute administrative tasks among locations in the Active Directory forest.

DNS zones

A DNS namespace can be divided into zones for more efficient management. There are a couple of simple rules that govern how a namespace can be divided into zones:

- A zone can only include a contiguous portion of the namespace, such as oreilly.com and windows.oreilly.com.

- A zone is tied to a specific root domain, such as oreilly.com or a subdomain, such as linux.oreilly.com.

A namespace like oreilly.com cannot be divided up into one zone for the root domain (oreilly.com) and another for all the subdomains (linux.oreilly.com, windows.oreilly.com, and so on). The problem would be that the linux and windows subdomains taken by themselves aren't a contiguous namespace. They're only contiguous when included with their oreilly.com root domain.

Integrating DNS zones

Every name server covers at least one zone, called its *primary zone*. In addition to the primary zone, if multiple name servers are used, a name server can contain a backup copy of other name servers' primary zones. This redundancy helps make DNS a very reliable naming system.

When one name server automatically queries another for a copy of its primary zone, the first name server sends a copy of the zone database file in a process called a *zone transfer*. By strategically placing name servers on different subnets, you can reduce lookup traffic on the network. The zone transfers cause traffic, so be sure to configure the zone transfers between areas of the network that will often share resources. Otherwise, you'll be generating needless traffic between the subnets.

Dynamic updates

Windows 2000 DNS servers can automatically synchronize zone information using a process called *Dynamic Domain Name Service* (DDNS). Whenever an IP address or hostname changes, the DDNS service makes sure that the zone database is updated.

DNS replication

The zone database is stored on at least one computer called the *primary name server*. To improve speed and reliability, you can host copies on the zone database on multiple *backup name servers*. Data within the zone file is updated automatically with DDNS. The primary name server can distribute updates out to the backup name servers in a process called a zone transfer. When a computer is first configured as a backup name server, the entire zone database must be copied using a full zone transfer. Subsequently, as changes are made to the zone database, only the changed data needs to be replicated. Partial replication of the changes to a zone database file is called an *incremental zone transfer*.

If the DNS zone file is stored in the Active Directory and all the name servers are also configured as part of the Active Directory, data transfer will be automatically handled by AD. If not, you can manually configure the name servers to replicate the zone file on a push basis using a process called *DNS notification*.

The DNS zone file maintains a serial number to keep track of which version of the database is current. Whenever there is a change to the zone database, the serial number is also modified, triggering the notification and subsequent replication of the zone file by the backup name servers.

Monitoring DNS

You can monitor DNS activity in a couple of different ways. You can keep an event log for DNS and view the results in the Event Viewer or set up more stringent debugging options. Troubleshooting DNS is covered in greater detail in the "Troubleshooting DNS" section at the end of this chapter.

Directory Maintenance and Replication

A good network administrator knows that thoroughly planning a network before actually implementing it will save a tremendous amount of time and effort in the long run. An experienced network administrator knows that no matter how well you plan a network, the network will have to be changed to meet the ever changing needs of its users.

The three main tasks you'll have to perform are: adding a new server, moving a server to a new replication site, and removing a server from the network. Because hardware is constantly improving, adding new servers or consolidating tasks performed by a few less powerful servers on a new server is commonplace. This type of activity can occur quite frequently if your company is growing rapidly.

Creating a Server Object

Everything in Active Directory is an object. In the case of a server, a *server object* is the logical representation of the physical machine in the hierarchical AD database. When you install a new server, you'll have to add it to the Active Directory using the following steps:

1. Choose Start → Programs → Administrative Tools → Active Directory Sites and Services.

2. Double-click on the site you would like to add the server to.

3. Right-click on the *Servers* folder and choose New → Server.

4. You'll see the New Object—Server screen. Type in a name for the new server and click the *OK* button.

Moving Server Objects Between Sites

Sites are areas of the network that have high interconnectivity bandwidth. They're used to divide up replication traffic in the most efficient way possible. When you start to change the number or types of servers on a network, you may have to move servers to other sites to maintain those high-speed connections.

Sometimes you need to change the replication site a server is currently a member of. You can do this by using the following steps:

1. Choose Start → Programs → Administrative Tools → Active Directory Sites and Services.

2. Right-click on the server you'd like to move and choose *Move*.

3. You'll see a list of available sites. Choose the site you want to move the server to and click the *OK* button.

IN THE REAL WORLD

When you replace a few slower servers with a higher capacity server, traffic on that part of the network can increase exponentially. Be sure that your new servers are on sites that can handle the increased traffic. You may have to create new sites or modify the physical layout of your network to maintain or improve speed.

Removing a Server Object

Hardware becomes obsolete fairly quickly. It's not that three-year-old servers become unusable, but time is money, so it's often your job to weed out slower machines.

IN THE REAL WORLD

Windows NT and 2000 have relatively high hardware requirements to run at peak performance. If the older servers have compatible hardware, they can sometimes be recycled using the free operating system Linux. Interoperability between Windows and Unix-based systems is increasing, and these older servers can be used for many worthwhile tasks on a primarily Windows 2000–based network.

Assuming you want to permanently remove a server, use the following steps to delete the server object from the Active Directory:

1. Choose Start → Programs → Administrative Tools → Active Directory Sites and Services.

2. Right-click on the server object you'd like to permanently remove and choose *Delete*.

3. Confirm that you want to do this by pressing the *Yes* button.

Active Directory Replication

In most network environments, significant and frequent changes are made to the files, folders, user accounts, and equipment. Active Directory has to share these

If a server object needs to be removed temporarily, the NTDS Settings object for that server should be removed. When the server is brought on-line again, these settings are automatically restored.

changes with all its domain controllers. Synchronizing this information across the entire enterprise can be a huge amount of work. To make this task as efficient as possible, the method of replication is specialized to the particular situation. Active Directory supports two main types of replication:

Single-master replication
> To prevent possible conflicts, one computer stores a master copy of the data and the replicating computers store a backup. This is a one-way process.

Multi-master replication
> Multiple computers store, send, and accept replication data at various times simultaneously around the network.

Operations master roles

Single-master replication is organized into five distinct tasks, called *operations master roles*. Some of the roles involve single domains, while other roles involve the whole forest. Only Windows 2000 domain controllers can be assigned operations master roles. The operations master roles are described in Table 3-5.

Table 3-5: Operations Master Roles

Role	Scope	Description
Infrastructure master	Domain	Updates and changes if a user or group is renamed. There can be only one infrastructure master per domain. If a user moves across domains, the two infrastructure masters will replicate the change during the next multi-master replication between domains.

Table 3-5: Operations Master Roles (continued)

Role	Scope	Description
Primary domain controller (PDC) emulator	Domain	If the network is running in mixed mode, the PDC emulator acts like a Windows NT PDC and replicates with the NT backup domain controllers. If the network is running in native mode, the PDC emulator will be the first DC to get replication of password changes. If replication hasn't occurred on a recent password change, a DC can check with the PDC emulator to see if it received the password change. This is especially important if a network has a lot of domain controllers and frequent password changes. There can be only one PDC emulator per domain.
Relative ID master	Domain	The relative ID master has two main functions. It assigns a group of consecutive IDs to domain controllers so that they can assign unique IDs to objects created on the DC. To move any Active Directory object between domains, you have to move it from the computer that is currently acting as the relative ID master. You can change which computer is the relative ID master, but there can be only one relative ID master at a time in a domain.
Domain naming master	Forest	Keeps track of domains that are added to or removed from the forest. There can be only one domain naming master in the forest.
Schema master	Forest	Changes to the Active Directory schema can only be made from the schema master. There can be only one schema master in the forest.

All the operations master roles are automatically assigned to the first domain controller in the forest. After your network has grown and there are multiple domain controllers, you may want to distribute the roles among different domain controllers.

Once you have two domain controllers in a domain, you can take some precautionary steps. The first domain controller will still have all the operations master roles, but the second domain controller can be configured as a *standby operations master* domain controller.

If the first computer fails, the backup machine will automatically assume any roles formerly handled by the original domain controller. If you have many domain controllers on your network, you may want to move some of the operations master roles onto separate machines for load balancing and reliability.

Because the operations masters have to replicate data frequently, be sure to choose domain controllers with fast network connections. You can assign any role to any domain controller by following a few steps. The process differs slightly, depending on which role you're changing.

Transferring operations master roles

All five roles can be reassigned using Microsoft Management Console (MMC) snap-ins. Unfortunately, not all of the snap-ins you'll need are installed by default. If you want to change the schema master, you'll have to install the Active Directory Schema snap-in by using the following steps:

1. Choose Start → Settings → Control Panel → Add/Remove Programs.

2. Choose *Change or Remove Programs.*

3. Choose *Windows 2000 Administrative Tools* and click the *Change* button.

4. You'll see the Welcome to the Windows 2000 Administration Tools Setup Wizard. As with most Windows 2000 wizards, you'll have to click the *Next* button to move to the next screen.

5. You'll see the Setup Options screen. Choose *Install All of the Administrative Tools.*

6. It will copy all the required files. Click the *Finish* button.

7. Start the Microsoft Management Console. Choose Start → Run, and then type mmc and click *OK.*

8. Choose Console → Add/Remove Snap-In.

9. You'll see the Add/Remove Snap-In screen. Click *Add.*

10. You'll see the Add Standalone Snap-In screen. Double-click on *Active Directory Schema.*

11. Click *Close* and then click *OK.*

12. Choose Console → Save.

Almost all of the administrative tasks in Windows 2000 are handled by MMC snap-ins. We're going to be using the MMC a lot in this chapter, so you'll be well prepared for the MMC simulation questions by the time you're done.

If you want to transfer the domain naming master role, you'll need to perform the following steps:

1. Choose Start → Run, type mmc, and click the *OK* button.

2. Open the Active Directory Domains and Trusts snap-in.

3. Right-click on the domain controller that you want to become the new domain naming master. Choose *Connect to Domain.*

Active Directory

4. You'll see the Connect to Domain screen. Click the *Browse* button and choose the correct domain name.

5. Right-click on *Active Directory Domains and Trusts* and choose *Operations Master.*

6. You'll see the Operations Master screen. Click on the *Change* button and then click *OK.*

You can change either the infrastructure master, PDC emulator, or relative ID master roles using roughly the same set of steps:

1. Choose Start → Programs → Administrative Tools → Active Directory Users and Computers.

2. Right-click on the domain in question and choose *Connect to Domain.*

3. You'll see the Connect to Domain screen. Click the *Browse* button and choose the correct domain name.

4. Right-click on *Active Directory Users and Computers* and choose *Operations Master.*

5. You'll see the Operations Master screen. Depending on which role you want to change, choose either *RID* (for Remote ID), *PDC* (for PDC emulator), or *Infrastructure* (for the infrastructure master).

6. After you've chosen the role you want to change, click on the *Change* button and then click *OK.*

There is one last role you may need to change, the schema master role. Assuming you've already installed the schema master snap-in, you can use the following steps to change which DC will act as the schema master:

1. Choose Start → Run, type mmc, and click the *OK* button.

2. Right-click on *Active Directory Schema* and choose *Change Domain Controller.*

3. Choose *Any DC* for automatic selection, or you can manually type in the name of the domain controller you want to be the new schema master. Click the *OK* button.

4. Right-click on *Active Directory Schema* and choose *Operations Master.*

5. You'll see the Change Schema Master screen. Click the *Change* button and then click *OK.*

If you only have one domain controller, all operations master roles will be on that computer. However, if you have multiple domain controllers and domain trees in your Active Directory forest, it can be difficult to remember which domain controllers are assigned each role.

There is a methodical way to find out which computers are playing each role. Remember, some roles are required in each domain, while others need only a single player for the entire forest.

If you want to find out which machines are acting as an infrastructure, PDC emulator, or relative ID master, you can perform the following steps:

1. Choose Start → Programs → Administrative Tools → Active Directory Users and Computers.

2. Right-click on *Active Directory Users and Computers* and choose *Operations Master.*

3. Depending on which computer you're trying to find, choose either *RID* (for Remote ID), *PDC* (for PDC emulator), or *Infrastructure* (for infrastructure master).

4. The name of whichever domain controller is currently acting in the role will appear. Click *Cancel* to close the dialog box.

If you want to find out which computer is acting as the domain naming master, use the following steps:

1. Choose Start → Run, type mmc, and click the *OK* button.

2. Open the Active Directory Domains and Trusts snap-in.

3. Right-click on *Active Directory Domains and Trusts* and choose *Operations Master.*

4. You'll see the Operations Master screen. Under *Domain Naming Operations Master,* you'll see the name of the current domain naming master.

5. Click the *Close* button without making any changes.

You'll have to follow a different set of steps to find out which computer is the current Active Directory schema master:

1. Choose Start → Run, type mmc, and click the *OK* button.

2. Open the Active Directory Schema snap-in.

3. Right-click on *Active Directory Schema* and choose *Operations Master.*

4. You'll see the Change Operations Master screen. Under *Current Operations Master,* you'll see the name of the current schema master.

Remote Installation Service (RIS)

You can remotely install Windows 2000 Professional on clients using a disk image or CD-ROM stored on a server using the *Remote Installation Service.* Client computers must have network cards that either are supported by the RIS boot disk, have Pre-Boot Execution Environment (PXE) ROMS, or are NetPC compliant.

IN THE REAL WORLD

RIS is a new technology with serious security issues. It doesn't use any encryption technology, yet it assigns file permissions during the installation process. Spoofing of an RIS server and subsequent permissions modifications, not to mention other damaging behavior, is a real possibility.

Creating an RIS Boot Disk

If the client computer on which you'd like to install Windows 2000 Professional, the only OS currently supported by RIS, doesn't have PXE ROMS, you'll have to create an RIS boot disk. You can create the disk by performing the following steps (be sure you have a formatted floppy disk available in the drive of the computer you're working on):

1. Start the RBFG.EXE program.

2. You'll see the Windows 2000 Remote Boot Disk Generator screen. Choose *Create Disk*.

3. A dialog box informing you that the process is complete will appear. Click on the *Close* button and remove the floppy disk.

Installing RIS on a Server

Choose a computer with a fast connection to the client computers to use as an RIS server. A lot of data must be sent from the server to the clients for the installation of Windows 2000 Professional. The RIS server setup will fail if it does not find a DNS server or the DHCP service running on the network, so be sure to verify this before proceeding.

Once you're ready to install RIS, use the following steps to complete the install:

1. Install the RIS service as an optional component. The Configure Your Server screen should indicate setup is not complete.

2. If you don't see the Configure Your Server screen, you can get it by choosing Start → Programs → Administrative Tools → Configure Your Server.

3. You'll see the Configure Your Server screen. Choose *Finish Setup* and you'll see the Add/Remove Programs screen.

4. Under *Configure Remote Installation Services*, click on *Configure*.

5. You'll see the Remote Installation Services Setup Wizard screen. Click the *Next* button.

The RIS Setup Wizard will ask for several configuration settings, such as where the Windows 2000 Professional installation source files are, where you'd like to create the disk image on the server, and whether it should start the client installation process as soon as possible.

Authorizing an RIS Server

RIS is not a highly secure environment, but you can limit your potential exposure by carefully selecting which computers can act as RIS servers. You have to *authorize* a server before it can perform RIS installations. As a safety feature, if an RIS installation is attempted by an unauthorized computer, that computer will automatically be cut off from the network. You can authorize an RIS server using the following steps:

1. Choose Start → Programs → Administrative Tools → DHCP.

2. Choose the DHCP server and choose Action → Manage Authorized Servers.

3. You'll see the Manage Authorized Servers screen. Click *Authorize*.

4. Type in the name or IP address of the proposed RIS server. Click the *OK* button and then click *Yes*.

5. You'll see the Manage Authorized Servers screen. Choose the new RIS server and click *OK*.

You can choose to configure your RIS server to install Windows 2000 without any prompts and using a default naming scheme. There is a custom setup available if you need any special settings on a particular client. If you have any trouble during the install, you can try to restart the installation or, if the problems persist, you can use third-party diagnostic software using the maintenance and troubleshooting option.

The Client Installation Wizard (CIW) will walk you through the steps needed to install, reinstall, or troubleshoot OS installation. The CIW gives you four options:

Automatic Setup
> This option allows users to simply log in and choose the operating system to be installed, then proceed without having to make any more input. Choices can be restricted by the Administrator, and a predefined naming scheme can be used.

Custom Setup
> This setup allows for two main customizations unavailable with an automatic setup. The automatic computer naming scheme can be overridden, and the location in AD where the computer account is created can be changed.

Maintenance and Troubleshooting
> This allows third-party diagnostic tools to be used to examine and potentially fix any problems with the disk image or setup files that will be used.

Restart a Previous Setup Attempt
> This can continue a previous installation where it left off, assuming you have resolved any problems that caused the installation to stop.

Pre-Staging RIS Clients

We've already discussed the need to authorize an RIS server to help ensure the integrity of the files being sent to the client. Keep in mind that it is technically possible to intercept and modify RIS installation data. You can further secure the RIS environment by making sure only authorized clients receive the installation files. The process of authorizing the client is called *pre-staging*. You can do this using the following steps:

1. Choose Start → Programs → Administrative Tools → Active Directory Users and Computers.

2. Right-click on the OU that will be the container for the RIS client. Choose New → Computer.

3. You'll see the New Object—Computer screen. Type in the name of the RIS client computer and click the *Change* button to authorize the computer's user to join the domain after RIS has installed the OS. Click the *Next* button.

4. You'll see the Managed screen. Click in the box next to *This is a managed computer.*

5. Unfortunately, you have to manually type in the client computer's GUID. This is a unique 32-digit hexadecimal code either located physically on the computer (usually a sticker), viewable in the BIOS, or both.

RIS Account Creation

If you are using RIS to install client computers, you are probably an administrator for a large, sophisticated network. Managing accounts for hundreds or thousands of users can be a lot of work that can be more efficiently handled by delegating some control to trusted users.

You can allow computer accounts to join a domain in one of two ways, depending on how the account was created. If the account was created in an OU container, you can use Group Policies for authorization. If the account was created in the Computers container, you can use the Delegation of Control Wizard for authorization. You can also authorize both user-created and pre-staged computer account creation to be delegated to a trusted user or group of users.

Active Directory Security

Active Directory is designed to allow a very large number of users to efficiently access potentially every network resource in the enterprise. Universal access can be great for productivity, but this freedom can pose a significant challenge to maintaining network security. It is absolutely essential that you take a systematic approach to ensuring security on your network. Security issues permeate all aspects of resource management. We cover various security topics throughout the entire book.

ON THE EXAM

Microsoft has decided to emphasize security by assigning an entire exam to the topic. Because security is such a fundamental part of managing a network, you'll find that security topics will be covered on every exam to some extent.

Security Templates

Active Directory is very good at displaying a lot of information in an easy-to-use directory structure. This approach is extended to managing your security configuration. You can store security settings in a single file, called a *security template.*

There is a Security Template Console snap-in available for the MMC, but it's not installed by default. Installing this console will simplify the process of creating security templates. You can install this snap-in using the following steps:

1. Open the Microsoft Management Console and choose Console → Add/Remove Snap-In → Add.

2. You'll see the Add Standalone Snap-In screen, shown in Figure 3-4. Choose *Security Templates*, click *Add*, and then press *Close*.

3. Click the *OK* button and then click *Save*.

4. Name the security console whatever you'd like and click the *Save* button.

Figure 3-4: The Add Standalone Snap-In dialog

You'll now be able to use this snap-in to configure and view security templates. There are many predefined security templates that you can modify to suit the needs of your network. You can create your own templates from scratch, but I recommend modifying an existing template until you become thoroughly familiar with all the possible security settings.

The Security Configuration and Analysis Console

The Security Configuration and Analysis Console is an MMC snap-in that can be used to configure, analyze, and modify security settings. Security templates can be imported into the console, modified if needed, and applied to the relevant policy to actually implement the changes. Most security needs can be met by the modification of existing security templates, rather than configuring an entire security policy from scratch.

The Security Configuration and Analysis Console will also check the current security settings and provide a report. This report not only will display areas that need to be secured, but will also allow you the option of letting the computer fix any potential security problems for you. Although this is very convenient, you should verify that the changes are adequate to ensure a secure environment.

You can create a security database into which you can import multiple security templates. You can import new templates into this database as needed. Both of these tasks can be performed using the following steps:

1. Right-click on the *Security Configuration and Analysis* node in the MMC and choose *Open Database*.

2. Type a name for a new security database and click *OK*.

3. You'll see the Import Template screen. Choose a template and click *OK*.

If you have an existing security database and you want to import another template, follow these steps:

1. Right-click on the *Security Configuration and Analysis* node in the MMC and choose *Open Database*.

2. Right-click on the appropriate database and choose *Import Template*.

3. You'll see the Import Template screen. Choose a template and click *OK*.

If you need to replace a template in the database rather than just merge one in, there is an option to clear the database before importing in the Import Template screen.

Audit Policies

One of the traditional tools network administrators use is the *log file*. A log file records events that have occurred on the network and can provide valuable clues in the event of a breach of security. They can be used to monitor and evaluate network performance and provide baseline data to compare with future activity.

An *audit policy* defines what will be recorded in the log file. You can audit activities, such as file access, login activity, resource usage, process tracking, and account management. You can apply an audit policy to a domain controller, standalone server, printer, or specific files or folders using the MMC. Auditing must be configured before the Event Viewer can be used to monitor audited events. You can create an audit policy for files and folders by using the following steps:

1. Right-click on the appropriate icon, choose *Properties*, and click on the Security tab.

2. Choose the *Advanced* button and click on the Auditing tab, then click the *Add* button.

3. Choose the users and groups for the policy to apply to and click *OK*.

4. You'll see a list of events with a *Successful and Failed* checkbox available. Click the boxes for the events you want to audit for the given users or groups.

Trust Relationships

Active Directory allows for two different types of *trust relationships.* A trust relationship is set up between a *trusting domain* and a *trusted domain.* The trusting domain allows users in the trusted domain to log in. Group Policy security in the trusting domain still applies to the users logging in from the trusted domain.

The default trust relationship between Windows 2000 domains in a tree and root domains in a forest is a two-way *transitive trust.* This means that if tree A trusts tree B and tree B trusts tree C, tree A automatically trusts tree C and vice-versa, without any separate trust relationships between A and C.

Because each subdomain in a tree trusts the root domain and the root domain trusts its subdomains, every subdomain in a tree automatically trusts every other subdomain in the tree. Because every root domain in a forest trusts every other root domain in the forest, every subdomain of every tree in the forest trusts every other subdomain in the forest. This greatly simplifies trusts in a Windows 2000 network compared to the Windows NT trust scheme.

IN THE REAL WORLD

Because users in any domain of the forest potentially have access to all other domains in the forest with a single logon, you should be very careful when assigning permissions to users.

The second type of trust relationship possible in Windows 2000 is a one-way *nontransitive trust.* This was the only option in Windows NT. In a nontransitive trust relationship, domain A decides to trust users in domain B. Domain A becomes the trusting domain in this relationship, because it trusts the users in domain B. Domain B becomes the trusted domain, because its users are trusted by domain A. Users in domain B can now log in to domain A, but users in domain A cannot log into domain B, unless a separate nontransitive trust relationship is established.

Nontransitive trusts can be set up between two Windows 2000 domains in different forests or between a Windows 2000 domain and a Windows NT domain. You can also set up a nontransitive trust between a Windows 2000 domain and a compliant Kerberos realm.

Active Directory Maintenance

Because Active Directory stores information about all the objects on the network, it is very important to make sure that the information contained in the AD is timely and accurate. Protecting the integrity of the data stored in your Active Directory and optimizing the directory's performance involves frequent monitoring and tweaking. I recommend assigning a set schedule for performing maintenance tasks.

Managing Accounts

The most important part of your network is its users. If you've created a good Organizational Unit structure and assigned Group Policies in an efficient manner, you shouldn't have much trouble maintaining user accounts. If an employee leaves the company and can potentially return, it is best to disable, rather than delete, the account.

IN THE REAL WORLD

If you delete an account, it is more difficult to reassign permissions for the objects that user owned to another user account. You'll have to own the objects to an administrator account before reassigning permissions.

Backing Up Active Directory

It is extremely important to back up data regularly. Users can lose data through malicious virus or worm attacks, by catastrophic hardware failure, or because of a simple mistake, such as accidentally deleting an important file. The safest policy is to keep frequent, multiple copies of data at separate locations.

The Active Directory can be backed up using the Windows Backup program included with Windows 2000. You'll probably have to schedule backups for late-night hours, because Windows Backup won't back up files that are in use and locked by applications. Also, the data transfer during a backup can use up quite a bit of network bandwidth.

Windows 2000 has a Backup Wizard to help you organize and implement a backup strategy. You can start the Backup Wizard using the following steps:

1. Choose Start → Programs → Accessories → System Tools → Backup.

2. You'll see the Welcome to the Windows 2000 Backup and Recovery Tools screen. Choose *Backup Wizard*.

3. The wizard will walk you through what you want to back up, where you want to put it, and when to perform the backup.

IN THE REAL WORLD

To back up Active Directory data, system state data must be selected in the Windows Backup Wizard. The wizard will automatically determine which system state data to back up.

Restoring Active Directory

There are two types of restoration options for an Active Directory domain controller, *authoritative* and *non-authoritative*. You must always perform a non-authoritative restore before you can perform an authoritative restore. You have to reboot into *Directory Services restore mode* before starting either type of restoration:

Non-authoritative restore

Restores only those settings that aren't replicated from other domain controllers. If any modifications have been made to the replicated data, that data will be automatically updated the next time the restored computer receives replication data.

Authoritative restore

If you accidentally delete an object or objects, you can use a backup from before the deletion to non-authoritatively restore the object(s). Then you can use the NTDSUTIL program to mark those objects as authoritative. This will give them precedence in the replication process, so the other domain controllers will replicate the restored objects.

Optimizing Performance

Network performance is determined by the combined speed and efficiency of many components working together. Potential bottlenecks can form because of a lack of bandwidth on the network media, slow hard drives on file servers, or too many authentication requests handled by an insufficient number of domain controllers.

Active Directory performance

You should frequently monitor Active Directory's performance to make sure everything is running smoothly. There are two tools you can use, the *Event Viewer* and the *Performance Console*:

Event Viewer

Monitors services and applications and stores information in event logs. These logs include information about applications, the directory and file replication services, security, and system errors.

Performance Console

Provides counters to keep track of the performance of both local and remote computers on the network. The Performance Console contains the System Monitor and Performance Logs and Alerts.

Performance logs can be used for instant feedback or kept as a baseline to be compared to future readings. Also, the NTDS object counters can be used in much the same way to trace Active Directory performance.

ON THE EXAM

The first step in troubleshooting Active Directory is to check the Directory Service logs in the Event Viewer.

Troubleshooting Active Directory

There are five operations master roles played by domain controllers in the forest. The severity of the problem depends on which DC fails. Table 3-6 lists the operations master roles and the consequences of their failure.

IN THE REAL WORLD

If you have enough well-connected domain controllers, be sure to assign a standby role to an alternate domain controller in case the primary DC fails. If you do this, the odds of a disruption are far less.

Most operations master failures will not immediately or drastically affect the performance or functionality of the network. There is one notable exception, the primary domain controller emulator.

Because it deals with user authentication, if the PDC emulator is unavailable it can cause serious problems. This is the one case where you might consider *seizing the role*.

Seizing an operations master role involves transferring the operations master role to another domain controller. This process was covered earlier in this chapter. You should only do this if it is absolutely necessary.

IN THE REAL WORLD

If you seize the role of either a domain naming master, relative ID master, or schema master, you'll have to format the hard drive and reinstall Windows 2000 on whichever domain controller you seized the role from before it can be safely returned to the network.

Table 3-6: Operations Master Failure

Operations Master Role	Consequence of Failure
Infrastructure master	Usually not an urgent problem, unless there have been a lot of user or group changes. Try to fix the problem before seizing the role.
Primary domain controller (PDC) emulator	Users may have trouble logging in, especially if the network is running in mixed mode. Unless you can make an immediate fix, seize the role and assign it to the standby unit.
Relative ID master	Usually not an urgent problem, unless enough objects are added to a domain to cause the current batch of relative IDs to be used up. Try to fix the problem before seizing the role.

Table 3-6: Operations Master Failure (continued)

Operations Master Role	Consequence of Failure
Domain naming master	Usually not an urgent problem, until you need to add or remove a domain from the forest. Try to fix the problem before seizing the role.
Schema master	Almost never a problem, unless an administrator wants to modify the Active Directory schema, either manually or through software.
Global catalog server	The GCS is replicated among domain controllers, so the odds of a total failure are small. But, if it becomes corrupted or otherwise unavailable, users will not be able to log on to access network resources. However, they will still be able to log on locally to those machines for which they have adequate permissions.

Troubleshooting DNS

If a DNS server is malfunctioning, it can cause quite a bit of trouble on the network. The Windows 2000 Event Viewer can be used to monitor and diagnose problems with DNS.

There are two levels of monitoring available, standard logging of events and *debug logging*. Debug logging can significantly slow down the DNS server's performance, so use it as a last resort. Debug information will be stored locally on the DNS server in a file named DNS.LOG, which can become quite large.

You should verify DNS entries in both forward and reverse directions. This can be done with the nslookup utility by first looking for the FQDN and matching the IP address, then using the IP address to match the FQDN.

Troubleshooting RIS

Remote installation can cause problems that you wouldn't experience during a normal installation. Table 3-7 lists some common problems and their solutions.

Table 3-7: Troubleshooting RIS

Problem	Solution
The wrong server is installing to an RIS client.	Either the data associating the RIS client and server hasn't been replicated yet (likely) or there is a rogue RIS server (unlikely).
A restored RIS volume no longer functions properly.	The SIS directory is missing or corrupt. Verify the source data and reinstall again.
Customized settings are not being implemented.	Check your configuration files for incorrect paths.

Troubleshooting Group Policies

Group Policies are a great way to manage resources because they can be layered and are cumulative. Unfortunately, when something goes wrong, you have to check the chain of inheritance to track down where the problem actually originates. If you're not careful, it's easy to either grant or deny access to a resource accidentally through the automatic accumulation of permissions.

Group Policies are also very flexible, allowing you to modify the normal inheritance rules. This is a convenient feature, but when something goes wrong, it can make it doubly difficult to track down the problem. Your best bet in troubleshooting Group Policies is to use a strict and consistent implementation of Group Policies right from the start.

Troubleshooting Software Deployment

Earlier in this chapter we discussed both publishing and assigning applications on the network. If you've distributed applications by Organizational Unit, you'll have an easier time making sure the correct people have access to applications. You should also take advantage of inheritance in the Active Directory to assign or publish applications the fewest number of times.

Active Directory Troubleshooting Tools

Windows 2000 includes several tools for maintaining and diagnosing problems with Active Directory, such as ReplMon, RepAdmin, DSStat, SDCheck, and ACLDiag. Even if you don't currently have a problem with your Active Directory, you should use these tools to get used to their functionality in case they are needed in an emergency.

Suggested Exercises

Active Directory is completely new to Windows 2000. Even if you've used Windows 2000 since its early betas as Windows NT 5.0, you can still benefit from a hands-on refresher of some important Active Directory topics.

The Study Guide in this part includes a lot of step-by-step instructions for performing specific tasks. If you'd like to test yourself, try performing these exercises without looking at the step-by-step instructions. If you can do this, you can feel confident that you are familiar with the day-to-day tasks required to maintain an Active Directory environment.

Installing Active Directory

1. Install Active Directory by creating a new domain controller for a new tree.

2. Install Active Directory again, this time creating a new domain controller for the existing tree.

3. Verify both installations.

Testing DNS

1. Perform a simple query.

2. Perform a recursive query.

Configuring Active Directory

1. Create a replication site.

2. Create a subnet.

3. Create a site link and assign it a cost of 80.

4. Create a site link bridge.

Organizational Units

1. Create an OU for each department at your company.

2. Create a few domain user accounts and add them to the appropriate OU.

Managing Objects

1. Search for an object by its description.

2. Move the object and perform the search again.

3. Publish a shared folder.

4. Delegate control of the shared folder to a user.

Group Policy Objects

1. Create a GPO for an OU.

2. Have a user try to delete a folder owned by an administrator.

3. Assign an OU Full Control of that folder.

4. Have a user in the OU try to delete the folder.

Remote Installation Service

1. Create a RIS boot disk.

2. Create a RIS Server.

3. Perform a remote installation.

Security

1. Create a security template.

2. Create an audit policy.

3. Have a user try to access a file they don't have permissions for and then check the log file.

Backup and Recovery

1. Use the Windows Backup Wizard to configure an overnight backup.

2. Delete an account the next day.

3. Perform an authoritative backup to restore the account.

4. Verify the account is functioning properly.

Practice Tests

Test Questions

1. When using the Active Directory Installation Wizard, which are valid options?

    a. Create a new tree

    b. Create a new Organizational Unit (OU)

    c. Join an existing tree

    d. a and c

    e. All of the above

2. Which servers need to be installed before Active Directory can run?

    a. A primary domain controller

    b. A backup domain controller

    c. A DNS server

    d. A web server

3. Where can you look to verify your domain is being recognized properly after a Windows 2000 installation?

    a. My Computer

    b. Control Panel

    c. My Network Places

    d. Network Neighborhood

4. What is the name of the universal configuration framework that can be customized to perform almost any configuration task in Windows 2000?

    a.   Microsoft Snap-in Console

    b.   Microsoft Administration Console

    c.   Microsoft Policy Console

    d.   Microsoft Management Console

5. What is the difference between intrasite and intersite replication?

    a.   Intrasite replication takes place between sites, and intersite replication takes place within a site.

    b.   Intersite replication takes place between sites, and intrasite replication takes place within a site.

    c.   Intrasite replication is used with mixed mode, and intersite replication is used with native mode.

    d.   Intersite replication is used with mixed mode, and intrasite replication is used with native mode.

6. Where can sites be created?

    a.   Within a subnet

    b.   Within a domain

    c.   Across domains

    d.   All of the above, if given adequate bandwidth

7. Which protocols can be used to transfer site replication data? (Select all that apply.)

    a.   IPX/SPX

    b.   TCP/IP

    c.   HTTP

    d.   SMTP

8. What does a site link cost determine?

    a.   The amount of money needed to link subnets

    b.   The total bandwidth needed between sites

    c.   The connection that will be used for intersite replication

    d.   The connection that will be used for Internet connectivity

9. Which topology best describes the path that replication follows in Active Directory?

    a.   Ring

    b.   Star

    c.   Bus

    d.   Mesh

10. Which server is automatically configured as the global catalog server?

    a.   The first domain controller in a subnet

    b.   The first domain controller in a forest

    c.   The first domain controller in a tree

    d.   The global catalog server isn't automatically configured

11. Which of the following could be a globally unique identifier (GUID) for an Active Directory object?

    a.   206.100.152.137

    b.   2cecfa7b-9316-11d4-bf01-004005a3ae74

    c.   www.oreilly.com

    d.   78/38*rbl

12. Which objects can't be moved between domains? (Select all that apply.)

    a.   Domain controllers

    b.   User accounts

    c.   Organizational Units

    d.   System files

13. What is the name of the utility that can move objects between domains?

    a.   Microsoft Management Console (MMC)

    b.   MOVETREE

    c.   Domain Transfer Console (DTC)

    d.   Windows Explorer

14. Object security information is stored in an Access Control List (ACL). Which permissions are stored in the ACL? (Select all that apply.)

    a.   NTFS permissions

    b.   Group permissions

    c.   FAT permissions

    d.   HPFS permissions

15. What type of trust relationship is automatically observed between computers running Windows 2000 in native mode who reside in the same tree?

    a.   Transitive trust

    b.   Nontransitive trust

    c.   Transitional trust

    d.   Transverse trust

16. Which of the following statements best describes how group policies affect permissions?

    a.   Permissions are not inherited from a parent group to a child group.

    b.   Permissions are inherited from a parent group to a child group as long as a parent group permission is not contradicted by the child group permission.

    c.   Permissions are inherited on a cumulative basis, from parent group to child group unless permission inheritance is disabled.

    d.   Groups cannot be nested, so there are no permission inheritance issues with groups.

17. You have 2 RIS servers which have been configured to install Windows 2000 Professional on 20 RIS-compatible clients. Each RIS server is copying a slightly different set of files and everything appears to be running smoothly. You check an RIS client and find out that the wrong files were copied to it. What is the most likely cause of this situation?

    a.   Only one RIS server is allowed per domain. Whichever RIS server was configured first will automatically perform all RIS client installations.

    b.   You made a mistake when assigning which server would configure that client.

    c.   Multiple RIS servers are allowed in a domain, but they must have the same configuration so they can automatically load balance.

    d.   There is a rouge RIS server on the network.

18. You have decided to become a Windows 2000 Networking consultant. Your first client has had a networking disaster, during which multiple operations masters have failed. Which operations master failure would you fix first?

    a.   Infrastructure master

    b.   Domain naming master

    c.   Relative ID master

    d.   Global catalog server

19. You've had to seize the role of a malfunctioning relative ID master. It turned out to be some bad RAM, which was replaced. What else must you do before putting that computer back on the network?

    a.   Format the hard drive and reinstall Windows 2000.

    b.   Just reinstall Windows 2000 without formatting.

    c.   Rename the computer and give it a new IP address.

    d.   Just put it back on the network and it will resume as the relative ID master after only changing the RAM.

20. Active Directory appears to be malfunctioning. What's the first step for troubleshooting Active Directory?

    a.   Reboot the global catalog server.

    b.   Check the Event Viewer for the Directory Service logs.

    c.   Check the global catalog server for the Directory Service logs.

    d.   Start changing permissions at random until you isolate the problem.

Case Study

Text Formatting Key:

- **Describes requirements**

- *Conflicts with requirement*

- Irrelevant background information

All the new designs for the 2003 model year have been approved from the design department, and these files need to be moved to a new domain in the prototyping division. To make the Active Directory more intuitive, **all designs are stored in folders under the control of the Designers Organizational Unit.** Permissions for most of the designs are set at the OU level, although **some files also have individual user permissions set. When you move the designs to the prototyping division, they will be stored in the Prototyping Organizational Unit.** All the prototype workers have permissions for the Prototyping Organizational Unit and *must be able to access all the designs immediately after the move* is made. You move the files and *check one* to make sure *the files inherited permissions of the destination OU.* All appears to be well with the move, so you turn off your cell phone and pager and go to lunch, confident in the fact that permissions were inherited.

Multiple Choice

1. Why can't the prototyping department open all of the newly moved files?

    a.   The prototyping department's domain controller hasn't been rebooted.

    b.   Any files transferred into an OU never inherit permissions.

    c. Individual file permissions override the destination OU's permissions.

    d. The source OU's permissions override the destination OU's permissions.

2. If you want to be certain permissions have been properly transferred, what is the minimum number of files you need to test permissions for after a move between OUs if those files are allowed to have both individual permissions and OU-based permissions?

    a. One

    b. One in each folder

    c. All of them

Answers

Comprehensive Test

1. d. You can either create a new tree or join an existing one with the Active Directory Installation Wizard. You can't create an OU with the AD Installation Wizard.

2. c. Active Directory requires a DNS server. There aren't any primary and backup domain controllers in a Windows 2000 network running in native mode, which is a prerequisite for Active Directory. All Windows 2000 domain controllers are peers.

3. c. You can look for your domain listed in My Network Places. Network Neighborhood has been replaced by My Network Places in Windows 2000. My Computer and the Control Panel won't provide easy verification of the domain's creation.

4. d. Microsoft Management Console is the name of the customizable configuration framework. The other choices don't really exist in Windows 2000.

5. b. Intrasite replication is within a site, intersite replication is between sites. Both types of replication take place in native mode only.

6. d. Sites are designed to facilitate information transfer between devices by available bandwidth, regardless of proximity to the other devices in the site.

7. b and d. You can use either TCP/IP or SMTP for site replication traffic. HTTP and IPX/SPX can't be used for site replication in Windows 2000.

8. c. Site link cost is a method of assigning values to multiple potential connections that could be used for replication traffic.

9. a. Both intersite and intrasite replication use a virtual ring topology for replication traffic regardless of the physical wiring of the network.

10. b. The first domain controller in a forest is automatically configured as the global catalog server.

11. b. A is an IP address, c is a web address, and d is just a random selection of characters.

12. a and d. Neither domain controllers nor system files can be moved between domains. User accounts and Organizational Units can be moved between domains.

13. b. MOVETREE is the name of the utility that can move objects between domains. A and d have multiple uses, but can't move objects between domains; c doesn't exist.

14. a and b. Neither FAT nor HPFS can store information in a Windows 2000 ACL.

15. a. Computers within an Active Directory tree have a transitive trust relationship.

16. c. Groups can be nested and permissions are inherited unless permission inheritance is disabled for the group.

17. b. Multiple RIS servers with different configurations are allowed in a domain. A rouge RIS server on a network is very rare compared to the chance that an Administrator could make an error configuring multiple RIS clients and RIS servers.

18. d. If a global catalog server is unavailable, users will not be able to log on to access network resources. None of the other operations masters are critical to network functionality on a short-term basis.

19. a. If you seize the role of a relative ID master, domain naming master or schema master, you have to format the hard drive before it can safely rejoin the network.

20. b. The Directory Service logs are viewable in the Event Viewer. They are the first place you should look when troubleshooting Active Directory.

Case Study: Multiple Choice

1. c. When you move objects to a new domain, the files inherit the destination OU's permissions, unless the files had individual permissions set, in which case they are retained, even after the move.

2. c. Take advantage of Windows 2000's extensive group- and OU-based permissions. The more granular level permissions are allowed to be set at, the more work it is to keep track of those permissions.

Highlighter's Index

Site Replication

- Intrasite replication: The replication of data within a single site
- Intersite replication: The replication of data between two or more sites

Organizational Unit Properties

Tab	Available Properties and Their Uses
General	Contains a general description and geographical location. Filling in these properties accurately is useful when doing a keyword search for Organizational Units.
Managed By	Contains the contact information for the department head of the OU. Keeping these properties up-to-date will make contacting a user easier if there is a security or maintenance problem with their account.
Group Policy	Contains information about the group policies assign to the OU. This information will make the future assignment of policies to similar Organizational Units easier.

Accounts

- Local user account: Grants access to resources that are on the local computer where the account was created
- Domain user account: Grants access to resources throughout the entire network, as long as trust relationships exist between domains

Moving Objects

- You can move more than one object at a time.

- Objects lose permissions that they inherited from their former OU and inherit permissions from their new OU.

- Permissions directly applied to the object itself remain unchanged.

Windows 2000 Permissions

Permission	Function
Read	View an object and its properties, such as its owner and permissions, without changing them
Write	Modify an object without changing its owner or permissions
Full Control	Includes Read and Write permissions and adds the ability to modify, delete, take ownership, and change permissions
Create All Child Objects	Add any object to an Organizational Unit
Delete All Child Objects	Remove any object from an Organizational Unit

Group Policy Objects

- Local GPO: Every Windows 2000 computer has one local GPO for storing its default settings, regardless of whether or not it is connected to a Windows 2000 network.

- Non-local GPO: These are applied to either users or computers and take precedence over a computer's local GPO. Non-local GPOs can control settings on a domain, OU, or site level. Permissions are cumulative.

Managing Applications

- Assigning a program: A program can be assigned to a particular computer or group of computers. This will allow users with access to the computer(s) to run the program.

- Publishing a program: A program can be published to a user or group of users. These users will have access to the program.

DNS Zones

- A zone can only include a contiguous portion of the namespace, such as oreilly.com and windows.oreilly.com.

- A zone is tied to a specific root domain, such as oreilly.com, or a subdomain, such as linux.oreilly.com.

Active Directory Replication

Single-master replication

    To prevent possible conflicts, one computer stores a master copy of the data and the replicating computers store a backup. This is a one-way process.

Multi-master replication

    Multiple computers store, send, and accept replication data at various times simultaneously around the network.

Operations Master Roles

Role	Scope	Description
Infrastructure master	Domain	Updates and changes if a user or group is renamed. There can be only one infrastructure master per domain. If a user moves across domains, the two infrastructure masters will replicate the change during the next multi-master replication between domains.
Primary domain controller (PDC) emulator	Domain	If the network is running in mixed mode, the PDC emulator acts like a Windows NT PDC and replicates with the NT backup domain controllers. If the network is running in native mode, the PDC emulator will be the first DC to get replication of password changes. If replication hasn't occurred on a recent password change, a DC can check with the PDC emulator to see if it received the password change. This is especially important if a network has a lot of domain controllers and frequent password changes. There can be only one PDC emulator per domain.
Relative ID master	Domain	The relative ID master has two main functions. It assigns a group of consecutive IDs to domain controllers so that they can assign unique IDs to objects created on the DC. To move any Active Directory object between domains, you have to move it from the computer that is currently acting as the relative ID master. You can change which computer is the relative ID master, but there can be only one relative ID master at a time in a domain.
Domain naming master	Forest	Keeps track of domains that are added or removed from the forest. There can be only one domain naming master in the forest.
Schema master	Forest	Changes to the Active Directory Schema can only be made from the schema master. There can be only one schema master in the forest.

Operations Master Failure

Operations Master Role	Consequence of Failure
Infrastructure master	Usually not an urgent problem, unless there have been a lot of user or group changes. Try to fix the problem before seizing the role.
Primary domain controller (PDC) emulator	Users may have trouble logging in, especially if the network is running in mixed mode. Unless you can make an immediate fix, seize the role and assign it to the standby unit.
Relative ID master	Usually not an urgent problem, unless enough objects are added to a domain to cause the current batch of relative IDs to be used up. Try to fix the problem before seizing the role.
Domain naming master	Usually not an urgent problem, until you need to add or remove a domain from the forest. Try to fix the problem before seizing the role.
Schema master	Almost never a problem, unless an administrator wants to modify the Active Directory Schema, either manually or through software.

Troubleshooting RIS

Problem	Solution
The wrong server is installing to an RIS client.	Either the data associating the RIS client and server hasn't been replicated yet (likely) or there is a rogue RIS server (unlikely).
A restored RIS volume no longer functions properly.	The RIS directory is missing or corrupt. Verify the source data and reinstall again.
Customized settings are not being implemented.	Check your configuration files for incorrect paths.

PART 4

Network Infrastructure

Exam Overview

Windows 2000 includes a wide variety of networking features, some of which are not available in previous versions of Windows NT. MCSE Exam 70-216, *Implementing and Administering a Microsoft Windows 2000 Network Infrastructure*, focuses on the protocols and services used in Windows 2000 networks.

Remember that Microsoft requires real-world networking experience for the Windows 2000 MCSE exams. This exam is a particularly important case in point. You should have experience with all of the protocols and services described in this chapter, preferably on a large network.

There is some overlap in Microsoft's objectives between the exams. We suggest that you review Part 6, *Designing Network Infrastructure*, in conjunction with this section.

To prepare for this chapter and the Network Infrastructure exam, you should be familiar with the basics of Windows 2000 Professional and Server, described in Parts 1 and 2 of this book. You should also be familiar with the basics of networking, including cables, hubs, and such standards as Ethernet and Token Ring.

Areas of Study

Network Basics

Need to Know	Reference
Protocols supported by Windows 2000	"Network Protocols" on page 221
Routable and non-routable protocols	"Network Protocols" on page 221
New Windows 2000 TCP/IP features	"TCP/IP" on page 221

215

TCP/IP

Need to Know	Reference
TCP/IP basics	"Managing TCP/IP" on page 223
DoD model layers and protocols	"TCP/IP Protocols and Services" on page 223
IP Address classes	"IP address classes" on page 226
Default subnet masks	"Subnet masking" on page 227

Need to Apply	Reference
Install TCP/IP on Windows 2000	"Installing TCP/IP" on page 230
Manage TCP/IP Configuration	"Managing TCP/IP settings" on page 230
Configure TCP/IP Packet Filtering	"Packet Filtering" on page 231

IP Routing

Need to Know	Reference
Static and dynamic routing	"IP Routing" on page 232
Information stored in routing tables	"Static Routing" on page 233
Dynamic routing protocols	"Dynamic Routing" on page 234

Need to Apply	Reference
Configure static routing	"Configuring Static Routing" on page 235
Configure dynamic routing	"Configuring Static Routing" on page 235
Install RIP and OSPF support	"Configuring Static Routing" on page 235

IPSec (IP Security)

Need to Know	Reference
IPSec components	"IP Security (IPSec)" on page 237
IPSec security settings	"Configuring IPSec" on page 237
IPSec authentication methods	"Authentication methods" on page 238

Need to Apply	Reference
Configure IPSec	"Configuring IPSec" on page 237
Configure security policies	"Security Policy Properties" on page 238

Host Name Resolution

Need to Know	Reference
Name resolution order	"Host Name Resolution" on page 217
HOSTS file format	"The HOSTS File" on page 240
Typical TLDs	"Domain Name Service (DNS)" on page 240

Need to Apply	Reference
Configure the HOSTS file	"The HOSTS File" on page 240
Install DNS Server	"Installing DNS Server" on page 241
Configure DNS Settings	"Configuring DNS" on page 242

NetBIOS Name Resolution

Need to Know	Reference
NetBIOS node types	"NetBIOS Name Resolution" on page 242
WINS process	"How WINS works" on page 244
WINS replication partner types	"WINS replication" on page 245
LMHOSTS file format	"The LMHOSTS File" on page 246

Need to Apply	Reference
Install WINS Server	"Installing WINS" on page 244
Configure WINS settings	"Configuring WINS" on page 245
Configure WINS replication	"WINS replication" on page 245
Create LMHOSTS files	"The LMHOSTS File" on page 246

NetWare Connectivity

Need to Know	Reference
NetWare-related components	"NetWare Connectivity" on page 217
Differences between CSNW and GSNW	"NetWare Connectivity" on page 217

Need to Apply	Reference
Install NWLink	"Installing NWLink" on page 248
Install CSNW	"Client Service for NetWare (CSNW)" on page 248
Install and configure GSNW	"Gateway Service for NetWare (GSNW)" on page 249

Network
Infrastructure

DHCP (Dynamic Host Configuration Protocol)

Need to Know	Reference
DHCP process	"How DHCP Works" on page 251
DHCP options and uses	"DHCP options" on page 253

Need to Apply	Reference
Install DHCP Server	"Installing DHCP Server" on page 252
Create a DHCP scope	"Creating a scope" on page 252
Create DHCP reservations	"DHCP reservations" on page 253
Configure DHCP clients	"Configuring DHCP clients" on page 254
Enable DHCP relay agent	"DHCP Forwarding" on page 254
Enable dynamic DNS updates	"Using DHCP with DNS" on page 255

Remote Access

Need to Know	Reference
RAS Authentication Methods	"Authentication" on page 256
RAS encryption options	"Remote Access Encryption" on page 257

Need to Apply	Reference
Install and configure Remote Access	"Configuring RAS" on page 255
Configure RAS to work with DHCP	"RAS and DHCP" on page 258

NAT (Network Address Translation)

Need to Know	Reference
NAT features	"NAT (Network Address Translation)" on page 258
Differences between NAT and ICS	"Internet Connection Sharing (ICS)" on page 260

Need to Apply	Reference
Install NAT	"Installing NAT" on page 258
Configure NAT settings	"Configuring NAT" on page 259
Configure special ports	"Using special ports" on page 259
Install and configure ICS	"Internet Connection Sharing (ICS)" on page 260

Certificate Services

Need to Know	Reference
Certificate Authority types	"Certificate Services" on page 260

Need to Apply	*Reference*
Install and configure a CA	"Installing a Certificate Authority" on page 261
Request and grant a certificate	"Requesting a certificate" on page 262
Revoke a certificate	"Revoking a certificate" on page 262

Monitoring Network Performance

Need to Know	*Reference*
Network Monitor components	"Using Network Monitor" on page 262
Logs available in Event Viewer	"Using Event Viewer" on page 264

Need to Apply	*Reference*
Capture and view packets with Network Monitor	"Using Network Monitor" on page 262
View Event Viewer logs	"Using Event Viewer" on page 264
Use IPSECMON to monitor IP Security	"Monitoring IPSec" on page 264

Study Guide

This chapter includes the following sections, which address various topics covered on the *Implementing and Administering a Microsoft Windows 2000 Network Infrastructure* MCSE exam:

Network Protocols
> Introduces the network protocols supported by Windows 2000, including TCP/IP, IPX/SPX, NetBEUI, and AppleTalk.

Managing TCP/IP
> Describes the TCP/IP protocol suite, its component protocols, and the organization of the TCP/IP reference model. Also describes the IP addressing scheme.

IP Routing
> Describes Windows 2000's routing features for the TCP/IP protocols and the process of configuring and managing IP routing.

IP Security (IPSec)
> Introduces Windows 2000's new secure IP features and presents procedures for installing and configuring IPSec features.

Hostname Resolution
> Describes the various methods of TCP/IP hostname resolution, including the HOSTS file and DNS (Domain Name Service).

NetBIOS Name Resolution
> Describes methods of NetBIOS name resolution, including traditional NetBIOS resolution and WINS (Windows Internet Name Service).

NetWare Connectivity
> Introduces Windows 2000's features for compatibility with NetWare networks, including NWLink (IPX/SPX protocols), CSNW (Client Service for NetWare), and GSNW (Gateway Service for NetWare).

DHCP (Dynamic Host Configuration Protocol)
> Describes the DHCP protocol, which dynamically assigns IP addresses, and how to configure and use this protocol in Windows 2000.

Remote Access Server (RAS)
> Introduces Windows 2000's implementation of RAS and how to configure and manage this service for dial-up access to networks.

NAT (Network Address Translation)
> Describes NAT, a Windows 2000 service that translates between private and public IP addresses to allow Internet access without the use of multiple public addresses.

Certificate Services
> Describes Windows 2000's certificate features. Digital certificates are used to authenticate encryption keys. Windows 2000 Server can act as a certificate authority (CA).

Monitoring Network Performance
> Describes several tools for monitoring the performance of the network and monitoring specific communications, such as IPSec.

Network Protocols

Network protocols specify the methods for communicating between computers and other devices on a network. Windows 2000 supports the same basic network protocols as previous versions of Windows NT, although protocols such as TCP/IP have been improved with new features.

TCP/IP

The TCP/IP protocol suite is the foundation of the Internet and the primary set of transport protocols used on Unix systems and on Windows NT and Windows 2000 networks. TCP/IP is named for two of its most important protocols, TCP (Transmission Control Protocol) and IP (Internet Protocol). TCP/IP is designed for large networks, and its transport protocols are routable.

Windows 2000 builds on the TCP/IP support of previous versions of Windows NT with a number of new and enhanced features. These include the following:

PPTP (Point-to-Point Tunneling Protocol)
> Allows the creation of VPNs (virtual private networks) that use the Internet or another large network as a virtual transport for a smaller network. This allows low-cost networking between machines in distant locations.

IPSec (IP Security)
> Uses keyed encryption to secure communication between TCP/IP nodes. This is particularly useful with VPNs.

L2TP (Layer 2 Tunneling Protocol)
> Combines L2F (Layer 2 Forwarding) with PPTP to create a more efficient virtual private network.

In addition, Windows 2000 includes an improved TCP/IP stack (the drivers that support the various TCP/IP protocols). This adds support for large transmission windows, selective acknowledgments, and better optimized traffic.

ON THE EXAM

TCP/IP is by far the most important protocol for Windows 2000 and for the *Implementing and Administering a Microsoft Windows 2000 Network Infrastructure* MCSE exam. Most of the remaining sections of this chapter will focus on various aspects of TCP/IP.

IPX and SPX

IPX (Internetwork Packet Exchange) and SPX (Sequenced Packet Exchange) are protocols developed by Novell for use with their NetWare network operating system. IPX and SPX are the primary protocols used in NetWare versions up to 4.1. NetWare 5.0, like Windows 2000, uses TCP/IP as its primary transport.

Like TCP/IP, the IPX/SPX transport protocols are routable and are suitable for large- and wide-area networks. Their chief disadvantages compared to TCP/IP are the less widely used protocols and the relative difficulty of managing addressing on a large network.

NetBEUI

NetBEUI (NetBIOS Extended User Interface) is a basic transport protocol developed by Microsoft and used as the primary network transport protocol in Windows NT 3.0 and earlier. Even Windows NT 4.0 required NetBEUI for some network configurations.

Windows 2000 does not rely on NetBEUI at all, but supports it for interoperability with earlier operating systems. NetBEUI is not routable and is not suitable for larger networks.

AppleTalk

AppleTalk was developed by Apple as a networking protocol for Macintosh computers. Although it is used almost exclusively by Apple computers, AppleTalk is a versatile, routable protocol that can be used on many types of networks. Windows 2000 supports AppleTalk for Macintosh connectivity.

IN THE REAL WORLD

Microsoft's next version of Windows 2000, code-named Whistler, is not expected to have AppleTalk support. Because modern Macintosh computers support TCP/IP, this should not be a serious deficiency.

DLC (Data Link Control)

DLC (Data Link Control) is a non-routable protocol used for communication with IBM mainframes using the SNA architecture. It is also supported by some printers with network interfaces, such as Hewlett Packard's JetDirect interface. Unlike the other protocols listed here, DLC cannot be used to support file sharing between computers or other generic communication between hosts.

IrDA (Infrared Data Association)

IrDA is a standard protocol for infrared communication and is typically supported by laptop computers and by desktop computers with an attached IR interface. Windows 2000 supports IrDA as a networking protocol.

Managing TCP/IP

TCP/IP is the default network protocol for Unix systems and is becoming popular as a protocol for Windows NT networks, even those unconnected to the Internet or Unix servers.

Most of the TCP/IP protocols were created by the Internet Activities Board (IAB), which consists of two task forces: the IETF (Internet Engineering Task Force) and the IRTF (Internet Research Task Force.) Most Internet protocols begin their lives as RFCs, or Request for Comments. These documents are created to propose new protocols or standards.

RFCs that have become standards are still referred to with an RFC number. RFC numbers are mentioned here for many of the protocols described in this chapter. The full text of RFCs is available from this URL:

http://www.internic.net/ds/rfc-index.html

TCP/IP Protocols and Services

The TCP/IP protocol suite includes a wide variety of protocols and services that are in common use on the Internet as well as on Windows NT and Windows 2000 networks. These include its namesake protocols, TCP (Transmission Control Protocol) and IP (Internet Protocol).

The various protocols that comprise the TCP/IP suite are organized according to the DoD (US Department of Defense) reference model, also known as the TCP/IP reference model. This model organizes protocols and services into four layers: Network Access, Internet, Host-to-Host, and Process/Application. The sections below describe each layer and give descriptions of the major protocols that act at each layer.

The Network Access layer

The Network Access layer is responsible for the physical transmission of data. This layer includes protocols that deal with the specific networking topologies and media used in the network. Table 4-1 describes some common network layer protocols.

Table 4-1: Common Network Layer Protocols

Protocol	Network Type
Ethernet	LANs using coaxial, twisted-pair, or fiber-optic cable
Token Ring	LANs using coaxial or fiber-optic cable
FDDI	LANS using high speed fiber-optic cable
SLIP (Serial Line Internet Protocol)	Dial-up Internet connections (older Unix systems)
PPP (Point-to-Point Protocol)	Dial-up Internet connections (Unix and Windows NT/2000)
X.25	Dedicated WAN connections
Frame Relay	Dedicated WAN connections

The Internet layer

The Internet layer deals with communication and routing between networks and also provides a common interface for upper-layer protocols. IP, described in RFC 791, is the most important protocol in the Internet layer. IP collects segments of data from the higher-layer protocols (TCP or UDP) and combines them into packets, or *datagrams*.

IP datagrams include IP addresses to identify the originating host and the destination host. IP addresses, described later in this section, provide a logical (software) addressing scheme that simplifies network routing.

IP and the other protocols of the Internet layer are summarized in Table 4-2.

Table 4-2: Common Internet Layer Protocols

Protocol	Description
IP (Internet Protocol)	Handles IP addressing; creates packets and facilitates communications between hosts by routing packets between networks
ARP (Address Resolution Protocol)	Translates IP addresses to hardware (MAC) addresses
RARP (Reverse Address Resolution Protocol)	Translates hardware (MAC) addresses to IP addresses
DHCP (Dynamic Host Configuration Protocol)	An extended version of BootP, used to dynamically assign IP addresses and other TCP/IP configuration
ICMP (Internet Control Message Protocol)	Provides management features for IP and serves as a messaging agent

The Host-to-Host layer

The Host-to-Host layer provides a layer of abstraction in communication between hosts and provides applications with a consistent interface independent of hardware and routing. The two host-to-host layer protocols, TCP and UDP, are explained in the following sections.

TCP (Transmission Control Protocol)

TCP is defined in RFC 793. TCP is a connection-oriented protocol: before any data is sent, a connection, or *virtual circuit*, is established between the originating host and the destination. This circuit provides a continuous connection and manages flow control.

TCP accepts blocks of data from an application at the process/application layer and breaks the data down into segments, which are sequenced for later reassembly. These packets are then processed by IP and sent over the network. The TCP protocol at the receiving end reassembles the segments into their original form for use by the application.

TCP is reliable and is considered a *full-duplex* protocol: after each segment is sent, the receiving end's TCP protocol returns a handshake, or acknowledgment. If the acknowledgment is negative, the segment is resent. The price for reliability is high bandwidth and a significant processing overhead.

UDP (User Datagram Protocol)

UDP is defined by RFC 768. UDP is a connectionless protocol: no virtual circuit is established between the source and destination. The destination does not know that UDP data is coming until the first segment arrives.

As with TCP, UDP accepts large blocks of data from the process/application layer and breaks them into segments. Segments are sequenced for later reassembly, but are not necessarily sent in the proper sequence or even all over the same route.

UDP provides no handshaking and is considered an unreliable protocol. However, it has a very low overhead in network bandwidth and processing, and it is ideal for situations where speed is crucial and small errors are tolerable (such as streaming audio).

The Process/Application layer

The Process/Application layer includes protocols and services that do actual work for a user. Because the complexities of the network are handled by the other layers, these protocols are generally platform-independent. Most of these protocols require server software on one machine and client software on another. Table 4-3 lists common process/application layer protocols.

Table 4-3: Common Process/Application Layer Protocols

Protocol	Description
Telnet	Emulates a terminal and allows you to access a Unix or other host
FTP (File Transfer Protocol)	Allows for two-way file transfer
TFTP (Trivial File Transfer Protocol)	A more basic file transfer protocol
HTTP (Hypertext Transfer Protocol)	A simple protocol used by the World Wide Web

Table 4-3: Common Process/Application Layer Protocols (continued)

Protocol	Description
NFS (Network Filesystem)	Allows filesystems on remote machines to be accessed as local drives
DNS (Domain Name System)	Resolves hostnames into IP addresses
SMTP (Simple Mail Transport Protocol)	Delivers email messages between servers and clients
POP (Post Office Protocol)	Allows client access to email messages
IMAP (Internet Mail Access Protocol)	Allows client access to email messages
NNTP (Netnews Transfer Protocol)	Transmits messages for USENET news discussion groups
SNMP (Simple Network Management Protocol)	Allows for statistical analysis and trouble-shooting on the network

IP Addressing

TCP/IP packets identify their destination with an *IP address*. The IP addressing scheme in use today was originally defined by the IETF in RFC 791.

An IP address is a 32-bit number that uniquely identifies a machine in the network. The address is divided into four bytes, or octets. IP addresses are usually represented in dotted decimal format, such as 128.110.121.6. However, addresses often make more sense in binary format.

An IP address is actually composed of two addresses: a *network address* and a *host address*. The location of the boundary between these addresses depends on the network class, explained below. All machines on a particular network have the same network address, but must have unique host addresses.

IP address classes

The original IETF standard defined five IP address classes, lettered A through E. Only Classes A, B, and C are in wide use. The main difference between the three supported classes is the number of bytes used for the network and host addresses, as described in Table 4-4.

Table 4-4: Classes of IP Addresses

Class	Network/Host Bytes	Number of Networks	Number of Hosts per Network
A	1/3	126	16,777,214
B	2/2	16,382	65,534
C	3/1	2,097,150	254

The three classes were designed to accommodate a wide range of networks, ranging from a small number of networks with large numbers of hosts (Class A) to a large number of networks with small numbers of hosts (Class C).

Network addresses are usually referred to with full four-byte IP addresses. For
example, in the Class C network address 209.68.11.152, the entire network is
referred to as 209.68.11.0, and the host is referred to as 209.68.11.152.

The actual number of hosts and networks for each class is limited by the fact that
each class is assigned a specific leading bit pattern and, thus, a range of decimal
addresses for the first byte. Table 4-5 lists the ranges and corresponding leading bit
patterns for each class.

Table 4-5: IP Address Class Ranges

Class	Leading Bits	First Byte Range
A	0	1–126
B	10	128–191
C	110	192–223

Subnet masking

You can add flexibility to the host/network addressing scheme by using subnet
masking. This technique steals a number of bits from the host address and uses
these bits to divide the network into smaller networks, or *subnets*. These subnets
can communicate via a router.

The subnet mask itself is, like the IP address, a 32-bit number. This number is
applied to the binary IP address with a logical AND operation to determine the
network address. In simpler terms, bits set to 1 in the subnet mask indicate the
network address, and bits set to 0 indicate the host address.

When you have not divided the network into subnets, the default subnet mask for
the class is used. The default subnet masks are shown in Table 4-6.

Table 4-6: Default Subnet Masks

Class	Default Subnet Mask
A	255.0.0.0
B	255.255.0.0
C	255.255.255.0

To divide the network into subnets, you can dedicate two or more bits to the
subnet address by adding corresponding bits set to 1 to the subnet mask. The
number of subnets available is 2^n-2, where n is the number of bits used for the

subnet address. It is necessary to subtract 2 because the binary subnet address cannot be all 1s or all 0s.

Depending on the number of subnets you have allocated, a different number of host addresses is available; the maximum number of hosts decreases as you increase the number of subnets. The maximum number of hosts is $2\wedge(x-n)-2$, where x is the total number of available bits for subnet and host addresses: 24 for Class A, 16 for Class B, or 8 for Class C.

You cannot use more than 6 bits for the subnet address in a Class C network, because you would be left with no available host addresses.

Reserved IP addresses

As mentioned above, certain addresses and ranges are not available for use. These values are reserved for various purposes, as described in Table 4-7.

Table 4-7: Reserved TCP/IP Addresses

Reserved Address	Description
0.0.0.0	Reserved for use by the RIP protocol.
127.0.0.1	Loopback—packets are sent back to the local machine without using the network.
255.255.255.255	Broadcasts to all nodes on the network.
Network address all 0s	Refers to "this network only."
Network address all 1s	Broadcast (all networks).
All 0s in node address	Refers to "this node."
All 1s in node address	Broadcast (all nodes).
First bytes 224–239	Multicasting addresses (Class D).
First bytes 240–254	Reserved for future use (Class E).

IP address assignments

If your network is not connected to the Internet, you can assign IP addresses in any way you see fit; in fact, you can even break the class addressing rules given above, although doing so can cause problems with routing. Nevertheless, to avoid problems in the future, it is best to use one of the available blocks of private IP addresses shown in Table 4-8.

Table 4-8: Private IP Addresses

Address Class	Starting Address	Ending Address
A	10.0.0.0	10.255.255.255
B	169.254.0.1	169.254.255.254
C	172.16.0.0	172.31.255.255
C	192.168.0.0	192.168.255.255

If your network is connected to the Internet, you must obtain a registered IP network address from Internet Assigned Numbers Authority (IANA), the agency that assigns IP addresses. Further information about registration is available at this URL:

http://www.internic.net

With the exploding popularity of the Internet, it is now virtually impossible to obtain a Class A or Class B address, and Class C addresses are becoming scarce. Because of this, InterNIC is now rather strict about issuing addresses.

For small company networks with Internet connectivity, one alternative is to connect to the Internet through an ISP (Internet Service Provider). The ISP may allocate you a small block of IP addresses, or it may assign them dynamically as machines on your network connect to the Internet.

Supernetting

Occasionally you may require the opposite of subnetting. For example, you may have three Class C networks and wish to address them as one large network. This can be accomplished using a process called supernetting.

To use supernetting, you steal bits from the last network address octet and use them as part of the host address. For example, the default Class C subnet mask is 255.255.255.0. To support three Class C addresses, you will need two extra bits, so the subnet mask to use is 255.255.252.0.

To calculate a mask for supernetting, AND the values of the last network address octets. For example, suppose your three Class C addresses are 132.124.4.0, 132.24.5.0, and 132.24.6.0. The last network address octets are 4, 5, and 6, or in binary 100, 101, and 110.

An AND operation with these three values results in 100. Use these three bits as the last bits of the subnet mask network address octet, with the remaining bits set to 1. In this example, the octet would be 11111100. In decimal this is 252, so the subnet mask is 255.255.252.0.

Supernetting only works if the addresses are consecutive and fall in the correct range; be sure the addresses are assigned specifically for this purpose. If the AND technique described earlier results in all 1s, supernetting cannot be used. Also, this technique only works if the routers support supernetting.

Many of the routers used in today's Internet backbones use CIDR (Classless Interdomain Routing), a system that uses a supernetting technique to treat groups of IP addresses assigned to the same organization as the same network.

Network
Infrastructure

ON THE EXAM

Supernetting is not stressed on the *Implementing and Administering a Microsoft Windows 2000 Network Infrastructure* exam, but you should understand how to calculate a supernet mask and understand that a group of consecutive IP addresses is required.

Configuring TCP/IP

TCP/IP configuration in Windows 2000 is similar to that of Windows NT, with certain improvements and differences. The following sections explain the installation and configuration of TCP/IP under Windows 2000.

Installing TCP/IP

TCP/IP is Windows 2000's default protocol suite and is normally installed during the installation of Windows 2000 Professional or Server. You will only need to install it manually if the installation options were changed, if it was removed, or if its required files have been corrupted.

ON THE EXAM

You should be familiar with the network protocol selections during the installation of Windows 2000 Professional or Server. These are explained in the Installation sections of Part 2 and Part 3 of this book.

To install TCP/IP, right-click the *My Network Places* icon and select *Properties*. This opens the Network and Dial-up Connections window, which contains icons for any configured connections. Right-click on the icon for your network (typically Local Area Connection) and select *Properties*.

The Properties dialog lists installed protocols, clients, and services. If there is no entry for Internet Protocol (TCP/IP), click *Install*. Select *Protocol* and click *Add*. Select *TCP/IP* from the list and click *OK*.

Managing TCP/IP settings

To manage settings for TCP/IP, highlight *Internet Protocol (TCP/IP)* in the Properties window for your network connection. Select *Properties* to display the settings dialog. The dialog is divided into several pages. The General page (shown in Figure 4-1) is displayed initially, and the remaining pages are available by clicking the *Advanced* button. The following categories of settings are available:

General
> Lets you choose whether to assign an IP address automatically (using DHCP, if available, or Automatic Private IP Addressing) or manually. You can also assign a default gateway (router) and choose whether to assign the DNS server address manually or automatically.

IP settings
> Allows you to configure IP addresses and Default Gateway settings. Unlike the General page, this page allows multiple addresses to be entered.

DNS
> Includes an option to specify multiple DNS server addresses and also includes DNS options. These are explained later in this chapter.

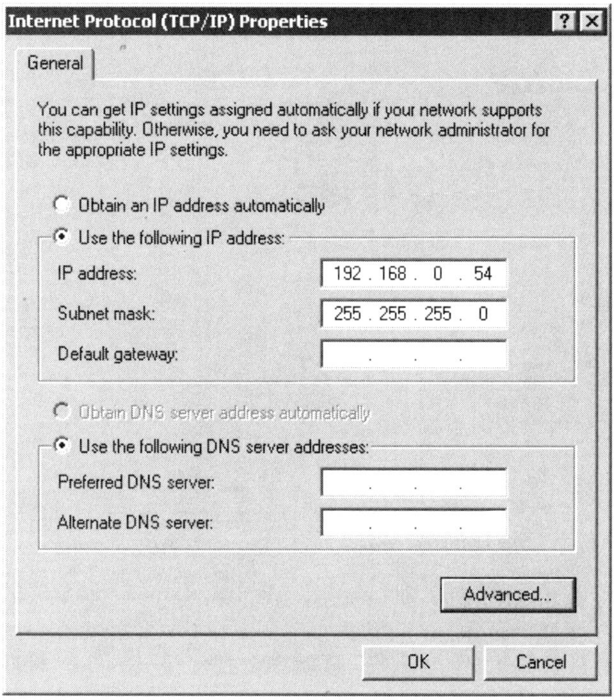

Figure 4-1: The General page of the TCP/IP Properties dialog

WINS
> Allows you to specify the addresses of one or more WINS servers and specify WINS options. WINS is explained later in this chapter.

Options
> Allows access to additional properties dialogs for advanced TCP/IP features. These include IP filtering and IPSec, described in the next sections.

ON THE EXAM

If you choose to assign the IP address automatically and a DHCP server is not available, Automatic Private IP Addressing (APIPA) is used. This automatically assigns a random IP address in the private range 169.254.0.1 to 169.254.255.254.

Packet Filtering

Packet filtering is a new Windows 2000 feature that allows you to block access to unauthorized TCP/IP ports or protocols on a server. To access packet filtering options, select *TCP/IP Filtering* from the TCP/IP Options dialog, then click *Properties*. The TCP/IP Filtering dialog is displayed, as shown in Figure 4-2.

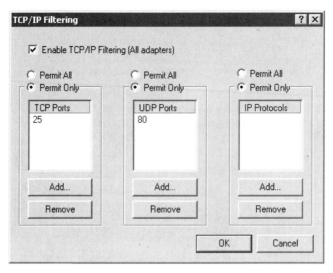

Figure 4-2: The TCP/IP Filtering dialog contains IP filtering options

IP filtering is enabled by default. To disable filtering, uncheck the *Enable TCP/IP Filtering* option at the top of the dialog. This option affects all network adapters. When filtering is enabled, you can control access to the computer with three settings:

TCP Ports

Select *Permit All* to allow access to all TCP ports or *Permit Only* to specify a list of accessible ports.

UDP Ports

Select *Permit All* to allow access to all UDP ports or *Permit Only* to specify a list of accessible ports.

IP Protocols

Select *Permit All* to allow access with any IP protocol or *Permit Only* to specify one or more protocols that can be used.

ON THE EXAM

If you wish to use IP filtering on one adapter but not on others, enable IP filtering and select the *Permit All* option for all three settings for the adapters that will not use filtering. This is the default state.

IP Routing

An IP router, or *gateway*, is a device that has more than one network adapter and thus is connected to multiple subnets. Routers can pass packets between the subnets, allowing them to act as a contiguous network. Routers can be either dedicated hardware devices or software services on hosts.

Any Windows NT or Windows 2000 computer can act as an IP router if it has multiple network interfaces attached to two or more subnets. This type of node is referred to as a *multihomed* computer.

There are two basic types of IP routing: *static routing* uses a fixed routing table specifying available destinations, and *dynamic routing* maintains a routing table dynamically by communicating with other routers. These are examined in the sections that follow.

Static Routing

In static routing, a *routing table* stores information about available destinations and the gateway (router) they can be reached through. Routing tables are not exchanged between routers in any way, so the routes must be specified for each multihomed computer.

The `route` command, described later in this section, allows you to modify or display the routing table. Type `route print` to display the current routing table. The following is an example of a simple routing table:

```
Network      Netmask        Gateway        Interface       Metric
Address                     Address
127.0.0.0    255.0.0.0      127.0.0.1      127.0.0.1       1
168.192.0.0  255.255.0.0    168.192.150.1  168.192.150.1   1
224.0.0.0    224.0.0.0      168.192.150.1  168.192.150.1   1
```

The route table includes the following fields:

Network address
> The network address of the destination network.

Netmask
> The subnet mask corresponding to the network address.

Gateway address
> The IP address of the gateway (router) that connects to the specified subnet.

Interface
> The IP address of the interface card in the local computer that connects to the gateway.

Metric
> The number of hops (cost) for the route. This number is used to optimize routes.

Default Gateways

Each Windows NT or 2000 client has a Default Gateway address defined in the IP Address tab of the TCP/IP Properties dialog. The *Advanced* button in that dialog allows a number of gateways to be listed in order of priority. The Default Gateway list can also be received by a DHCP client.

The Default Gateway is listed in the route table with a network address of 0.0.0.0. The defined gateways are used in order when no explicit route is found in the route table for a destination network.

In a network with only two subnets, you can create a functional static route setup with only the Default Gateway parameter. Configure a multihomed computer on each subnet as a router and enter each machine in the other's Default Gateway field. In this scheme all destinations not recognized as part of the local subnet are automatically sent to the other subnet.

Dynamic Routing

Dynamic routing uses a *routing protocol* (rather than a manually configured routing table) to exchange information between routers. Two routing protocols are widely supported on today's networks and the Internet: RIP and OSPF. These are described in the following sections.

RIP (Router Information Protocol)

RIP was formally documented in RFC 1058 and then expanded in RFCs 1387–1389. RIP is the most popular routing protocol in use today. RIP is a *distance vector routing protocol*, meaning that the primary information routers exchange is a measure of the distance (in hops) between destinations, and these distances are used to calculate optimal routes.

RIP keeps an internal routing table similar to the table used for static routing, but the table is maintained strictly by receiving updates from adjacent routers. The following information is maintained for each entry in the RIP database:

Address
> The IP address of the host or network the route points to.

Gateway
> The first router (gateway) to which packets should be sent in order to reach the destination.

Interface
> The IP address of the network adapter in the local machine that is connected to the gateway's subnet.

Metric
> A measure of the number of hops required to reach the destination, or *cost*. Metric values range from 1 to 15.

Timer
> A measure of the amount of time since the record was updated.

Along with Version 1 of RIP, supported by Windows NT, Windows 2000 supports RIP Version 2. RIP v2 improves on v1 by sending updates only when routes change and, also, supports a basic form of router authentication.

OSPF (Open Shortest Path First)

OSPF is documented in RFC 1131 (Version 1) and RFC 1247 (Version 2). OSPF is a *link state routing protocol*, meaning that routing is based not only on distance, but also on the current status of links in the network.

OSPF is an autonomous system, meaning that all routers use the same algorithm and a copy of the same database. Each OSPF router keeps a database that keeps track of the entire routing system and receives updates from other routers. OSPF is considered superior to RIP for most purposes, but has not yet been implemented as widely.

Configuring Static Routing

You can configure a Windows 2000 computer acting as a static router by using the `route` command. This command can display routing information, add entries, or modify or delete entries in the static routing table. The options of the `route` command are described in Table 4-9.

Table 4-9: Route command options

Option	Description
add	Adds a route to the routing table. User specifies the destination IP address and the gateway address for routing.
change	Changes an existing entry in the route table.
delete	Deletes a route table entry. User specifies the IP address.
print	Displays the route table including the network address, subnet mask, gateway address, interface IP address, and metric (number of hops).
--f	Flushes the routing table (deletes all routes).
-p	When used with –a, makes the added route permanent (not lost at reboot).

Configuring Dynamic Routing

Dynamic routing, like many other Windows 2000 features, is managed through Microsoft Management Console (MMC). To configure routing, select Programs → Administrative Tools → Routing and Remote Access from the Start menu. The Routing and Remote Access MMC snap-in is displayed, as shown in Figure 4-3.

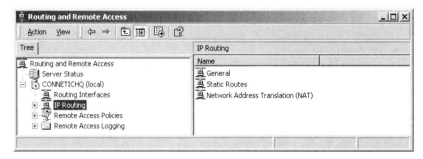

Figure 4-3: The Routing and Remote Access console

From this dialog, you can manage one or more servers designated as routers. Select *Add Server* from the Action menu to add a server to the list; the local computer is normally on the list by default in Windows 2000 Server.

To initially configure routing, select *Configure and Enable Routing and Remote Access* from the Action menu. This prompts you with a series of dialogs to configure routing:

1. A welcome screen is displayed. Click *Next.*

2. A variety of options, such as *Remote Access Server* and *Internet Connection Server,* are displayed. Select *Network Router* and click *Next.*

3. A list of current protocols is displayed, and you can optionally add protocols. If TCP/IP is already on the list, simply click *Next.*

4. Choose whether to allow demand-dial connections, which use dial-up networking to route to a remote network. This option is disabled by default. Click *Next.*

5. A final screen is displayed. Click *Finished* to complete the installation process. This starts the routing services and returns you to the Routing and Remote Access console.

ON THE EXAM

When using Windows 2000 computers as software routers, be sure to use the same routing protocol (RIP or OSPF) on all of the machines so that they will be able to exchange routing tables.

After routing is installed, you can access the following options under each server in the console:

Routing Interfaces
Displays a list of network adapters that can be used for routing. You can add a new entry for a demand-dial route or an IP tunneling (PPTP) route.

IP Routing: General
Displays statistics for each enabled router interface, including bytes sent and received and operational status. Right-click on an interface to access additional information dialogs, such as Show IP Routing Table, which displays the current static or dynamic route table.

IP Routing: Static Routes
Provides an interface to the static routing table as an alternative to the route command, described earlier in this section. Right-click to add a new static route or right-click on a highlighted route to remove or modify it.

IP Security (IPSec)

IPSec, new to Windows 2000, allows encryption for TCP/IP traffic. IPSec was developed by the IETF and is an open standard for a variety of encryption tech-nologies. IPSec can be configured to provide security between any two Windows 2000 Server computers. IPSec is supported in Windows 2000 by the following components:

IPSec Policy Agent

This is a service that runs under Windows 2000 and manages IPSec policies. The policies are stored in the Active Directory or in the local computer's registry.

ISAKMP/Oakley Key Management Service

This combines two protocols: ISAKMP, a key management protocol, and the Oakley protocol, which generates keys for data encryption. The IPSec Policy Agent automatically starts and manages this service.

IP Security Driver

This driver (IPSEC.SYS) acts as a filter for all IP communication, determining whether security is required for each packet. Secured packets are encrypted using the key provided by the Key Management Service.

Configuring IPSec

You can configure IPSec by setting security policies, which can be set either for the Active Directory or for individual computers. To manage a computer's security policies, select Administrative Tools → Local Security Policy from the Start menu.

From the Local Security Settings snap-in, double-click the entry for *IP Security Poli-cies* on local machine. The following default policies are available from this window:

Client (Respond Only)

Allows the computer to act as a client when a server requests or requires a secure connection.

Secure Server (Require Security)

When the computer is accessed as a server, clients are required to use a secure connection.

Server (Request Security)

When the computer is accessed as a server, clients are requested to use a secure connection. If the client does not support this, a standard non-secure connection is used.

Right-click one of these options and select *Assign* to assign the policy to the local computer. You can also right-click in the window and select *Create IP Security Policy* to create a new policy.

Security Policy Properties

To modify a default or new security policy, right-click its entry and select *Properties*. Each policy consists of basic settings and one or more rules for securing data. To add a rule, click *Add*. If the *Use Add Wizard* box is checked, a wizard prompts you for settings; otherwise, the Rule Properties dialog is displayed. The Rule Properties dialog is divided into a number of pages, described in the following sections.

Authentication methods

This page allows you to select the methods used to authenticate between the client and the server before initiating secure communications. The following authentication methods are available:

Windows 2000 default (Kerberos)
> The default setting, this uses the Kerberos v5 protocol to authenticate the connection.

Use a certificate from this certificate authority
> If Certificate Server is in use and a valid certificate authority (CA) is configured, this option can be selected to use certificate-based encryption.

Use this string to protect the key exchange
> If selected, a particular string can be used to specify a pre-shared key used for authentication. This key must be entered on both computers that will support the secure connection. (The key is used only during authentication, not for the actual data encryption.)

ON THE EXAM

When you configure IPSec between two computers, be sure that they are both configured with at least one authentication method in common; otherwise, they will be unable to communicate.

Tunnel setting

If the rule is used for IP tunneling, specify the endpoint IP address of the tunnel. This option is disabled by default. To use tunneling, you must configure each endpoint of the tunnel with the IP address of the other endpoint.

Connection type

Choose which types of connections to include in the encryption rule: all network connections, the local area network, or remote access (RAS) connections. Each rule can apply to only one of these connection choices.

IP filter list

This property page displays a list of filter rules that can be applied to IP data. These rules are used to determine whether each packet will be encrypted and sent, sent in its unencrypted state, or blocked. Each entry in this list represents a list of filters; only one entry can be selected.

Click *Add* to add a filter list or *Edit* to modify an existing list. Each list can include one or more filters. Click *Add* to add a filter. Each filter includes the following properties, which you can add either using a wizard or through the Properties dialog:

Addressing
Specify the source and destination IP addresses that will be matched by the filter. Each can be set to the local IP address, any address, or a specific address, range of addresses, or DNS name. Choose the *Mirrored* option to also match packets from the destination to the source address.

Protocol
Select *Any* to match all TCP/IP protocols, or you can choose a specific protocol. For TCP and UDP, you can also specify source and destination port addresses to match.

Description
Enter a description of the filter rule, if desired. This will be displayed in the Description column of the Filter List dialog.

Filter action

The Filter Action property page allows you to choose the action that will be performed for packets matching the specified filter rule list. Default actions allow you to permit the packet communication, request security, or require security.

To add an action to the list, click *Add*. As with other Add options, you can choose whether to use a wizard or the standard property dialog. This dialog includes the following property pages:

Security methods
Choose whether to Permit, Block, or Negotiate security for the filtered packets. If Negotiate is selected, you can specify a list of one or more security methods that can be used, in order of preference.

General
Specify a name and description for the filter action.

Hostname Resolution

TCP/IP supports hostnames, or alphanumeric aliases corresponding to particular IP addresses. These provide a user-friendly alternative to IP addresses and can be used in most places an IP address would be accepted.

When you attempt to access a remote machine via its hostname, a process called *hostname resolution* occurs. Windows NT clients use the following methods, in order, to attempt to resolve a hostname:

1. Comparison with the local hostname

2. The HOSTS file

3. Any configured DNS servers

4. NetBIOS name resolution

Steps 1–3 deal with TCP/IP hostname resolution. If these methods fail, the client attempts to use NetBIOS resolution, described in the next section. The following sections discuss the methods of TCP/IP hostname resolution.

The HOSTS File

The simplest method of hostname resolution uses the HOSTS file. This is a lookup table formatted as an ASCII text file and stored in \systemroot\drivers\etc\HOSTS. This file follows the format of the HOSTS file in BSD Unix 4.3.

The HOSTS file lists IP addresses, each followed by one or more hostnames to act as aliases for that address, separated by spaces or tabs. The # symbol begins a comment. The following is a simple example of a HOSTS file:

```
# HOSTS file
# (This is a comment)
127.0.0.1       localhost     # Loopback to local host
192.168.0.1     thismachine   # Alias to my actual address
209.68.11.152   starling      # A frequently used host
```

Entries in the HOSTS file are resolved very quickly and do not require connection to a name server, so this file is convenient to use for hosts that you will frequently access via FTP, Telnet, or other utilities.

IN THE REAL WORLD

The HOSTS file is convenient, but it's no substitute for a true name database such as DNS. Maintaining a large HOSTS file is difficult, and it must be manually updated when addresses change. An extraneous HOSTS entry is something to check for when a host is not resolving properly, because it overrides DNS.

Domain Name Service (DNS)

DNS is a standard for hostname resolution that was first developed for Unix; it is defined by RFCs 1034 and 1035. DNS is the standard for name resolution on the Internet and is also used locally in many networks. Windows NT machines can act as DNS clients or servers.

A DNS client sends a hostname to the server and receives an IP address in response. Hostnames can range from simple machine names on a local network to subdivided names, such as www.figby.com, used on the Internet. Internet hostnames use a hostname, a domain name, and a top-level domain name (TLD). The most common TLDs are listed in Table 4-10. An entire hostname with its TLD is referred to as an FQDN, or *fully qualified domain name.*

Table 4-10: Top-Level Domain Names

Domain	Purpose
COM	Commercial organizations
EDU	Educational institutions
ORG	Organizations (usually non-profit)
NET	Internet service providers
GOV	U.S. government organizations
MIL	U.S. military organizations
INT	International organizations
US, CH, and other country codes	Geographic domains

As with IP addresses, the InterNIC formerly assigned domain names under the COM, NET, and ORG TLDs. This task has now been turned over to an ever-expanding group of competing registrars, managed by the Internet Corporation for Assigned Names and Numbers (ICANN).

IN THE REAL WORLD

ICANN is currently considering several proposals to add additional TLDs to the available list, but there is not yet a concrete plan for the expansion of this system. In the meantime, the rules have been relaxed on COM, NET, and ORG: these domains can be registered by anyone.

Installing DNS Server

Windows 2000 Server includes Microsoft DNS Server, an implementation of a standard DNS server. This component can be installed during the installation of Windows 2000. If the DNS server is not already installed, follow these steps to install it:

1. Select *Add/Remove Programs* from the Control Panel.

2. Click *Add/Remove Windows Components* to start the Windows Components Wizard.

3. Highlight the *Networking Services* entry in the list and select *Details.*

4. Check the box next to *Domain Name Service (DNS)* and click *OK.*

5. Click *Next* to complete the installation.

Configuring DNS

After the DNS server is installed, you can manage the service from the DNS Manager MMC snap-in. To access this utility, select Programs → Administrative Tools → DNS from the Start menu. The DNS Manager snap-in is shown in Figure 4-4.

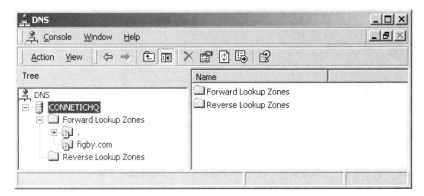

Figure 4-4: The DNS Manager MMC snap-in

You can add either forward- or reverse-lookup zones from this window or modify existing zones. To add a zone, right-click in the empty window or select *New Zone* from the Action menu. This displays the New Zone Wizard, which prompts you for the following information:

1. A welcome dialog is displayed. Click *Next* to continue.

2. Choose a zone type: *Active Directory-integrated*, which stores the DNS information in the Directory; *Standard Primary*, which creates an NT 4-style primary zone; or *Standard Secondary*, which creates a secondary copy of a primary zone.

3. Click *Next* to continue.

4. Choose whether the zone will be forward-lookup (returns IP addresses for names) or reverse-lookup (returns names for IP addresses) and click *Next*.

5. Choose a name for the zone. This typically includes the domain name, such as zone2.figby.com. Click *Next* to continue.

6. For a non-Active Directory zone, choose whether to create a new zone file or to load the contents of an existing file (typically from a backup or another computer). Click *Next* to continue.

7. A final summary dialog is displayed. If the information shown is correct, click *Finish* to create the zone and exit the wizard.

NetBIOS Name Resolution

The NetBIOS API provides support for the naming scheme used by Windows networking: computer names, domains, and workgroups. Windows 2000 includes

NetBIOS over TCP/IP (NBT), a service that allows NetBIOS communications and name resolution through TCP/IP.

After the HOSTS file and DNS fail to locate an IP hostname, Windows 2000 clients can use NetBIOS resolution. NetBIOS names have their own rules for domain resolution and their own name server service (WINS).

The steps involved in NetBIOS name resolution depend on the client's NetBIOS node type or name resolution mode. The following are the five possible node types and their name resolution methods:

B-node (broadcast)
These nodes send a broadcast (NetBIOS name query) to the entire local subnet when they need to resolve a name. The broadcast is repeated three times, if necessary. Each machine on the subnet compares the NetBIOS name in the broadcast with its own name. If a machine finds a match, it sends a reply (NetBIOS name query response) to the original node, and the NetBIOS session is established.

Enhanced B-node
This is Microsoft's nonstandard version of the B-node method and is Windows NT's default if a WINS server is not used. The broadcasts are sent as in the previous method. If no response is received from any machine on the local subnet, the client searches its local LMHOSTS file (explained later in this section) for an entry corresponding to the name.

P-node (peer-to-peer)
This type of node sends a NetBIOS name query message directly to a defined WINS server (described later in this section). No further resolution attempts are made.

M-node (mixed)
These nodes first attempt to use B-node broadcasts. If no response is received, they send a query to a WINS server. Primary and secondary WINS servers are tried, if specified in the client's configuration.

H-node (hybrid)

These nodes use the opposite of the M-node method: they first send a query to the defined WINS servers. If there is no response or the response is negative, they resort to B-node broadcasts. This is Windows NT's default method when a WINS server is available; it minimizes network traffic.

Windows Internet Name Service (WINS)

The P-node, M-node, and H-node methods of NetBIOS name resolution can make use of an NBNS (NetBIOS Name Service) server. Microsoft's implementation of NBNS is called WINS, or Windows Internet Name Service. A properly configured WINS server allows clients to avoid bandwidth-heavy B-node broadcasts.

How WINS works

Several processes, each involving a type of message sent between the client and the server, make up WINS resolution:

1. When a client initializes, it sends a NAME REGISTRATION REQUEST message to its defined primary WINS server. If it does not receive a response, it sends the same request to its secondary WINS server.

2. If the server hasn't already registered the same name to another client, it sends a POSITIVE NAME REGISTRATION RESPONSE message, specifying a TTL (Time-to-Live) indicating how long the name will remain registered. Otherwise, the server sends an END-NODE CHALLENGE message, and the client must challenge the already-registered node.

3. After 50% of the TTL has expired, the client attempts to renew the registration by sending a NAME REFRESH REQUEST message. If the response is positive, a new TTL is specified.

4. When the client needs to resolve a NetBIOS name, it sends a NAME QUERY REQUEST message to the server. The server replies with a positive response if the name is registered or with a negative response if the name is not found.

5. When the client shuts down, it sends a NAME RELEASE REQUEST to the server and receives a NAME RELEASE RESPONSE releasing the name. The client stops using the name, and the server removes it from the WINS database.

Installing WINS

Windows 2000 Server includes a WINS server. This can be selected for installation during the Windows 2000 installation, or it can be installed manually. If the WINS server is not already installed, use the following procedure to install it:

1. Select *Add/Remove Programs* from the Control Panel.

2. Click *Add/Remove Windows Components* to start the Windows Components Wizard.

3. Highlight the *Networking Services* entry in the list and select *Details.*

4. Check the box next to *Windows Internet Name Service (WINS)* and click *OK*.

5. Click *Next* to complete the installation. The Windows 2000 Server CD-ROM may be required during the installation process.

Configuring WINS

After WINS Server is installed, you can manage it from the WINS MMC snap-in. To access this utility, select Programs → Administrative Tools → WINS from the Start menu.

The Active Registrations item under a WINS server displays a list of currently registered names and their corresponding IP addresses. Because WINS configures itself automatically, you do not need to configure this list yourself; however, you can add static mappings for machines that are unable to register themselves in WINS, such as Unix and other non-Windows machines.

To add a static mapping, select *New Static Mapping* from the Action menu. The New Static Mapping dialog includes the following options:

Computer name
Specify the NetBIOS name for the computer.

NetBIOS scope
Specify an optional NetBIOS scope. Only nodes with the same scope can participate in the same network.

Type
Specify the type of node or nodes: Unique, Group, Domain Name, Internet Group, or Multihomed.

IP address
Specify the IP address corresponding to the NetBIOS name. For the Domain, Internet Group, and Multihomed mapping types, you can specify multiple IP addresses.

WINS replication

The Windows 2000 WINS server includes support for automatic database replication between servers. The replication scheme uses a system of partners:

Push partners
Automatically send updates to partner servers whenever changes are made to the WINS database. This provides for the best database synchronization.

Pull partners
Periodically poll partner servers and receive updates for any changes since the previous polling. This system works best over wide-area links where constant synchronization updates would inflate bandwidth.

To configure WINS replication, highlight the *Replication Partners* item under the server name in the WINS snap-in. This displays a list of current replication partners, if any.

To add a partner, select *New Replication Partner* from the Add menu. You are prompted for the IP address of the WINS server to partner with. After the partner is added, right-click its entry and select *Properties* to access the Partner Properties dialog, shown in Figure 4-5. This dialog includes the following options:

Replication partner type
> Choose the type of partner: Push, Pull, or Push/Pull (allows both types of replication).

Pull replication
> For pull partners, choose whether to use a persistent connection for the replication. You can specify a start time and replication interval for the regular updates.

Push replication
> For push partners, choose whether to use a persistent connection. You can also specify the number of updates to the WINS database that will be allowed before forcing a replication session.

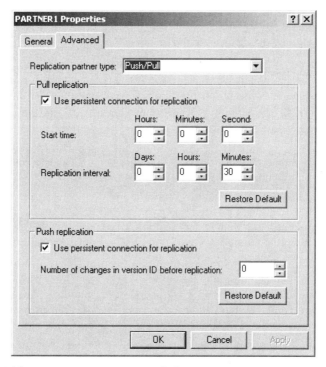

Figure 4-5: The WINS Partner Properties dialog

The LMHOSTS File

In Enhanced B-node NetBIOS resolution, the LMHOSTS file is checked if a negative response is received from the WINS server. This file is similar to the HOSTS file, but uses IP addresses and NetBIOS names. To enable the LMHOSTS file, select the *Enable LMHOSTS Lookup* option in the WINS tab of the TCP/IP Properties dialog.

LMHOSTS is a standard ASCII file stored in \\systemroot\system32\drivers\etc\ lmhosts.sam. The following is an example of a simple LMHOSTS file:

```
168.192.150.1      East1      # this is a comment
168.192.150.2      East2      #PRE    # see below
168.192.150.6      North1
```

Entries in the LMHOSTS file can be suffixed with #PRE to indicate that they are to be directly loaded into the local NetBIOS cache for fast resolution. Entries suffixed #DOM are domain entries, which can be used to support network browsing and domain authentication.

The LMHOSTS file supports a rudimentary form of remote name resolution through the use of block inclusion. Entries from the LMHOSTS file on a remote server can be included using the following syntax:

```
BEGIN_ALTERNATE
#INCLUDE \\East1\public\lmhosts
END_ALTERNATE
```

The files you include are searched only if no match was found in the local LMHOSTS file. If more than one remote LMHOSTS file is included in this fashion, they are searched in order; if a name is resolved by one file, the remaining files will not be searched.

NetWare Connectivity

Windows 2000 includes software to act as a client in a NetWare network and access resources on NetWare servers. NetWare support is provided by the following components:

NWLink (IPX/SPX protocols)
The protocols used for NetWare connectivity.

Client Service for NetWare (CSNW)
The NetWare client software included with Windows 2000 Professional.

Gateway Service for NetWare (GSNW)
The NetWare client software included with Windows 2000 Server; GSNW also acts as a gateway to allow Windows NT/2000 clients to access NetWare resources.

Directory Services Migration Tool
A tool for converting user accounts, files, and other information from a NetWare server to a Windows 2000 server.

File and Print Services for NetWare
Allows a Windows 2000 computer and printer to service NetWare clients. FPNW is available separately from Microsoft.

Windows 2000's key NetWare connectivity features are described in more detail in the following sections.

NWLink (IPX/SPX Protocols)

Novell NetWare networks include the IPX (Internetwork Packet Exchange) and SPX (Sequenced Packet Exchange) protocols. These protocols were developed by Novell and are the default protocols for NetWare 4.0 and earlier networks.

NWLink is Microsoft's implementation of the IPX/SPX protocols and is included with Windows 2000. This protocol is automatically installed when you install CSNW or GSNW, or it can be manually installed.

Installing NWLink

To install NWLink manually, follow these steps:

1. In the Network and Dial-up Connections Control Panel applet, right-click the icon for the appropriate local area network and select *Properties*.
2. Select the General tab and click the *Install* button.
3. Choose to add a protocol, then choose *NWLink IPX/SPX Protocol* from the list.

ON THE EXAM

CSNW and GSNW only support the NWLink IPX/SPX protocols. NetWare 5 uses the TCP/IP protocol by default and may not include IPX. Windows NT clients using NWLink will only be able to connect if the NetWare server supports IPX.

Client Service for NetWare (CSNW)

Client Service for NetWare (CSNW) is Windows 2000 Professional's included NetWare client. This allows direct access to resources on NetWare servers. To use CSNW, it must be installed on each client that will access the NetWare network; each client also must have an account on the NetWare server.

To install CSNW, follow these steps:

1. In the Network and Dial-up Connections Control Panel applet, right-click the appropriate local area network and select *Properties*.
2. Select the General tab, then click the *Install* button.
3. Choose to add a client, then choose *Client Service for NetWare* from the list.

CSNW requires NWLink to operate. If it is not already installed, NWLink will automatically be installed during the installation of CSNW.

ON THE EXAM

CSNW has a few advantages over GSNW in that it provides a faster, more direct connection to the NetWare server. It also provides better security, because each client can be given access to separate files through a NetWare account. However, it requires NWLink to be installed on all clients, rather than simply on a gateway machine. It also requires separate maintenance of NetWare and Windows 2000 user accounts.

Gateway Service for NetWare (GSNW)

Gateway Service for NetWare (GSNW) is included with Windows 2000 Server and acts as a NetWare client for the server machine. In addition, it can serve as a gateway to allow Windows clients to access NetWare resources. When this is used, you do not need separate NetWare client software on each client.

GSNW uses a single user account on the NetWare server to authorize all access to resources, and everything is accessed through the gateway machine. It requires NWLink on the gateway machine, but can communicate with Windows clients via TCP/IP. To install GSNW, follow these steps:

1. In the Network and Dial-up Connections Control Panel applet, right-click the appropriate local area network and select *Properties*.

2. Select the General tab, then click the *Install* button.

3. Choose to add a client, then choose *Gateway (and Client) Service for NetWare* from the list.

If NWLink is not already installed, it will be added during the installation of GSNW.

Configuring GSNW

After GSNW is installed, you can configure it using the Gateway Service for NetWare applet in the Control Panel. This dialog is shown in Figure 4-6 and includes the following options:

Preferred Server
For non-NDS networks, choose the default NetWare server.

Default Tree and Context
For NDS networks, choose the default tree and context.

Print Options
Choose whether to add form feeds during printing, notify users after print jobs complete, or print banners.

Login Script Options
Choose whether to run a NetWare login script.

Gateway
Press this button to display a separate dialog allowing you to enable and configure the gateway.

DHCP (Dynamic Host Configuration Protocol)

DHCP (Dynamic Host Configuration Protocol) provides an alternative to manually assigning IP addresses to computers. DHCP automatically assigns, or *leases*, IP addresses to hosts from a centrally managed pool.

DHCP is an extension of the BootP protocol defined in RFC 951 and is itself described in RFCs 1531, 1533, 1534, 1541, and 1542. Windows 2000 fully supports

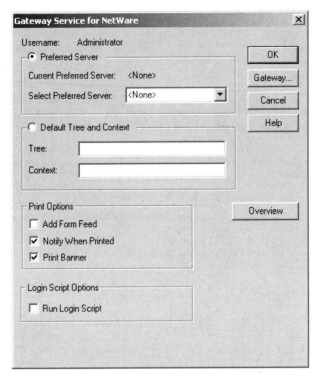

Figure 4-6: The Gateway Service for NetWare options dialog

ON THE EXAM

NDS (Novell Directory Services) is a global directory of servers, computers, users, and other resources used in NetWare 4.x and 5.x. It is similar in function to the Windows 2000 Active Directory, and it is organized similarly.

---

this standard. Any Windows 2000 computer can act as a DHCP client, and Windows 2000 Server can be configured to act as a DHCP server.

DHCP provides obvious advantages over manual address assignment: there is less administrative hassle, and new machines can be added to the network without dedicated IP addresses. In situations where all machines on the network are not used at once, DHCP allows a small pool of addresses to serve a larger number of machines.

DHCP is simple to install and practical for use in all but the smallest networks. Its disadvantages include the necessity of managing the address pool, the potential for conflicts between DHCP-assigned and manually assigned addresses, and the lack of a consistent address needed for some client applications.

How DHCP Works

DHCP clients and servers communicate with various messages, defined by RFC 1531. Communication is via UDP and uses ports 67 and 68. When a DHCP client initializes, the following process occurs:

1. The client broadcasts a DHCPDISCOVER message, requesting an IP address lease from any DHCP server. This message includes the client's MAC address and NetBIOS name. If there is no response to the discover message, it is rebroadcast at intervals until a response is received.

2. Any DHCP servers that receive the message respond with DHCPOFFER messages. These messages include the DHCP server's IP address, an available IP address, its corresponding subnet mask, and the lease's duration in hours. DHCP servers reserve the offered addresses for a period of time and await a request.

3. The client selects one of the offered leases (in NT, always the first one offered) and sends the server a DHCPREQUEST message, which includes the client's MAC address, the offered IP address, and the server's IP address.

4. The DHCP server responds to the request by broadcasting a DHCPACK (acknowledgment) message if the requested address is still available. In this case, the client is now ready to access the network, and the DHCP server marks the address as unavailable to other clients. If the address is no longer available, the server sends a DHCPNAK (negative acknowledgment) message, and the client begins the process again with a DHCPDISCOVER message.

5. After 50% of the IP address lease duration given in the offer message has expired, the client attempts to renew the lease by sending another DHCPREQUEST message directly to the DHCP server. If there is no response, the renewal request is rebroadcast after 87.5% of the lease has expired, and any available DHCP server can respond.

6. If the address is still available, the DHCP server responds with DHCPACK, and a new lease period begins. If the address has become unavailable, the server responds with DHCPNAK; in this case, the client restarts the discovery process after the lease period expires.

The DHCP server *releases* an IP address, making it available to other clients, when the lease duration expires without a renewal, when a renewal request is denied, or when the client sends a DHCPRELEASE message.

Windows NT and Windows 2000 clients store their assigned IP addresses in the registry; other clients use a file for this purpose. When the client reinitializes, it first attempts to request the address stored from a previous session.

Configuring DHCP

Windows 2000 Server includes a DHCP Server service. The following sections describe the process of installing and configuring DHCP Server and other configurations you may need to specify to complete the DHCP configuration on your network.

Installing DHCP Server

DHCP Server can be installed during the Windows 2000 Server installation or can be added to the installation later. Perform the following steps to install DHCP Server:

1. Select *Add/Remove Programs* from the Control Panel.

2. Click *Add/Remove Windows Components* to start the Windows Components Wizard.

3. Highlight the *Networking Services* entry in the list and select *Details*.

4. Check the box next to *Dynamic Host Configuration Protocol (DHCP)* and click *OK*.

5. Click *Next* to complete the installation.

Creating a scope

After DHCP is installed, you can manage it using the DHCP MMC snap-in. To access this snap-in, select Programs → Administrative Tools → DHCP from the Start menu. This utility is shown in Figure 4-7.

Figure 4-7: The DHCP Management MMC snap-in

To use DHCP, you must specify at least one scope, or range of IP addresses for assignment to clients. A scope is created by default when you install DHCP Server. To create an additional scope, select *New Scope* from the Action menu. A wizard displays the following dialogs:

1. A welcome dialog is displayed. Click *Next* to continue.

2. Type a name and description for the scope, then click *Next*.

3. Enter the range of IP addresses to be used for the scope and specify the subnet mask. This can be specified in the usual dotted decimal format or as a number of bits.

4. You can now optionally add one or more *exclusions*, ranges of IP addresses that will be excluded from the scope. Specify a start and end address and click *Add* to add an exclusion.

5. Specify the lease duration for IP addresses in the scope as a number of days, hours, and minutes. The default is eight days.

6. Choose whether to specify DHCP options. If you choose *Yes*, you are further prompted for Default Gateway, DNS, and WINS Server addresses to send to

clients. These options can also be set manually, as described later in this section.

7. A final screen is displayed. Click *Finish* to create the scope.

After a scope is created, it must be activated before its addresses will be available to clients. If you specified options while creating the scope, you are prompted to activate it immediately. If not, you can right-click on a scope in the list and select *Activate* to make the scope active.

DHCP authorization

Before Windows 2000 clients can access a DHCP server, it must be authorized in Active Directory. This prevents unauthorized DHCP servers from gaining access to the network. To authorize servers, highlight the DHCP entry in the DHCP snap-in's left pane and select *Manage Authorized Servers* from the Action menu. From this dialog you can authorize or unauthorize servers.

ON THE EXAM

The Windows 2000 DHCP service checks Active Directory for an authorization entry when it starts and will not respond to client requests if it is unauthorized.

DHCP reservations

DHCP reservations are reserved IP addresses. This feature is useful for computers that must have consistent IP addresses, such as WINS servers. To add reservations, highlight the *Reservations* item within a scope and select *New Reservation* from the Add menu. The reservation requires the following options:

Reservation name
A name for the reservation, to be displayed in the Reservations window.

IP address
The IP address to be assigned to the client. This address must be part of the scope, must not be excluded, and must not be currently leased.

MAC address
The hardware (MAC) address for the client.

Description
An optional description to be displayed in the Reservations window.

Supported types
Specify whether DHCP, BootP, or both are allowed for this reservation. (BootP is typically used for diskless workstations.)

DHCP options

DHCP options allow the DHCP server to send clients additional information, such as router, DNS server, or WINS server addresses. Many options are available.

You can set options for a scope using the *Scope Options* entry in the scope, or you can set global options with the *Server Options* entry in the DHCP console. You can also set options for a reserved client. Right-click on any of these and choose *Configure Options* to set option values.

Highlight an option in this dialog, check its corresponding box, and set a value to use the option. Although you can set values for the full list of DHCP options and even define your own options, a limited set of options is recognized by Windows clients. These are described in Table 4-11.

Table 4-11: Common Numeric DHCP Options

Option Number	Option Name	Value type	Description
003	Router	Array of IP addresses	Preferred routers (gateways), in order of preference
006	DNS Servers	Array of IP addresses	Available DNS servers, in order of preference
044	WINS/NBNS Servers	Array of IP addresses	Available WINS servers, in order of preference
046	WINS/NBT Node Type	Byte	WINS node type; see the previous section "NetBIOS Name Resolution"
047	NetBIOS Scope ID	String	Identifier for NetBIOS over TCP/IP

Configuring DHCP clients

DHCP client configuration is simple for Windows 2000 or other Windows clients: choose the *Obtain an IP Address Automatically* option. If a DHCP server is available, the IP address and other configuration details will be obtained via DHCP.

DHCP Forwarding

DHCP requests do not normally pass through a router, unless it is specifically configured for DHCP (or BootP) forwarding. You can enable DHCP forwarding on a Windows 2000 computer as part of the IP routing configuration.

To add the DHCP relay service, choose Programs → Administrative Tools → Routing and Remote Access from the Start menu. Select the General item under IP Routing and then select *New Routing Protocol* from the Action menu. Choose *DHCP Relay Agent* from the list and click *OK.*

After the installation, a DHCP Relay Agent item will appear in the server tree. To enable the relay agent, highlight this entry, select *New Interface* from the Action menu, and add the *Local Area Connection* interface or the interface you wish to use. After an interface is added, you can modify its settings by selecting *Properties* from the Action menu. The following options are available:

Relay DHCP packets
   If this option is enabled, DHCP forwarding is enabled.

Hop-count threshold
   Specify the maximum number of hops a request can travel via relay agents.

Boot threshold (seconds)

If a value is specified, the agent will not relay DHCP requests until the specified number of seconds. This allows the relay to act as a backup for a local DHCP server when it fails to respond in the allotted time.

Using DHCP with DNS

Normally DNS cannot be used with computers that obtain IP addresses via DHCP, because their IP address may be different at each boot. Windows 2000's DHCP service provides a way around this. The DHCP server can contact the DNS server and update its information using the *dynamic DNS updates* feature.

Windows 2000 clients can contact the DNS server directly to update their DNS records when their IP address changes. For older clients, the DHCP server can provide this feature. To enable this feature, select the *Enable Updates for DNS Clients that Do Not Support Dynamic Update* option in the DNS zone Properties dialog.

Remote Access Server (RAS)

RAS allows dial-up connections (modem connections, or on-demand connections such as ADSL) to be used for TCP/IP networking and routing. The following sections describe Windows 2000's RAS features and the utilities used to configure RAS settings.

ON THE EXAM

The following sections describe dial-in (server) configuration for RAS. Dial-up (client) RAS settings are configured using the Network and Dial-up Connections window, available by right-clicking the *My Network Places* icon and selecting *Properties*.

Configuring RAS

You can configure RAS settings using the Routing and Remote Access snap-in to MMC, which was described earlier in this chapter as used for IP Routing configuration. The majority of RAS settings are contained within one or more remote access policies.

A policy specifies remote access settings for a configurable group of users. A default policy is included to allow access to any user with the dial-in permission set in their user policy. You can modify this policy or add separate policies to modify RAS settings.

The policy Properties dialog allows you to grant or deny permissions based on a number of conditions. You can use the *Edit Profile* button to edit the full range of RAS settings for the policy. The Profile dialog is divided into a number of property pages, described in the following sections.

Dial-in Constraints

The Dial-in Constraints page allows you to restrict the use of dial-up connections. The following options are available:

Disconnect if idle for
> If this option is enabled, the user will be disconnected after the specified number of minutes with no network activity.

Restrict maximum session to
> If this option is enabled, the user will be disconnected after the specified number of minutes, regardless of activity.

Restrict access to the following days and times
> Specify dates and times to allow access.

Restrict dial-in to this number only
> If multiple numbers are in use, select this option to allow the user access to only one specified number.

Restrict dial-in media
> If this option is enabled, you can choose dial-up media (DSL, ISDN,VPN, etc.) that can be used by the policy's users.

IP

This page includes IP addressing options. You can choose whether the server always supplies an IP address or only does so when requested by the client. You can also define packet filters to be used for the policy's users.

Multilink

The multilink feature allows two or more modem devices to be aggregated into a single higher-bandwidth link. This page allows you to enable or disable multilink for the policy's users.

This page also includes settings for Bandwidth Allocation Protocol (BAP). This protocol allows you to reduce the number of multilink lines available to this policy's users when the dial-up line usage exceeds a specified level for a specified amount of time.

Authentication

This page allows you to choose the types of authentication allowed for the policy's users when dialing in. You can choose one or more of the following authentication methods:

CHAP (Challenge Handshake Authentication Protocol)
> An Internet-standard protocol that exchanges encrypted tokens for authentication.

MS-CHAP
> Microsoft's proprietary version of CHAP, supported by Windows and Windows NT.

MS-CHAP v2

A new version of MS-CHAP, available only to Windows 2000 clients and servers.

Extensible Authentication Protocol (EAP)

A dynamic authentication protocol that can use certificates, smart cards, or other authenticated methods.

Unencrypted authentication

Allows use of the PAP (Password Authentication Protocol) and SPAP (Shiva PAP) protocols, which provide authentication using plain-text passwords.

Unauthenticated access

If this option is enabled, clients can complete PPP connections with no authentication. It is disabled by default and is a serious security risk.

Which types of authentication you allow will depend on your need for security and the types of systems you are supporting. In a Windows network, MS-CHAP and MS-CHAP v2 will support all clients securely. If you need to support Unix clients, you may need to enable CHAP, PAP, or perhaps even unauthenticated access, but each of these you enable reduces security.

Encryption

This page allows you to enable encryption for RAS clients. The options here include *No Encryption*, *Basic*, and *Strong* encryption. The encryption features of RAS are explained in detail in the next section.

Advanced

This page allows you to configure a number of additional named RAS options. Press *Add* to display a complete list of available options and add an option if desired.

Remote Access Encryption

Windows 2000 includes a number of options for encrypting TCP/IP dial-up and VPN connections for enhanced security. The following sections describe the encryption protocols available and their intended use.

Dial-up connections

Dial-up connections typically use the PPP protocol. This protocol allows secure authentication to initiate a connection, but does not normally include encryption. Windows 2000 includes the MPPE (Microsoft Point-to-Point Encryption) to add encryption to the PPP transport.

VPN connections

VPN (virtual private network) connections can use either the PPTP or L2TP protocols. Windows 2000 uses MPPE to secure PPTP communication and uses IPSec to secure L2TP communications.

RAS and DHCP

Windows 2000 RAS can use DHCP to assign IP addresses. Although clients cannot directly issue DHCP requests or receive responses from a DHCP server, the RRAS service leases addresses from DHCP in groups of ten and assigns them to clients.

ON THE EXAM

RRAS also works with the DHCP relay agent. Although clients cannot request IP addresses through the relay agent, they can request WINS and DNS addresses and other information available through DHCP options.

You can modify the number of IP addresses RRAS leases at a time. This value is stored in the registry under this subkey:

`\System\CurrentControlSet\Services\RemoteAccess\Parameters\Ip\`

Within this subkey, the `InitialAddressPoolSize` key stores the number of addresses to lease.

NAT (Network Address Translation)

There are two basic ways to connect a network to the Internet: a *routed connection*, which uses a router and requires public IP addresses for each connected computer; or a *translated connection*, which uses a single computer to access the Internet with a public address and translates the data to allow use of private IP addresses elsewhere in the network. Network Address Translation (NAT) translates private IP addresses to public addresses, allowing a single computer to provide Internet access for a private network and eliminating the need for public addresses for all machines on the network. NAT actually provides three separate services to clients on a Windows 2000 network:

Translation
Translates between public and private IP addresses.

IP address assignment
Includes a simple DHCP server and can assign IP addresses to clients. NAT uses the pools of private IP addresses listed earlier in this chapter.

DNS name resolution
Acts as a DNS server. Rather than maintaining a name and address database, the NAT server forwards DNS requests to an Internet DNS server and returns the results to its clients.

Installing NAT

NAT is configured as a routing protocol and must be used on a Windows 2000 computer running Routing and Remote Access Services. To install NAT, follow these steps:

---

1. In the Routing and Remote Access console, open the *Routing and Remote Access* key in the left pane. Open the entry for the server, then select *IP Routing*.

2. Highlight the *General* entry. Right-click and select *New Routing Protocol.*

3. Select *Network Address Translation* from the list and click *OK.*

Configuring NAT

After NAT is installed, you must configure the network a certain way to allow NAT to be used. These considerations include the following:

- The IP address of the NAT server should be set to the first address in the chosen range of private IP addresses; for example, 192.168.0.1.

- A dial-up (or persistent, such as DSL) connection to an Internet Service Provider (ISP) must be configured.

- The NAT protocol must be installed, as described earlier, and configured to use the LAN interface and the dial-up (or other) interface to the Internet.

To enable NAT addressing, select *NAT* in the left pane of the Routing and Remote Access console and select *Properties.* Choose the Address tab, then enable the *Automatically Assign IP Addresses by Using DHCP* option. You can also specify the private address range to use from this dialog.

ON THE EXAM

NAT can also be configured to use a pool of two or more public IP addresses. You can configure this from the Address Pool tab of the NAT Properties dialog.

Using special ports

NAT normally allows only outbound access to the Internet. To allow inbound access, you can configure a special port. This is useful if you are running a public server, such as a web server, on a machine in the private network. To configure a special port, follow these steps:

1. Assign the server machine a static private IP address and exclude the address from NAT's address range.

2. In the Routing and Remote Access console, select *Network Address Translation* in the left pane. Right-click the interface that provides Internet connectivity and select *Properties.*

3. Select the Special Ports tab. Choose whether to use a TCP or UDP port, then click *Add.*

4. Specify the incoming port number (for example, 80 for most web servers). If you have multiple public IP addresses, you must also select the address to use.

5. Specify the outgoing port number and private IP address for the server machine.

Internet Connection Sharing (ICS)

Internet Connection Sharing (ICS) is a simplified version of NAT that can be used for basic address translation. ICS differs from NAT in the following ways:

- ICS uses a single checkbox rather than complex configuration information.

- ICS uses a fixed range of private IP addresses.

- ICS allows only one public IP address.

- ICS can only be used on one internal LAN interface.

To install ICS, follow these steps:

1. In the Routing and Remote Access console, open the *Routing and Remote Access* key in the left pane. Open the entry for the server, then select *IP Routing*.

2. Highlight the *General* entry. Right-click and select *New Routing Protocol*.

3. Select *Connection Sharing* from the list and click *OK*.

4. In the Network and Dial-up Connections window, right-click the *Internet* interface to share and select *Properties*.

5. Select the Sharing tab and activate the *Enable Internet Connection Sharing for this Connection* option. You can also choose whether ICS will dial the connection automatically when it is accessed by a client.

IN THE REAL WORLD

Windows 98 SE and Windows Me also include an implementation of ICS. These operating systems don't support a full-featured NAT implementation.

Certificate Services

Windows 2000's Public Key Infrastructure (PKI) manages public-key encryption. This type of encryption uses two keys: a public key and a private key. Messages encrypted with the private key can be decrypted with the public key, and vice versa.

Windows 2000 Certificate Services manages the issuing of certificates. These are documents that verify identity and can include a public/private key pair. Certificates are issued by a certificate authority (CA). There are several types of CA:

Standalone root CA
> Standalone CAs are used when the organization will be issuing certificates to third parties. The root CA is the most trusted CA and can authorize subordinate CAs. Standalone CAs do not require Active Directory.

Standalone subordinate CA
> Standalone subordinate CAs are authorized by and subordinate to the root CA.

Enterprise root CA
> Enterprise CAs are used when the organization will be issuing certificates internally, i.e., to employees or students. The enterprise root CA is the highest authority and can authorize subordinate CAs. Windows 2000 allows one enterprise root CA per certificate hierarchy and any number of root CAs per network. Enterprise CAs require Active Directory.

Enterprise subordinate CA
> Enterprise subordinate CAs are authorized by and subordinate to the root CA.

Installing a Certificate Authority

You can configure a certificate authority on any Windows 2000 Server computer. Follow these steps to install a CA:

1. In the Control Panel, select *Add/Remove Programs*, then select *Add/Remove Windows Components*.

2. Check the *Certificate Services* option.

3. You are warned that the computer cannot be renamed or removed from the domain; click *OK*.

4. Select the CA type from the four types listed in the previous section.

5. Enter the name, organization, city, and other details for the CA and click *Next*.

6. Specify a directory for the CA database. The default is C:\WINNT\System32\ CertLog. Click *Next*.

7. The CA is now installed; this may take several minutes, and the Windows 2000 CD-ROM may be required.

Network Infrastructure

ON THE EXAM

After a Windows 2000 Server computer is configured as a certificate authority, it cannot be renamed, moved to another domain, or removed from the domain. Consider these options carefully before installing a CA.

Managing Certificates

The Windows 2000 Certificate Authority can be managed using the Certificate Authority Manager MMC snap-in, available from the Administrative Tools menu after installation. There is also a web-based interface for enrolling certificates. Various certificate management tasks are described in the following sections.

Requesting a certificate

The process of requesting and being granted a certificate is called enrollment. Follow these steps to request and grant a certificate:

1. With a web browser, connect to *http://servername/certsrv/default.asp*.
2. Select the *Request a Certificate* option and click *Next*.
3. In the Certificate Authority Manager, select *Pending Requests* in the left pane.
4. Right-click the pending request and select *Issue*.
5. In the browser, access the same URL. Select the *Check on a pending certificate* option and click *Next*.
6. You can now view and use the certificate.

Revoking a certificate

Occasionally, you may need to revoke an issued certificate. To revoke a certificate, highlight it in Certificate Authority Manager, right-click, and select *Revoke Certificate*. You are prompted for a reason for the revocation.

Monitoring Network Performance

Windows 2000 includes a number of utilities for monitoring network performance and troubleshooting problems. These are described in the following sections.

Using Network Monitor

Network Monitor is a utility for monitoring traffic on the network. Network Monitor consists of three components:

Network Monitor tools
> The network monitoring utility.

Network Monitor agent
> A service that runs in the background and provides data to Network Monitor.

Network Monitor driver
> An optional driver that can provide additional information to the Network Monitor agent.

Installing Network Monitor

To install Network Monitor under Windows 2000 Server, follow these steps. The installation includes the monitoring tools and the monitoring agent.

1. In the Add/Remove Programs Control Panel applet, select the *Add/Remove Windows Components* option.
2. Open the Management and Monitoring Tools entry by clicking *Details*.
3. Select *Network Monitor Tools* and click *OK*.
4. Follow the instructions to complete the installation. You may need the Windows 2000 CD-ROM.

The Network Monitor driver is installed separately. Follow these steps to install the driver:

1. In the Network and Dial-up Connections Control Panel applet, right-click the local area connection and select *Properties.*

2. Click the *Install* button. Choose *Protocol* from the list of network component types and click *Add.*

3. Select *Network Monitor Driver* from the list and click *OK.*

4. Follow the instructions to complete the installation. You may need the Windows 2000 CD-ROM.

Capturing packets

After Network Monitor is installed, you can access it by selecting Programs → Administrative Tools → Network Monitor from the Start menu. The main Network Monitor dialog is shown in Figure 4-8.

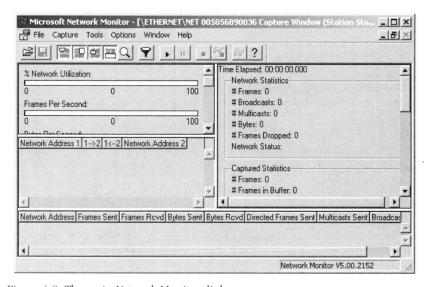

Figure 4-8: The main Network Monitor dialog

To start capturing packets, select Capture → Start from this utility. You can also use the other settings in the Capture menu to select the types of data that will be captured.

Viewing Capture results

After capturing packets and stopping the capture, select Capture → Display Captured Data to display the data. While you are viewing, select Display → Filter to choose which types of data are displayed. You can also use File → Save As to save the current capture data to a file.

Using Event Viewer

Event Viewer displays error messages and other information about past events. In Windows 2000, Event Viewer is an MMC snap-in. To access this snap-in, select *Event Viewer* from the Administrative Tools Control Panel applet. Event Viewer is available in Windows 2000 Professional and Server.

Event Viewer displays three separate logs. For each log, events are displayed with their corresponding type, date, time, and source. Events are categorized by type, including Information, Warning, and Error. The following logs are available:

Application log
> Includes events logged by applications and problems such as application crashes.

Security log
> Includes messages relating to security. Security problems, such as incorrect logons, are included in this log if auditing is enabled. Security auditing is disabled by default.

System log
> Includes system error messages and status messages for system reboots and other events. If system events are selected for auditing, these are also included in this log.

Monitoring IPSec

Windows 2000 includes IP Security Monitor, a tool for measuring IP Security statistics. To run this utility from Windows 2000 Professional or Server, type IPSECMON at the command prompt or the Run prompt.

IPSECMON displays a list of currently enabled IPSec policies and indicates whether IPSec is enabled on the computer. It also displays a window of IPSec statistics, including counters of the number of bytes sent and received securely, authenticated bytes sent and received, bad packets and errors, and key additions. A separate window displays ISAKMP/Oakley statistics.

Suggested Exercises

For the Network Infrastructure exam, you should be familiar with all of the protocols and services described in this chapter, particularly all aspects of TCP/IP.

If at all possible, you should practice using a network with several workstations and servers. Experience with larger networks (multiple locations, subnets, and routers) is even better.

The following sections describe exercises you can perform to become more familiar with Windows 2000 network infrastructure.

Installing and Configuring TCP/IP

1. For each machine in your network, perform these steps:

    a. Add TCP/IP to the list of protocols if it is not already installed.

    b. Assign an IP address. Use the private IP address ranges listed in the Study Guide to avoid conflicts.

    c. Use the ping utility from another computer to verify that the computers can communicate.

2. Either on paper or in a real network, divide a class C IP network into subnets and calculate the correct subnet masks.

3. Enable the Packet Filtering feature and configure several filters, then test to ensure that the ports have been blocked. (You can use the `telnet` command to connect with any port number.)

Configuring IP Routing

1. Configure a computer to act as a static router. Use the `route` command to add several routing table entries.

2. Set a default gateway address for all computers on the network.

3. Configure two or more Windows 2000 Server computers to act as dynamic routers and install the RIP or OSPF routing protocol.

Managing IPSec

1. Configure two Windows 2000 computers with IPSec security policies.

2. Verify that the computers can communicate and use IPSECMON to ensure that encrypted data is being transmitted.

3. Use the filtering built into IPSec to allow traffic only between the two computers' IP addresses and block several TCP and UDP ports. Verify that the security restrictions are effective.

Configuring Name Resolution

1. Set up a HOSTS file on a computer and ensure that it is interpreted correctly when you use a web browser.

2. Install a DNS server under Windows 2000 Server.

3. Set up a DNS zone.

4. Install a WINS server under Windows 2000 Server.

5. Configure clients with the appropriate DNS and WINS server IP addresses.

6. Configure WINS replication between two Windows 2000 Server computers.

7. Set up an LMHOSTS file on a computer.

Setting up NetWare Connectivity

1. Install NWLink on a Windows 2000 computer.

2. Install CSNW on a Windows 2000 Professional computer. If you have a NetWare server available, verify that you can access its resources.

3. Install GSNW on a Windows 2000 Server computer. If you have a NetWare server available, verify that you can access its resources from several different computers.

Installing and Configuring DHCP

1. Install a DHCP server on a Windows 2000 Server computer.

2. Authorize the DHCP server in Active Directory.

3. Configure a DHCP scope with a pool of addresses.

4. Configure several clients to obtain addresses from the DHCP server and verify that they are able to connect to the network.

5. Configure a DHCP relay agent and use it to access a DHCP server.

6. Configure a DHCP reservation for a computer. Boot the computer and verify that it was assigned the correct IP address.

7. Use DHCP options to provide a WINS server address to clients.

Installing and Managing Remote Access

1. Install Remote Access Server on a Windows 2000 Server computer.

2. Configure the server correctly to allow remote connections, then try connecting over a modem, if available.

3. Experiment with different RAS authentication methods.

Installing and Using NAT

1. Install NAT on a Windows 2000 Server computer. Configure a local area interface and a connection to the Internet.

2. Configure a pool of private IP addresses.

3. Configure clients to use NAT (DHCP) to obtain their IP address. Verify that they are assigned an address and that they can access the Internet via the NAT server.

4. Configure a NAT special port and verify that the server can be accessed via the Internet.

Installing and Using Certificate Services

1. Install Certificate Services on a Windows 2000 Server computer and configure a certificate authority.

2. Use the web interface to request a certificate.

3. Use Certificate Authority Manager to issue the certificate and verify that the client can view the certificate.

4. Revoke the certificate.

Monitoring the Network

1. Install Network Monitor on a Windows 2000 Server computer.

2. Install the Network Monitor driver.

3. Use Network Monitor to capture packets on the network for several minutes; make sure the network is in use during this time.

4. View the captured data, then try using filters to view only selected types of data.

5. Use Event Viewer to view the application, security, and system logs.

6. Use IPSECMON to monitor an IPSec connection between two computers.

Practice Tests

Comprehensive Test

1. Which of the following is Windows 2000's default transport protocol?

    a. TCP/IP

    b. IPX/SPX

    c. DLC

    d. NetBEUI

2. Which of the following protocols are routable? (Select all that apply.)

    a. TCP/IP

    b. IPX/SPX

    c. NetBEUI

    d. AppleTalk

3. Which of the following is not a network transport protocol?

    a. TCP/IP

    b. IPX/SPX

    c. DLC

    d. NetBEUI

4. Which TCP/IP protocols operate at the Host-to-Host layer of the DoD model? (Select all that apply.)

    a. TCP

    b. IP

c. UDP

d. ICMP

5. Which of the following protocols translates IP addresses to hardware (MAC) addresses?

    a. IP

    b. ARP

    c. RARP

    d. ICMP

6. HTTP (Hypertext Transfer Protocol) operates at which layer of the DoD model?

    a. Network Access

    b. Host-to-Host

    c. Internet

    d. Process/Application

7. Of the following IP address classes, which allows for the greatest number of network addresses?

    a. Class A

    b. Class B

    c. Class C

8. Which of the following techniques is used to divide an IP network into smaller network segments?

    a. Supernetting

    b. Subnetting

    c. CIDR

    d. DHCP

9. Which of the following techniques is used to combine several consecutive network addresses into a single network?

    a. Supernetting

    b. Subnetting

    c. CIDR

    d. DHCP

10. Which of the following protocols are related to email? (Select all that apply.)

    a. POP

    b. SNMP

c. SMTP

d. IMAP

11. Which of the following Windows 2000 features is used to prevent unauthorized ports or protocols from being accessed on a computer?

   a. IPSec

   b. IP Filtering

   c. Certificate Authority

   d. ISAKMP

12. Which type of routing uses routing protocols rather than a manually configured routing table?

   a. Static routing

   b. Dynamic routing

13. Which of the following are routing protocols used with Windows 2000? (Select all that apply.)

   a. RIP

   b. IPX

   c. RRAS

   d. OSPF

14. Which of the following IP Security options should you choose on a server to maintain the highest level of security?

   a. Respond Only

   b. Require Security

   c. Request Security

   d. All of the above

15. Which of the following name resolution methods is used first when Windows 2000 resolves a name?

   a. DNS

   b. WINS

   c. The HOSTS file

   d. The LMHOSTS file

16. Which of the following are used for NetBIOS name resolution? (Select all that apply.)

   a. DNS

   b. WINS

   c. HOSTS

   d. LMHOSTS

17. Which of the following NetWare compatibility tools are included with Windows 2000 Server? (Select all that apply.)

    a. CSNW

    b. GSNW

    c. NWLink

    d. FPNW

18. Which of the following services allows multiple Windows-based clients to access resources on a NetWare server without installing NetWare client software on each client?

    a. CSNW

    b. GSNW

    c. NWLink

    d. FPNW

19. What is the term used to refer to a group of IP addresses that can be allocated by a DHCP server?

    a. Zone

    b. Scope

    c. Pool

    d. Lease

20. Which of the following is a protocol used to manage RAS's multilink feature?

    a. DHCP

    b. CHAP

    c. MS-CHAP

    d. BAP

21. Which of the following dial-up authentication methods has the highest level of security?

    a. PAP

    b. CHAP

    c. MS-CHAP

    d. SPAP

22. You want to provide Internet access to your private network and have two public IP addresses to use. Which of the following services could be used to translate between public and private addresses?

    a. NAT

    b. IPSec

c.   ICS

d.   DHCP

23. Which of the following functions are provided by Windows 2000's NAT protocol? (Select all that apply.)

    a.   Network address translation

    b.   IP address assignment

    c.   Managing a DNS database

    d.   Incoming connections from the Internet

24. Which of the following services cannot be used at the same time as NAT?

    a.   DHCP

    b.   DNS

    c.   ICS

    d.   RAS

25. Which of the following certificate authorities require Active Directory?

    a.   Standalone root CA

    b.   Standalone subordinate CA

    c.   Enterprise root CA

    d.   Enterprise subordinate CA

26. Which of the following is used by clients to request a certificate from a CA?

    a.   Certificate Authority Manager

    b.   MMC

    c.   A web browser

    d.   An email program

27. Which of the following options are not available after installing a certificate authority?

    a.   Rename the server

    b.   Move the server to a different domain

    c.   Revoke a certificate

    d.   Set up a subordinate CA

28. Which of the following utilities can be used to capture and view packets transmitted over the network?

    a.   Event Viewer

    b.   Network Monitor

    c.   IPSECMON

    d.   Performance Monitor

Network Infrastructure

29. Which of the following utilities can keep a count of encrypted bytes transmitted using IP Security?

    a.   Event Viewer

    b.   Network Monitor

    c.   IPSECMON

    d.   Performance Monitor

30. Which of the following utilities can display a list of application errors that have occurred?

    a.   Event Viewer

    b.   Network Monitor

    c.   IPSECMON

    d.   Performance Monitor

Case Study

Text Formatting Key:

- **Describes requirements**
- *Conflicts with requirement*
- Irrelevant background information

You are a network consultant working for the law firm of Figby, Tillman, and Figby. You are setting up a **new network** with **2 servers running Windows 2000 Server**, **15 workstations running Windows 2000 Professional**, and **various other computers running Windows 98** and *Linux*.

The network will span **two locations** with a *router and a WAN link* connecting them. One server will be placed at each location. Your goals are to create a **cohesive network** that will be **easy to administer and expand** in the future.

Multiple Choice

1. Which would be the best network transport protocol for the new network?

    a.   TCP/IP

    b.   IPX/SPX

    c.   NetBEUI

    d.   None of the above

2. You want to automatically assign IP addresses using DHCP. How many DHCP servers are required?

    a.   One

    b.   Two

    c.   None

3. Later, you are setting up a third location. You have added a server running Windows 2000 Server at the new location. The server has two network cards and has been connected to the WAN and to its local network. Which of the following additional hardware or software will be required to complete the configuration of the new location? (Select all that apply.)

    a.   Router

    b.   Routing and Remote Access installed on server

    c.   DHCP server installed on server

    d.   DHCP relay activated on server

Create a Tree

1. Place the following network protocols under the headings *Routable* and *Not Routable*.

    a.   TCP/IP

    b.   IPX/SPX

    c.   NetBEUI

    d.   AppleTalk

    e.   DLC

2. You are arranging for some of the workstations to be used remotely via dial-up connections. Place each of the following operating systems under the maximum level of dial-up security they can support: *CHAP, MS-CHAP,* or *MS-CHAP v2.*

    a.   Windows 95

    b.   Windows 98

    c.   Linux

    d.   Windows NT 4.0

    e.   Windows 2000 Professional

    f.   Windows 2000 Server

Answers

Comprehensive Test

1. a. TCP/IP is Windows 2000's default transport protocol.

2. a, b, d. TCP/IP, IPX/SPX, and AppleTalk are routable protocols. NetBEUI (choice c) is not routable.

3. c. DLC is not a network transport protocol; it is used mainly for mainframe communication and printing.

4. a, c. TCP and UDP are protocols at the Host-to-Host layer of the DoD model. IP and ICMP (choices b and d) operate at the Internet layer.

5. b. ARP (Address Resolution Protocol) translates IP addresses to MAC addresses. RARP (choice c) performs the opposite duty. IP and ICMP (choices a and d) are unrelated to this function.

6. d. HTTP operates at the Process/Application layer of the DoD model.

7. c. Class C provides for the greatest number of network addresses.

8. b. Subnetting divides the network into smaller segments. Supernetting (choice a) provides the opposite function, combining separate networks into a single network.

9. a. Supernetting combines several consecutive networks into a single network.

10. a, c, d. POP (Post Office Protocol), SMTP (Simple Mail Transport Protocol), and IMAP (Internet Mail Access Protocol) are used for email. SNMP (choice b) is used for network management.

11. b. IP filtering can block access to unauthorized ports or protocols. IPSec (choice a) is used for encrypted communication.

12. b. Dynamic routing uses routing protocols to maintain the routing table.

13. a, d. RIP (Router Information Protocol) and OSPF (Open Shortest Path First) are routing protocols.

14. b. The Require Security option does not allow unencrypted communication and is thus the most secure.

15. c. The HOSTS file is examined first in name resolution.

16. b, d. WINS (Windows Internet Naming Service) and the LMHOSTS file are used for NetBIOS resolution.

17. a, c. CSNW (Client Services for NetWare) and NWLink (IPX/SPX protocols) are included with Windows 2000 Professional. GSNW (choice b) is included with Windows 2000 Server. FPNW (choice d) is available separately from Microsoft.

18. b. GSNW (Gateway Services for NetWare) allows multiple Windows clients to access NetWare resources without NetWare client software.

19. b. A scope is a group of available IP addresses that can be issued by a DHCP server.

20. d. BAP (Bandwidth Allocation Protocol) is used to manage multilink connections.

21. c. MS-CHAP is the most secure authentication method.

22. a. NAT can be used to provide access to the Internet from a private network. ICS (choice c) provides similar features, but can only support one public IP address.

23. a, b, d. NAT provides address translation, IP address assignment, and allows incoming connections. Although NAT acts as a DNS server, it does not maintain a DNS database (choice c), but forwards DNS requests to a separate server.

24. c. ICS (Internet Connection Sharing) provides the same function as NAT and should not be used concurrently.

25. c, d. Enterprise CAs require Active Directory. Standalone CAs (choices a and b) do not.

26. c. Clients use a web browser to access the web interface and request a certificate.

27. a, b. Once Certificate Authority is installed, you cannot rename the server or move it to a different domain.

28. b. Network Monitor can be used to capture and view packets transmitted on the network.

29. c. IPSECMON can keep a count of encrypted bytes transmitted.

30. a. Event Viewer can display a list of application errors.

Case Study: Multiple Choice

1. a. TCP/IP would be the best choice of a transport protocol. It provides easy administration and works across the router. IPX/SPX (choice b) would work as well in these respects, but would not support the Linux workstations. NetBEUI (choice c) is not routable; it is supported only for legacy networks.

2. a. Only one DHCP server is required, because this is a small network. The remote subnet can access the DHCP server if the router supports DHCP forwarding, or by using a DHCP relay.

3. b, d. Routing and Remote Access should be installed on the server. Because this will act as a router, a hardware router (choice a) is not required. A DHCP server (choice c) is not required if you use a DHCP relay.

Case Study: Create a Tree

Create a Tree Answer # 1

Routable	Not Routable
TCP/IP	NetBEUI
IPX/SPX	DLC
AppleTalk	

Create a Tree Answer # 2

CHAP	MS-CHAP	MS-CHAP v2
Linux	Windows 95	Windows 2000 Professional
	Windows 98	Windows 2000 Server
	Windows NT 4.0	

Highlighter's Index

Network Protocols

TCP/IP

Named for protocols: Transport Control Protocol and Internet Protocol
Default protocol for Windows 2000
Routable
Uses logical (IP) addresses
New Windows 2000 features: enhanced PPTP, L2TP, and IPSec

IPX/SPX

Developed by Novell for NetWare
Default protocol in NetWare 4.x and earlier (NetWare 5 uses TCP/IP)
Supported in Windows 2000 by NWLink
Routable

NetBEUI

NetBIOS Extended User Interface
Developed by Microsoft for basic networking
Non-routable
Not used by default in Windows 2000

AppleTalk

Developed by Apple for Macintosh networking
Routable
Supported by Windows 2000 for Macintosh connectivity

DLC

Data Link Control
Developed by IBM for mainframe use
Used by some print servers
Non-routable; not a network transport option

IrDA

Used for short-distance infrared communication
Supported by Windows 2000, Windows 98/Me
Used primarily for laptop computers

TCP/IP

Network Access Layer

Handles physical network topology and media
Protocols: Ethernet, Token Ring, SLIP, PPP, Frame Relay, etc.

Internet Layer

Handles routing and communication between networks
IP (Internet Protocol): Combines data into packets; handles IP addressing
ICMP (Internet Control Message Protocol): Network management, diagnostics, and messaging
ARP (Address Resolution Protocol): Converts IP to MAC addresses
RARP (Reverse ARP): Converts MAC addresses to IP addresses
DHCP (Dynamic Host Configuration Protocol): Assigns IP addresses and other configuration.

Host-to-Host Layer

Provides a layer of abstraction in communication between hosts
Provides applications with a consistent interface
TCP: Connection-oriented, reliable, full-duplex
UDP: Connectionless, unreliable, slightly faster transmissions

Process/Application Layer

Supports applications and high-level services
Protocols: Telnet, FTP, TFTP, HTTP, NFS, DNS, SMTP, POP, IMAP, NNTP, SNMP, etc.

IP Address Classes

Class	Network/Host Bytes	Number of Networks	Number of Hosts per Network
A	1/3	126	16,777,214
B	2/2	16,382	65,534
C	3/1	2,097,150	254

Subnet Masking

Subdivides a network by using bits from host address

Number of subnets available: $2^{(number\ of\ bits)}-2$

Class	Default Subnet Mask
A	255.0.0.0
B	255.255.0.0
C	255.255.255.0

Private IP Address Ranges

Address Class	Starting Address	Ending Address
A	10.0.0.0	10.255.255.255
B	169.254.0.1	169.254.255.254
C	172.16.0.0	172.31.255.255
C	192.168.0.0	192.168.255.255

IP Filtering

Blocks access to unauthorized ports or protocols

Enabled by default

Can filter TCP ports, UDP ports, or protocols

IP Routing

Static Routing

Uses a static routing table.

Uses route command to maintain routes.

Routers do not communicate.

Dynamic Routing

Routers communicate using a routing protocol.

Routing table is created automatically.

RIP: Distance-vector routing.

RIP v2: Adds authentication and reduced bandwidth.

OSPF: Link state routing.

IPSec (IP Security)

IPSec Components

IPSec Policy Agent

ISAKMP/Oakley Key Management Service

IP Security Driver

IPSec Options

Client (Respond Only): Acts as a client when a server requests or requires a secure connection.

Secure Server (Require Security): Clients are required to use a secure connection.

Server (Request Security): Clients are requested to use a secure connection, and a standard non-secure connection is used if necessary.

IPSec Authentication Methods

Windows 2000 default (Kerberos)
Uses Kerberos v5 to authenticate the connection (default)

Use a certificate from this certificate authority
Uses certificate-based encryption; requires Certificate Server and a valid certificate authority (CA)

Use this string to protect the key exchange
Uses a pre-shared key; must be entered on both computers

Name Resolution

Hostname Resolution Order

1. Comparison with the local hostname
2. The HOSTS file
3. Any configured DNS servers
4. NetBIOS name resolution

NetBIOS Name Resolution Order

1. Local name cache
2. WINS Server
3. B-node broadcast
4. LMHOSTS file
5. Hostname resolution

DNS (Domain Name Service)

Internet standard for hostname resolution; requires a DNS server.
Windows 2000 Server includes DNS Server software.
Zone: Defined group of names and IP addresses.
At least one zone must be defined for use.
Configure with DNS Manager snap-in.

WINS (Windows Internet Naming Service)

Uses a dedicated server; WINS Server included with Windows 2000 Server.
Used with P-node, M-node, and H-node resolution.

Configure with WINS snap-in.
Clients require WINS server address.
Server address can be set with DHCP.

NetWare Connectivity

NWLink (IPX/SPX Protocols)
> The protocols used for NetWare connectivity.

Client Service for NetWare (CSNW)
> The NetWare client software included with Windows 2000 Professional.

Gateway Service for NetWare (GSNW)
> The NetWare client software included with Windows 2000 Server; GSNW also acts as a gateway to allow Windows NT/2000 clients to access NetWare resources.

Directory Services Migration Tool
> A tool for converting user accounts, files, and other information from a NetWare server to a Windows 2000 server.

File and Print Services for NetWare
> Allows a Windows 2000 computer and printer to service NetWare clients. FPNW is available separately from Microsoft.

DHCP (Dynamic Host Configuration Protocol)

DHCP Basics

Maintains a pool of addresses (scope) and assigns them dynamically.
Can assign IP address, subnet mask, default gateway, DNS server, WINS server.
Uses broadcasts and one or more DHCP servers.
Clients only need DHCP enabled; address of server is not required.
Manage with DHCP snap-in.

DHCP Features

Authorization: Windows 2000 authorizes DHCP servers; Windows 2000 Server DHCP service will not start without authorization.
Reservations: IP addresses can be reserved for specific computers.
Options: Sends gateway, DNS, and other information along with IP address.
DHCP relay: Forwards DHCP requests between subnets when a router is not configured to forward DHCP.
Dynamic DNS updates: DHCP server contacts DNS server to update addresses of clients; Windows 2000 clients can do this themselves.

Remote Access

Remote Access Basics

Supported in Windows 2000 by RRAS (Routing and Remote Access Services)

Managed using Routing and Remote Access snap-in

Supports dial-in and dial-out use; dial-in limited in Windows 2000 Professional

Authentication Methods

CHAP (Challenge Handshake Authentication Protocol)

An Internet-standard protocol that exchanges encrypted tokens for authentication.

MS-CHAP

Microsoft's proprietary version of CHAP, supported by Windows and Windows NT.

MS-CHAP v2

A new version of MS-CHAP, available only to Windows 2000 clients and servers.

Extensible Authentication Protocol (EAP)

A dynamic authentication protocol that can use certificates, smart cards, or other authenticated methods.

Unencrypted Authentication

Allows use of the PAP (Password Authentication Protocol) and SPAP (Shiva PAP) protocols (plain-text passwords).

Unauthenticated Access

If this option is enabled, clients can complete PPP connections with no authentication. It is disabled by default and is a serious security risk.

NAT (Network Address Translation)

NAT Features

Translation: Translates between public and private IP addresses

IP address assignment: Includes a simple DHCP server and can assign IP addresses to clients; uses private IP addresses

DNS name resolution: Acts as a DNS server; forwards DNS requests to an Internet DNS server and returns the results to clients.

NAT Versus ICS

- ICS uses a single checkbox rather than complex configuration information.

- ICS uses a fixed range of private IP addresses.

- ICS only allows one public IP address.

- ICS can only be used on one internal LAN interface.

Certificate Services

Basics

Part of Windows 2000's Public Key Infrastructure (PKI)
Windows 2000 Server can act as a CA
Manage using Certificate Authority Manager snap-in
Request certificates from web interface: *http://servername/certsrv/default.asp*

CA Types

Standalone root CA: Used when the organization will be issuing certificates to third parties; most trusted CA; can authorize subordinate CAs; does not require Active Directory
Standalone subordinate CA: Authorized by and subordinate to the root CA; does not require Active Directory
Enterprise root CA: Used when the organization issues certificates internally; highest authority; can authorize subordinate CAs; requires Active Directory
Enterprise subordinate CA: Authorized by and subordinate to the root CA; requires Active Directory

Network Monitoring

Network Monitor

Captures and displays packets
Only captures packets to or from the monitored computer
Components: Network Monitor Tools, Network Monitor Agent, Network Monitor Driver

Event Viewer

Application log

Includes events logged by applications, and problems such as application crashes.

Security log

Includes messages relating to security. Security problems, such as incorrect logons, are included in this log if auditing is enabled.

System log

Includes system error messages and status messages for system reboots and other events; includes system events if auditing is enabled.

IPSECMON

Available in Windows 2000 Professional or Server
Monitors an IPSec connection
Runs IPSECMON.EXE from command prompt or from Run prompt
Displays remote access policy list
Counts encrypted and authenticated bytes, errors, etc.

PART 5

Designing Active Directory

Exam Overview

The majority of Microsoft MCSE exams have been designed to test your knowledge of the hardware and software required for a functional and efficient networking environment. Although there were some short scenario questions that involved deciding which solution was best for a fictitious company, there was no real focus on how your decisions would affect the company in detail on a day-to-day basis and over the long term. You were never asked to make a compromise based on departmental chain of command or the type of IT staffing the company has on board. You were only concerned with the technical feasibility of a particular solution.

That has now changed. In an effort to make the tests a better judge of real-world performance, the actual business environment must be taken into account. Consider the Designing series of tests to be a middle-ground between the old MCSE tests and a Cisco exam where they put you into a room with a disabled network and say "Okay, you want to get certified . . . fix it."

Don't be afraid of these exams. Be afraid of your first two weeks on the job if you can't pass these exams. If you have any on-the-job experience in technical support or network administration, you'll be fine with the business end of these questions. You will, however, need to be very organized and be able to read through a list of requirements to decide the priority and feasibility of each piece of your solution. Just like real life. Be sure to have read the Active Directory chapter before you continue.

Objectives

Need to Know	Reference
How to analyze the business needs for a unified directory structure	"Analyzing the Company" on page 292
How to manage the interconnectivity of hardware and data	"Domain Structure" on page 297

Need to Know	Reference
How to analyze the geographic requirements of a business model	"Physical locations" on page 294
How to analyze business communication requirements	"Analyzing the Company" on page 292
How to analyze a company's IT infrastructure	"IT structure" on page 296
How to analyze Active Directory's interactions with other directory types	"Directory Services Overview" on page 290

Need to Apply	Reference
Plan a replication strategy	"Replication" on page 309
Plan a desktop operating system strategy	"Active Directory Architecture" on page 296
Analyze Active Directory's impact on the existing network	"Active Directory Architecture" on page 296
Design an Active Directory forest and tree structure	"Domain Structure" on page 297
Design an Active Directory naming scheme	"DNS Naming" on page 306
Design an Active Directory Organizational Unit structure	"Domain Structure" on page 297
Design the placement of operations masters	"Operations masters placement" on page 297
Design the placement of global catalog servers	"Global catalog server placement" on page 298
Design the placement of domain controllers	"Domain controller placement" on page 297
Design the placement of DNS servers	"Organizing a DNS structure" on page 306

Study Guide

This chapter includes the following sections, which address various topics covered on Exam 70-219, *Designing A Microsoft Windows 2000 Directory Services Infrastructure*:

Directory Services Overview
  Discusses the functionality and role of the Active Directory in a business environment. Compares Active Directory to the Windows NT directory model. Describes the major components that make up an Active Directory.

Balancing Technical and Business Requirements
  Describes the major focus of this exam: applying your knowledge of Active Directory to design a solution that meets the business needs of any organization, large or small.

Analyzing the Company
  Describes how to map an organization using the physical layout, the departmental structure, and the functional structure. It also describes how to evaluate the Information Technology structure and how that will impact the management of your solution.

Domain Structure
  Describes Windows 2000 security groups, Organizational Units, and Active Directory objects. Discusses the use of multiple domains and multiple domain trees. Describes the empty root domain tree structure, multiple forests, and multiple tree forests. Describes where to place domain controllers, operations masters, and global catalog servers.

Designing Trust Relationships
  Describes the use of transitive trusts within a forest and external trusts between forests. Also discusses shortcut trusts and the authentication issues involved with trust relationships.

Designing Group Policies

Describes the goals of an effective Group Policy architecture. Describes security group filtering and Group Policy blocking.

Delegating Authority

Describes how to transfer object ownership and distribute responsibility throughout the Active Directory. Also describes permission inheritance issues.

DNS Naming

Describes how to organize a Domain Name Service naming structure for Active Directory. Also describes child and parent domains and efficient naming practices.

Schema Modification

Describes the relationship between attribute-schema objects and class-schema objects. Also describes how applications can modify the schema and how to manage and modify schema definitions through the Microsoft Management Console.

Replication

Describes how data is replicated between domain controllers throughout the Active Directory. Describes how to optimize site topology to decrease network traffic. Describes site links, site link bridges, and bridgehead servers. In addition to the replication information available in this section, I've described the implications that certain design choices have on replication performance in their respective sections throughout the chapter.

Directory Services Overview

Active Directory defines and arranges all of the elements of the network. It creates a single hierarchical database of the physical components, user accounts, programs, and data. It makes defining relationships and rules flexible through the use of organizational units, inherited permissions, and trusts. You'll need to have a firm grasp on the organizational qualities of Active Directory before you can blend in the business requirements to design a complete directory solution. This chapter helps reinforce how Active Directory is modeled and concentrates on leveraging Active Directory in real-world business scenarios.

Active Directory Versus the NT Domain Model

The Windows NT domain model included primary domain controllers (PDCs) and backup domain controllers (BDCs), which could only be linked by a series of one-way trusts. The PDC acted as a master server, while the BDCs acted in a subordinate way. Windows 2000 has a much more distributed, peer-to-peer relationship among its servers.

The wiring and physical layout of NT networks was often influenced and somewhat limited by the older, more strictly structured NT domain model. Windows 2000 allows for a lot more flexibility in the placement and functionality of servers. The processes that used to run mostly on the NT PDC can be reassigned to other servers in a much more flexible way. This also allows for a more robust replication environment, with servers disregarding traditional domain borders and replicating over the most efficient routes, based on how much bandwidth is currently available.

In an Active Directory network, all the Windows 2000 servers are essentially peers. Trusts are two-way, and the network is arranged in a tree structure with a true DNS naming scheme, just like on the Internet. This setup is much more flexible than the old NT domain model; and, as you'll see later, it will give you more options for planning to meet the complex business requirements discussed later in this chapter.

Windows 2000 is moving toward embracing the open Internet networking standards, like DNS, Kerberos, and Telnet. Microsoft could have gone much further by providing for more interoperability with open standards, but these are big steps in the right direction for making the "CSE" portion of your title more important than the leading "M."

Active Directory Components

You'll need to be absolutely comfortable with the following terms throughout the rest of the chapter:

- Domain
- Forest
- Tree
- Organizational Unit
- Object

If you have any questions about the definition and practical use of these components, you'll find them covered in detail in the Active Directory chapter. This chapter and this test will concentrate heavily on the implementation of these basic building blocks of Active Directory as they apply to achieving specific business goals. The ability to translate business requirements into an Active Directory design is stressed in almost all of the questions. Some questions will go into great detail describing multiple business requirements, goals, and wishes. If you can quickly associate the AD component with a particular need, it will make designing the overall solution much easier.

ON THE EXAM

Always write down the business requirements in the long questions. A single missed requirement buried deep within a question will ruin a solution that meets every other aspect of what the company wanted you to accomplish. MCSE questions are often overly long and have confusing sentence structure. Don't be tempted to skip past seemingly unimportant filler when you read the questions.

Balancing Technical and Business Requirements

If you've never actually worked in or managed an IT department, you'll be at a bit of a disadvantage while taking this test. Many of the questions will involve giving you a series of requests and requirements, along with an overall goal. You'll be asked to make judgement calls based on not only what is technically possible, but what makes the most sense given the structure and politics of the people side of the business.

ON THE EXAM

The test questions are very in-depth, and you'll probably have to take notes. The first thing you should do is read the whole question through and write down only what is required. By separating this out, when you read through the question the second time, you can eliminate any conflicting goals from the proposed solution.

Always keep it in the back of your mind that Microsoft is aiming this exam at the network architect, rather than the IT staff that will actually run the network on a day-to-day basis. You have to think like a consultant for this exam. Organization and judgment are top priorities.

Analyzing the Company

Now that I've thoroughly emphasized the different approach you'll have to take on this exam, it's time to get to work on what skills you'll have to display to be successful.

The first task is to gather information about the company. There are three general categories you'll need to look at:

Requirements and goals
> You'll need to make a list of everything that is required, such as limited access to the billing system and nightly backups. You'll also need to prioritize a list of goals that must not conflict with the requirements. Goals might include the ability to access files from a certain branch office. You'll have to decide whether the security and physical structure of the network will allow for that goal to be included, given the strict adherence to the requirements. No number of secondary goals is equal to the importance of a single requirement.

Planning for the future
> Active Directory is modular, so growth or reorganization is usually easily accommodated. The one area where you'll have to be particularly careful is planning replication sites. They have very specific bandwidth requirements, and growth can disrupt the process and require the addition of expensive dedicated circuits, like T1, DSL, or coaxial cable connections. Adding an

Ethernet hub and some Cat5 cable is usually not an issue, but be careful if you're replicating between remote locations. I can't think of a single question that has ever mentioned downsizing, so when questions talk about the future, plan on managing growth.

Business structure and personnel considerations

It is fairly straightforward to model an Organizational Unit (OU) structure after the company's departmental structure. Permissions can usually be inherited by departments intact, but it gets a bit more complex when companies have more than one location with similar departments and managers who need access to multiple departments in multiple domain trees. You can also manage business modeling efficiently using the empty root domain structure discussed later in this chapter.

Microsoft has included a bit of jargon to help you organize your notes when designing a solution. The jargon will probably show up, so it's a good idea to memorize these decisions. Also, the authors of the questions will probably have this model in mind when designing the questions, so using the same model may make deciphering the questions a bit easier.

Remember that some of the questions will be quite long and include several pages of requirements, goals, suggestions, and distracting filler. By using the four-point model shown in Table 5-1, you may be better able to prioritize both the requirements and the secondary goals.

ON THE EXAM

For many of the questions, you won't be able to see all of the text on the screen at once. Be sure to ask the test center for at least two or three pages to take notes on before you start. I once had to bang on the glass partition repeatedly and with increasing vigor to finally get the attention of the test center receptionist to give me another page for notes.

Table 5-1: Analyzing Your Notes

Analysis Step	Purpose
Decision point	An individual item that is either required or suggested. You should separate the requirements from the goals and then prioritize the goals, grouping them so the goals that aren't mutually exclusive are listed together. You can then score each group of goals by importance and create a packaged solution.
Implications	When you score the goals, be sure to take into account the effect that each goal has on the implementation of the others. If one goal would negatively impact many other goals, you may want to reconsider, even if the first individual goal is slightly more important than individual goals in the group it affects.

Table 5-1: Analyzing Your Notes (continued)

Analysis Step	Purpose
Risks	You have to consider both the technical and financial costs of each solution. If adding a convenience feature poses an undue security risk, a client such as a lawyer or a bank has to abandon that feature.
Trade-offs	On the questions, you'll sometimes have one group that wants a feature that could adversely affect another group. You'll have to do your best to weigh all of the options and be very careful with the precise wording of these sorts of questions.

Mapping Organizational Structure

You should make a chart of all the departments, who is in them, and what their job functions are. You should also determine all of the data- and equipment-sharing relationships between departments. If two departments need to share access to the same network resources, that should be considered when you design the Organizational Unit (OU) structure.

There are a few different ways to map the structure of an organization, and you may not be able to immediately pick out which way is best. In the next sections, you'll find descriptions of the common ways to map an organization.

IN THE REAL WORLD

Although I've listed the different ways of mapping a company separately, don't forget that you have the freedom to combine these techniques to form a hybrid structure. Most businesses have a functional structure that blurs the lines between departments, while retaining relatively strict departmental administrative and budgetary boundaries.

Physical locations

Because almost every organization has different departments, but not every company has multiple locations, it may be easier to start with locations. If a company has multiple physical locations, especially if the different physical locations have the same departments, you may want to create a physical locations chart first and have it handy when making the functional chart.

After you define all the physical locations, you'll want to map out the network connections available between them. For Active Directory to function efficiently, high-speed replication of network data is a must. If a remote location has a slow or intermittent connection to the rest of the organization, that will have to be resolved before they can fully participate in the AD. Careful placement of servers can often overcome some weakness in the bandwidth available for remote sites, especially in the case of domain controllers' being able to handle user logon traffic locally, without having to cross the slow connection for authentication.

By creating a physical locations map first, then overlaying the departmental structure afterwards, you may find a more efficient way to organize the communication, workload, and administration of the company as a whole. Mapping how information flows through the physical and departmental charts can be a real eye-opener for an organization. If you get the brick and mortar company organized before you start designing an Active Directory, creating the AD structure will be a vastly easier task.

Departmental structure

Within each physical location, you should chart the different departments and interview the managers and employees to find out which resources they need access to and which they need to share with other departments. The main departmental divisions will likely be the main OU divisions, so access permissions planning is a must at the departmental level. Always try to assign permissions to the largest groups possible for easier administration.

The advantages of the departmental structure are that it's very easy to convert to an OU structure, employees are already familiar with it, and employee transfers between departments are easy. Assuming the departmental manager has the necessary knowledge, departmental OU structure also facilitates the delegation of authority to local department managers.

Functional structure

The Active Directory system is all about managing data. How does it go from place to place and who has access to it? The division of data access does not always follow strict departmental lines. If the company is designed in such a way that billing and sales need access to customer financial records and customer service and technical support need access to customer product records, you can divide by function rather than department. Instead of having four separate OUs based on department, you may be better off with two OUs, based on the data they need to access.

Don't forget that OUs are automatically arranged in a hierarchical structure with permissions inheritance. You can create top level OUs based on the data they need to access and lower level OUs by department. Then you can move an entire department in and out of data access OUs whenever the department's needs change.

Because permissions would be automatically inherited from the top level data access OU to the lower level departmental OU, you wouldn't have to change permissions for employees on an individual basis. They would inherit permissions from their departmental OU, which in turn inherits permissions from the data access OU.

Most of the time departments have many unrelated or conflicting functions that may cause this type of organization to be difficult, if not impossible, to create and maintain. Technically, you can block some permissions inheritance to solve these types of problems, but experience has shown that repeated blocking of permissions inheritance is more trouble than it's worth.

The whole point of the OU structure is to have a clean, inherited, hierarchical structure. The more you alter this by blocking permissions inheritance, the more it resembles the old group-based permissions scheme. The larger the organization, the more difficult it becomes to do it the old way.

IT structure

This exam will probably make you feel like a consultant. Microsoft wants you to be able to design an Active Directory solution that can be managed by someone other than yourself, namely the IT staff at the fictitious enterprise mentioned in their questions. There are several types of IT management structures based on the size and purpose of the company. They are described in Table 5-2. You'll need to know about each one and how it will impact your decision making.

Table 5-2: IT Structure Types

Type	Definition	Issues
Centralized	All IT decisions and operations are handled by a single department in a single location.	Good communication with outside departments and locations is essential.
Decentralized	IT decisions are handled independently at each location.	Interoperability, security, and cooperation are essential.
Mixed	IT management is distributed, but technology is relatively consistent.	Affected by both the centralized and the decentralized issues.
Outsourced	IT decisions are implemented and maintained by an outside interest.	Response time and communication are essential.

Remember that you can mix and match these structuring techniques to create a hybrid structure. It's often easiest to divide first by location, then by department, and finally by function. In any case, you may be better off creating all three charts and checking to see if the IT structure tips the scales at all.

Active Directory Architecture

For this exam, you are asked to be a network architect. The process of learning how to design an efficient and effective Active Directory follows the same pattern as learning a foreign language. Consider someone asking you a question in a foreign language. When you are just learning a new language, you have to translate, think in your native language, and translate again to respond. When you become fluent, you begin to think in the foreign language. With practice, you will become a much more efficient conversationalist, and eventually you'll talk as fast as a native speaker.

As far as being a network architect goes, the proper use of concepts like Organizational Units and permissions inheritance should become as familiar to you as the placement of windows and walls are to a traditional architect. Once you've reached that point, you'll be able to look beyond the complexities of what makes up an Active Directory and directly translate physical locations, departments, and job duties into trees, Organizational Units, and domain local groups.

Domain Structure

You'll need a solid understanding of the objects in the domain structure and how they relate to and interact with each other. The topics covered on the Windows 2000 MCSE tests overlap much more than they did on the older exams. Microsoft has interwoven the Networking Essentials, DNS, Active Directory, and Security topics throughout all of the exams. Although Active Directory and Security have their own tests, you'll need to know how Organizational Units, permissions inheritance, and Group Policies work for almost all of the exams, including this one.

Domain controller placement

Domain controllers authenticate users and perform many other administrative functions that keep AD running smoothly. If at all possible, you should try to include one domain controller for each replication site where interactive logins occur. Funneling all the login traffic for a network into a small number of remote computers significantly decreases overall network performance and user satisfaction.

Domain controllers tend to use more expensive hardware than typical workstations. If cost is an issue and you are limited in the number of domain controllers, don't skimp on the connectivity speed between domain controllers. If you are using an Ethernet network, try to have 100 Mbit connections between domain controllers and, if possible, across the entire network.

Operations masters placement

The first domain controller in an Active Directory network usually hosts the different operations master roles. There are a few different types of operations masters, and they aren't all used or manually modified very often. You can usually just allow the first domain controller to retain the operations master's functions.

Active
Directory

IN THE REAL WORLD

Although you probably won't deal with operations masters on a regular basis and you can usually keep the default settings, there is one thing to be especially careful of: be sure that a domain controller that is acting as an infrastructure master is not also acting as a global catalog server. This may interfere with the infrastructure master's ability to cross-reference changes to objects on the network.

Global catalog server placement

Global catalog servers keep track of just about everything to do with objects and replicate that information on a regular basis. This means that global catalog servers need a lot of bandwidth. You have to strike a balance between the number of global catalog servers and the amount of available bandwidth you have supporting them.

The more global catalog servers you have, the faster the response for each request, assuming there is enough bandwidth to run at full capacity with room to spare for periodic fluctuations in network traffic.

Multiple domains

Although it's possible to have multiple domains sharing a single Active Directory, most of the time a well-designed single domain with multiple subdomains is an easier and more efficient solution to create and maintain. Active Directory can encompass multiple domains, sites, and forests. This can become very complex, so if you're given a choice between single or multiple domains, always choose single unless there is a compelling reason to do otherwise. In a few cases, a multiple domain strategy is the best solution:

Remote locations
> If remote locations have low bandwidth connections between them, the frequent replication traffic generated in a single domain setup may be enough to overwhelm the connection. The cost of maintaining faster interconnection lines may outweigh the benefits of a single domain, especially if each location has qualified network administrators already on staff.

Limited partnerships
> If two essentially separate organizations want to keep their own administrative controls in place, a multiple domain setup would keep domain Administrator accounts separate. This is especially important if companies are keeping secrets from one another.

Policy separation
> If one company has a more stringent password policy, it may be necessary for the security of one company and the convenience of another to keep the policies separate. The only way to do that is with separate domains. For example, suppose a defense contractor requires passwords of at least 10 random characters changed every 48 hours without reusing the same password. The less sensitive areas of the company may not want such a strict policy.

Multiple domain trees

Domains within an Active Directory are automatically arranged in a hierarchical tree structure. The first domain in a tree is called a *root tree*. Every domain tree has a single root tree. Root trees and their child domains can be linked into a forest of domain trees. All trees in the forest have two-way transitive trust relationships, which means all user accounts in a forest can potentially access all resources in all domains in the forest.

The domain that will act as the root tree is created first. Most of the time, the root domain contains many of the resources and structures that will be used throughout all the child domains. You can name the root domain with the company name and create child domains for each department within a company. Sometimes, a company will want to further separate the branches of a tree from a common root domain without resorting to creating a multiple tree domain. This is made possible by creating an *empty root domain.*

Empty root domains

Suppose two companies merge and they want to have the benefits of automatic two-way trusts and a single domain tree while still maintaining a bit of separation between each domain. If the departmental structure of the companies is quite different, it might be easier not to have a common Organizational Unit structure.

If the first domain in a tree is left relatively empty, the child domains will be starting with a nearly clean organizational slate. This is a good way of organizing a company with one name and many separate divisions. In a smaller company, the same principle applies to a single domain's Organizational Unit structure. Each parent OU can be separated from the other's while still being connected with a hierarchical tree structure.

IN THE REAL WORLD

An empty root domain configuration separates the master administrator account from the administrator account of each child domain. If you want to give relative autonomy to local administrators within each of the company's divisions, yet keep them from all having control over each other's subdomains, keep the root domain's Administrator account tightly controlled and let each location create an Administrator account for each subdomain independent of one another.

Multiple forests

You probably won't want to create a multiple forest structure for a single organization, regardless of how many divisions they have. Because they only allow for specific one-way trusts between two domains, linking the forests can be an administrative nightmare. In a few specific cases, a multiple forest may be your best option:

- If two forests need to set up a limited relationship between a small number of domains, but otherwise remain autonomous, having a few one-way trusts is an acceptable way to share information.

- If two large and complex forests already exist and companies are merging, the pragmatic approach may be to just link the domains that need to be linked on a case-by-case basis as the merger goes through. You should document each other's network for a potential full merger in the future.

Make sure that the domains linked in a multiple-forest trust relationship have sufficient bandwidth between them to handle the amount of traffic passing between the two networks. If users in one domain can have access to the other, but not vice versa, check to make sure you have two separate one-way external trust relationships.

Multiple-tree forests

Many businesses have a central ownership, but have separate names to describe each division. It is especially important to maintain name identification throughout the company if you choose to use the same domains for internal and external use. You can maintain brand identity through separate names while maintaining all the benefits of a single forest structure by naming each domain root for each separate division.

A multiple-tree forest is far easier to manage than a multiple forest. All trust relationships are two-way and are configured automatically. Replication among domains is easy to accomplish by the strategic division of replication sites that can encompass just about any well connected area of the forest, regardless of domain.

Organizational Units

An Organizational Unit (OU) is a group of related objects that share access permissions. They are used similarly to the way groups were used in Windows NT, except that OUs can contain just about any type of object, not only user accounts.

Organizational Units provide a logical way to group and collectively manage such network resources as user accounts, files, folders, and printers. Usually, the OU matches a real-life department or team within a company. There are many benefits to dividing up the Active Directory into OUs.

The most obvious benefit is the ability to quickly map a company's departmental structure to permissions-based groups, where all the objects that need to perform job functions can be administered together as a unit.

The other benefit is the ability to easily delegate authority. You can assign administrator-like privileges to the manager of the web design department for all the scanners, printers, and web directories used by the department without giving that manager an Administrator account for the whole network.

By repeating this process, you can allow departmental managers to have day-to-day control over their work environment without any undue security risks. This will free more time for you to manage, monitor, and maintain the network as a whole without micromanaging every department.

The best part is that, when a new resource or employee is added or removed, you can simply drag and drop that resource in or out of the OU. What you'll do is create a domain for the company, create subdomains where appropriate, and divide the remaining resources into OUs based on departmental divisions.

Objects

This is the easiest component to remember. Any individual network resource in the Active Directory is considered an object. User accounts, files, folders, printers, and Organizational Units are all objects.

Objects have properties that describe what they are and permissions to control who has access to them. Objects can generally be moved around the Active Directory by dragging and dropping them in the Microsoft Management Console (MMC). The definitions of all objects are stored in the schema, which is covered in more detail later in this chapter as well as in other sections of the book.

Windows 2000 groups

It's a lot easier to manage security for a group of similar users rather than to assign permissions to each individual user account. Windows 2000 has three types of security groups detailed in Table 5-3.

Table 5-3: Security Groups

Group	Description
Domain local	Used to grant permissions within only the local domain. May contain user accounts and global groups from any trusted domain. Permissions granted are valid only within the local domain, regardless of where the account or group originated.
Global	Used to grant permissions across the entire forest. May contain only global groups and user accounts. Replicates only the group name between domains, not the group membership list, so replication traffic is less than with universal groups.
Universal	Used to grant permissions across the entire forest. Usually contains other groups, rather than individual user accounts. Can contain any type of group. Must replicate to all domains in the forest, so frequent changes to group membership can generate significant network traffic.

All of the groups can contain other groups. Putting one group inside another is called *nesting*. Nesting is an efficient way to manage permissions for a large number of users while limiting the number of groups you have to directly manage on a regular basis. You can take the following approach to help organize groups:

1. Start by adding user accounts to global groups by department or job function.

2. If more than one department needs access to the same resources, nest the departmental global groups into a larger global group. Try to minimize the total number of independent global groups by nesting as many as possible. Keeping track of permissions will be easier with fewer separate groups.

3. If you can see a need for universal groups, add the global groups to universal groups; otherwise, simply add the global groups to the appropriate domain local groups to lessen replication traffic, as compared to just using universal groups to distribute permissions across the forest.

4. Once all the user accounts are grouped as efficiently as possible, start granting the needed permissions and test to make sure everyone can access what they are supposed to and nothing else.

5. After everything is running smoothly, you can delegate control of departmental group membership to each department head. Changes at the departmental level automatically replicate up through the group structure, and you should have a nearly self-sufficient group structure.

Designing Trust Relationships

The ability to share information securely and conveniently is important to almost all businesses. Windows 2000's trust scheme will make it a bit easier to manage than the cumbersome NT trust scheme. You'll still need to map out which domains need to trust which and whether or not those domains are within the same forest. There are two main types of trust relationships in Windows 2000, *transitive* and *external*. There is also a third type, called a *shortcut trust*, which I'll discuss later.

Transitive trusts

Transitive trusts are by far the most common type of trusts you'll run into. They are automatically created between parent and child domains within a tree structure and between domain roots. This means that every domain within a forest automatically has a two-way trust relationship with every other domain in the forest. This is why it is so important that permissions be assigned properly, especially if certain domains in the forest need tight security.

External trusts

Sometimes domains in different forests need to trust each other. This type of relationship is not automatic. There are a couple of rules you'll need to know about external trusts in order to determine if they meet a company's goals:

1. External trusts are one-way only. If you need a two-way external trust, you have to create two separate one-way trusts between domains in different forests.

2. External trusts only connect two domains in different forests. The transitive trust relationships that each domain shares within its own forest are not shared by the remote domain. The rest of the domains in each forest are isolated from the remote computer.

Authentication issues

The Active Directory uses a totally different method of authentication than Windows NT. Windows 2000 uses the Kerberos model of authentication, which involves the use of keys. The Kerberos model is discussed throughout the book and in detail in the security chapter.

Only Windows 2000 networks running in native mode can take full advantage of all the trust relationships described in this section. When attempting to make a trust relationship with a remote Windows 2000 domain, be sure to check to see if their network is in mixed mode or native mode.

Shortcut trusts

All child domains have a transitive trust with their parent domains, but domains may be in different trees with several transitive trusts separating them from each other. This can cause more authentication overhead than is necessary. Active Directory allows you to specifically create a two-way transitive trust between two domains within the forest without having to rely on the series of two-way transitive trusts that automatically link them via the tree structure.

IN THE REAL WORLD

If two domains will often need to share information and user logins, it will reduce authentication traffic if you specify a shortcut trust between them. You can use an SMTP program to analyze traffic on the network before and after you create a shortcut trust, to quantify the benefits. If you see large benefits, you may want to add more shortcut domains.

Designing Group Policies

When you are designing a Group Policy, you'll have to figure out what the company's priorities are. You'll need to weigh several options: security vs. convenience, control vs. flexibility, and up-front effort vs. recurring effort. As a consultant, you might run into a client who wants security, convenience, flexibility, and control with maximum up-front effort (yours) and minimal recurring effort (theirs). This is not possible with Group Policies.

The main sticking points are security and flexibility. If you want to restrict access to objects on the network, the people who have permission must make the changes themselves. This is more secure, but it diminishes convenience. Consider this situation:

Your supervisor calls to tell you her son has broken his arm and she's on the way to the hospital. You'll have to give her sales presentation to the assembled crowd in twenty minutes. You try to open sales.ppt and get "Permission Denied." No problem, just call the Network Administration department to change permissions. The last you checked, there were three network administrators, but when you call them you find out that one is on vacation, one's out on an emergency hardware installation 45 miles away, and the third one quit yesterday.

The alternative extreme can result in having a disgruntled employee modify the sales presentation to include just about anything. Your job is to explain this and convince the company to balance the needs of security and convenience by allowing you to implement a responsible Group Policy structure.

It's almost always easier to apply permissions to groups of similar users, rather than to each individual user on a case-by-case basis. Windows 2000 gives you many different types of groups to choose from. Groups are smaller divisions than Organizational Units and only contain user accounts, whereas OUs can contain all kinds of objects. No matter which groups you use, the reasons for the policies will remain the same. Getting to know what the policies can do will help you determine which groups to use. Group Policies are applied through the use of a Group Policy Object (GPO) containing the rules that make up the policy.

Group Policy goals

Group Policies can be used to define which programs are to be installed on which computers. This can be done by department, with web development getting Photoshop and Flash, sales getting Outlook and Excel, and technical support getting Quake. Actually, the Group Policy can be used to make sure technical support doesn't install unauthorized programs, which brings us to another of GPO's benefits: security.

Group Policies can allow certain users to log in to any workstation and have access to only their authorized applications, regardless of whether the unauthorized application is installed on the workstation that they are locally logged in to. GPOs can also restrict physical and remote access to sensitive computers, such as domain controllers.

IN THE REAL WORLD

Group Policies are inherited throughout the Active Directory. Although Group Policy Objects can be applied at the domain or site level, you may be better off applying most policies at the OU level to give yourself greater flexibility. Remember that a Deny permission overrides all others.

If you've created the OU structure to match the company's real-world departmental structure, assigning permissions by OU is a convenient way to provide access to those who need it and deny access to everyone else. Also, if you arrange to have the employee transfer process include a notification to the network administrator, employees can be moved in and out of OUs faster than they can clean out their cubicle.

ON THE EXAM

Be careful if a Group Policy is applied on the site level. A site level GPO affects the whole local domain, and, because a site can span multiple domains, a Group Policy change at that level can have wide-ranging effects. Only the Enterprise Admins group can apply Group Policies at the site level.

If you want to create a Group Policy that applies to the whole domain or multiple domains, it's better to apply the policy on the domain level rather than the site level. This is more work initially, because Group Policies only apply to the local domain. You'll have to apply the same policy to each domain separately. This should help avoid accidental policy application.

Overall, I think the best approach is to apply no Group Policies at the site level, general policies at the domain level, and specific policies at the OU level. This hierarchical approach has less risk and gives you more granular control over policies. The up-front investment in time usually pays off later.

IN THE REAL WORLD

Group Policy Objects add to the network traffic and can increase login times, especially if policies are applied across multiple domains. Try to draft as few policies as possible, but remember that combining too many rules in a single policy can make assigning policies to slightly different groups problematic.

Security group filtering

Members of a security group can be prevented from inheriting a GPO, even it if applies to their entire domain. This is especially useful for users with elevated privileges who need to retain access to secure objects.

Group Policy blocking

In addition to blocking GPOs with security groups, you can also block GPOs at the OU level. Normally, Group Policies are automatically inherited from any parent OU. You can set an OU to block policy inheritance, but it only works if the parent OU doesn't have a No Override setting. You're better off just taking the time to plan Group Policies thoroughly, rather than worrying about whether or not they will apply and what the exceptions are.

Delegating Authority

Everything in Active Directory is an object that has an access list of permissions. Efficiently assigning these permissions can save you and the users a lot of grief in the day-to-day operations of the network. There are a few different strategies for designing a delegation scheme.

You need to transfer, or *delegate*, the authority to access objects throughout the Active Directory. These objects can number into the hundreds of thousands in moderate sized businesses. Properly grouping and then assigning permissions by group is essential. How you divide the groups depends on the type of organization and the type of objects you're dealing with.

Object ownership

The first step to creating a solid delegation plan is to create an inventory of the type and number of objects you have. Every object must be owned by somebody who will be responsible for its safekeeping. If you find an object that is improperly owned, a member of the Domain Administrators group can take ownership and temporarily or permanently assign ownership to themselves or another user.

You can delegate permissions by object or by task. A task might be backing up files or clearing a print spool. Task-based delegation is generally more difficult and time consuming, so it is used much less frequently than object-based delegation.

Permissions inheritance

Objects automatically inherit permissions from their containers further up the AD structure. Sometimes, it is necessary to prevent this from happening. Be very careful if you block permissions inheritance, because if you forget you did it, making a change to the parent object will no longer be passed on down the line to the blocked object. Be sure to document every case of blocked inheritance.

IN THE REAL WORLD

Blocking inheritance is particularly dangerous when a subsequent No Access permission is assigned to a parent container. The child objects that were blocked from inheriting permissions will still have access to the object even though their parent container doesn't. Without proper documentation procedures, this can easily go unnoticed until it's too late.

DNS Naming

If you have experience with the Domain Name System (DNS) used on the Internet, you'll have no problem designing a DNS naming scheme for your Active Directory. The first thing you'll have to decide is whether or not you'll be using the same domain name for the internally (company) and externally (Internet) accessible network resources.

IN THE REAL WORLD

Many companies choose to use different domain names for their internal and external networks. Often, companies will use non-routable (from the outside world) IP addresses for their internal network and create a gateway or proxy server to act as a buffer to the Internet. Internally, some companies use a non-Internet protocol, such as IPX/SPX, to prevent open TCP/IP access to parts of their network.

Organizing a DNS structure

One of the simplest and most effect ways to organize a hierarchical naming scheme like DNS is to mirror the actual geographic and departmental hierarchy of the company. You have to take into account whether or not the business wants to use the same domain name for internal and Internet addressing. Table 5-4 shows an example of DNS Naming Scheme.

Table 5-4: DNS Naming Scheme

Company Breakdown	DNS Name Used
Parent company name: O'Reilly & Associates	oreilly.com
Geographic locations: Sebastopol, Cambridge	sebastopol.oreilly.com cambridge.oreilly.com
Sebastopol's Departments: editorial, production, and marketing	editorial.sebastopol.oreilly.com production.sebastopol.oreilly.com marketing.sebastopol.oreilly.com

The DNS naming system is from left to right, specific to general. A final example would be if the marketing office in Sebastopol had a server named zookeeper. In that case, that server's DNS address would be zookeeper.marketing.sebastopol.oreilly.com. Every unique DNS name has to have a unique Internet Protocol (IP) address.

You'll notice that the parent company name is part of all the subdomain names. You can create as many subdomains as you'd like. However, you cannot change the original parent domain name. The name is called the *forest root* domain.

Because the forest root domain name cannot be changed, if the company is going to merge or otherwise change names in the near future, you may want to consider registering the new name and using it internally, especially if it's going to be a hyphenated name. When the merger is finalized, the new domain name can be made public.

If you choose to use the same domain name both internally and externally, you'll probably want to set up a *firewall*. A firewall can separate DNS *zones* from one another. You may put network resources in any zone you'd like and make any zone either public (accessible from the Internet) or private (accessible only from within your local network).

If the company wants the least amount of risk, you should suggest that they use separate domain names for internal and external use. It's conceivable that a resource could be accidentally (or intentionally) put in the wrong DNS zone or otherwise made accessible to the outside world. Not only is the use of separate internal and external domain names a bit more secure, it makes it easy to determine which resources are public just by the domain name.

Schema Modification

The *schema* is a database that contains a listing of all the types of objects and their properties. The schema determines which properties are both necessary and optional for each object. A faulty schema modification can have a disastrous and unexpected impact across the entire AD. If you're not absolutely sure of all the possible consequences a particular schema modification can cause, don't even consider doing it.

Some AD aware programs will modify the schema to include new functionality. New types of objects with different access permissions may be needed as technology changes. The ability to modify AD's schema is mostly for future compatibility. Most installations will never have to be modified directly. You should still understand how the schema works, because applications you install may be modifying it for you.

Attribute-schema objects

The attribute-schema objects define the rules and structure of an attribute of an object. A folder is an object that needs many different attributes to describe it in its entirety. Each attribute, such as its name, will need rules to define it and make sure it behaves in a similar way to all other folders. Can a folder have the same name as another folder in the same location? How long can that name be? These attributes can be combined into a group called a *class*.

Class-schema objects

An object usually has multiple attributes. Because each attribute is defined in a separate attribute-schema object, these objects have to be unified to create an encompassing definition of the familiar object, such as a file, folder, or user account. The collection of attribute-schema objects that define a common object (like a folder) is called a class-schema object.

A class-schema object can require certain attribute-schema objects and allow others if needed. For example, a file has to have a name, but not necessarily an application-mapped file extension.

Class-schema objects also determine the structural hierarchy attributes of an object. You can put a file in a folder or a folder in a folder, but you can't put a folder in a file.

IN THE REAL WORLD

Compression programs like WinZip can take folder structures, put them in a compressed file, and restore them later. WinZip modifies the normal way Windows stores files and folders. This is done without modification to the Active Directory schema.

Modifying the schema

There are two ways the schema can be modified: by using the Active Directory Schema snap-in for the Microsoft Management Console (MMC) or through the installation of an application that modifies the schema automatically. Objects in the schema have a unique identification number called an *object identifier*. There is a worldwide hierarchical numbering scheme that is similar to the IP address system used on the Internet. The International Organization for Standardization (ISO), an international standards body, maintains this hierarchy and can assign numbers for use in the schema.

The are a few potentially negative side effects of modifying the schema that you should consider. Before you change the attributes of an object, check to make sure you won't have conflicts with existing objects. Modifying the schema requires that all domain controllers replicate the change. This can cause a lot of traffic, so you may want to time it when network usage is low. Also, replication is not instantaneous throughout the domain, so inconsistencies can occur until the replication is completed.

Replication

A Windows 2000 network consists of peer-to-peer domain controllers. There is no longer an NT-style hierarchy of primary domain controllers and backup domain controllers. The Windows 2000 domain controllers need to exchange information among themselves on a regular basis. Unlike OUs, which are best designed to match the departmental makeup, replication sites have to be designed to physically link over a fast part of the network regardless of departmental boundaries.

Sites

Sites are the basic physical structures that allow the replication of data on the network. The strategy for creating an efficient replication environment is fairly straightforward: find the best available bandwidth between potential sites, look at bandwidth utilization on each subnet, and link sites accordingly. Your goal is to link sites so that they have the greatest bandwidth between them (see Table 5-5).

Table 5-5: Site Replication Strategy

Domain Controller Name	Average Available Bandwidth to DCA	Average Available Bandwidth to DCB	Average Available Bandwidth to DCC
DCA	N/A	7.8 Mbit	5.2 Mbit
DCB	7.8 Mbit	N/A	6.1 Mbit
DCC	5.2 Mbit	6.1 Mbit	N/A

By creating a table like Table 5-5, you can easily to see that you want to avoid the DCA to DCC connection of 5.2 Mbit and link DCA to DCB at 7.8 Mbit and DCB to DCC at 6.1 Mbit. Keep in mind that bandwidth usage can change very rapidly on a network, and you should consistently monitor network utilization.

IN THE REAL WORLD

If your network allows open access to the Internet, be sure to look out for potentially high-bandwidth programs, like Napster. The ease with which multimedia is distributed over the Internet, legally and otherwise, is increasing rapidly. A few employees downloading music eight hours a day could severely impact the bandwidth available for replication.

Proper division of replication sites can help the overall performance of Active Directory. Many of the features of Active Directory that were not present in the NT directory structure require the efficient transfer of information throughout the entire network. Some of this traffic can be optimized by placing commonly needed resources within a site. A decrease in the number of sites, so that each site has access to the servers it needs to operate relatively autonomously, may outweigh the raw replication speed achieved by having smaller sites. Table 5-6 shows some examples of where site design can pay traffic dividends.

Table 5-6: Site-Level Traffic Optimization

Traffic Area	Benefits
Replication	The interval between exchanges of information between replication sites can be customized to fit the needs of each network segment.
Logons	If a domain controller is available in the current site, all logon traffic will stay within the site and will be handled by that domain controller if possible.
File Replication Service	The processing of Group Policies and logon scripts is handled by the File Replication Service (FRS). The FRS uses site settings to determine when and how to replicate its data.
Distributed Filesystem	The Distributed Filesystem (DFS) allows multiple linked copies of network resources to be distributed among many servers. DFS will look within a replication site for a copy of the resource before searching the rest of the network.
Site-aware programs	Programs that can take advantage of FRS and DFS will automatically benefit from their cooperation with replication site topology to reduce network traffic generated by the program.

Replication of data within a site is called intrasite replication. Replication between sites is called intersite replication. It is important that bandwidth between domain controllers be as high as possible, because they will be involved in both intersite and intrasite replication. You should always map out the physical location of all the domain controllers and the nearby hubs and switches that connect them. If possible, try to have 100 Mbit connections between all domain controllers and have at least one domain controller in each replication site.

The amount of time it takes to exchange replication data between domain controllers is called *replication latency*. Don't confuse the amount of time it takes to complete a transfer, *replication latency*, with the total amount of bandwidth needed for the transfer, *replication cost*. Each replication session has a certain amount of setup and teardown traffic, in addition to the actual data transfer. If you configure the site replication to save changes in a batch and send them all at once, you'll reduce the overall replication latency and lower the replication cost by transferring fewer setup and teardown packets.

Sites can be adjusted after they are created. Whenever there are changes to the network, you should re-evaluate your site borders to make sure you still have the most efficient replication setup. Adding a single computer to a site can significantly change the available bandwidth, which can have a cascading effect on the performance of seemingly unrelated parts of the network. Always perform a check on the current situation, called a *baseline*, so you'll have something to compare the new numbers to after a change.

ON THE EXAM

There is a big difference between replication latency and replication cost. If you increase the bandwidth between replication sites, you'll decrease the latency, but not the cost. You'll be sending the same amount of data, only faster.

Site links

All the sites in Active Directory have to be able to share information. The way in which they replicate information is not random, you can choose which sites share a replication link and when they transfer data. You have to take into account employee shift schedules and sometimes differences in time zone when determining the most efficient timing of replication on large networks. The connection between two sites for the purpose of replicating data is referred to as a site link.

Site link bridges

Most site links connect two locations, but each of those locations probably has a site link to somewhere else. Site links on fully routed IP networks are transitive, which means that, if site A is connected to site B and site B is connected to site C, then site A is effectively connected to site C via a site link bridge.

Bridgehead servers

Because sites can span multiple domains and some domains have several domain controllers, you may want to specify which domain controller in a site will handle replication duties. The chosen domain controller is referred to as a bridgehead server. The domain controller that has the most unused bandwidth to another site is a good choice to be a bridgehead server.

Suggested Exercises

The Designing Active Directory exam requires you to make decisions based not only on technical knowledge of Windows 2000 and Active Directory, but also on business needs. To achieve proficiency in both the objective technical and subjective business sections of the test, you should try to work through some business consulting scenarios, ranging from small departmental planning to multinational corporate consulting.

Obviously, not everyone who is taking the certification exams has the opportunity to actually consult with such a wide range of businesses, so I've made a list of exercises that should help get you thinking about some of the situations you might run into on the tests.

Domain Naming

1. Map out the geographical, divisional, and departmental structures for at least one small, medium, and large company.

2. Create flow charts and determine the best hierarchical domain naming strategies for each of them.

3. Visit *http://www.networksolutions.com* and go as far through the process of registering a domain name as you can without actually submitting the request.

Company IT Mapping

1. Try to map out at least three companies' IT structures.

2. Determine which are centralized, decentralized, mixed, or outsourced.

3. Rate them by efficiency, taking into account the size of the operation compared to the number of IT staff.

Trust Relationships

1. Verify that two-way transitive trust relationships exist within a tree.

2. Try to configure an external trust. See if it is really a one-way trust.

3. Configure two external trusts to simulate a transitive trust relationship.

DNS

1. Look at a DNS zone file on a Unix server and a Windows 2000 server. Note any differences.

2. Manually edit a zone file on a Windows 2000 DNS Server and ping the machine that you've made the change for.

3. Move a machine between DNS zones.

Site Replication

1. Create at least two replication sites.

2. Assign one to be a bridgehead server.

3. Make sure one site has a server with multiple connectivity options, such as Ethernet and a dial-up modem. Assign a site link value to each connection.

4. Modify the site link value so each connection type has a turn at being the least costly.

5. Monitor which connection is used, based on the site link cost.

Practice Tests

Test Questions

1. What should you know about a company before you install an Active Directory for them?

    a. The geographic, divisional, and departmental layout of the company

    b. The security requirements of each location and department

    c. The predicted growth pattern for the next five years

    d. All of the above

2. Which domain structure is generally easier to maintain?

    a. A single domain with multiple subdomains sharing a single AD

    b. Multiple domains sharing a single AD

    c. A single domain with multiple subdomains with individual ADs

    d. Multiple domains with multiple ADs

3. Two companies are merging, neither of which has a computer network. They decide they want to use Windows 2000 and Active Directory. They have a small IT staff and would like to have a single domain. However, they'd like to keep their naming systems relatively separate. What can you do to best accommodate their needs?

    a. Create two domains and create two one-way trust relationships between them.

    b. Create a single domain, giving one company the root domain name and making the other a sub-domain.

    c.   Create an empty root domain and give each company a sub-domain name.

    d.   Tell them they must use a hyphenated name if they wish to have a single domain.

4. Which type of Active Directory container is most useful in mapping company departmental structure for the assignment and inheritance of permissions?

    a.   Domain local accounts

    b.   Global accounts

    c.   Trees

    d.   Organizational Units

5. What is the process of putting one group inside of another called?

    a.   Hive management

    b.   Nesting

    c.   Inheritance

    d.   Subfolders

6. When can external trusts be used in Windows 2000?

    a.   Between trees in a forest

    b.   Between domains in a tree

    c.   Between trees in a domain

    d.   Between domains in different forests

7. When can shortcut trusts be used?

    a.   Between two domains in the same forest

    b.   Between two domains in different forests

    c.   Between two users in the same OU

    d.   Between two users in the same forest

8. Which group can apply Group Policies at the site level?

    a.   Domain Admins

    b.   Enterprise Admins

    c.   Replication Admins

    d.   Power Users

9. Which of the following changes will decrease the replication cost value between sites?

    a.   Upgrading from a 10 Mbs to 100 Mbs Ethernet setup

    b.   Decreasing the number of domain controllers

    c.   Increasing the number of domain controllers

    d.   None of the above

10. If site A is connected to site B for replication and site B is connected to site C for replication, what is the connection between A and C called?

    a.   A transitive trust

    b.   A bridgehead

    c.   A site link bridge

    d.   A shortcut trust

11. You are designing groups to be used across an entire Active Directory forest that contains several domains. The domains are at different physical locations and the available bandwidth between these locations is very low. Which type of group allows for access across the entire forest with the minimum amount of replication traffic?

    a.   Domain local

    b.   Global

    c.   Universal

    d.   All of the above

12. You are trying to create the most efficient site replication strategy possible for a very large network. It has been decided that you should configure bridge-head servers. Which computers are the best candidates to be bridgehead servers?

    a.   Domain controllers with the most unused RAM

    b.   Domain controllers with the most unused bandwidth

    c.   Workstations with the most unused RAM

    d.   Standalone servers with the most unused RAM

13. You are designing an efficient replication strategy for a mid-sized network. What should be your number one priority?

    a.   Making sure there are sufficient services available within each site

    b.   Increasing the number of replication sites

    c.   Decreasing the number of domain controllers per site

    d.   Increasing the number of bridgehead servers

14. You have a publicly registered domain name and class 2 block of IP addresses. You're running your own DNS server. Part of the network will be accessible over the Internet and part will be private for the next six months. Then the whole network will be publicly available. What should you do to keep these areas separate for now and make the transition as easy as possible?

a. Assign valid IP addresses to the public parts of the network and non-routable IP addresses to the private parts. Reassign IP addresses in six months.

b. You must have two separate DNS servers running on separate subnets. In six months, append the zone files together on the public DNS server.

c. Create zone files for the public and private parts of the network and keep them separated using a firewall. Use routable IP addresses for both zones. In six months, change the appropriate zone from private to public while retaining the originally assigned IP addresses.

d. Make all IP addresses public, but use DHCP to randomly assign the private addresses.

15. The group hierarchy for the programmers of your company is as follows: the parent group is called Programmers. The Programmers group has three sub-groups, Database, Web Design and Accounting. The Accounting group previously was the only Programming group to have access to the Billing folder. Since the Accounting programmers no longer need that access and none of the other programmers do either, you've decided to deny all access to the Billing folder to the parent Programmers group. You notice that Pamela, who is in the Accounting group, can still access the Billing folder. What should you do first?

a. Disable Pamela's account immediately.

b. Check other Accounting accounts to see if the permissions were inherited properly.

c. Deny access to the Billing folder specifically for Pamela.

d. Deny access to the Billing folder for the Accounting group.

16. How can you make sure that permissions will be inherited all the way down the Organizational Unit tree and will not be blocked by a child OU?

a. Double-check every OU's permissions manually after every change.

b. Make sure the all the child OUs have No Override set.

c. Make sure the parent OU has No Override set.

d. You can't prevent permissions inheritance blocking.

17. What is the best way to prevent inheritance of permissions for a small number of users across the domain?

a. Put them in the Enterprise Administrator's group.

b. Let them all share a single Administrator account.

c. Put them in a separate OU and configure the OU's permissions appropriately.

d. Put them in a security group and configure that group's permissions appropriately.

18. You notice that login times have increased for your Active Directory forest. Which of the following are possible causes?

    a. Group Policy Objects that apply across multiple domains have increased traffic.

    b. Replication traffic has increased despite adding more individual sites.

    c. A couple of global catalog servers have crashed and haven't been replaced.

    d. All of the above.

19. You have been given a budget that allows you to buy five new servers. What should you do with this hardware to get biggest performance benefit for your Active Directory network?

    a. Create five new DNS servers

    b. Create five new bridgehead servers

    c. Create five new global catalog servers

    d. Create five new FTP servers

20. You are running Active Directory within a forest. Two workstations in separate trees need to share a Distributed Filesystem folder. What changes to the trust relationship(s) must be made for this folder to be shared between workstations in different trees?

    a. You must create two separate one-way trusts between the trees.

    b. You must create two separate one-way trusts between the workstations.

    c. You must manually create a two-way trust between the trees.

    d. All computers in the forest automatically have two-way trust relationships, so you don't need to change any trust relationships.

Case Study

Text Formatting Key:

- **Describes requirements**
- *Conflicts with requirement*
- Irrelevant background information

You have been given a list of **requirements to implement a replication strategy for the sales department. Sales has 3 Windows 2000 domain controllers,** 2 standalone servers, and 28 workstations. **The domain controllers have the following interconnection speeds.**

Domain Controller Name	Average Available Bandwidth to DCA	Average Available Bandwidth to DCB	Average Available Bandwidth to DCC
DCA	N/A	7.8 Mbit	5.2 Mbit
DCB	7.8 Mbit	N/A	6.1 Mbit
DCC	5.2 Mbit	6.1 Mbit	N/A

You must determine which domain controllers will be linked together for replication purposes to make the most efficient connections.

Multiple Choice

1. How many computers in the sales department will be involved with the intra-site replication?

    a. 3

    b. 5

    c. 33

    d. None

2. What does the above chart indicate regarding replication?

    a. Latency

    b. Cost

    c. Distance

    d. Security

Create a Tree

Place each domain controller under the domain controller to which it would connect, given the most efficient replication configuration. Each domain controller must be connected to another domain controller. A domain controller may share a connection with more than one domain controller.

DCA	DCB	DCC

Answers

Comprehensive Test

1. d. You should know as much as possible about the company before you begin to configure Active Directory. You can't take full advantage of Active Directory without this information.

2. a. It's easiest to maintain a single domain that uses multiple subdomains and a single Active Directory.

3. c. An empty root domain will allow the subdomains to retain naming separation, while taking advantage of the single domain for administrative and maintenance purposes.

4. d. Organizational Units are the best way to model Active Directory after a company's departmental structure.

5. b. Putting groups inside of other groups is called nesting.

6. d. External trusts can only occur between two domains residing in different forests.

7. a. Shortcut trusts can only be used between two domains in the same forest.

8. b. Only members of the Enterprise Admins group can apply Group Policies at the site level.

9. d. You can decrease the latency of a connection by providing more bandwidth, but that won't decrease the cost. Cost is determined by the amount of information being sent over the connection, not by the speed or the percentage of available bandwidth.

10. c. A site link bridge is the virtual connection formed between multiple sites that are linked to the same site.

11. b. Global groups are valid across the entire forest and replicate only the group name between domains, not the individual members of the group. This uses less bandwidth than universal groups, which replicate the member information for the group along with the group name. Domain local groups are only valid in the local domain and do not replicate to other domains in the forest.

12. b. Only domain controllers can be bridgehead servers. The amount of available bandwidth will be the most important factor for site replication duties.

13. a. Making sure there are enough services within a site prevents requests from having to be served outside the site, which improves response time. Just making sites smaller could be counterproductive.

14. c. A single DNS server can have public and private zones that can be easily changed. Using non-routable IP addresses would technically work, but reassigning all those IP addresses would be inefficient.

15. b. It is likely that the permissions were not inherited for the entire Accounting group, not just Pamela's account. You shouldn't just block the Accounting group from the Billing folder, because if permissions inheritance is disabled for the Accounting group, you'll have to change permissions for the Accounting group separately from the other programming subgroups. It's better to fix the inheritance problem at its source, rather than dealing with it on a case-by-case basis.

16. c. The easiest and most effective way to prevent inheritance blocking is to make sure the parent container has No Override set.

17. d. Security groups are the best solution for assigning permissions across the domain. Don't give non-administrators an Administrator account and never allow users to share a single account.

18. d. All of these scenarios can increase login times. You should always create baselines for all aspects of network performance to make it easier to quantify change.

19. c. Adding global catalog servers is by far the best choice to improve network performance because requests are load balanced and just about every network request has something to do with the global catalog.

20. d. All computers in the forest automatically share two-way transitive trust relationships.

Case Study: Multiple Choice

1. a. Only domain controllers are involved in intrasite replication.

2. a. Latency is based on how much available bandwidth is available for replication. Cost is a constant value, regardless of the available bandwidth.

Case Study: Create a Tree

DCA	DCB	DCC
DCB	DCA	DCB

Highlighter's Index

Analyzing Your Company Evaluation Notes

Analysis Step	Purpose
Decision point	An individual item that is either required or suggested. You should separate the requirements from goals and then prioritize the goals, grouping them so goals that aren't mutually exclusive are together. You can then score each group of goals by importance and create a packaged solution.
Implications	When you score the goals, be sure to take into account the effect that each goal has on the implementation of the others. If one goal would negatively impact many other goals, you may want to reconsider, even if the first individual goal is slightly more important than individual goals in the group it affects.
Risks	Consider both the technical and the financial costs of each solution. If adding a convenience feature poses an undue security risk, a client such as a lawyer or a bank has to abandon that feature.
Trade-offs	On the questions, you'll often have one group that wants a feature that would adversely affect another group. You'll have to do your best to weigh the options and be very careful with the wording of the questions of this sort.

IT Structure Types

Type	Definition	Issues
Centralized	All IT decisions and operations are handled by a single department in a single location.	Good communication with outside departments and locations is essential.

Type	Definition	Issues
Decentralized	IT decisions are handled independently at each location.	Interoperability, security, cooperation.
Mixed	IT management is distributed, but technology is relatively consistent.	Both centralized and decentralized issues.
Outsourced	IT decisions are implemented and maintained by an outside interest.	Response time, communication, control.

Reasons for a Multiple Domain Structure

Remote locations

If remote locations have a low bandwidth connection between them, the frequent replication traffic generated in a single domain setup may be enough to overwhelm the connection. The cost of maintaining faster interconnection lines may outweigh the benefits of a single domain, especially if each location has qualified network administrators already on staff.

Limited partnerships

If two essentially separate organizations want to keep their own administrative controls in place, a multiple domain setup would keep domain Administrator accounts separate. This is especially important if companies are keeping secrets from one another.

Policy separation

If one company has a more stringent password policy, it may be necessary for the security of one company and the convenience of another to keep the policies separate. The only way to do that is with separate domains. For example, suppose a defense contractor requires passwords of at least 10 random characters changed every 48 hours without reusing the same password. The less sensitive areas of the company may not want such a strict policy.

Security Groups

Group	Description
Domain local	Used to grant permissions within only the local domain. May contain user accounts and global groups from any trusted domain. Permissions granted are valid only within the local domain, regardless of where the account or group originated.
Global	Used to grant permissions across the entire forest. May contain only global groups and user accounts. Replicates only the group name between domains, not the group membership list, so replication traffic is less than with universal groups.
Universal	Used to grant permissions across the entire forest. Usually contains other groups, rather than individual user accounts. Can contain any type of group. Must replicate to all domains in the forest, so frequent changes to group membership can generate significant network traffic.

External Trusts

- External trusts are one-way only. If you need a two-way external trust, you have to create two separate one-way trusts between domains in different forests.

- External trusts only connect two domains in different forests. The transitive trust relationships that each domain shares within its own forest are not shared by the remote domain. The rest of the domains in each forest are isolated from the remote computer.

DNS Naming Conventions

Company Breakdown	DNS Name Used
Parent company name: O'Reilly & Associates	oreilly.com
Geographic locations: Sebastopol, Cambridge	sebastopol.oreilly.com cambridge.oreilly.com
Sebastopol's departments: editorial, production, and marketing	editorial.sebastopol.oreilly.com production.sebastopol.oreilly.com marketing.sebastopol.oreilly.com

Site Level Traffic Optimization

Traffic Area	Benefits
Replication	The interval between exchanges of information between replication sites can be customized to fit the needs of each network segment.
Logons	If a domain controller is available in the current site, all logon traffic will stay within site and will be handled by that domain controller if possible.
File Replication Service	The processing of Group Policies and logon scripts is handled by the File Replication Service (FRS). The FRS uses site settings to determine when and how to replicate its data.
Distributed Filesystem	The Distributed Filesystem (DFS) allows multiple linked copies of network resources to be distributed among many servers. DFS will look within a replication site for a copy of the resource before searching the rest of the network.
Site-aware programs	Programs that can take advantage of FRS and DFS will automatically benefit from their cooperation with replication site topology to reduce network traffic generated by the program.

PART 6

Designing Network Infrastructure

Exam Overview

As a network administrator or consultant, your job can involve planning, analyzing, and designing networks as much as implementing them. This may include choosing protocols and services to use, designing addressing and Internet access schemes, and providing other services, such as remote access.

MCSE Exam 70-221, *Designing a Microsoft Windows 2000 Network Infrastructure*, deals with the high-level design and planning of network protocols and services. This exam can be used as an optional core exam or as an elective.

There is some overlap in Microsoft's objectives between this exam and the basic Network Infrastructure exam (Exam 70-216), which focuses more on the technical implementation of network protocols and services. You should study Part 4, *Network Infrastructure*, as well as this chapter before taking the *Designing a Microsoft Windows 2000 Network Infrastructure* exam.

To prepare for this chapter and the Network Infrastructure exam, you should have studied Part 4 and Parts 1 and 2 (*Windows 2000 Professional* and *Server*). You should also have real-world experience with computers in a networked environment that uses the services and protocols covered in this chapter.

Areas of Study

Designing a Network Infrastructure

Need to Know	Reference
Phases of network design	"Designing a Network Infrastructure" on page 332
Typical network services	"Network Services Overview" on page 332

Need to Apply	Reference
Analyze business and technical requirements for a network design	"Examining Requirements" on page 333

Designing TCP/IP Networks

Need to Know	Reference
IP addressing format and classes	"IP Addressing" on page 334
Difference between public and private addresses	"Public addresses" on page 335; "Private addresses" on page 335
Private IP address ranges	"Private addresses" on page 335

Need to Apply	Reference
Design an IP addressing scheme	"IP Addressing" on page 334
Determine whether to use packet filtering or a firewall	"Packet filtering" on page 337
Plan the use of IPSec	"IPSec encryption" on page 338
Improve TCP/IP availability and performance	"Optimizing TCP/IP Networks" on page 339

Designing DHCP Services

Need to Know	Reference
Advantages of DHCP	"Designing DHCP Services" on page 340
DHCP options available	"Basic DHCP Design" on page 340
How DHCP works with other services	"DHCP and Other Services" on page 341

Need to Apply	Reference
Plan the use of DHCP	"Designing DHCP Services" on page 340
Integrate DHCP with other services	"DHCP and Other Services" on page 341
Improve DHCP availability and performance	"Optimizing DHCP Services" on page 342

Designing Name Resolution Services

Need to Know	Reference
Name resolution types	"Designing Name Resolution Services" on page 344
DNS zone types	"Basic DNS Design" on page 344

Need to Apply	Reference
Design name resolution using DNS and WINS	"Designing Name Resolution Services" on page 344
Choose the correct DNS zone type for an application	"Choosing zone types" on page 345
Secure a DNS solution	"Planning DNS Security" on page 345
Improve DNS availability and performance	"Optimizing DNS" on page 346
Integrate WINS with other services	"WINS and other services" on page 347
Improve WINS availability and performance	"Optimizing WINS" on page 348

Designing Internet Connectivity

Need to Know	Reference
Methods of Internet connectivity	"Designing Internet Connectivity" on page 349
Benefits of NAT	"Network Address Translation (NAT)" on page 349
Benefits of Proxy Server 2.0	"Microsoft Proxy Server" on page 352
Proxy server types	"Basic proxy server design" on page 352

Need to Apply	Reference
Design Internet connectivity and choose the required services	"Designing Internet Connectivity" on page 349
Choose between NAT and ICS	"Network Address Translation (NAT)" on page 349
Determine placement of NAT servers	"Placement and connectivity of the NAT server" on page 350
Use NAT to support DHCP and DNS	"Replacing DHCP and DNS services" on page 350
Plan the use of NAT address pools and special ports	"Allowing Internet access" on page 351
Secure a NAT solution	"NAT security" on page 352
Optimize NAT performance	"Optimizing NAT" on page 352
Secure a proxy server solution	"Proxy server security" on page 353
Improve proxy server availability	"Optimizing proxy server availability" on page 354
Improve proxy server performance	"Optimizing proxy server performance" on page 354

Designing
Network

Designing Routing and Remote Access

Need to Know	Reference
Router types	"Static and dynamic routing" on page 355
Typical routing protocols	"Routing protocols" on page 356
Remote access authentication methods	"Remote access security" on page 358
VPN protocols	"Tunneling protocols" on page 359

Need to Apply	Reference
Determine placement of routers	"Router placement" on page 355
Choose the routing protocols to use	"Routing protocols" on page 356
Secure a routing solution	"Planning Routing Security" on page 356
Improve routing availability and performance	"Optimizing the Routing Design" on page 357
Design a remote access solution	"Planning Remote Access" on page 358
Secure a remote access solution	"Remote access security" on page 358
Choose VPN protocols	"Tunneling protocols" on page 359
Optimize remote access	"Optimizing remote access" on page 360
Use RADIUS for remote access	"Remote access using RADIUS" on page 360

Study Guide

This chapter includes the following sections, which address various topics covered on the *Designing a Microsoft Windows 2000 Network Infrastructure* MCSE exam:

Designing a Network Infrastructure
Describes the scope of a network infrastructure design and presents an overview of the network services you will use in planning the network. Also introduces the process of examining the business requirements, technical requirements, and existing network infrastructure to plan a design.

Designing TCP/IP Networks
Describes the process of creating a TCP/IP design as a basis for a complete network infrastructure.

Designing DHCP Services
Examines the requirements and process of creating a design for DHCP (Dynamic Host Configuration Protocol).

Designing Name Resolution Services
Provides techniques for developing designs for name resolution services, including DNS (Domain Name Service) and WINS (Windows Internet Naming Service).

Designing Internet Connectivity
Describes the design considerations for Internet connectivity services, including Microsoft Proxy Server and NAT (Network Address Translation).

Designing Routing and Remote Access
Provides methods for planning routes between networks, routing protocols, and on-demand routing. Examines planning considerations for remote access solutions, including RAS (Remote Access Service) and RADIUS (Remote Authentication Dial-In User Service).

Designing a Network Infrastructure

This chapter deals with the process of designing a *network infrastructure*: the protocols and services that comprise a network. Microsoft divides network service design into three phases:

Design
> The initial planning, design, and testing for a network or a service within a network

Implementation
> The process of putting the planned design into action on the network

Management
> The administration and management required for day-to-day management of the network or service

---

ON THE EXAM

The term network infrastructure may bring to mind the physical cabling and devices that comprise a network, but the *Designing a Microsoft Windows 2000 Network Infrastructure* exam focuses on network protocols (such as TCP/IP) and services (such as DNS, DHCP, and Routing and Remote Access).

Network Services Overview

This chapter describes the considerations you should use when designing a Windows 2000 network infrastructure. This can include any number of network protocols and services. The main protocols and services you will use in most Windows 2000 design include the following:

TCP/IP
> TCP/IP (Transmission Control Protocol/Internet Protocol) is the main transport protocol used in Windows 2000 networks, as well as the Internet.

DHCP
> DHCP (Dynamic Host Configuration Protocol) allocates IP addresses to clients from a pool of available addresses, eliminating the need for manual address allocation, and can also assign DNS addresses and other configuration.

DNS and WINS
> These services provide name resolution, translating resource names to IP addresses. DNS (Domain Name Service) supports IP hostname resolution, and WINS (Windows Internet Name Service) supports NetBIOS name resolution.

NAT
> NAT (Network Address Translation) translates private IP addresses to public addresses, allowing a single computer to provide Internet access for a private network and eliminating the need for public addresses for all machines on the network.

Microsoft Proxy Server

Microsoft Proxy Server acts as an intermediary between a private network and the public Internet, similar to NAT. Unlike NAT, Proxy Server provides user-based and site-based security, caching, and support for web publishing.

Routing

Network routing uses either hardware-based routers or computers running routing software, including Windows 2000, to transmit network traffic between subnets. Routers combine subnets into a single coherent network.

Remote Access

Windows 2000's Remote Access services allow remote users to access the network through dial-up modems. Remote Access can also be used with routing to allow dial-on-demand routing to the Internet or other networks.

ON THE EXAM

While design considerations for these protocols and services are covered here and in the *Designing a Microsoft Windows 2000 Network Infrastructure* exam, the technical details of their implementation are part of the *Implementing and Administering a Microsoft Windows 2000 Network Infrastructure* exam, and covered in Part 4.

Examining Requirements

An essential part of the design of a network infrastructure involves examining the requirements of the business, the technical requirements, and the existing network. The following sections discuss these considerations.

Business requirements

When you are designing a new network, business requirements will be the primary source of information. These include the needs of users (access to files, printers, and other resources) and the needs of management (security, user management, and administration).

Technical requirements

Whether you plan to design a network from scratch or augment an existing network, there are technical requirements. These include the operating systems that will be used, the network wiring, and the features of available hardware and software. Carefully note these requirements to avoid creating technical problems when the design is implemented.

Analyzing the existing network

In many cases, an existing network is already present and you must design additions to the network, or support for additional services. You should document the existing network thoroughly and take its configuration into account when planning the new network.

Planning for change

Last but not least, any network design should account for the certainty of change in the future. Networks will require support for more computers and more users, as well as support for future technologies and operating systems. A good network design should be flexible and anticipate as many of these changes as possible.

Designing TCP/IP Networks

TCP/IP, as you learned earlier in this book, is a suite of network protocols used in Unix systems, on the Internet, and as the primary protocol suite for Windows NT and Windows 2000 networks. TCP/IP is named for two of its key protocols, Transport Control Protocol and Internet Protocol.

ON THE EXAM

The *Designing a Microsoft Windows 2000 Network Infrastructure* MCSE exam focuses on higher-level planning and strategy rather than technical details. Nevertheless, you should understand the technical side of TCP/IP, as discussed in Part 4 of this book, in order to create a workable network design.

As the transport protocol, TCP/IP forms the fundamental backbone of a network infrastructure, and thus your network design should begin with a plan for the configuration of these protocols. All of the network services discussed in the remainder of this chapter are built upon the foundation of TCP/IP.

The basic considerations when designing a TCP/IP implementation include the assignment of IP addresses and the method (manual or automatic) of assigning them; IP security, filtering, and encryption; and ways of ensuring optimum availability and performance. These are discussed in the following sections.

IN THE REAL WORLD

Although the *Designing a Microsoft Windows 2000 Network Infrastructure* MCSE exam deals solely with TCP/IP as a network transport, your network may require the use of other protocols, such as IPX/SPX for connectivity with NetWare networks, or AppleTalk for Macintosh connectivity.

IP Addressing

As discussed earlier in this book, each node in a TCP/IP network has a unique logical address called an IP address. Each IP address is a 32-bit number divided

---

into 4 bytes, or octets. These are usually expressed in dotted-decimal format, such as 209.68.11.152.

An IP address is divided into a network address and a host address; the division between the two depends on the IP address class. Table 6-1 presents an overview of the three main IP address classes and their distinctions.

Table 6-1: Classes of IP Addresses

Class	Network/Host Bytes	Number of Networks	Number of Hosts per Network
A	1/3	126	16,777,214
B	2/2	16,382	65,534
C	3/1	2,097,150	254

In addition to these basic divisions between network and host addresses, subnetting can be used to create finer divisions; for example, using 28 bits for the network address and 4 bits for the host address.

The key factor in planning IP addressing for a network is its connectivity to the Internet. Any machines that will be accessible across the Internet must have public IP addresses; machines that are inaccessible can use private addressing. These address schemes are described in the following sections.

Public addresses

Public IP addresses are assigned by the Internet Assigned Numbers Authority (IANA). Because there is a finite number of addresses in the standard IP addressing scheme, a limited number of addresses are available; Class C addresses are generally the only ones available to most companies.

Fortunately, for all but the largest companies, it is rarely necessary to assign public addresses to more than a few machines on a network. In fact, each machine with a public address increases the security risk. Public addresses are typically needed for the following situations:

- Machines running NAT or a proxy server to provide Internet access to other machines

- Web servers and machines running other publicly accessible services, such as FTP

Your network design should include a list of the machines that will initially require public addresses, because these will need to be registered before configuring Internet connectivity.

Private addresses

Private addresses are used on machines that cannot be accessed from the Internet and have no need for Internet access or will access the Internet through a proxy server or NAT device. Private addresses are assigned by the network administrator and do not require registration of any kind.

When you assign private addresses, using ranges specifically intended for use as private addresses ensures that traffic from these machines will never be routed to the Internet and, also, prevents conflicts with Internet addresses.

ON THE EXAM

NAT allows machines with private IP addresses to access the Internet through a gateway machine; the machine running NAT is the only one required to use a public address. NAT is explained in detail later in this chapter.

Private addresses are set aside by the IETF in RFC 1918 and are guaranteed to never be registered as valid public addresses. Table 6-2 lists the IP address ranges that can be used for private IP addressing.

Table 6-2: Private IP Addresses

Address Class	Starting Address	Ending Address
A	10.0.0.0	10.255.255.255
B	169.254.0.1	169.254.255.254
C	172.16.0.0	172.31.255.255
C	192.168.0.0	192.168.255.255

How addresses are assigned

Another facet of your IP addressing design should address the method of assigning IP addresses, whether public or private addresses are used. The following are the basic methods of assigning IP addresses in Windows 2000 networks:

Manual assignment
　　Certain machines can be manually assigned a public or private IP address. This should be restricted to machines that require a consistent address, such as DHCP, DNS, and WINS servers, and machines that cannot use DHCP.

DHCP scopes
　　DHCP (Dynamic Host Configuration Protocol) can be used to assign addresses from a scope (a pool of available addresses) automatically to clients. This is typically the main method of address allocation in large networks.

DHCP reserved addresses
　　DHCP also allows IP addresses to be reserved for certain machines. Reservations can be used for application servers or other machines that require a consistent address.

Automatic Private IP Addressing
　　Automatic Private IP Addressing (APIPA) is a Microsoft standard for assigning IP addresses in small networks that do not support DHCP. Addresses are assigned from the pool of private Class B addresses in the 169.254.x.x range.

TCP/IP Network Security

Another important aspect of a TCP/IP network design is security. TCP/IP networks have significant security flaws when implemented with default settings, and you should plan to use such features as filtering and encryption to improve security. These are discussed in the following sections.

Packet filtering

Packet filtering refers to a node analyzing TCP/IP packets based on certain criteria—for example, the packet type, the source or destination addresses, or the ports used—and discarding packets that do not match these criteria. Packets can be filtered in several locations within the network:

- Firewalls and proxy servers include filtering and are an ideal place to implement this feature.

- Windows 2000 includes per-node packet filtering as part of the TCP/IP stack. This feature allows complete control over incoming IP packets, but can be complex to implement on every machine.

- TCP/IP routers may also include packet filtering features.

Windows 2000's per-host IP filtering is most useful for hosts with special functions, such as dedicated web, FTP, or application servers. The filters for such a server can be set to disallow all inappropriate incoming traffic—for example, on a machine used strictly as a web server, HTTP requests on port 80 should be the only incoming packets allowed.

ON THE EXAM

Windows 2000's IP filtering operates at the Application layer of the OSI model. For more information about the technical details of IP filtering, consult Part 4 of this book.

The main alternative to packet filtering is a proxy server or *firewall*. This is a dedicated machine that acts as an intermediary between the Internet and your network. A proxy has certain advantages over simple filtering:

- Proxies can perform more specific filtering—for example, content-based filtering of web access.

- Proxies support additional features, such as caching.

On the other hand, IP filtering has some advantages over a proxy server:

- Proxies need to explicitly support each protocol used. IP filtering can support any protocol and can support new protocols without software changes.

- Proxy servers introduce a slight delay; IP filtering does not.

IPSec encryption

IPSec (IP Security) is an IETF standard for the encryption of TCP/IP traffic. Windows 2000's implementation of IP security allows an encrypted connection to be established between any two Windows 2000 computers. IPSec is supported in Windows 2000 by the following components:

IPSec Policy Agent

> This is a service that runs under Windows 2000 and manages IPSec policies. The policies are stored in the Active Directory or in the local computer's registry.

ISAKMP/Oakley Key Management Service

> This combines two protocols: ISAKMP, a key management protocol, and the Oakley protocol, which generates keys for data encryption. The IPSec Policy Agent automatically starts and manages this service.

IP Security Driver

> This driver (IPSEC.SYS) acts as a filter for all IP communication and determines whether security is required for each packet. Secured packets are encrypted using the key provided by the Key Management Service.

IPSec supports two key features: *encryption* (encoding network traffic to prevent snooping) and *authentication* (verifying that the data comes from a specific known source). Depending on your network's needs, a network infrastructure design can include either or both of these features.

Under Windows 2000, each computer can be configured with an IP Security policy. The policy determines when encrypted connections are used. Policies may be customized, or use one of the following default policies:

Client (Respond Only)

> Allows the computer to act as a client when a server requests or requires a secure connection.

Secure Server (Require Security)

> When the computer is accessed as a server, clients are required to use a secure connection.

Server (Request Security)

> When the computer is accessed as a server, clients are requested to use a secure connection. If the client does not support this, a standard plain-text connection is used.

ON THE EXAM

You should understand how Windows 2000 computers are configured for IPSec for the *Designing a Microsoft Windows 2000 Network Infrastructure* MCSE exam. This process is explained in Part 4, *Network Infrastructure*.

Optimizing TCP/IP Networks

As the final step in creating a design for a TCP/IP network, you should consider how the design will affect network availability and performance. These factors are discussed in the following sections.

Improving availability

In any network, especially one with WAN connections, availability is a concern. Services needed by users may become unavailable due to factors ranging from cable failure to software bugs. For a TCP/IP network design, the availability of the network transport and its protocols are the main concern.

ON THE EXAM

Microsoft measures network availability as the percentage of time users are able to access the data they need over the TCP/IP network.

The chief way to improve availability is to provide redundant links. Routers can be used to automatically route traffic to the most available link and temporarily bypass problems, provided there are redundant connections.

Routing protocols, such as RIP, can use link cost metrics to route traffic; for example, you can set a dial-on-demand connection using a modem to have a high cost, both because it may incur telephone company charges and because the modem will be unavailable for other tasks. If the dial-up connection has the highest cost, it will only be used when other connections fail.

Improving performance

Finally, your TCP/IP network infrastructure design should be structured to provide optimum performance. To improve the performance of a design, consider the following factors:

IP address space
> Public IP addresses are scarce and should be conserved. You may need to use variable-length subnetting to better divide the addresses in a range or use supernetting to combine a block of addresses (for example, those issued by an ISP) into a contiguous address space.

Traffic considerations
> Consider which types of traffic you will have on the network: latency-sensitive traffic, which causes user delays (for example, HTTP requests); and bandwidth-sensitive traffic, which requires a continuous flow of data.

Optimizing TCP/IP
> On some networks, TCP/IP performance can be improved by changing TCP/IP parameters in the registry settings, such as Receive Window Size and Bandwidth/Delay Product.

Designing Network

QoS (Quality of Service)

QoS, a new feature of Windows 2000, can be used to allocate bandwidth to specific needs, so that bandwidth-critical applications are not restricted by regular network traffic.

ON THE EXAM

You should understand the process of changing TCP/IP parameters in the registry for the *Designing a Microsoft Windows 2000 Network Infrastructure* MCSE exam. These settings are described in detail in Part 4.

Designing DHCP Services

As mentioned in the previous section, DHCP (Dynamic Host Configuration Protocol) can be used to dynamically allocate IP addresses to clients as needed. Including DHCP in your network design can greatly decrease the amount of time required for configuring and debugging individual clients.

DHCP is an extension of the simpler BOOTP protocol, which is generally used by diskless workstations that boot using a disk image stored across the network. DHCP's key advantages in a network design include the following:

- IP addresses are assigned automatically rather than requiring manual configuration for each client, reducing administrative costs.

- IP addresses can be managed from a central location.

- When not all nodes are used concurrently, DHCP can allow a group of IP addresses to serve a larger number of nodes than the number of IP addresses.

DHCP assigns IP addresses using a *lease*, which grants a client the address for a specific length of time. The client must request a renewal of the lease before the lease time expires; Windows clients automatically request a renewal after 50% of the lease time has elapsed.

Any Windows 2000 computer can act as a DHCP client, and Windows 2000 Server can be configured to act as DHCP server. The DHCP Client Service is automatically configured on Windows 2000 computers and runs whether you are using DHCP or not. Windows 95/98/Me and NT, Unix, and Macintosh machines can also act as DHCP clients.

DHCP is relatively simple to use, but your network design should include the number of DHCP servers, the scopes available, and other DHCP considerations, such as placement of DHCP relay agents. These are discussed in the following sections.

Basic DHCP Design

DHCP uses scopes, or individual ranges of IP addresses, to provide addresses to clients. Windows 2000's DHCP server also allows the use of *superscopes*: two or more scopes treated as a single pool of addresses. This is useful when the addresses available are not contiguous.

Along with IP addresses, DHCP includes *options*, which can configure other aspects of a client with centralized administration. Commonly used options are described in Table 6-3.

Table 6-3: Common Numeric DHCP Options

Option Number	Option Name	Value Type	Description
003	Router	Array of IP addresses	Preferred routers (gateways) in order of preference
006	DNS Servers	Array of IP addresses	Available DNS servers in order of preference
044	WINS/NBNS Servers	Array of IP addresses	Available WINS servers, in order of preference
046	WINS/NBT Node Type	Byte	WINS node type; see "Basic WINS Design"
047	NetBIOS Scope ID	String	Identifier for NetBIOS over TCP/IP

DHCP and Other Services

DHCP can be integrated with other Windows 2000 network services to provide better network management. Some services designed to integrate with DHCP are described in the following sections.

DHCP and routing

Windows 2000 includes the *DHCP relay agent*, which acts as a router and forwards DHCP traffic between subnets. Without this service, you must have one DHCP server per subnet; with the relay agent, a single DHCP server can handle several subnets.

ON THE EXAM

Some routers support DHCP (or BOOTP) forwarding. If this feature is enabled, DHCP broadcasts are forwarded between the subnets, eliminating the need for the DHCP relay agent. Windows 2000 computers acting as routers must have the relay agent enabled to support DHCP forwarding.

DHCP and remote access

DHCP can be used with Remote Access Server (RAS) to dynamically assign IP addresses to remote clients. This is ideal when you have a large pool of dial-up users; your DHCP scope needs only one IP address for each port configured for remote access, rather than one per user.

DHCP and DNS

DNS converts IP hostnames to IP addresses. However, when IP addresses are dynamically assigned, the DNS server cannot keep a static list of names and addresses. Fortunately, Windows 2000's DHCP server can automatically update the DNS server each time a client is issued a new IP address.

The DHCP server only needs to be integrated with DNS to support older (non-Active Directory) clients. Windows 2000 clients using Active Directory automatically send updates the DNS server upon being issued an IP address.

ON THE EXAM

Technically, the DHCP server updates the PTR records in DNS for Windows 2000 clients. Windows 2000 clients update their A records themselves. With older clients, which do not support dynamic updates, the DHCP server updates both records.

DHCP and Active Directory

Along with providing updates to DNS, Windows 2000's Active Directory also provides authentication for DHCP servers. This prevents the security risk of an unauthorized DHCP server's providing incorrect IP address and gateway information to clients.

ON THE EXAM

Active Directory authorization works with Windows 2000 DHCP servers, but because other DHCP servers (such as the one included with Windows NT Server 4.0) do not register with Active Directory, they can work without authorization.

Optimizing DHCP Services

To design an optimal DHCP structure for a network, you must consider the number of servers, their placement within the network, and the need for routing or forwarding services. Methods of optimizing a DHCP design are described in the following sections.

Single servers

A Windows 2000 DHCP server can manage IP addressing for several thousand clients, either all within a single subnet or using DHCP relay agent to support more than one subnet. Because DHCP uses broadcasts, relay agents must be used in any situation where a router or switch does not forward broadcast or DHCP traffic.

Multiple servers per subnet

New to Windows 2000 is the concept of superscopes, or combinations of several scopes. This feature can be used to allow multiple DHCP servers in a single subnet (or in two or more subnets with the appropriate routing or relay agents).

To configure multiple servers, you divide the addresses in the DHCP scope into smaller scopes for each server. Then configure a superscope on each server that encompasses all of the available scopes. This is known as a *distributed scope*.

ON THE EXAM

You cannot use the same IP address scope on two DHCP servers without using the superscope feature. Without this, one server may assign an address already assigned by another server, thus causing conflicts.

Servers in separate subnets

It is sometimes more practical to have a separate DHCP server for subnets rather than using the DHCP relay agent. In particular, when a subnet is separated from the main network by a WAN link, including a separate DHCP server in the subnet prevents delays and keeps broadcast traffic separate between the subnets.

Supporting non-Windows clients

Because DHCP is an IETF standard, Windows 2000's DHCP server can be used to provide IP addresses to other clients, such as Unix, Macintosh, and previous versions of Windows. However, some clients may not support DHCP options, such as default gateway or DNS address assignment.

Unlike previous versions of Windows NT, Windows 2000's DHCP server includes specific support for BOOTP clients. Because these clients use the simpler BOOTP protocol, they do not release DHCP leases; the server automatically checks whether their IP addresses are still in use when the lease expires and makes the addresses available to other clients.

Improving performance

A DHCP server's performance can be improved in most of the typical ways of improving Windows 2000 performance, beginning with the basics: adding memory and adding fast disk drives or RAID arrays. The DHCP server is also multithreaded and can take advantage of multiprocessor computers.

In some cases, the computer running the DHCP service has quite a bit more power than is needed to serve a small subnet. In this case, you can install multiple network adapters and create a multihomed DHCP server. This server can provide DHCP service for several subnets without the use of forwarding or routing.

If a single server is inadequate for the needs of a network, you can add additional servers for separate subnets. In a single large subnet, you can use distributed scopes and multiple servers, as described earlier in this section.

Last but not least, you can improve DHCP server performance by setting the correct lease length in the server's parameters. If leases are too long, an IP address shortage can result; if leases are too short, clients are required to renew frequently, which increases network traffic and places a higher load on the DHCP server.

ON THE EXAM

Windows 2000 clients can also explicitly release their DHCP lease on shut-down, which allows the IP address to be immediately available for other clients.

Designing Name Resolution Services

As discussed earlier in this chapter, TCP/IP supports hostnames, or alphanumeric aliases corresponding to particular IP addresses. These provide a user-friendly alternative to IP addresses and can be used in most places an IP address would be accepted.

When a client attempts to access a machine via its hostname, a process called *host-name resolution* occurs. Name resolution is typically accomplished by two services:

- DNS (Domain Name Service) for IP hostnames (fully qualified domain names, or FQDNs)

- WINS (Windows Internet Name Service) for NetBIOS hostnames, used to support versions of Windows prior to Windows 2000

The following sections describe the process of designing a DNS implementation for a network, including WINS support if needed.

Basic DNS Design

DNS is a standard for hostname resolution that was first developed for Unix and is defined by RFCs 1034 and 1035. DNS is the standard for name resolution on the Internet and is also used locally in many networks. Windows 2000 machines can act as DNS clients or servers.

DNS servers use zones, or databases of names and their corresponding addresses. Windows 2000's DNS server supports three basic types of zones:

Traditional DNS zone (primary)
   Traditional zones store the zone database in a file on the computer running DNS Server. There can only be one primary zone per network, and this is the only zone that allows updates to the DNS database.

Traditional DNS zone (secondary)
   Secondary zones store a read-only copy of a primary zone's database. They provide redundancy and can fill DNS requests, but do not allow updates to the database.

Active Directory integrated zone

New to Windows 2000, Active Directory integrated zones store their data in the Active Directory. The data is replicated along with other Active Directory information. You can have several Active Directory zones in a network, and any of them can allow updates to the DNS database.

In addition to these types, *reverse lookup zones* function similarly, but translate IP addresses to hostnames instead of names to IP addresses. Any of the above zone types can also be created as a reverse lookup zone.

Choosing zone types

Which types of DNS zone you use depends on the needs of the network. The following are the basic criteria for choosing the DNS zone types to use in your network design:

- Choose Active Directory integrated zones if the network is based chiefly on Windows 2000, and Active Directory is supported on the network.

- Choose traditional zones if integrating with existing non-Windows 2000 DNS services (for example, Unix or Windows NT 4.0 DNS servers).

- If Active Directory support is planned but not yet implemented, you can use an Active Directory integrated zone as a delegated domain. This provides the advantages of Active Directory for the Windows 2000 portion of the network and allows integration with existing DNS services.

Planning DNS Security

DNS does not by itself provide a high degree of security, but you can secure it using Active Directory and normal network security. The following sections describe key security concerns for DNS servers.

Securing DNS replication

In the process of DNS replication, portions of the DNS database are sent over the network. The following measures ensure that the DNS data is kept secure during this process:

- Use Active Directory integrated zones if possible. These replicate using Active Directory, which encrypts its replication traffic. In addition, Active Directory authenticates all such zones to prevent unauthorized servers.

- If DNS replication is performed over a VPN (virtual private network), use the strongest security levels available.

- Consider using IPSec to encrypt replication traffic between DNS servers.

Securing DNS updates

Windows 2000's DNS server allows *dynamic updates*. For example, Windows 2000 clients can dynamically update their DNS records when they are assigned IP addresses, and the DHCP server can send updates to the DNS server as addresses are assigned.

Dynamic updates are secure when Windows 2000 is used for the DNS server, but only when Active Directory integrated zones are in use. Traditional zones can be updated automatically, but are not secure.

Optimizing DNS

DNS is a vital network service, and a failed or unavailable DNS server can prevent a client from accessing other network services. The following sections introduce methods of improving the performance and availability of DNS services.

Measuring and improving performance

DNS server performance is measured based on the time it takes to receive a result for a DNS query and the amount of network bandwidth used. In order to improve performance beyond that of a single DNS server, you may consider one of the following strategies:

- Caching-only DNS servers can be used to keep a local cache of DNS requests and their results. These are particularly useful at the remote end of a WAN link, because the cache can be used to answer many requests without requiring WAN traffic.

- Consider using delegated DNS zones and separate servers to handle portions of the DNS namespace.

- Windows 2000's DNS Server supports load balancing, or dividing requests between redundant servers. This is useful in situations with extremely high DNS traffic.

Designing for availability

A single DNS server may not always be available, due to potential hardware and network problems. The first step in improving availability is to install multiple DNS servers. You can use multiple servers in a single subnet or use separate servers for each subnet or location.

For Active Directory integrated zones, you can set up more than one replicated copy of the zone. For traditional zones, configure a primary zone and one or more secondary zones. Distant locations are typically served with secondary zones.

ON THE EXAM

To improve DNS performance and availability within a single network, you can use Windows 2000 Advanced Server's clustering feature to create a server cluster. However, the DNS Server is not cluster-aware and will not take full advantage of a cluster.

Basic WINS Design

WINS is similar to DNS, but translates NetBIOS (network basic input/output services) names to IP addresses. NetBIOS names are not required by Windows 2000 computers, but are relied upon by previous versions of Windows.

NetBIOS includes a broadcast-based method of name resolution. Using this system, for example, a small network of Windows 98 computers can resolve each other's names without the need for a WINS server. However, because NetBIOS broadcasts are not routable, WINS servers are needed for larger networks.

All Windows-based computers can act as WINS clients, and Windows NT Server and Windows 2000 Server include WINS server software. Clients can be supplied with the address of the WINS server with manual configuration, or the address can be issued via DHCP.

WINS and other services

The WINS server integrates with other Windows 2000 services. The following are the most important services you may wish to configure to work with WINS:

- DHCP can be integrated with WINS in the same way as DNS. The DHCP server updates the WINS server whenever a client is issued a new address.

- DNS can be integrated with WINS, which allows WINS to automatically update the DNS server. Because WINS updates its database of NetBIOS names and addresses automatically, this eliminates the need to manually add them to a DNS zone.

Number of WINS servers

In a small network with a single subnet and relatively few nodes, NetBIOS broadcasts prove sufficient and a WINS server is not needed. In a network with a great number of nodes or a need to reduce broadcast traffic, a WINS server can improve client response times.

Multiple WINS servers can replicate their database, and thus you can use two or more WINS servers when a single server is inadequate for a network. WINS servers can also be placed at remote subnets, so that name resolution traffic does not have to travel across WAN links.

ON THE EXAM

Due to the replication traffic, adding too many WINS servers can decrease rather than increase speed. A single WINS server per subnet is sufficient in all but the largest networks.

Windows 2000 clients can be configured with as many as 12 WINS server addresses; previous versions of Windows support two addresses. If you are using one WINS server per subnet, a WINS server in a remote subnet can be used as a secondary address, to provide redundancy in cases where the primary server does not respond.

ON THE EXAM

Although Windows 2000 supports as many as 12 WINS server addresses, Microsoft does not recommend the use of more than two WINS server addresses per client.

Optimizing WINS

The WINS service is largely automatic and requires less configuration than DNS. Nevertheless, there are factors you can include when you plan your network design to ensure high availability and performance for WINS servers. The following sections discuss these measures.

Improving availability

When WINS servers are in use, clients may be hampered by a temporarily unavailable server. You can ensure WINS availability in several ways:

- Always specify at least two WINS server addresses for clients and ensure that replication is configured correctly between multiple servers.
- WINS replication can be used both to support redundant servers and to ensure that no data is lost.
- Using the clustering features of Windows 2000 is another way to ensure availability, but only for a single server. Even if clustering is used, separate WINS servers should be used in remote locations.

Improving performance

The following are methods of reducing the WINS server's response time and ensuring high performance:

- Use a fast machine as the WINS server; monitor its performance to determine if CPU speed, memory, or network bandwidth are becoming a bottleneck.
- Schedule push-and-pull partner replication to perform major updates during non-peak hours, but update often enough to prevent discrepancies when IP addresses change.

ON THE EXAM

Windows 2000 clients support burst-mode name registration, which can be configured to reduce the network bandwidth used by WINS registrations. Using this feature is another way to improve performance.

Designing Internet Connectivity

Internet connectivity is important in just about every network today, and Windows 2000 can use a number of services to make Internet connectivity easier. Several services are available to implement Internet connectivity for a network:

- Network Address Translation (NAT) provides a method of allowing Internet connectivity on a network with private IP addresses, eliminating the need for public addresses for every machine that accesses the Internet.

- Internet Connection Sharing (ICS) is a simplified form of NAT that has easy configuration; it is also included with Windows 98/Me. ICS is best for small networks.

- Microsoft Proxy Server 2.0 acts as a caching proxy and firewall for clients accessing Internet services.

NAT is included as part of Windows 2000; Microsoft Proxy Server 2.0 is a separate product available from Microsoft. At their most basic, both of these products provide an interface between a private network and the Internet. Which service to use depends on a number of factors:

Security
> NAT provides a global way of allowing Internet access, but does not provide security. If you need to provide different Internet access to different users or different access to different Internet resources, Proxy Server is a better solution.

Routing and locations
> NAT and ICS cannot be used on a routed network, unless separate NAT servers are used for each subnet. Proxy Server is a better solution for routed networks and for networks with multiple physical locations.

Resource sharing
> NAT does not provide for clients' sharing resources with Internet-based clients; Proxy Server allows you to control this access.

ON THE EXAM

For the *Designing a Microsoft Windows 2000 Network Infrastructure* MCSE exam, you should be able to determine whether NAT, ICS, or Proxy Server is the better solution for a particular network's Internet connectivity needs.

Network Address Translation (NAT)

Network Address Translation (NAT) is part of Windows 2000's Routing and Remote Access Service. NAT, as discussed in Part 4, translates between public and private IP addresses. This provides the following benefits:

- The private network is isolated from the Internet and secure from unauthorized access; only the NAT server is accessible from the Internet.

- Private IP addresses can be used on most machines in the network, eliminating the difficulty of obtaining public IP addresses for all machines.

- Acts as a simple DHCP server to assign addresses to clients from the pool of private addresses. This may eliminate the need for a separate DHCP server.

- Forwards DNS requests, so clients on the private network can resolve Internet hostnames without the use of a local DNS server.

The technical details of configuring and using NAT are described in Part 4. The following sections discuss the factors you should consider when using NAT in your design for a network infrastructure.

ON THE EXAM

Internet Connection Sharing (ICS) is a simple version of NAT for smaller networks. See Part 4 for details about installing and using ICS.

Placement and connectivity of the NAT server

The NAT server can be any Windows 2000 Server machine, and one NAT server should be used per network. The NAT server needs at least two network adapters: one for the local subnet and one for Internet access. These can be interfaces to similar networks (i.e., Ethernet) or dissimilar networks (i.e., Ethernet and DSL Internet).

The NAT server should be placed in the network with easy connectivity to the entire subnet; each NAT server can serve only one subnet. NAT servers do not require a consistent or dedicated IP address, because clients contact the NAT server using DHCP broadcasts.

Replacing DHCP and DNS services

As mentioned above, a NAT server can perform the services of a basic DHCP server for a single subnet. The NAT server issues addresses from the private range of 192.168.0.1–255 by default and responds to broadcasts in the same way as a DHCP server.

You can configure whether the NAT server assigns IP addresses. Client configuration for NAT is the same as for DHCP: with Windows clients, simply set the *Obtain an IP Address Automatically* option.

The NAT server can also be configured to forward local DNS requests to a public DNS server (often, the DNS server of an ISP). This eliminates the need for a local DNS server. When this feature is enabled, the NAT server specifies its own address as the DNS server when it configures clients.

NAT should not be used to forward DNS requests if a DNS server is already present on the network. Instead, the local server can communicate with Internet-based DNS servers as needed to resolve external hostnames.

Allowing Internet access

An essential part of Internet connectivity is the ability for Internet servers to send data back to the client that requested it, and NAT allows for this. However, in the default configuration, NAT does not allow external clients to access computers on the private network.

If you wish to make one or more computers accessible from the public network, you can use one or both of the following NAT features:

Address pools

If you have more than one public address available, you can set aside an address to be mapped to a specific private network address.

Special ports

You can also set up a mapping for requests sent to a specific port number on the NAT server to be sent to a specific IP address and port number in the local network. This is useful for allowing Internet access to an internal web or other server.

Designing Network

NAT security

NAT is reasonably secure by default, allowing access only to the NAT machine and any other addresses or ports you have specifically made available. You can enhance NAT's security by following these guidelines:

- Use IP filtering on the Internet connection or on the NAT machine's interface to the private network.
- Use Windows 2000's VPN features in combination with NAT to control user access to the network via the Internet.

Optimizing NAT

NAT can be optimized to provide better Internet connectivity and faster response times. Follow these guidelines to optimize your NAT design:

- Consider dedicating a machine to NAT. On smaller networks you can use this machine for other services, such as DHCP.
- Add additional modems or additional Internet connections to provide redundancy and increase bandwidth.
- Dial-up Internet connections are affordable, but there is a significant delay when dialing. Consider a permanent Internet connection: DSL, in particular, is often equally affordable.

Microsoft Proxy Server

Microsoft Proxy Server 2.0 is the latest version of Microsoft's proxy server product. Previous versions were included with Windows NT 4.0's Option Pack; Windows 2000 Server does not include Proxy Server, but it is available separately from Microsoft.

A proxy server provides access to the Internet or a public network, similar to NAT. However, proxy servers also add the following features:

- Security based on individual users, nodes, or Internet addresses
- Caching for HTTP and FTP requests
- Support for networks that span multiple subnets or locations

Microsoft Proxy Server 2.0 supports the new features of Windows 2000, including Active Directory integration. Proxy Server can also use Windows 2000's IPSec feature to authenticate and encrypt data.

Basic proxy server design

A single proxy server is sufficient for small to medium networks. The proxy server should be placed within the private network and provided connectivity to the Internet or public network.

For larger networks, multiple proxy servers can be used. These can either offer services to separate subnets or act together as a proxy chain. This allows secondary proxies to add caching and availability to the main proxy server.

Proxy server clients can be configured to connect with the proxy server in one of three ways:

Proxy server client (WinSock Proxy)
> Windows machines can use this client to automatically contact the proxy server for any IP request other than to the local network.

SOCKS proxy
> For non-Windows machines, SOCKS supports a number of protocols and provides an alternative to the Windows-specific client.

Web proxy (HTTP/FTP)
> With no client software, clients can simply contact the proxy server through a web browser. This works only for HTTP and FTP protocols.

Proxy server security

One of the key advantages to using Proxy Server for Internet connectivity rather than NAT is the built-in security features. Proxy Server's security can be configured in one of two ways:

Active Directory integration
> Proxy Server can be integrated with the Windows 2000 Active Directory, and users and groups in the Directory can be used to control Internet access.

Non-Active Directory
> In networks based on operating systems other than Windows 2000, Active Directory integration cannot be used. Instead, the proxy server computer's local users and groups can be used to secure Internet access.

Proxy Server 2.0 supports *packet filtering*, which allows you to restrict access to specific source or destination addresses, ports, or protocols. This allows you to specify exactly which sites can be accessed (grant access) or which cannot be accessed (deny access).

ON THE EXAM

Proxy Server's packet filtering is independent of Windows 2000's TCP/IP packet filtering. Both can be used to secure the proxy server.

Domain filters, another Proxy Server feature, allow you to restrict access to Internet sites by domain name or IP address. As with packet filters, domain filters can be set to grant all access or deny all access by default, and you can specify exceptions to this rule.

Web publishing

The Web Publishing feature of Proxy Server allows the proxy server to act as a gateway for incoming HTTP and FTP requests. After passing the proxy server's security tests, these requests are forwarded to the specified internal web or FTP server.

Designing Network

This feature provides two main benefits: first, it allows the proxy server's security mechanisms to prevent inappropriate access to the web server. Second, it allows you to operate one or more web or FTP servers on the internal network, without the need for public IP addresses.

Optimizing proxy server availability

Because a proxy server acts as the single gateway between a private network and the public Internet, a failure in the proxy server or its network connection can affect the whole network. The best way to prevent this is to have at least two proxy servers acting in an array. This not only improves performance, but also allows one proxy server to serve the entire network if the other fails.

ON THE EXAM

You can also configure a proxy array with only one proxy server. This is the only way to use Active Directory with one server, and it allows for future expansion with multiple servers.

For incoming requests, a proxy array also provides redundancy. In addition, the load balancing feature of Microsoft Proxy Server 2.0 allows incoming requests to be divided evenly between servers to prevent a slowdown of any one server. Round-robin DNS entries can also provide load balancing.

Optimizing proxy server performance

As the network grows, a proxy server can become a bottleneck, either for internal requests to access the Internet for or Internet-based access to an internal web or FTP server. Caching is one important way you can improve proxy server performance.

Proxy server supports two caching methods: *passive caching*, which simply caches requests as they are handled, and *active caching*, which anticipates requests and updates often-requested resources automatically. Use passive caching to conserve bandwidth; use active caching to provide increased performance.

Multiple servers may be needed if a single network is unable to quickly handle all requests. These can be configured in an array, or you can create a hierarchical arrangement with proxy servers in remote locations to minimize WAN traffic.

ON THE EXAM

Load balancing, discussed in the previous section, can also improve performance for incoming requests to a proxy server.

Designing Routing and Remote Access

Routers are used to connect subnets in a network, and are an essential element for all but the smallest networks. Routers can either be hardware devices or computers; Windows 2000 and Windows NT computers can act as routers.

Remote access is another important feature for most of today's networks, allowing access to employees or customers across modem connections. Routing and remote access can also be combined, for example, to allow dial-up access to a remote portion of the network.

The following sections describe what you should consider when planning to use the routing and remote access features of Windows 2000 in your network design.

Basic Routing Design

Routers are an important part of most networks. They not only connect subnets, but also provide security and provide communication between dissimilar networks. The following sections describe the basics of planning a network routing design.

Router placement

Routers are generally placed between subnets; a router typically has at least two network interfaces, one for each subnet. Routers can support both persistent network connections (such as Ethernet or DSL) and non-persistent connections, such as dial-up PPP.

Routers are chiefly used in two positions: first, as a connection between subnets in a LAN or WAN, and second, as an interface to a public network, such as the Internet.

ON THE EXAM

Routers can be used to connect a private network to the Internet, much like NAT or Proxy Server; the chief difference is that a router does not provide address translation, so all machines on the private network must have public IP addresses to use a router for connectivity.

Static and dynamic routing

Routers use a routing table to keep track of potential network destinations and their paths. There are two basic types of IP routers:

Static routers
> Use a fixed routing table specifying available destinations, configured by the administrator.

Dynamic routers
> Maintain a routing table dynamically by communicating with other routers.

Static routing is typically used in smaller networks; when several routers are used in a network, dynamic routing provides greater efficiency, greater availability, and easier administration.

IN THE REAL WORLD

Although dynamic routing has many advantages, its use of routing protocols also opens it up to certain types of attacks. Be sure you keep security in mind when configuring dynamic routing.

Routing protocols

Dynamic routers use one or more *routing protocols* to communicate between routers. The following routing protocols are supported by Windows 2000:

RIP (Router Information Protocol)
RIP is the most basic router protocol. Routers running RIP keep a table of destinations and the number of hops (intermediate nodes) they require. RIP is known as a *distance vector routing protocol.*

RIP v2
RIP Version 2 is an improved version of RIP supported by Windows 2000. Its chief advantages are that it sends updates only when needed rather than repeating them unnecessarily, and it provides for router authentication.

OSPF (Open Shortest Path First)
OSPF is a *link state routing protocol,* meaning that routing is based not only on distance, but also on the current status of links in the network. OSPF uses a more efficient method to transmit changes between routers and, thus, conserves network bandwidth.

IGMP
IGMP is a specialized protocol that allows multicast transmissions, such as those used in streaming media, to route within a subnet. It can be used in combination with other routing protocols to support multicasts.

ON THE EXAM

RIP is the best choice for simple routing, with few changes to the routing table. OSPF is a better choice when routes change frequently and when redundant paths are provided. IGMP is specifically for multicast transmissions.

Planning Routing Security

Because routers form the backbone of a complex network, they are an important place to consider the security of the network. The following sections describe ways you can build security into your network routing design.

Authentication

Routers can be authenticated to prevent unauthorized access to the network. The simplest form of authentication is the passwords used by the RIP v2 and OSPF protocols. All routers must be set to the same password, which prevents unauthorized routers from participating in the network.

ON THE EXAM

RIP v2 and OSPF passwords use clear-text authentication and are vulnerable to network snooping.

You can improve upon basic router authentication in the following ways:

- For demand-dial routing, use the encrypted authentication supported by Remote Access.
- IPSec can be used to authenticate routers and to encrypt communications.

IP filtering

The IP filtering feature of Windows 2000's Routing and Remote Access service provides additional security for routing. You can use this feature to control the IP addresses and protocols that routers can use to communicate. Windows 2000's TCP/IP filters provide an additional layer of security.

VPNs and IPSec

To further secure traffic between routers, you can use encrypted tunnels for the transmission of data. Use one of the following features of Windows 2000:

- For routers that communicate via the Internet, use VPN tunneling. IPSec can be used on VPN tunnels if the L2TP protocol is used.
- For Windows 2000 routers within a local subnet, use IPSec to create an encrypted tunnel between routers.

Optimizing the Routing Design

Routers that operate inefficiently can bog down an entire network. Although Windows 2000's routing features are reasonably efficient, you can optimize routing to improve availability and performance. Follow these guidelines to optimize routing:

- If Windows 2000 computers are used as routers, consider using a faster machine or a cluster to provide increased performance and reliability. If the machine is also performing other services, consider dedicating the machine to routing.
- Use multiple routers to ensure availability.

- Use redundant routes to ensure connectivity when a portion of the network is unavailable.

- Consider using persistent connections (such as DSL) for Internet access instead of dial-up connections.

Planning Remote Access

Windows 2000's Remote Access features allow dial-up modems to be used for network connectivity. Although this feature is often used for remote access by users, it also works with Windows 2000 routing to allow dial-up routing to portions of the network.

As discussed earlier in this chapter, Remote Access works with DHCP to assign IP addresses to modem users. It is also integrated with Windows 2000's DNS, WINS, and Active Directory services.

Important considerations when designing a remote access solution include server placement, security, and authentication for remote users. The following sections describe items you should consider when planning remote access for a network.

Placement of remote access servers

A remote access server can be placed in a subnet to provide dial-up access to public networks for users of the subnet and to provide dial-in access to the subnet for remote users. The server should be configured with a fast network connection, because remote users already experience delays caused by modem use.

ON THE EXAM

If a remote access server handles a large number of modems it can quickly exceed the bandwidth of a typical network connection, because it needs to provide the combined bandwidth needed by all of the concurrent modem users.

Remote access security

Remote access is particularly vulnerable to security breaches, because access by modem is available to anyone who has the phone number. Thus, Windows 2000 remote access includes a number of security options. Security begins with the authentication of clients. Windows 2000 supports the following authentication types:

CHAP (Challenge Handshake Authentication Protocol)
An Internet-standard protocol that exchanges encrypted tokens for authentication

MS-CHAP
Microsoft's proprietary version of CHAP, supported by Windows and Windows NT

MS-CHAP v2

A new version of MS-CHAP, available only to Windows 2000 clients and servers

Extensible Authentication Protocol (EAP)

A dynamic authentication protocol that can use certificates, smart cards, or other authenticated methods

Unencrypted Authentication

Allows use of the PAP (Password Authentication Protocol) and SPAP (Shiva PAP) protocols, which provide authentication using plain-text passwords

In addition to authentication, Windows 2000 remote access supports encryption of communications. The following types of encryption are supported:

- MPPE (Microsoft Point-to-Point Encryption) provides basic encryption using 40-, 56-, or 128-bit encryption keys based on the RSA standard.

- IPSec is used for L2TP tunneling, described in the following section.

Tunneling protocols

Another important use of remote access is to support virtual private networks, or VPNs. This refers to the use of a public network, such as the Internet, to provide a transport for two or more otherwise unconnected portions of a private network.

Because VPN data travels over public networks, security is of great concern. Windows 2000's VPN protocols support *tunneling*, or encrypting VPN traffic and encapsulating it in standard network protocols, to prevent snooping on the public network. Windows 2000 supports two tunneling protocols:

PPTP (Point-To-Point Tunneling Protocol)

The basic VPN protocol, created as an extension to the dial-up protocol PPP (point-to-point protocol). PPTP connections are encrypted with MPPE.

L2TP (Layer 2 Tunneling Protocol)

A protocol that combines L2F (Layer 2 Forwarding) with PPTP to create a more efficient virtual private network. L2TP uses IPSec for encryption.

Your choice of the protocol to use mainly depends on the operating systems in use on the network. PPTP is supported by older Windows systems (beginning with Windows 98 SE) and by other platforms; L2TP with IPSec is more secure, but requires Windows 2000.

ON THE EXAM

Windows 2000's Remote Access supports five PPTP or L2TP ports by default; you must create any additional ports you need separately.

Optimizing remote access

Remote access can provide an essential link in the network infrastructure, and your design should ensure the optimum availability and performance of remote access. The following are guidelines for improving availability and performance:

- Use redundant dial-in servers and modems.

- Add additional servers at remote locations to provide local availability.

- Consider using Windows 2000 clustering or DNS load balancing to divide remote access tasks among multiple servers.

- Use the highest-speed modems available.

- Consider dedicating a server to remote access or using a faster machine or faster disk storage to support large numbers of remote users.

Remote access using RADIUS

RADIUS (Remote Access Dial-In User Services) is a new Windows 2000 feature that centralizes remote access management and provides accounting features. This can be used as a more sophisticated management tool for remote access.

RADIUS uses existing mechanisms for user authentication rather than providing its own authentication and is a standard defined in RFCs 2138 and 2139. RADIUS allows remote users to authenticate with a Windows NT domain or with the Windows 2000 Active Directory.

For security, RADIUS supports the same encryption and authentication methods as standard remote access. RADIUS also uses a system of secrets (passwords) for authentication between RADIUS servers.

ON THE EXAM

For optimum security, Microsoft recommends that RADIUS secrets be at least 16 characters long and include lowercase and uppercase letters, numbers, and punctuation.

Suggested Exercises

Even more than most exams, the Designing series of MCSE exams require you to have real-world experience working with the issues they cover. Because the emphasis is often on larger networks, you may have to design conceptual networks if you do not have access to a large network to experiment with.

The following exercises will provide a framework for your preparations for the *Designing a Microsoft Windows 2000 Network Infrastructure* MCSE exam.

Designing a Network Infrastructure

Practice analyzing a company's needs and existing infrastructure and designing a network. Ideally, use your network or a client's as a model or arrange to visit a company and interview its IS personnel. Your analysis should include the following components:

- Business requirements
- Technical requirements
- Existing network infrastructure
- Planned upgrades, expansions, or changes

TCP/IP and DHCP Design

Design a public/private IP addressing scheme for a network. Include the use of DHCP for addressing and determine the number of DHCP servers and relays required.

Name Resolution Design

Design one or more DNS zones for a network. Choose whether to use traditional or Active Directory integrated zones. Determine whether DNS, WINS, or both will be required.

Internet Connectivity

Determine whether NAT, ICS, or Proxy Server would be the best application to provide Internet connectivity for your network. Determine the best placement for NAT or proxy servers.

Routing and Remote Access

Design a remote access system for your network. Your design should include the following:

- Authentication methods
- Support for non-Windows systems
- Security
- Placement and configuration of remote access servers

Practice Tests

Comprehensive Test

1. You are running NAT to provide Internet access to 10 computers on a network. How many public IP addresses are required?

    a.   0

    b.   1

    c.   10

    d.   11

2. Which of the following is *not* a reserved private IP address?

    a.   192.168.0.12

    b.   10.0.10.10

    c.   209.68.11.152

    d.   169.254.0.5

3. Which of the following protocols can assign IP addresses to clients from a pool of available addresses? (Select all that apply.)

    a.   DHCP

    b.   NAT

    c.   DNS

    d.   ICS

4. Which of the following are advantages of a proxy server over IP filtering for security? (Select all that apply.)

    a.   Protocol-specific filtering

    b.   Caching

    c.   Improved speed

    d.   Support for new protocols

5. Which of the following IPSec policies should you choose for maximum security?

    a.   Respond Only

    b.   Require Security

    c.   Request Security

6. Which of the following is a routing protocol new to Windows 2000?

    a.   RIP v1

    b.   RIP v2

    c.   OSPF

    d.   L2TP

7. Which of the following operating systems can operate as a DHCP server? (Select all that apply.)

    a.   Windows Me

    b.   Windows NT Server

    c.   Windows 2000 Professional

    d.   Windows 2000 Server

8. Which of the following is a Windows 2000 DHCP feature that allows multiple non-consecutive pools of IP addresses to be used?

    a.   Scopes

    b.   Superscopes

    c.   DNS updates

    d.   DHCP relay

9. Which of the following can be used to forward DHCP requests between subnets in a network? (Select all that apply.)

    a.   DHCP relay

    b.   RIP

    c.   Hardware routers

    d.   Superscopes

10. In Windows 2000, how many WINS server addresses can a client be configured with?

    a.   1

    b.   2

    c.   6

    d.   12

11. Which of the following is *not* included with Windows 2000 Server?

    a.   NAT

    b.   Proxy Server 2.0

    c.   ICS

    d.   DHCP

12. Which of the following services are performed by NAT along with address translation? (Select all that apply.)

    a.   DNS

    b.   DHCP

    c.   WINS

    d.   RAS

13. Which NAT feature allows you to configure a web or other Internet server on a machine with a private IP address?

    a.   Web Publishing

    b.   Proxy Server

    c.   Special ports

    d.   Connection sharing

14. Which Proxy Server feature allows you to support a web or other Internet server on a machine with a private IP address?

    a.   Web Publishing

    b.   Proxy Server

    c.   Special ports

    d.   Connection sharing

15. Which of the following routing protocols support router authentication? (Select all that apply.)

    a.   RIP v1

    b.   RIP v2

    c.   OSPF

    d.   L2TP

Designing Network

16. How many PPTP or L2TP ports are supported by default in routing and remote access?

    a.   1

    b.   2

    c.   5

    d.   16

17. Which one of the following Internet connectivity methods requires a public IP address for each computer that will access the Internet?

    a.   Proxy Server

    b.   NAT

    c.   Router

    d.   ICS

18. For client computers running Windows 2000 Professional, which of the following DNS records are updated by the DHCP server?

    a.   PTR record

    b.   A record

    c.   MX record

    d.   None of the above

19. Which of the following DNS zones is available only in Windows 2000?

    a.   Traditional primary zone

    b.   Traditional secondary zone

    c.   Active Directory integrated zone

    d.   Reverse lookup zone

20. Which of the following is the encryption method used with PPTP virtual private networks under Windows 2000?

    a.   IPSec

    b.   MS-CHAP

    c.   MPPE

    d.   SPAP

Case Study

Text Formatting Key:

- **Describes requirements**
- *Conflicts with requirement*
- Irrelevant background information

You are designing a network that will have **40 Windows 2000 Servers** distributed between **10 locations** with WAN connections. The clients in the initial network will include **200 Windows 2000 Professional machines**, *50 Windows 98 machines,* and *10 Macintosh computers.* You are also running *web servers* on 2 of the Windows 2000 Server machines.

You need to develop a **plan for IP addressing** on the network. You also need to support **name resolution** and provide **Internet access** to all of the clients.

Multiple Choice

1. You are considering using ICS (Internet Connection Sharing) to provide IP addresses and Internet connectivity. Which of the following might be a problem with this approach? (Select all that apply.)

   a. No support for Macintosh clients

   b. No support for incoming connections to the web servers

   c. No support for Windows 98 clients

   d. No support for multiple subnets

2. Along with the requirements mentioned above, you want to ensure that the web servers are secured against attacks and to monitor and control Internet access by employees. Which of the following would be the best choice for Internet connectivity?

   a. ICS

   b. NAT

   c. Proxy Server 2.0

   d. A router

3. After installing the service you chose above, which additional services will be required to provide for the original requirement of Internet access and IP addressing?

   a. DNS

   b. DHCP

   c. NAT

   d. WINS

Create a Tree

1. Place the following protocols under the headings *name resolution* or *IP addressing*:

   a. DNS

   b. DHCP

c.   WINS

d.   NAT

e.   ICS

2. Place the following RAS authentication methods under the headings *encrypted* or *unencrypted*:

a.   CHAP

b.   PAP

c.   SPAP

d.   MS-CHAP

e.   EAP

Answers

Comprehensive Test

1. b. Only a single public IP address is required, although more than one can be used.

2. c. 209.68.11.152 is not a reserved private IP address. The other addresses listed fall into one of the reserved ranges.

3. a, b, d. DHCP, NAT, and ICS can assign IP addresses. DNS (choice c) is used to resolve names and addresses.

4. a, b. Proxy servers offer advanced filtering options and support for caching. Improved speed (choice c) and support for new protocols (choice d) are advantages of IP filtering over a proxy.

5. b. Use the Require Security (Secure Server) option for maximum security.

6. b. RIP v2 is new to Windows 2000. RIP v1 and OSPF (choices a and c) are supported by earlier versions of Windows NT; L2TP (choice c) is not a routing protocol.

7. b, d. Windows NT Server and Windows 2000 Server can act as DHCP servers.

8. b. Superscopes allow multiple, non-consecutive pools of IP addresses to be treated as a single scope.

9. a, c. DHCP relay can be used to forward DHCP requests between subnets. Many hardware routers also support this feature.

10. d. Windows 2000 supports up to 12 WINS server addresses.

11. b. Proxy Server 2.0 is a separate product and is not included with Windows 2000 Server.

12. a, b. Although limited, NAT acts as a DNS and DHCP server.

13. c. The special ports feature allows you to configure a machine with a private IP address to be accessible from the Internet as a web server.

14. a. The Web Publishing feature of Proxy Server allows you to make an internal server available over the Internet.

15. b, c. The RIP v2 and OSPF routing protocols support router authentication.

16. c. Five PPTP or L2TP ports are supported by default in Routing and Remote Access.

17. c. When a router is used for Internet connectivity, each machine that will access the Internet requires a public IP address. The other solutions listed use private addressing.

18. a. The PTR record is updated by the DHCP server. The A record (choice b) is updated directly by the client running Windows 2000 Professional.

19. c. Active Directory integrated zones are available only in Windows 2000.

20. c. MPPE (Microsoft Point-to-Point Encryption) is used to encrypt traffic on PPTP VPNs.

Case Study: Multiple Choice

1. b, d. ICS does not support incoming connections or multiple subnets. It can support non-Windows clients (choice a) and Windows 98 clients (choice c).

2. c. Proxy Server 2.0 would be the best choice, because it supports advanced security features and can filter Internet access by clients.

3. b. Because Proxy Server does not handle IP addressing, you would need to use DHCP to allocate IP addresses.

Case Study: Create a Tree

Create a Tree Answer # 1

Name Resolution	IP Addressing
DNS	DHCP
WINS	NAT
	ICS

Create a Tree Answer # 2

Encrypted	Unencrypted
CHAP	PAP
MS-CHAP	SPAP
EAP	

Highlighter's Index

TCP/IP Design

TCP/IP Basics
Named for protocols: Transport Control Protocol and Internet Protocol
Default protocol for Windows 2000
Routable
Uses logical (IP) addresses
New Windows 2000 features: Enhanced PPTP, L2TP, and IPSec

IP Address Classes

Class	Network/Host Bytes	Number of Networks	Number of Hosts per Network
A	1/3	126	16,777,214
B	2/2	16,382	65,534
C	3/1	2,097,150	254

Subnet Masking
Subdivides a network by using bits from host address
Number of subnets available: $2^{(number\ of\ bits)} - 2$

Class	Default Subnet Mask
A	255.0.0.0
B	255.255.0.0
C	255.255.255.0

Private IP Address Ranges

Address Class	Starting Address	Ending Address
A	10.0.0.0	10.255.255.255
B	169.254.0.1	169.254.255.254
C	172.16.0.0	172.31.255.255
C	192.168.0.0	192.168.255.255

IP Filtering

Blocks access to unauthorized ports or protocols
Enabled by default
Can filter TCP ports, UDP ports, or protocols

DHCP Design

DHCP Basics

Maintains a pool of addresses (scope) and assigns them dynamically.
Can assign IP address, subnet mask, default gateway, DNS server, WINS server.
Uses broadcasts and one or more DHCP servers.
Clients only need DHCP enabled; address of server is not required.
Manage with DHCP snap-in.

DHCP Features

Authorization: Windows 2000 authorizes DHCP servers; Windows 2000 Server DHCP service will not start without authorization.
Reservations: IP addresses can be reserved for specific computers.
Options: sends gateway, DNS, and other information along with IP address.
DHCP relay: forwards DHCP requests between subnets when a router is not configured to forward DHCP.
Dynamic DNS updates: DHCP server contacts DNS server to update addresses of clients; Windows 2000 clients can do this themselves.

Name Resolution Design

DNS (Domain Name Service)

Internet standard for hostname resolution; requires a DNS server.
Windows 2000 Server includes DNS Server software.
Zone: Defined group of names and IP addresses.
At least one zone must be defined for use.
Configure with DNS Manager snap-in.

WINS (Windows Internet Naming Service)

Uses a dedicated server; WINS Server included with Windows 2000 Server.
Used with P-node, M-node, and H-node resolution.
Configure with WINS snap-in.
Clients require WINS server address.
Server address can be set with DHCP.

Internet Connectivity

NAT (Network Address Translation)

Translation: Translates between public and private IP addresses
IP address assignment: Includes a simple DHCP server and can assign IP addresses to clients; uses private IP addresses
DNS name resolution: Acts as a DNS server; forwards DNS requests to an Internet DNS server and returns the results to clients

Internet Connection Sharing (ICS)

Simplified version of NAT
Uses a single checkbox rather than complex configuration information
Uses a fixed range of private IP addresses
Allows only one public IP address
Can only be used on one internal LAN interface

Proxy Server 2.0

Provides security based on individual users, nodes, or Internet addresses
Caches HTTP and FTP requests
Supports networks that span multiple subnets or locations
Integrates with Active Directory
Provides user-based and site-specific security

Routing and Remote Access

Remote Access Basics

Supported in Windows 2000 by RRAS (Routing and Remote Access Services)
Managed using Routing and Remote Access snap-in
Supports dial-in and dial-out use; dial-in limited in Windows 2000 Professional

Authentication Methods

CHAP (Challenge Handshake Authentication Protocol)
An Internet-standard protocol that exchanges encrypted tokens for authentication.

MS-CHAP
Microsoft's proprietary version of CHAP, supported by Windows and Windows NT.

MS-CHAP v2

A new version of MS-CHAP, available only to Windows 2000 clients and servers.

Extensible Authentication Protocol (EAP)

A dynamic authentication protocol that can use certificates, smart cards, or other authenticated methods.

Unencrypted authentication

Allows use of the PAP (Password Authentication Protocol) and SPAP (Shiva PAP) protocols (plain-text passwords).

Unauthenticated access

If this option is enabled, clients can complete PPP connections with no authentication. This option is disabled by default and is a serious security risk.

PART 7

Designing Security

Exam Overview

As a network administrator or consultant, your job can involve planning, analyzing, and designing networks as much as implementing them. Security should be a major consideration in any network design.

MCSE Exam 70-220, *Designing Security for a Microsoft Windows 2000 Network*, deals with the design and planning of network security services and protocols. This exam can be used as an optional core exam or as an elective.

Because Active Directory is the fundamental data store for Windows 2000 security, most security techniques involve the Directory. You should be familiar with all aspects of Active Directory, as discussed in Part 3. You should also consider the design of Active Directory (Part 5) and Network Infrastructure (Part 6) when developing a security design.

To prepare for this chapter and the Designing Security exam, you should have studied Parts 1 and 2 for the basics of Windows 2000 Professional and Server. You should also be familiar with Windows 2000's Active Directory and should, ideally, have real-world experience managing and securing a Windows 2000 network.

Areas of Study

Planning Network Security

Need to Know	Reference
Types of security	"Windows 2000 Security Overview" on page 382
Network role types	"Mapping Network Roles" on page 386

Need to Apply	Reference
Analyze business requirements for a security design	"Analyzing Business Requirements" on page 383
Analyze technical requirements for a security design	"Analyzing Technical Requirements" on page 384
Map information flow	"Mapping Company Information" on page 385
Identify network roles	"Mapping Network Roles" on page 386
Analyze current security risks	"Analyzing Security Risks" on page 386
Design a plan for upgrades and changes	"Planning for Change" on page 388

Designing Basic Security

Need to Know	Reference
Basic components to secure	"Creating a Security Baseline" on page 389
Operations master types	"Operations masters" on page 390
Windows 2000 authentication methods	"Planning Authentication" on page 391
Certificate authority roles	"Certificate server roles" on page 398

Need to Apply	Reference
Create a baseline for security	"Creating a Security Baseline" on page 389
Choose authentication methods	"Planning Authentication" on page 391
Install Certificate Services	"Certificate authority (CA) hierarchies" on page 397
Manage certificates	"Managing certificates" on page 398

Encrypting Filesystem (EFS)

Need to Know	Reference
EFS features, advantages, and disadvantages	"EFS Basics" on page 401
EFS terminology	"EFS Basics" on page 401
EFS process	"How EFS works" on page 402
Key storage locations	"Key storage locations" on page 403

Need to Apply	Reference
Determine whether to use EFS	"EFS Basics" on page 401
Encrypt and decrypt files	"How EFS works" on page 402

Designing Auditing

Need to Know	Reference
Built-in audit policies	"Creating an Audit Policy" on page 404
Typical events to audit	"Creating an Audit Policy" on page 404

Need to Apply	Reference
Create an audit policy	"Creating an Audit Policy" on page 404
Determine events to audit	"Creating an Audit Policy" on page 404
Plan for the use of audit data	"Planning Use of Audit Data" on page 406

Securing Network Services

Need to Know	Reference
Windows 2000 DNS security features	"DNS Security" on page 407
Dynamic DNS support for different operating systems	"DNS Security" on page 407
RIS features and requirements	"Remote Installation Services (RIS) Security" on page 410
Terminal Services modes	"Terminal Services Security" on page 412

Need to Apply	Reference
Configure DNS for higher security	"DNS Security" on page 407
Configure RIS naming schemes	"Remote Installation Services (RIS) Security" on page 410
Secure Terminal Services	"Terminal Services Security" on page 412

Designing Secure Connectivity

Need to Know	Reference
Differences between NAT and Proxy Server	"Securing Public Network Access" on page 413
VPN protocols	"VPNs (Virtual Private Networks)" on page 414
Windows 2000 SMB security features	"SMB Signing Security" on page 415

Need to Apply	Reference
Secure Internet access with NAT or Proxy Server	"Securing Public Network Access" on page 413

Need to Apply	Reference
Choose VPN protocols	"VPNs (Virtual Private Networks)" on page 414
Enable SMB signing	"SMB Signing Security" on page 415

Planning IP Security

Need to Know	Reference
IP Security features and advantages	"Planning IP Security" on page 416
IPSec terminology	"Creating an Encryption Scheme" on page 417
IPSec negotiation phases	"IPSec Negotiation" on page 418
Common TCP/IP ports	"IP Filtering" on page 419
Types of filter policy	"IP Filtering" on page 419

Need to Apply	Reference
Create an IPSec encryption scheme.	"Creating an Encryption Scheme" on page 417
Configure IPSec packet filters.	"IP Filtering" on page 419
Define IPSec security levels.	"Defining security levels" on page 420

Study Guide

This chapter includes the following sections, which address various topics covered on the *Designing a Microsoft Windows 2000 Network Infrastructure* MCSE exam:

Planning Network Security
> Discusses the basics of network security and the tasks you should perform to begin designing a secure network

Designing Basic Security
> Introduces the basic security features of Windows 2000 and the process of creating a security baseline

Encrypted Filesystem (EFS)
> Presents information about the Encrypted Filesystem, Windows 2000's system for storing encrypted files within the NTFS

Designing Auditing
> Discusses Windows 2000's auditing features and how they can be used to monitor network security

Securing Network Services
> Presents methods of adding security to Windows 2000's network services, including DNS, RIS, and Terminal Services

Designing Secure Connectivity
> Discusses methods of securing connectivity to public networks, VPNs, and SMB (file sharing)

Planning IP Security
> Presents the details of how IPSec (IP Security) can create secure communication channels between Windows 2000 computers

Planning Network Security

Security is an important consideration in any network, whether it means keeping highly confidential files private or simply allowing users access to the files and other resources they need. Windows 2000 adds a number of security features to those of Windows NT:

- Active Directory replaces the SAM database in NT 4.0 for domain-level security, but retains SAM for workstation security.

- More sophisticated IP filtering allows any computer to receive only specific types of packets, or packets from trusted addresses.

- IP Security (IPSec) uses encrypted network traffic to increase the security of TCP/IP networks.

The following sections explore the basics of Windows 2000 security and discuss the analysis and planning you should perform to begin designing a secure network.

IN THE REAL WORLD

Like any relatively new operating system, Windows 2000 has a few security holes not found in previous versions. To maintain a truly secure network, watch Microsoft's web page and other sites for news of security problems and download and install patches as soon as they are available.

Windows 2000 Security Overview

A secure network requires more than a secure operating system—it requires a consistent design and plan followed by network administrators as well as other employees. The basic tasks involved in maintaining a secure network are discussed in the following sections.

Authentication

Authentication is what most users immediately recognize as a form of security—the logon dialog box that is presented when Windows 2000 starts. This process involves verifying that the password and user account are correct and then allowing access to the network.

The authentication process is far more complex than it appears, because it provides security by not sending passwords directly across the network. The Windows 2000 authentication process uses *Kerberos* authentication, an Internet standard specified by RFC 1510. This is explained in detail later in this chapter.

Controlling access to resources

Although authentication identifies a specific, authorized user, this does not in itself provide security. The next key component of a security design is the control of user access to such resources as files, printers, and modems.

Using the NTFS, you can control a user's ability to access files. Using Active Directory, you can control the user's ability to access printers and other resources, referred to as objects, as well as access to the Active Directory itself.

Auditing resource access

A third component of a secure network is auditing. Windows 2000's auditing features allow user actions (such as logon or file access) to be logged in whatever level of detail you desire.

Although a perfectly secure network would not require auditing, no network is perfectly secure. An audit trail and regular analysis allow you to determine whether unauthorized access is happening and to further analyze problems that do occur so as to prevent future problems.

Encryption

A network is only as secure as the wires its data is carried on, and in large networks, an immense amount of wire is involved—from the local building's cabling to WAN connections and modem lines. In many networks, this is complicated further by the use of VPNs (virtual private networks). These networks use the Internet—which is inherently very insecure—as their transport.

Encryption is a way to prevent unauthorized access to data in these networks. Although the cabling may be relatively insecure (and the Internet even more so), encrypted data is useless without the ability to decrypt it. Of course, the quality of the encryption scheme is critical. Windows 2000's available encryption methods are explained later in this chapter.

Analyzing Business Requirements

Before you begin to configure Windows 2000 for a secure network, you should look at the company itself. To begin designing a secure network, analyze the company's security needs—which can vary widely within the company:

- Users need to access their personal files and certain shared files.
- Management needs to restrict access to certain areas.
- The IS department needs simple methods of adding users to the network or changing privileges.

Your security design should begin with a list of requirements for all users, managers, and departments, from general items like those listed above to specific names of files, directories, and printers. The following sections discuss the information you should examine.

Company structure

The company's organizational structure is an important element of a security design. It specifies which managers should assign the privileges to certain users and, ideally, describes the different departments and divisions that will require different security settings.

Size and locations

The scope of a company is a critical factor in a security design. For tiny companies, for example, a design may simply define three types of users and the resources they have access to. An example of this would be creating three user groups for customer service representatives, database programmers, and network administrators. Customer service employees may have Read access to billing information, the database programmers may have Read and Write access, and the network administrators might have full control over the customer database. For a company with multiple locations, each location may have a different organizational structure and different security requirements.

At the extreme, international companies may have different requirements for each location and for different organizations and may even have separate security administrators and IS departments to manage separate locations. With some companies, the locations can be treated similarly; with others, there is more similarity to a group of companies with certain communication channels than to a single, cohesive organization.

ON THE EXAM

Although you may work, or intend to work, in a relatively small network with a simple organization, you should be prepared to analyze and design security for large, multinational companies for the Designing Security MCSE exam.

Analyzing Technical Requirements

Although business requirements are an essential part of a security design, technical requirements are also important. You should work with the IS department to determine technical needs and factor these into the design. The following sections describe typical technical considerations.

Connectivity and bandwidth

Although not strictly a security issue, the connectivity and bandwidth available between departments or locations is an important consideration. Methods of connectivity are part of the network infrastructure design, but they may also have an impact on security:

- Some types of WAN links are more secure than others.

- Internet links in particular require strong encryption to ensure security.

- Several security methods (such as encryption) may have an impact on the bandwidth or response time available to users.

Performance requirements

Performance effects of security measures are another consideration. Although heavy use of IP filtering and encryption can provide strong security, they can also

---

slow down the performance of servers and the network. You may need to plan to use faster machines or multiple servers to meet the performance and security needs of the company.

IN THE REAL WORLD

To secure a network, you need to understand the protocols and services that form its basic infrastructure. These are discussed in Part 6, *Designing Network Infrastructure.*

Mapping Company Information

To continue your security design, you should map the flow of information in the company. This includes information transmitted across the network, as well as information that travels through other channels. The following section describes aspects of information you should map.

Information flow

Whether the company currently uses the network for communication, you should map the flow of information in the company. This includes information sent through memos, email, or phone conversations.

This can facilitate setting up improved communication systems, and it is also important to security; for example, if several users work as a team at adjacent stations, it would be pointless to give them different access privileges. On the other hand, if a user has to repeatedly ask a supervisor to look up information, the user may need more privileges to be efficient.

Product life cycle

The life cycle of a company's product can also affect information flow. For example, a company that produces physical products would have different communication needs during the processes of design, production, inventory management, sales, and service.

By contrast, a software company might divide its product life cycle into design, feasibility testing, programming, debugging, alpha testing, beta testing, production, sales, shipping, and support. During different phases, users may require different types of network access, and different aspects of security may be important.

In a well-organized company, its organizational chart may already divide the components of the product life cycle into departments: for example, the Testing department handles all testing, and the Sales department handles all sales. This makes it easy to assign security by department. On the other hand, in a smaller company these roles may be shared by one or more departments.

Decision-making structure

To complete your map of company information flow, you should document how decisions relating to security will be made. Will a single administrator have complete discretion to grant privileges to users? Will a single manager direct the IS department for all security needs? Or are several people or departments involved in the decision-making process?

Mapping Network Roles

Your security design should also include a list of *network roles*. These are the various types of users that will require network access. Rather than listing current users and their security needs, the design should focus on the roles the users hold, such as Payroll Administrator or Backup Administrator.

These roles can be given the appropriate privileges for their responsibilities, and the users who currently handle the job can be assigned to the roles. The following sections discuss different types of roles you may wish to include in your security design.

End-user roles

End-user roles are those that apply to a specific user or group of users, such as Payroll Administrator or Accounts Payable Manager. These roles should be based on the company's organizational chart, and each should have specific needs.

Resource ownership

In the Windows 2000 security system, such resources as files are typically owned by a user. Your design should specify which user role owns each resource and thus has control over it.

Administrative roles

Administrative roles include tasks usually performed by the IS department: for example, Backup Administrator, Security Manager, or Internet Access Manager. You should define a list of roles and specify the resources that each will need to access.

Service roles

Service roles do not usually represent actual users. These represent user accounts that will be used by applications and network services: for example, IIS (Internet Information Server) uses a user account to define its access to files, and automated backup routines use a user role that has limited access to a large number of files.

Analyzing Security Risks

Securing a network always involves some degree of *risk*: the chance that security will be compromised. No matter how secure the operating system or how secure your security policies, there is always a certain element of risk. The key to good security lies in determining the level of risk that is acceptable and eliminating unacceptable risks.

Finding current security risks

Whether you are dealing with a company currently running a previous version of Windows NT, a different operating system, or no computers at all, there is a potential for security risks. These range from the highly technical (OS bugs that allow a determined cracker to gain access) to the logistical (secure documents left in easily accessible or public locations).

A vital part of your security design is a list of current security risks and the ways your design can correct them. The following are typical examples of common security risks:

- Employees using easy-to-guess passwords or keeping written notes of their passwords

- Poorly managed file security allowing employees to read, modify, or delete (either deliberately or accidentally) inappropriate files

- Physical security that makes network security useless: for example, an unlocked door to the room containing the file server or printouts of confidential information in trash cans

- The potential for malicious attacks from crackers, current or former employees, or competitors

These are only a few examples. The best way to find security risks is to attempt to attack the network yourself, without using administrative passwords, and to see how easy or difficult this task is.

Determining acceptable risks

It's impossible to eliminate all security risks. Rather than attempt to, you should determine the level of risk that is acceptable. This may vary wildly, depending on the type of company you are working with: a small company may tolerate a great number of unlikely risks, while a bank or government organization may need to guarantee that very few or no significant risks exist.

You may wish to deem a risk acceptable if it is difficult to prevent and has a relatively small risk of serious impact (for example, employees taking printouts of their own files home) or if the cost of preventing it is greater than the potential cost of the data lost or compromised due to the risk.

ON THE EXAM

Although certain types of risk are unavoidable, you may be able to use auditing to at least determine the damage and decide whether further steps should be taken to eliminate the risk. Auditing is discussed later in this chapter, in the section "Design Auditing."

Designing
Security

Analyzing new systems

Every new component you add to the network, or to the company's infrastructure in general, adds new security risks. This includes major changes, such as a new operating system, as well as small changes, such as installing new software or creating new user accounts.

You should analyze your security design at every step to determine whether the added components will introduce new risks, and then decide on the best way to prevent those risks.

Planning for Change

Network security is an ongoing task, and your security design should include a plan to regularly reevaluate the security of the existing network, hardware, and software and make necessary changes. Security can also be affected by incidental changes to the network.

The following sections discuss these changes and other final issues you should consider when planning a secure network.

Identifying upgrades and patches

In most networks, upgrades are regularly performed. These may include any or all of the following:

- New software versions
- New operating system versions
- New hardware
- New WAN or LAN infrastructure equipment

Any of these upgrades may cause changes to the security of the network, and you should review the security design and assess the impact before making any changes. In particular, new versions of operating systems always create new security holes.

Another upgrade you should regularly perform is to check for updated security patches for operating systems (such as Windows 2000) and other software you may have on the network (web browsers, email programs, etc.).

Technical support

Supporting users with technical problems is necessary in all but the simplest networks, and your network design should include a plan for managing the technical support personnel with security in mind. If technical support personnel are not mindful of security, they can cause more harm to the network's security than mere users.

System administration

Last but not least, your security design should consider the impact security will have on the system administrators. Here are some potential problems to watch out for:

- If too many security measures are used, the administrative work to set up users, grant access, and perform other tasks becomes overwhelming.

- If users are forced to deal with complicated security mechanisms, administrators and technical support personnel will have to spend time training users and correcting any problems they encounter.

IN THE REAL WORLD

The more inconvenient a security measure is, the more likely employees will try to circumvent it. I've actually witnessed a voice mail consultant advocating changing your password five times in immediate succession every Monday morning if you want to use the same password continuously.

Designing Basic Security

Although Windows 2000 is not necessarily more secure than previous versions of Windows NT, it does include new security features which can be quite effective if designed and implemented in a thoughtful and thorough way. The following sections discuss the fundamental aspects of Windows 2000 security.

Creating a Security Baseline

Networks are traditionally divided into two basic types of computers: workstations and servers. One or more servers can handle a variety of tasks for the network: file and printer sharing, administration and security, and other services. Current network operating systems, including Windows 2000, allow the division of these responsibilities between several servers. The following sections discuss the different types of servers and clients that form the baseline of Windows 2000 security.

Domain controllers

Windows NT uses domains (groups of servers that share a single security database) as the basic unit of security. Windows 2000 expands this system with Active Directory. In older Windows NT networks, servers could be assigned one of three roles:

Primary domain controller
> The authoritative controller for a domain. Only one PDC can be used per domain, and this is the only server that allows changes to the security database.

Backup domain controller
> One or more backup domain controllers (BDCs) provide redundancy and can be used for authentication. They cannot make changes to the security database.

Member server
> A server that does not act as a domain controller and has its own separate security database.

Windows 2000 still follows this basic system, with one exception: rather than PDCs and BDCs, all Windows 2000 domain controllers act as peers. Any domain controller can be used for authentication, and any controller can be used to make changes to the Active Directory database.

Operations masters

Although Windows 2000 domain controllers act as peers in most respects, certain operations require one server to act as an operations master. There are five separate roles held by operations masters, which may be one server or several different servers:

Schema master

Acts as the authority for changes to the Active Directory schema (the specification of the object types and properties stored in the Directory). One server per forest acts as the schema master.

Domain naming master

Manages additions, deletions, and changes to the domains contained within the Active Directory forest. One server per forest acts as domain naming master.

Relative ID master

Manages the identifiers used to associate objects with containers and allows objects to be moved between containers. One server per domain acts as relative ID master.

PDC emulator

Emulates a Windows NT 4.0 PDC for compatibility with older systems. One server per domain acts as PDC emulator.

Infrastructure master

Manages associations between users and groups. One server per domain acts as infrastructure master.

ON THE EXAM

The first server configured as a domain controller when the Active Directory forest is created is assigned the schema master and domain naming master roles. The first domain controller configured in each domain is assigned the relative ID master, PDC emulator, and infrastructure master roles.

File and print servers

Windows 2000 servers that will be used to share files and printers may require additional consideration in your security design. NTFS security and printer security should be configured to allow access to groups, and users should be assigned to those groups to allow them access.

Application servers

Often, a Windows 2000 Server is dedicated to a specific application: for example, a database server. The security considerations for these servers depend on the application. Some applications, such as database servers, may have their own security systems separate from that of Windows 2000.

RAS servers

RAS (Remote Access Service) allows users to access Windows 2000 networks by dialing in to modems. RAS requires its own security considerations. RAS security can be configured in two ways:

- From the Dial-in property page of each user account's properties
- From the Remote Access Policy settings in the Routing and Remote Access console

Another consideration is the type of authentication used by RAS. The available authentication methods are discussed later in this chapter.

Desktop computers

Desktop computers are basic network clients and typically use such operating systems as Windows 95/98/Me or Windows 2000 Professional. You typically control the security of these computers' activity on the network by managing the user accounts used to log on to the network.

Your security design should specify these settings, as well as basic security measures—for example, training users to store data in a secure area of the network rather than on a local hard disk.

Portable computers

Portable computers are treated similarly to desktop computers, but introduce additional risks: for example, they can easily be lost or stolen, allowing unauthorized access to their disks and potentially to the network. Your security design should include a plan to deal with these risks.

Kiosks

Kiosks are application-specific computers or terminals. These may include special-purpose machines (such as point-of-sale terminals) as well as ordinary computers that are made available for public use running an application. These should be carefully secured by using a user account with the bare minimum of privileges needed, because they may be open to the public.

Planning Authentication

When a user logs on, the authentication process verifies the username and password, grants access to the user, and identifies subsequent network activities with the user account. The following sections discuss the various authentication methods used in Windows 2000 networks.

Clear-text passwords

The most basic form of authentication uses clear-text (plain ASCII text) passwords transmitted across the network. This is the least secure method: because passwords are transmitted across the network as text, they are vulnerable to snooping.

Clear-text authentication is not used by any critical Windows 2000 services, but it may be required for certain applications. These include the following:

- SLIP (Serial Line Internet Protocol) connections to Unix systems
- PPP (Point-to-Point Protocol) when required by older clients
- FTP clients and servers
- Telnet

ON THE EXAM

Clear-text authentication has an almost complete lack of security. Whenever possible, it should be replaced with a more secure authentication method.

LM and NTLM authentication

Windows 9x computers use the *LM* (LAN Manger) authentication protocol for user authentication. Windows NT and Windows 2000 use a more secure authentication protocol called *NTLM*. Windows NT and 2000 have to support the older, less secure LM protocol to be compatible with Windows 9x computers. There are a few important differences between LM and NTLM:

- LM is not case sensitive; NTLM is, which makes LM passwords exponentially easier to crack.
- LM passwords can be cracked seven digits at a time, even for passwords longer than seven digits.
- Windows NT and 2000 may store a copy of the NTLM password in the easier-to-crack LM format. If the LM password is cracked, all that needs to be done to crack the corresponding NTLM password is to try changing the case of letters in the LM password.

IN THE REAL WORLD

Instead of trying to perform complex tasks on one powerful computer, many successful projects, such as Distributed.net and SETI@Home, are dividing the workload among thousands of computers. This means that password and encryption cracking is both faster and less expensive than it used to be.

Kerberos authentication

Windows 2000 introduces Kerberos authentication, a new system that can be used instead of NTLM if both clients and servers are running Windows 2000 and are configured to use Kerberos. Kerberos is based on RFC 1510. When a client attempts to log on to the network in this system, the following process occurs:

1. The client encrypts the current time using the password entered and sends a packet containing the result and the user ID to the authenticating server.

2. The server looks up the user in the Active Directory database and uses the key stored with the user to encrypt the time. If the result matches the client's result, access is allowed.

3. When the user attempts to access a file or printer, a session key is sent if the client is allowed access. This enables the client to access that resource without further authentication until logout.

Digest authentication

Digest authentication is an alternate means of authenticating users accessing resources on Internet Information Server (IIS). Normally, users trying to access protected files on IIS must have a user account on either IIS itself or another server that IIS has a trust relationship with.

There are many security issues both with the standard Windows authentication and with digest authentication. Neither IIS nor Windows (any version) has a reputation of having impenetrable security, so you'll usually have to balance security, convenience, and interoperability when designing a networking solution. There are pros and cons to both types of IIS authentication:

- Standard Windows authentication transmits passwords as clear text. This makes them especially vulnerable to capture on an Ethernet network.

- Digest authentication doesn't send passwords as clear text, but it requires the server to permit the use of passwords that can't be encrypted.

IN THE REAL WORLD

Digest authentication is supported only by Microsoft Internet Explorer Version 2.0 and newer. If users are using other web browsers, digest authentication may not work properly. Microsoft is trying to get digest authentication approved as a standard via RFC 2069.

There are a few things to check to make sure that the domain controller and user accounts are set up to work with digest authentication:

- User accounts must be set to *Save Password as Encrypted Clear Text.*

- User accounts must be set to *User Must Change Password at Next Logon.*

- Check the domain controller to make sure IISUBA.DLL is installed.

Designing Security

Users won't be able to use digest authentication until they have changed their passwords. Digest authentication can be set up with Windows 2000 and IIS 5.0 by using the following steps:

1. In the Microsoft Management Console, choose either the *IIS* or *Computer Management Console.*

2. Right click on the *IIS tree* for the whole server or the specific web site you want to use digest authentication with.

3. Choose *Properties*, select the *Server* tab, and click the *Edit* button.

4. Select the *Directory Security* tab and click the *Edit* button under the *Anonymous Access and Authentication Control.*

5. Choose *Digest Authentication for Windows Domain Servers* and click *OK.*

Smart cards

Smart cards are credit card–sized devices with enough storage to contain numerous encryption and authentication keys, as well as encrypted data. For example, the encryption key used to store EFS files can actually be stored on the smart card, so that files cannot be decrypted without it. Smart cards are meant to address some of the inherent security limitations of the traditional username/password, but there are also drawbacks. The physical card and a *personal identification number* (PIN) are used together for identification, just as the username and password are used together. Table 7-1 addresses some of the advantages of smart cards.

Table 7-1: Smart Cards Versus Usernames and Passwords

Issue	Smart Card	Username and Password
Stolen identification	The PIN is useless without the card.	Account is compromised in most cases.
Temptation to write the password down	Because the PIN is usually a lot shorter than a good password and is usually never changed, most people will memorize the PIN.	If you enforce a strong password policy of random numbers, letters, and symbols changed on a regular basis, many people will write down their passwords.
Loss of card/forgotten password	It's more difficult and expensive to issue a new card than to look up a user's password.	Passwords can be easily reset or given to users if forgotten.
Cost	More expensive and needs physical equipment and special software.	Included in Windows 2000; no special hardware or software is needed.

Smart cards don't have to be deployed as the only means of authentication on a network. You can use smart cards for only those resources that require additional security and continue to use usernames and passwords in other areas.

The first thing you should do before proceeding in implementing a smart card authentication system is map out which resources would be more secure in a smart card environment. After you determine where they will be used and who will use them, you can figure out how much equipment you need to buy.

Once you have the physical equipment (the smart cards and the smart card readers), you can get started with converting some or all computers to require smart card authentication. There a few steps you'll need to do in order to get the system up and running:

1. Install Microsoft Certificate Services and set up a certificate authority (CA).

2. Use the CA to issue certificates and configure the level of security needed for each location.

3. Issue the physical cards and install the readers on the appropriate machines. Be sure to set up a PIN for each card.

4. Test each location and card to be sure they are all working properly.

RADIUS

The RADIUS client-server authentication protocol is commonly used by Internet Service Providers to authenticate incoming connections. RADIUS is an acronym for Remote Authentication Dial-In User Service and is often used in conjunction with other authentication protocols, such as Point-to-Point Protocol (PPP).

As with Kerberos, Microsoft has its own implementation of RADIUS that differs slightly from the standard. The most significant difference is that the Microsoft version, called *Internet Authentication Service* (IAS), uses Active Directory to authenticate users.

You won't need to memorize each step of the authentication process for the exam, but you should be familiar with the basic process that happens during authentication. Following is a list of the steps involved with IAS authentication on a Windows 2000 RAS server:

1. When the remote user either dials in (via PPP) or attempts to connect via a virtual private network (VPN), the RAS server sends a RADIUS Access Request packet to the IAS server.

2. The IAS server tries to find the user account in Active Directory. If found, and if the user's permissions are valid for that type of connection, the IAS server sends an Access-Accept packet to the RAS server. Otherwise, the connection is terminated.

3. To determine the level of access granted to the user, the RAS server uses permissions information that was included in the Access-Accept packet.

4. The RAS server sends an Accounting-Start packet to the IAS server, requesting it to monitor the connection. This continues until the session is disconnected and the RAS server sends an Accounting-Stop packet.

A few options will cause this list of steps to vary. If at any time the RAS server doesn't receive a response from the IAS server, the RAS server will automatically try to connect to a backup IAS server. Also, the RAS server will attempt to connect the user with the most secure protocol possible. Its first choice is Extensible Authentication Protocol (EAP), which can be used with smart cards and certificates, MS-CHAP, CHAP, and PAP.

IN THE REAL WORLD

Both RAS and RADIUS are used to authenticate dial-up connections to the network. RADIUS has the advantage of being good at handling a large volume (thousands of connections a day) and for centralized record-keeping across multiple RADIUS servers. RAS is for lower volumes and has less sophisticated reporting options.

Certificates

Certificates are documents that include identification and a public key used for encryption. These provide a more secure method of authentication than basic authentication methods, such as Kerberos. Certificates are discussed further in the next section of this chapter.

SSL

SSL (Secure Sockets Layer) is an encrypted protocol used to access secure web documents. IIS supports SSL with compatible browsers. SSL uses public-key encryption, using certificates granted by a certificate authority.

Integration with other systems

Despite Microsoft's positioning of Windows 2000 as the answer to all networking questions, many networks still include non-Windows systems. Your security design should include policies for these systems. The following are third-party systems supported by Windows 2000:

- The current AppleTalk protocol allows Macintosh clients to access Windows 2000 shares without the need for File Services for Macintosh. Further interoperability is made possible with Print Services for Macintosh.

- NetWare servers are supported by Microsoft Services for NetWare.

- Unix computers can be interconnected using Microsoft Services for Unix and for such Unix-based systems as Samba.

- IBM mainframe and mini (AS/400) computers are supported by SNA Server 4.0.

Certificate-Based Security

Windows 2000 uses Kerberos for most authentication duties, as long as it's supported by both parties. In the case of a mixed-mode environment, where there are both Windows 2000 and Windows NT computers, NTLM authentication can be used.

Although Kerberos is more secure than NTLM, certificate-based authentication is even more secure, and it can be used by many operating systems and within several third-party programs. To use certificates, there has to be a certificate authority to issue them. You can create a certificate authority on your own local network or use a third-party certificate authority, like VeriSign. In either case, you'll have to plan ahead to make sure that you design a system that actually works with no loopholes.

Certificate-based authentication uses private and public keys for the verification of identity. Public and private keys always come in matching pairs. Data encrypted with the public key can only be decrypted by the matching private key. Certificate authorities use a special private key called a *root key*. Root keys are combined with a user's public key to make a certificate. Keys are discussed in more detail in the "Encrypted Filesystem (EFS)" section later in this chapter.

IN THE REAL WORLD

To a certain extent, as long as the private key remains secure, the system works. However, keys thought to be impenetrable a few years ago can be cracked by the ordinary personal computers of today. The Internet has made it feasible to pool the resources of several hundred thousand personal computers to create a virtual supercomputer, the power of which far exceeds that of any commercially available supercomputer.

Certificate authority (CA) hierarchies

A certificate authority verifies the identity of users and issues certificates using a key-based system. Windows 2000 comes with Certificate Services, which can be used for issuing certificates. It's also used to help manage EFS encryption and smart card authentication. The use of certificate services allows you to become your own certificate authority. Assuming you're logged with an administrator account, you can install certificate services by performing the following steps:

1. Choose Start → Settings → Control Panel.

2. Double click on *Add/Remove Programs.*

3. On the Windows Components tab, click the *Components* button.

4. Select *Certificate Services,* click *Yes* to acknowledge the name change warning, and then click the *Next* button.

5. Choose the type of root certificate server and click the *Next* button.

6. Fill in the required identification information and click the *Next* button.

7. Choose a secure area for the data storage location and click the *Next* button.

8. After the required files are copied and verified, click the *Finish* button.

Certificate server roles

Most large organizations will need more than one server to handle all the certificate traffic. Certificate authority servers are arranged in a trust hierarchy, with a root certificate authority being the master. Certificate Services allows the following CA server roles:

Enterprise root CA
> If you are using Active Directory, this is the master CA. It issues the certificates for the enterprise subordinate CA servers, so its security must not be compromised. Otherwise, your whole certificate system can be compromised by hijacked or impersonated CA servers. The enterprise root CA requires both Active Directory and Windows 2000 DNS.

Standalone root CA
> If you're not using Active Directory, this is the master CA. It issues the certificates for the standalone subordinate CA servers, so its security must not be compromised. Otherwise, your whole certificate system can be compromised by hijacked or impersonated CA servers.

Enterprise subordinate CA
> Receives its authorization certificate from the enterprise root CA and can issue certificates to users. An enterprise root CA can be responsible for many enterprise subordinate CA servers.

Standalone subordinate CA
> Receives its authorization from the standalone root CA or another standalone subordinate CA. It can issue certificates to users or issue a certificate to authorize other standalone subordinate CA servers.

Managing certificates

Certificates can be managed using the Microsoft Management Console (MMC). Some certificates will have a time limit and expire automatically; on occasion, a certificate may even have to be revoked. The CA server handles most of the certificate issuing and expiring by itself, and a certificate revocation list (CRL) is published periodically by the CA.

The easiest way to manage a large number of certificates is by creating policies and templates. You'll need to create a public key policy to allow computers to automatically receive certificates from a CA. You can do this by using the following steps:

1. Start the Active Directory Users and Computers snap-in.

2. Choose the Organizational Unit for the computer you want to authorize and open its properties.

3. Choose *Group Policy* and click the *New* button. Select *Edit* to edit the current policy. The Group Policy dialog is displayed, as shown in Figure 7-1.

4. Browse to the *Public Key Policies* folder and right-click on *Automatic Certificate Request Settings*.

5. Choose *New,* then choose *Automatic Certificate Request* and click the *Next* button.

6. Choose the computer you want to authorize, assign it a CA, and click the *Finish* button.

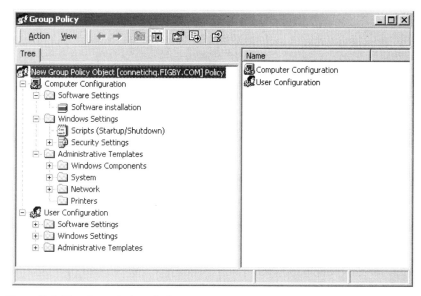

Figure 7-1: The Group Policy dialog

Follow those steps for all the computers you want to authorize. If you ever need to check to see if a certificate was processed, you can look at all the pending certificate requests in the certification authority snap-in of the MMC. There is a pending requests folder that lists all the requests that have not been processed yet. If a requested certificate isn't in the pending folder, it should be in either the issued or revoked folder, both of which are located in the same place as the pending folder.

Mapping certificates

Outside users or groups of users, connecting from another domain or another Active Directory, can be authenticated with the use of certificates, but the outside certificate must be linked to an actual user account in the local Active Directory. This mapping is required to allow Windows 2000 to employ its native user management security while also having the additional security of a certificate issued by a trusted CA.

There a few different ways to map certificates, depending on how many people you want to authorize and the level of monitoring required. Table 7-2 lists the different certificate mapping options.

Although issued certificates are listed in the issued folder, they're really stored in the Active Directory, in the local machine's registry, or on a smart card.

Table 7-2: Mapping Certificates

Name	Relationship	Description
Standard	One-to-one	One certificate is mapped to one account.
Use Issuer for Alternate Security Identity	Many-to-one	All certificates for a given CA are mapped to a given account.
Use Subject for Alternate Security Identity	Many-to-one	All certificates with the same subject (purpose) are mapped to a given account.

Third-party certificate authorities

Some companies need to have a very high level of security, and some companies don't have the personnel needed to manage the certificate process efficiently. If you don't have the resources or time to securely manage certificates, you can hire an outside organization to handle your certificates. In any case, you can outsource the CA process.

Although Windows 2000 can work with outside certificate authorities, many of the tools and options are unavailable when you use an outside certificate authority. One example is that computer certificates cannot be automatically granted or renewed. Another is that smart card certificates must be issued from a CA within its own Active Directory.

Using an outside certificate authority may save work and can be more secure, but the trade-off of flexibility and response time to problems should be considered. Also, U.S.-based third-party certificate authorities can be legally required to turn over a client's keys by court order.

If an outside company is used as the certificate authority, you also risk that the company can go out of business or have a catastrophic security failure. Also, the reason you have certificates in the first place is to have a higher level of security. If your company's business plan is dependent on keeping information private, keep in mind that with an outside certificate authority another company is potentially holding the keys to your network.

Encrypted Filesystem (EFS)

Windows 2000 includes the ability to encrypt files and folders. This type of encryption involves the use of software keys to scramble and restore data. The different types of keys and how they work together are described later in this section. First, you have to determine if the benefits of encryption outweigh the possible consequences.

Because encryption is standard on every Windows 2000 computer, by default, almost anyone with a user account on the network can encrypt files and folders. If a user has encrypted files and folders and leaves the company or otherwise loses the recovery key, it can cause a lot of headaches. Most of the time, with some effort, the encrypted files can be fully recovered. This can become very time consuming if there is a large number of files in multiple locations or if many different encryption keys were used.

EFS Basics

The Windows 2000 encryption and decryption process is transparent to the user. After a folder has been configured to encrypt its contents by checking a box in the folder's advanced properties, the owner of the file can treat the file just like an unencrypted file. The decryption is performed automatically when the authorized user opens the file. The file is reencrypted when the user closes the file. Storing a file in a folder that's set up to encrypt its contents is all that's needed to take full advantage of the built-in Windows 2000 encryption system.

There are a few basic limitations of EFS that may convince you not to bother with EFS at all. If you choose not to use EFS, you have to explicitly disable its use. Otherwise, anyone who wants to can use EFS. These limitations include the following:

- There is no multiple-user or group encryption. Encrypted files are associated with a particular user account.

- Encryption and compression are mutually exclusive.

- Encrypted data may be left in the paging file as clear text.

- If an encrypted file is in a shared folder, any user with permissions to delete files from that folder can delete another user's encrypted file.

There are a few terms you'll have to be familiar with to understand how the Encrypted Filesystem actually works. Remember, a *key* is the piece of software that scrambles and unscrambles the data:

File encryption key (FEK)
> A key that is associated with a particular user account.

Recovery agent key
> The recovery agent key is also used to encrypt and decrypt files along with the FEK. If the FEK is unavailable, the recovery agent key can be used to decrypt the file.

Data recovery field (DRF)
> The section of an encrypted file that contains information regarding the FEK and recovery agent keys.

Public key
> The key that is used to encrypt files. It is stored within the files it has encrypted.

Private key
> The key that is used to restore encrypted files. It is kept private and is used to restore files that were encrypted with its matching public key.

Key store
> The location where private keys are stored.

Protected storage service
> Generates a master key that is used to encrypt a user's private key.

Master key
> An EFS key that encrypts the user and recovery keys so that either key can recover the file.

System key
> An optional security measure that can be used to encrypt all the master keys generated by the protected storage service.

How EFS works

The Windows 2000 Encrypted Filesystem is designed to be to be as transparent to the user as possible. All you have to do to encrypt your files is right-click on their folder and change the properties to encrypt the contents of that folder. From then on, the owner of the files uses them normally and won't even notice they're encrypted.

A file is encrypted using a user's public file encryption key (FEK). The FEK is stored inside the encrypted file in an area called the *data decryption field* (DDF) The user's FEK is also encrypted with the recovery agent's private key, and that copy of the FEK is stored within the encrypted file in the data recovery field (DRF). Every encrypted file has its own data decryption field and data recovery field.

The protected storage service encrypts the user's private recovery key and the recovery agent's private recovery key with a master key. For added security, all the master keys can be encrypted with the system key.

IN THE REAL WORLD

When you open an encrypted file, some programs will create a decrypted temporary file, which may become compromised. Although most programs, like those in Microsoft Office, usually delete their temporary files after the file is closed, it may be possible to recover decrypted data from them.

Key storage locations

There are two types of keys public and private. Public keys are readily accessible, but private keys need to be kept in a more secure location. Users' public keys are stored inside certificates. These certificates are stored in the Certificates folder of the My subdirectory. The My folder is buried quite a few folders down in the Documents and Settings folder.

IN THE REAL WORLD

You should create a shortcut to the Certificates folder if you plan on visiting often. It's buried seven folders deep. An example path, if my username were Kirt, would be: Documents and Settings\Kirt\Application Data\Microsoft\SystemCertificates\My\Certificates.

Private keys are stored in encrypted form in the RSA folder. RSA refers to Rivest, Shamir, and Adleman, who developed cryptographic algorithms, which are used by many operating systems, including Windows 2000. The path to the RSA folder is similar to the public key path, but at the Microsoft folder, instead of going into the SystemCertificates folder, you go into the Crypto folder, inside of which is the RSA folder. If you want to find a master key, look in the Protect subfolder of the Microsoft folder using the same upstream path.

IN THE REAL WORLD

EFS isn't truly secure unless the private keys are stored on a smart card or removable media that isn't kept with the data when it's not being used. All certificates stored on the computer itself can be recovered and used by security professionals or hackers.

Planning Recovery

A default recovery policy is included with Windows 2000, but you can modify the policy using the Microsoft Management Console's Group Policy snap-in. In addition to your normal data protection plan, which should include nightly backups and anti-virus software, you can maintain the security of your encrypted files by limiting access to computers that store the master and private keys.

As long as the recovery agent's keys are kept safe, you should be able to recover any file on your network. If a recovery agent key is lost, be sure to reencrypt the file and obtain a valid recovery agent key for it as soon as possible, just in case the user's private key also becomes unavailable.

EFS Options

There are a few options you might want to consider if the standard EFS setup doesn't meet your needs. If you need more security, you can become your own certificate authority (CA) or establish a relationship with a trusted outside CA. The

Designing
Security

CA would then issue certificates instead of using the standard certificates generated by the EFS. You can also use the system key to encrypt all of your master keys and store them in a highly secure location.

The most important option for EFS is who is allowed to use it. Only use EFS when it is necessary and when it will improve security. Remember, there are performance and convenience costs to encrypting files. There is also a small risk that the file will be unrecoverable if all the relevant keys are lost.

Designing Auditing

Windows 2000 makes it easy to keep track of events that happen on your network. These include file and folder access and modification, password changes, and logon sessions, just to name a few. The automatic recording of information about the events that happen on your network is called *auditing*. The file that stores this information is called a *log*.

How many times a day do you open, close, or save a file? How many times do you log in to or out of a system? Have you changed your password or moved a folder lately? Multiply these numbers by the number of people who have access to your network, and you begin to see that the amount of information that can be stored in log files can be enormous.

You have to decide what really needs to be audited. It's very easy to tell Windows 2000 to keep track of an event, so you may be tempted to just track everything. That way if something goes wrong, you can search the log files for evidence of what happened. Many security-conscious system administrators take this approach, but you have to balance that with the actual benefits and the workload it will add.

If you've never set up auditing or dealt with log files before, the process can seem a bit overwhelming. The trick to designing a good audit system is to make a plan ahead of time, implement it, and, most importantly, use it. It is useless to tell Windows 2000 to monitor all failed and successful login attempts if you aren't going to check the logs for suspicious activity.

Creating an Audit Policy

Windows 2000 comes with nine built-in audit policies that can track the success, failure, or both for different types of events. The more of these policies you implement, the greater the disk space, RAM, and CPU usage you take away from the rest of the system. You should create a baseline of server performance before turning auditing on and check it after each policy you implement. If performance is suffering significantly, you should add a dedicated machine or load balance across multiple machines.

Most of the information you store through auditing is stored in the security log and can be viewed using the event viewer. Be sure to look at each type of log file to see if the information is both legible and useful to you. Otherwise, you may want to adjust the audit policies to optimize the log files. Table 7-3 shows the nine built-in audit policies and the type of event they can track.

IN THE REAL WORLD

You should make sure that the log files are stored on a secure system. If someone is trying to break in, they may try to cover their tracks by altering or destroying the log files.

Table 7-3: Built-in Audit Policies

Policy Name	Events Tracked
Audit account logon events	Success and failure
Audit account management	Success
Audit directory service access	Success and failure
Audit logon events	Success and failure
Audit object access	Success and failure
Audit policy changes	Not defined
Audit privilege use	Not defined
Audit process tracking	Not defined
Audit system events	Success and failure

In addition to providing built-in audit policies, Windows 2000 has several security templates that can get you started on deciding which events should be tracked. When you first install Windows 2000, the *basic security template* is applied. The basic security template is simply the default security settings that come with Windows 2000.

If you need to add to that security, there are two incremental templates to help you, *secure* and *highly secure*. The secure template mainly applies to local files and folders; the highly secure policy also applies to network communication. A highly secure template requires IPSec to be used.

Two other templates are part of the incremental template set, *compatible* and *dedicated domain controller*. Compatible allows non-Windows 2000 certified applications to be run with minimal security risk. Dedicated domain controller applies to local security on a domain controller. These templates are available when the Security Configuration and Analysis Tool snap-in is installed.

Following is a list of the types of events you might want to audit and a description of why auditing them can be helpful in maintaining a secure network environment:

Logon and logoff
Password guessing is one of the oldest and simplest ways to try to gain unauthorized access to networked computers. Keeping close track of the who, when, and where of all successful and unsuccessful logon attempts is a great place to start.

Account changes
You can keep track of the addition, deletion, or modification of accounts. Pay special attention to all new accounts to make sure permissions are set properly and that the new account is associated with only one authorized user.

Monitoring logon/logoff patterns of new accounts to get a baseline of their activity will help you spot anomalies later on.

Policy changes
> In addition to manually setting security for objects, policies (especially Group Policies) can have wide-ranging effects on security settings. If a new policy changes security settings, that change will be noted.

Active Directory
> Files, folders, and just about every object in a Windows 2000 environment are stored in the Active Directory (AD). Changes to the AD structure also can have wide-ranging effects due to the built-in inheritance structure.

Access to objects
> Almost everything in Windows 2000 is an object. Objects have attributes. You can monitor any modifications to these attributes, which include permissions and ownership. You can also monitor how the objects are used, such as whether a folder was opened or whether its contents have been changed.

System events
> You can keep track of when a computer was turned on and off or rebooted and other events having to do with the system itself, rather than any particular files, folders, or users.

Planning Use of Audit Data

Once you've decided what to audit and you actually start generating log files, you have to schedule and plan what you are going to monitor and how often you're going to monitor it. You'll also need to determine how far back you want the log files to go. Luckily, log files can pretty much maintain themselves by periodically eliminating older events.

The most important thing to remember about auditing is that it is useless to generate log files if you aren't going to look at them. There is quite a bit of overhead to this monitoring, so choose the events you want to track wisely.

Securing Network Services

The main goal of networking is the sharing of information and resources. However, sharing is usually done on a limited basis. One of the most challenging aspects of designing network security is balancing how easy it is for an authorized user to gain access to a resource versus how difficult it is for an unauthorized person to do the same.

The protocols and services that are designed to legitimately provide identification and communication can be manipulated to provide unauthorized access to the network. The best way to begin securing your network is to divide it into manageable sections and then document each area that is potentially vulnerable. After you have a good idea of the number and potential severity of risks, you can begin the process of securing the network.

The documentation is also useful after a successful attack. You'll immediately know the other areas where you'll be susceptible to the same vulnerability. Thorough documentation allows network administrators to learn from past mistakes and to explain to management exactly what went wrong. If you know what happened and why, you're more likely to keep your job after a security disaster. This section will concentrate on the networking services that are likely to be present in a Windows 2000 environment.

IN THE REAL WORLD

In addition to learning about the general principles of network security, you should use email lists, newsgroups, and the Web to keep up to date. New vulnerabilities are discovered and made public on the Internet almost every day. Sometimes the information and tools used for breaking into a network are the best way to figure out how to secure it.

DNS Security

The traditional Domain Name Service (DNS) that is commonly used on the Internet has been modified for use with Windows 2000. Normally, DNS zone files are manually updated text files that contain a lookup table of a resource's fully qualified domain name (FQDN) and its Internet Protocol (IP) address. In Windows 2000, these DNS files can be dynamically updated. As is usually the case, this added functionality also adds a security risk.

Most of the modifications to the Windows 2000 version of DNS are to allow it to integrate with Active Directory. Following is a summary of the major changes that are included with Windows 2000 DNS:

Service (SRV) records
> Windows 2000 domain controllers often run many services that other computers need, such as DHCP. SRV records allow Windows services to be registered in the DNS zone file, so client computers can find services located on other machines via DNS.

Dynamic Host Configuration Protocol (DHCP)
> A DHCP server can automatically assign a network identification configuration to a client computer. This process can now be used in conjunction with Dynamic DNS (DDNS) to also automatically update a DNS zone file to include the newly configured client computer's settings.

Dynamic DNS (DDNS)
> Dynamic DNS is the process of automatically updating zone files.

DNS can be used to look up the IP address for a given FQDN or find an FQDN based on a given IP address. The process of finding an IP address for a given FQDN is called a *forward lookup* and uses a DNS *A record* (host record). The process of finding an FQDN given an IP address is called a *reverse lookup* and uses a DNS *pointer (PTR) record*.

Not all threats to the security and functionality of your network are from malicious attacks. Sometimes a simple configuration error can have a domino effect throughout your network. It's difficult enough to find and fix changes that people make to the network. When computers configure themselves and don't keep track of what they've done, there is potential for mass confusion.

It's too expensive and time consuming for a network administrator to make every single change manually. Usually, software can be written to perform mundane configuration tasks, such as the assignment and tracking of IP addresses. You can maximize the benefits of automation and minimize its risks with careful planning. To be able to plan for Dynamic DNS, you should know the information contained in Table 7-4.

Table 7-4: DHCP and Dynamic DNS

Client OS	With DHCP	Without DHCP
Windows 9x	DHCP server updates both the A and PTR records.	No dynamic updating is available.
Windows NT	DHCP server updates both the A and PTR records.	No dynamic updating is available.
Windows 2000	Client updates A record only, DHCP server updates PTR record.	Client updates both the A and PTR records.

The default behavior is that the DHCP server updates both the A and the PTR records for all Windows client computers, except for Windows 2000. Security and documentation are easier to maintain if you can be sure that all DNS updates came from the DHCP server. You can prevent Windows 2000 clients from updating their A records and offload that responsibility to the DHCP server by performing the following steps:

1. Right-click on *My Network Places* and choose *Properties.*
2. Right-click on the local-area connection you wish to configure and choose *Properties.*
3. Choose *TCP/IP* and click *Properties.*
4. Click the *Advanced* button and choose the *DNS* tab, shown in Figure 7-2.
5. Uncheck *Register this connection's addresses in DNS.*
6. Click *OK.*

You may be surprised to know that the default behavior of Windows 2000 is to allow computers to change existing IP/FQDN mappings without question. This means that if my computer were configured to have the FQDN of mcse.oreilly.com and the IP address of 10.10.1.1 and mcse.oreilly.com was already assigned to the IP address of 10.10.1.7, my computer would overwrite the previous IP address and assume its identity. Luckily, you can disable this behavior in the registry by doing the following:

1. Choose start → run, type `regedt32`, and click *OK.*
2. Open the HKEY_LOCAL_MACHINE folder.

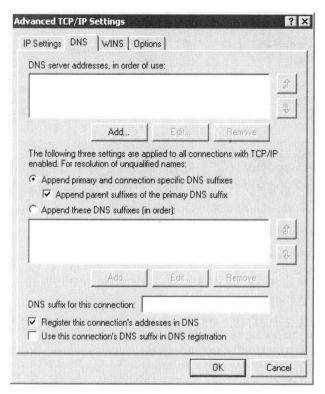

Figure 7-2: The DNS Properties dialog

3. Open the SYSTEM folder and open the following subfolders in order: Current-ControlSet, Services, Tcpip, and Parameters.

4. Add the key for DisableReplaceAddressesInConflicts and set the DWORD to 1.

5. Save and reboot.

Now that you've narrowed legitimate DNS changes to the DHCP server, you have another serious security issue to deal with: Windows 2000 doesn't automatically prevent unauthorized DHCP servers from assigning configurations and updating DNS. It's fairly easy to prevent other Windows-based DHCP servers from running on your network, but it's much more difficult to prevent non-Windows based DHCP attacks. An unauthorized DHCP server is called a *rogue DHCP server*. Here's how to prevent unauthorized Windows-based DHCP servers from operating on your network:

1. Open the DHCP Microsoft Management Console (MMC) snap-in by selecting *DHCP* from the Administrative Tools menu.

2. Right-click *DHCP* and choose *Manage Authorized Servers*. A list of authorized servers is displayed, as shown in Figure 7-3.

3. Click *Authorize* and fill in the name and IP address of the authorized DHCP server. Click *OK* to save the entry.

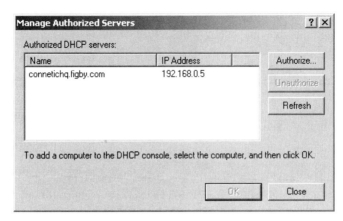

Figure 7-3: The Manage Authorized Servers dialog for DHCP

Although DNS might already seem to be rife with security holes, there are at least two more areas you'll want to secure. Earlier, I discussed how to prevent Windows 2000 clients from modifying their A record. Now, you'll find out another reason that I like to prevent client A record modification.

DHCP servers will only remove records they modified when the DHCP lease expires. This means they'll delete the PTR record, but leave the orphaned A record. If a Windows 2000 client created the A record, it stays in the DNS table, even though it has expired. If you still want to let Windows 2000 clients register their own A records, be sure to configure DHCP to remove expired A records that it didn't create. You can do this by performing the following steps:

1. Open the Microsoft Management Console (MMC).

2. Under the DHCP server section, right-click on *Scope* and choose *Properties*.

3. Under the DNS tab, choose *Discard Forward Lookups When Leases Expire*.

If Dynamic DNS seems like its more trouble than its worth, you can disable its use altogether. This can be done on a zone-by-zone basis. To disable Dynamic DNS for a particular zone, use the following steps:

1. Open the Microsoft Management Console (MMC).

2. Under the DNS section, right-click on the proper zone and choose *Properties*.

3. Under General, you'll see a pull-down box to the right of *Allow Dynamic Updates?*; choose *No*.

Remote Installation Services (RIS) Security

Windows 2000 Professional Edition can be installed and restored on remote client computers automatically, using Remote Installation Services (RIS). This is a great time-saver if you have to create or maintain a large number of Windows 2000 Professional clients. You can create a pre-configured disk image of the Windows 2000 operating system, its settings, and additional software and use RIS to copy the files to the client and register its computer account in Active Directory.

Just as with Dynamic DNS, the added convenience also adds some potential security holes. Before you can create an RIS environment, a few other services have to be present and running, along with the client hardware requirements. Following is a list of the requirements for an RIS environment (all these devices must be members of the same Active Directory domain):

- Clients must meet the normal Windows 2000 Professional requirements in addition to being Pre-boot Execution Environment (PXE)–enabled with a remote boot capability.
- At least one RIS server.
- At least one DNS server.
- At least one DHCP server.

IN THE REAL WORLD

RIS is normally used in brand new installations or to update the operating system configuration of Windows 2000 Professional clients. RIS cannot upgrade an existing Windows 3.1x, 9.1x, or NT based computer to Windows 2000 Professional.

Because RIS can automatically install and configure a large number of client computers, it's a good idea to have RIS name these clients in a systematic and understandable fashion. If your network spans multiple buildings, floors, or geographic locations, you'll probably want to create a simple code to determine where the client is by its name. A computer name of B3F7D5 may sound no better than R2D2, but it could mean the client computer is in building number three, on the seventh floor, on desk number five. You can easily and instantly locate thousands of computers by name, and RIS can be configured to allow a similar naming scheme by using the following steps:

1. Open the Microsoft Management Console (MMC).
2. Choose the *Active Directory Computers and Users* console.
3. Right-click on the *RIS server* and choose *Properties.*
4. Choose *Remote Install/Advanced Settings.*
5. Choose *New Clients* and use the naming rules as defined in the Windows 2000 Resource Kit.

IN THE REAL WORLD

If you are going to be responsible for creating or maintaining a Windows 2000 Active Directory environment, tell your boss that you absolutely must have the Windows 2000 Resource Kit. It will likely pay for itself the first time you use it. In addition to the information contained in the kit, several useful programs and utilities are included.

Some of the same security issues involving rogue DHCP servers are present with rogue RIS servers. An unauthorized RIS server could hijack legitimate client configuration requests and configure those clients with less than optimal settings. You can take almost the same steps as with DHCP to make sure only authorized RIS servers are able to operate on your network. Following is a list of steps necessary to ensure RIS server authorization, assuming you're logged in as a member of the Enterprise Administrators security group:

1. Open the Microsoft Management Console (MMC).

2. Choose the *DHCP Management* snap-in.

3. In the scope (right) pane, right-click on *DCHP root description* and choose *Manage Authorized Servers.*

4. Choose *Authorize*, then type in the name and IP address for the authorized RIS server.

5. Click *OK* and then click *Yes.*

Terminal Services Security

Windows 2000 Terminal Services is now included as a standard feature of Windows 2000 Server. Terminal Services allow for a *thin-client* network, which means much of the processing and storage needed to run applications is handled remotely on the server. This is especially useful and economical if you already have a large base of older client hardware that is incapable of running Windows 2000 Professional locally. Because the RAM and storage needs are provided by the server, the client can be relatively low powered and still perform well in a Windows 2000 environment.

IN THE REAL WORLD

Don't skimp on RAM for the terminal server hardware. In large or busy environments, it's best if there is more than one terminal server available, so that you can balance the processing and storage load; and, if there is a catastrophic failure on one server, the other can take over while repairs are made.

Terminal Services can be run in two modes, remote administration mode and application sharing mode. These modes are selected during the installation and cannot be changed afterwards without reinstalling Terminal Services:

Remote administration mode
> Only members of the Administrators group can log on locally. This mode is used mainly to provide remote configuration and maintenance for system administrators.

Application sharing mode
> This mode allows access to programs and services stored and run on the server. Client computers run programs on the server as if they were running locally.

There are a few security issues that you should be very careful with when using Terminal Services:

- Don't install Terminal Services in application sharing mode on a Windows 2000 domain controller. If you do, all the permissions you grant users on that particular domain controller are valid on every domain controller in Active Directory.

- Terminal Services traffic uses port 3389 by default. Be sure to disable that port if you want to block traffic with a firewall or router.

- Smart card authentication is incompatible with Terminal Services.

- Be sure that your normal NTFS, Group Policies, user permissions, and user profiles are in order before you allow Terminal Services to be run.

Designing Secure Connectivity

The connections between computers in a network are a potential security vulnerability, because network data can be read on the computers it passes through. This becomes a much more serious issue when public networks, such as the Internet, are involved.

The following sections discuss some key methods of securing network connectivity:

- Providing secure access to public networks, such as the Internet

- Using the Internet to create virtual private networks (VPNs)

- Using Server Message Block (SMB) signing to add security to network file sharing

Securing Public Network Access

The simplest method of providing a network with connectivity to the Internet is to assign a public IP address to each computer on the network and use a router to provide all computers with connectivity to the network. This works, but has several disadvantages:

- A limited number of public IP addresses are available, and you may not be able to obtain enough for all of the computers on the network.

- All computers are accessible by anyone on the Internet, providing infinite possibilities for security problems.

- There is no way to control which local resources can be accessed from the Internet or which Internet resources can be accessed.

The solution to these problems is to use a separate internal IP addressing scheme and use a translation system or a proxy server to provide connectivity between public and private networks. Windows 2000 provides two methods of accomplishing this:

NAT (Network Address Translation)
> NAT translates between local (private) IP addresses and public addresses. This provides a simple method of allowing Internet access and a limited way of allowing access to local resources from the Internet.

Proxy Server
> Proxy Server acts as a proxy between local computers and the Internet. The proxy's IP address is the only one exposed to the public network. Proxy Server also provides additional security features, such as customizable filters and user-based security.

Regardless of the method you use, you should include policies in your network security design for two critical items: access to the Internet from local computers and access to local computers from the Internet. These are discussed in the following sections.

Securing Internet access

Your security design should specify who can access the Internet and whether you will limit the sites that can be accessed. If you wish to limit access to individual sites or control access based on users and groups, you will require a firewall, such as Microsoft Proxy Server.

It is also important to provide a single access point to the Internet, typically the NAT or Proxy Server machine. If separate modems throughout the network can be used for Internet access, there is no way to centralize security.

Providing access to local resources

Both Proxy Server and NAT allow you to make one or more local computers reachable over the Internet, without exposing their IP address. This is useful for web servers and other public services. Proxy Server allows precise filtering, management, and logging of incoming traffic.

VPNs (Virtual Private Networks)

A VPN, or virtual private network, allows two or more computers to form a virtual LAN connection using a public network, such as the Internet, as the transport. Because all of the data travels across public channels, VPNs require encryption.

Windows 2000 supports two VPN protocols, PPTP and L2TP. These are described in the following sections.

PPTP

PPTP (Point-to-Point Tunneling Protocol) is a VPN protocol based on the PPP (Point-to-Point Protocol) dial-up protocol. PPTP encapsulates local data within IP packets for transmission via the public network.

PPTP does not itself include encryption. Windows 2000 encrypts PPTP data using MPPE (Microsoft Point-to-Point Encryption). MPPE is based on an RSA encryption scheme, which uses an algorithm to generate cipher keys that change with each packet.

L2TP

L2TP (Layer 2 Tunneling Protocol) is an IETF standard for VPN tunneling. L2TP is based on a combination of L2F (Layer 2 Forwarding) and PPTP.

As with PPTP, L2TP does not in itself provide encryption. Windows 2000's implementation of L2TP is designed to be used with IPSec to encrypt data. IPSec is explained in detail later in this chapter.

ON THE EXAM

You should understand the differences between PPTP and L2TP and their advantages and disadvantages for the Designing Security MCSE exam. These protocols are explained in more detail in Part 6 of this book.

SMB Signing Security

SMB (Server Message Block) is the protocol Windows NT and Windows 2000 servers use for file sharing. Windows 2000 improves upon the security of the basic SMB protocol by adding two features:

Mutual authentication
Requires both the SMB client and server to identify themselves, preventing an unauthorized node from intercepting file sharing messages

SMB signing
Adds digital signatures to SMB messages, further preventing the possibility of unauthorized access

SMB signing is also supported by Windows NT 4.0 SP3 or later and by Windows 98, but not enabled by default. To enable SMB signing on these systems, edit the following registry key:

```
HKEY_LOCAL_MACHINE\SYSTEM\CurrentControlSet\Services\LanManServer\
Parameters
```

To enable signing, add one or both of the following values under this key. Both are word values and should be set to 1 to enable or 0 to disable:

EnableSecuritySignature
If this feature is enabled, SMB signing is supported and will be used whenever a file sharing connection is made with a client that also has this feature enabled.

RequireSecuritySignature
If this feature is enabled, SMB signing is required: only clients that support SMB signing and have the feature enabled will be able to share files. The EnableSecuritySignature key should also be set.

Planning IP Security

Absolute security on any network is nearly impossible to achieve. When we share information, the processes and mechanisms we use to transfer that information can usually be compromised. Normally, the tighter the security, the less convenient it is to share information. Because the fundamental purpose of a network is the sharing of resources, network administrators have to balance the need for easy and efficient access to resources against the level and layers of security necessary to maintain the privacy and integrity of shared resources.

As the world has become networked, the standards and protocols of the Internet have come to play a more prominent role in all computer-to-computer communication. The vast majority of this communication is done through *packet-switching* networks using the Internet Protocol (IP).

When information is sent across an IP network, it is divided up into discrete chunks, each of which has its own routing information. These chunks, or *packets*, are sent relatively independently across the network and are reassembled on the other end of the connection. Their journey may span several independent telephone, cable, and Internet networks. At almost any point along this journey, the packets and their precious information cargo can be compromised. Your job is to make sure that this doesn't happen.

It is difficult to secure everything all of the time. So, your first job in building an IP Security scheme is to prioritize the communications that definitely need to be secure. Usually this can be done on a departmental or Organizational Unit level. Windows 2000 has many security tools to make it easier to maintain private communication across your network. The most prominent of these tools is IPSec.

Internet Protocol Security (IPSec) allows for the encryption of data packets. There are many tools, such as *packet sniffers*, and programs that allow a computer to imitate, or *spoof*, a trusted computer. Normally, the data portion of a captured packet can be read. If enough sequential packets are compromised, the entire communication can be reassembled by someone other than the intended recipient. If a packet is encrypted, the act of capturing it loses some of its importance. Each captured packet must then be decrypted, which is not an easy chore. Usually, if you encrypt all of your data, sophisticated data thieves will move on to an easier way of capturing your secrets.

IN THE REAL WORLD

The most straightforward and devastatingly effective way to attack any organization's security is through its trusted employees. One of the most important and often overlooked questions a qualified system administrator should ask when planning a secure environment is, "Do all of our employees have reason to be loyal to us?" If the answer is anything but a resounding "Yes," you should pay extra close attention to auditing and encryption. The vast majority of successful attempts to break security are perpetrated from within the organization itself.

IPSec provides solutions for the most common attacks your network might face. Table 7-5 presents some of the common attacks you might face and how IPSec protects you from them.

Table 7-5: IPSec Solutions

Type of Attack	IPSec Solution
Packet sniffing	Encryption protects the information contained in captured packets.
Packet reuse	The packet sequence pattern is protected to make sure captured packets can't be modified and reused in an attack.
Elevated application permissions	Packet filtering and IP address limitations limit the risk of a rogue application compromising security.

Creating an Encryption Scheme

There are always choices to be made when designing security. These choices usually involve deciding where, along the curve between ease of use and absolute security, your needs are best served. When you're designing an encryption scheme to be used with IPSec, the main decisions you have to make are whether or not to encrypt data inside a packet and, if you chose to encrypt, how often the encryption keys should change. Following are some terms and abbreviations to get familiar with before we move on:

Internet Key Exchange (IKE)
> IKE is the protocol IPSec uses to negotiate a security association (SA) between two computers. IKE also assigns a shared secret key to be used for the length of the SA.

Security association (SA)
> An SA is a relationship between two computers for the purposes of secure communication. An SA is created using the IKE protocol, and the particular SA an IPSec connection will use is determined by negotiation between the connecting computers.

Authentication header (AH)
> One of the two IPSec packet security services. This service allows the sender of a packet to be authenticated, but does not encrypt the contents of the packet. AH is more efficient, but less secure, than ESP.

Encapsulating security payload (ESP)
> The second of the two IPSec packet security services. This service allows for both the authentication of the sender and the encryption of the contents of the packet. ESP is more secure, but less efficient, when compared to AH.

When you use IPSec, you not only have to choose between encrypted packets and sender authentication (ESP) or just sender authentication (AH), but also have to choose how the packets are packaged and delivered across the network.

There are two modes that IPSec can operate in, *transport mode* and *tunnel mode*. With transport mode, the packet itself is sent across the network; with tunnel mode, the packet is encapsulated inside another packet and sent through a virtual private network (VPN) tunnel. This packet encapsulation process is sometimes referred to as *IP tunneling*.

IPSec Negotiation

There are two distinct phases of IPSec negotiation. These processes are affectionately known as *Phase One Negotiation* and *Phase Two Negotiation*. Choices made during these phases will determine the level of security and processing overhead involved with the connection.

Phase One Negotiation

The first phase of negotiation is mainly concerned with creating a secure connection between the two computers. The IKE protocol negotiates any secure associations to be used and generates the *master key*, which is used to encrypt communications.

Phase two also uses keys to further secure communications, but unless you use *Perfect Forward Security* (PFS), the initial phase one key is reused, even when the phase two keys change. This is less secure because, the longer a single key is in use, the greater the risk of interception and decryption by an outside party.

IN THE REAL WORLD

With Windows 2000, you can choose to use either the Data Encryption Standard (DES) or a newer, more secure version of DES called 3DES. DES has been repeatedly cracked and is not suitable for extremely secure communication if the information sent needs to be secure for a long period of time. DES does take some time to crack; if you switch keys often, it may be enough to satisfy your encryption needs.

If you've used a web browser to shop online, you're probably already familiar with the concept of key length determining the level of encryption. Basically, the longer the key, the harder it is to crack. There are two lengths of keys available with Windows 2000 IPSec, 768 bits and 1024 bits.

IPSec uses the Diffie-Hellman (DH) algorithm, which allows duplicate keys to be generated independently on the IPSec-connected computers without ever sending the key itself over the network. If the generation of DH keys fails, the communication between the two computers ceases. New DH keys can be regenerated during an IPSec connection. The more often you change keys, the better the odds that your communication will remain secure.

Phase Two Negotiation

The second phase of negotiation is where the real work of getting a secure connection up and running takes place. The first decisions have to do with the packets. A choice between AH or ESP is made, and the type of encryption for the packets is chosen. ESP is more secure than AH.

Keys will be used to encrypt the data flowing across the connection. In phase two, the amount of time a certain key will be used is determined. The shorter the time, the better the security. As always, you pay a performance penalty for greater security. So, an AH connection with long key intervals will deliver information faster, but an ESP connection with short key intervals will be more secure.

IP Filtering

If you've ever configured and used a firewall, you're probably already familiar with IP filtering. There are three things that you should know about every packet: where it came from and where it's going, the protocol used to get it there, and the port it left from and will arrive at. With TCP/IP, the port isn't a physical place, but a marker to determine which program the computer should send the information to.

The best way I can think of to describe TCP/IP ports is with an analogy to cable TV. Although a single coaxial cable delivers the TV signals into a house, different people at different TVs can watch different channels simultaneously, even though all of the TVs are fed by the same upstream wire. In the same way, the telephone or Ethernet wire hooked up to your computer can deliver information to many programs simultaneously.

IN THE REAL WORLD

The concept of a TCP/IP port may seem a bit odd to the hardware-oriented among us. A serial or parallel port is an actual metal object that you can plug a wire into. It's easy to visualize little bits marching to and from your computer in single file or in rows, but a TCP/IP port is just a virtual place data can be routed to. Programs listen for data assigned to their port.

The most common type of filtering allows communication to occur based on a computer's IP address. Although this type of filtering is useful, it is by no means impossible to manipulate IP addresses to make one computer look like another. If a packet is captured, modified, and resent, it will look like it came from wherever the third party wants it to.

Certain programs use well known default ports. Table 7-6 lists some common TCP/IP ports and the programs or services that commonly use them.

Table 7-6: Common TCP/IP Ports

Port	Program or Service
21	File Transfer Protocol (FTP)
23	Telnet
25	Simple Mail Transfer Protocol (SMTP)
79	finger
80	WWW
750	Kerberos

Designing
Security

You can filter out packets addressed to certain ports and thereby theoretically prevent that type of program from communicating. The reason I say theoretically is that most programs allow you to choose an alternate port. You should block all ports other than ones you have a specific use for.

IN THE REAL WORLD

Although the Unix `finger` program isn't as popular or useful as it once was, I included it and SMTP on the list so you can test port security at places you're friendly with. I often telnet to port 25 and use the `vrfy` command to check email addresses. Without annoying the system administrators, try connecting to port 25, then to 79. Usually, you'll get a response from 25, but get refused access on 79.

The last type of filtering you might want to use is *protocol filtering*. If you don't want anyone browsing the web, you can block all HTTP packets. It's difficult to implement this type of filtering because many employees really need access to their web browsers and email programs for legitimate work. If that's the case and you still need to prevent unauthorized use, you can install a proxy server or monitor the data sent to and from your employees. Although this type of draconian spying activity is legal in the United States, it's usually bad for employee morale.

What happens when a filter runs across a packet that meets its criteria is determined by the filter policy. There are four types of policies for filters:

Blocking policy
    If a packet meets the criteria defined in the filter as unauthorized, the packet will be blocked. A blocking policy applies to both incoming and outbound traffic.

Negotiated policy
    If both computers are running IPSec, all the rules and filters apply. If one computer is not running IPSec, communication will still be allowed. You have to be very careful when using this policy, because it may allow unfriendly computers to communicate and potentially circumvent other security measures on your network.

Passthrough policy
    IPSec does nothing to filter the traffic. If you still need security, be sure the traffic is otherwise protected through the use of encryption.

Permit policy
    Blocks all traffic that doesn't have a specific filter defined for it. This is the most secure policy.

Defining security levels

The Windows 2000 MCSE Designing series exams test your ability to take real-world information and categorize, prioritize, and determine which solution meets the requirements. When you're deciding how to secure communications using IPSec, you might want to use the following procedure:

1. Take an inventory of all the computers on your network and list all the computers they will communicate with.

2. For each potential connection, determine what type of information might get sent and rate how secure that communication must be.

3. Determine which computers will be allowed to communicate outside your network, and install gateways and firewalls as necessary.

4. Compare the relative values of security versus convenience for all the IPSec options, such as encryption and filter types.

5. Install and configure all the relevant software and prepare to monitor and improve the setup as more information becomes available.

Managing IPSec

Assuming you have configured a secure network communications strategy perfectly on the first attempt, management will be easy. But that isn't likely to happen, so you should spend some time testing your own security. Try to break in and steal packets. Try to guess passwords with brute force password crackers. Monitor the traffic patterns and determine where bottlenecks occur. Most importantly, keep up to date with what your users need to accomplish with their network communications. Although security is very important, remember it's the job of the network and its administrator to ensure that communication is as easy and efficient as possible.

Suggested Exercises

Even more than most exams, the Designing series of MCSE exams require you to have real-world experience working with the issues they cover. Because the emphasis is often on larger networks, you may have to design conceptual networks if you do not have access to a large network to experiment with.

The following exercises will provide a framework for your preparations for the Designing Security MCSE exam.

Planning Network Security

For your network or one you have decided to analyze, determine the requirements and create a security design. This should include the following:

- Business requirements
- Technical requirements
- Company information flow
- Network roles
- Current security risks
- Planned upgrades and changes
- System administration

Designing Basic Security

Continue your security design by making notes about the baseline security of each of these network components:

- Domain controllers and operations masters
- File and print servers

- Application servers
- Remote access
- Desktop computers
- Mobile computers
- Kiosks

Encrypting Filesystem (EFS)

1. Compress several files and directories on a Windows 2000 Server computer. Attempt to access them locally and through the network and verify that access is forbidden without the decryption key.

2. View the directories where private and public keys are stored.

3. Unencrypt the files and verify that they can be accessed normally.

Designing Auditing

1. Create a user account and then create an audit policy to audit that user's activities.

2. Log on as the user and perform a number of operations (log on, access files, delete files, change properties).

3. Log on as the administrator and use Event Viewer to view the audit data gathered for the user's activities.

4. Continue your network design by specifying the audit policies that will be used.

Securing Network Services

1. Configure DNS to prevent unauthorized changes to IP/FQDN mappings, as described in the Study Guide section.

2. Configure DNS to interact securely with DHCP.

3. Configure security for RIS (Remote Installation Services).

4. Install Terminal Services on a Windows 2000 Server computer and try connecting to a terminal.

Designing Secure Connectivity

1. For your network security design, decide whether NAT or Proxy Server would be a better choice for Internet connectivity.

2. Install NAT on a Windows 2000 Server computer and verify that you can access the Internet from another computer on the network.

Designing
Security

3. Configure a VPN between two Windows 2000 computers using L2TP.

4. Enable SMB signing on a Windows 2000 Server computer.

Planning IP Security

1. Install IPSec on two Windows 2000 computers and configure them to connect. Use IPSECMON to verify that encrypted information is being transmitted and received.

2. Configure IP filtering to allow access to a specific set of ports.

3. For your security design, specify whether IPSec should be used and which computers should be equipped with IPSec configurations.

Practice Tests

Comprehensive Test

1. Which of the following are the three basic roles of Windows 2000 Server computers? (Select two answers.)

    a. Primary domain controller

    b. Backup domain controller

    c. Domain controller

    d. Member server

2. You have just installed a new Windows 2000 Server computer as a domain controller for a new domain in an existing Active Directory forest. Which of the following roles will be assigned to this server by default? (Select all that apply.)

    a. Schema master

    b. Domain naming master

    c. Relative ID master

    d. PDC emulator

    e. Infrastructure master

3. Which of the following services use clear-text authentication? (Select all that apply.)

    a. Telnet

    b. FTP

    c. PPTP

    d. SLIP

4. Which of the following is a dial-up service designed for high volume and centralized accounting?

    a.   RAS

    b.   RRAS

    c.   RADIUS

    d.   PPP

5. Which of the following certificate authorities require Active Directory? (Select all that apply.)

    a.   Standalone root CA

    b.   Standalone subordinate CA

    c.   Enterprise root CA

    d.   Enterprise subordinate CA

6. Which of the following is used by clients to request a certificate from a CA?

    a.   Certificate Authority Manager

    b.   MMC

    c.   A web browser

    d.   An email program

7. Which of the following Windows 2000 features is incompatible with EFS?

    a.   NTFS

    b.   File compression

    c.   File sharing

    d.   Certificate Services

8. Which of the following are the two modes Windows 2000 Terminal Services can operate in? (Select two.)

    a.   Remote administration mode

    b.   RIS mode

    c.   Application sharing mode

    d.   Thin client mode

9. Which of the following are Windows 2000 VPN protocols? (Select all that apply.)

    a.   PPTP

    b.   SMB

    c.   PPP

    d.   L2TP

10. Which of the following refers to Microsoft's implementation of RADIUS?

    a. RAS

    b. IAS

    c. SMB

    d. PPTP

11. Which of the following is Windows 2000's standard authentication method?

    a. LM

    b. NTLM

    c. Kerberos

    d. Certificate authority

12. Which of the following operating systems support NTLM? (Select all that apply.)

    a. Windows 3.1

    b. Windows 98

    c. Windows NT 4.0

    d. Windows 2000

13. Which of the following is required to allow a new Macintosh computer to access shares on a Windows 2000 server?

    a. File Services for Macintosh

    b. AppleTalk protocol

    c. Both of the above

    d. None of the above

14. Which of the following protocols is used for encryption between web servers and clients?

    a. NTLM

    b. SSL

    c. IAS

    d. EFS

15. Which of the following certificate types are used to authenticate outside organizations or individuals? (Select all that apply.)

    a. Standalone root CA

    b. Standalone subordinate CA

    c. Enterprise root CA

    d. Enterprise subordinate CA

16. Which of the following operating systems use case-sensitive passwords by default? (Select all that apply.)

    a.   Windows 3.11

    b.   Windows 98

    c.   Windows NT

    d.   Windows 2000

17. You are designing a smart card login solution for your Windows 2000 network. You have already bought the smart cards and the readers and installed Certificate Services. What else must you do before you can begin using smart card logins?

    a.   Make sure the Enable Ctrl-Alt-Del policy is set

    b.   Make sure the Disable Ctrl-Alt-Del policy is set

    c.   Make sure the Require Ctrl-Alt-Del policy is set

    d.   None of the above

18. What is RADIUS commonly used for?

    a.   Dial-up authentication with an ISP

    b.   Dedicated T1 or cable authentication with an ISP

    c.   Storing the IP addresses of all computers behind a firewall

    d.   Storing the IP addresses of domain controllers behind a firewall

19. What is Microsoft's implementation of RADIUS called?

    a.   MS-RADIUS

    b.   Kerberos

    c.   Active Directory Authentication Service (ADAS)

    d.   Internet Authentication Service (IAS)

20. Which two objects are combined to make a certificate?

    a.   A password and a private key

    b.   A root key and a user's public key

    c.   A root key and a user's private key

    d.   A user's public and private keys

21. Which functions can a standalone subordinate certificate authority perform?

    a.   Issue certificates to users

    b.   Issue certificates to authorize other standalone subordinate certificate authorities

    c.   Accept certificates from users

d. Accept certificates from other standalone subordinate certificate authorities

e. All of the above

Case Study

Text Formatting Key:

- **Describes requirements**
- *Conflicts with requirement*
- Irrelevant background information

You are in charge of a small network with **20 workstations** running **Windows 2000 Professional**, **2 servers** running **Windows 2000 Server**, and 2 computers running **Windows 98**. You have never given much thought to security and have had a number of *security problems*.

Your goal is to plan a security design to **improve** all aspects of **security** for the network, while *causing a minimum of trouble for users.*

Multiple Choice

1. Two of the Windows 2000 Professional workstations and one of the Windows 98 machines are used remotely via dial-up connections. You have recently had a number of outside attempts to gain access via the dial-up modems. Which of the following dial-up authentication methods could you use to provide the most improvement in security?

   a. PAP

   b. CHAP

   c. MS-CHAP

   d. MS-CHAP v2

2. You suspect that one or more users have been accessing files they should not have access to. Which of the following could you use to help determine whether this is a problem?

   a. NTLM

   b. Auditing

   c. EFS

   d. Smart cards

3. One of the users is storing files on the hard disk of his Windows 98 machine and has noticed that they are not secure. What can you do to improve security?

   a. Install EFS.

   b. Use smart card authentication.

Designing
Security

c. Move the files to another machine.

d. Require the user to change passwords more frequently.

Create a Tree

1. Create a table with the headings *Less Secure* and *More Secure*. Place each of the following pairs of items into the appropriate columns on a line of the table.

   a. LM vs. NTLM

   b. NAT vs. Proxy Server

   c. SSL vs. HTTP

   d. Digest authentication vs. standard Windows authentication

   e. Smart cards vs. username and password

Answers

Comprehensive Test

1. c, d. Windows 2000 uses domain controllers and member servers. Domain controllers are not divided into primary and backup controllers (choices a and b).

2. c, d, e. The first controller in a domain (but not the first in the forest) is assigned the relative ID master, PDC emulator, and infrastructure master roles.

3. a, b, d. Telnet, FTP, and SLIP use clear-text authentication.

4. c. RADIUS (Remote Access Dial-In User Service) is designed for high volume and centralized record-keeping.

5. c, d. Enterprise CAs require Active Directory.

6. c. Clients use a web-based interface to request certificates.

7. b. EFS (Encrypted Filesystem) and file compression cannot be used on the same files or directories.

8. a, c. Terminal Services can operate in remote administration mode or application sharing mode.

9. a, d. PPTP and L2TP are VPN protocols.

10. b. IAS (Internet Authentication Service) is Microsoft's implementation of RADIUS.

11. c. Kerberos is Windows 2000's standard method of authentication.

12. c, d. Windows NT 4.0 and Windows 2000 support NTLM.

13. d. New Macintosh computers support TCP/IP and can access Windows 2000 shares without File Services for Macintosh.

14. b. SSL (Secure Sockets Library) is used for encrypted communication between web clients and servers.

---

15. a, b. Standalone CAs are used to authenticate outside individuals or organizations.

16. c, d. Both Windows NT and Windows 2000 use case-sensitive passwords. Windows 3.11 and Windows 98 don't differentiate password case by default.

17. b. The Disable Ctrl-Alt-Del policy must be set before Windows 2000 can use smart card authentication.

18. a. RADIUS (Remote Authentication Dial-In User Service) is used along with other protocols in managing dial-up user authentication.

19. d. Microsoft's implementation of RADIUS is called Internet Authentication Service (IAS).

20. b. A certificate is made with a user's public key and a certificate authority's root key.

21. a, b, d. A standalone subordinate certificate authority can issue and accept certificates to and from other SSCAs and can issue a certificate to a user, but it can't accept a certificate from a user.

Case Study: Multiple Choice

1. c. MS-CHAP would provide the most security while supporting the computers. MS-CHAP v2 is more secure, but would not support the Windows 98 machine.

2. b. Auditing could help you determine whether there is a security problem. EFS and smart cards (choices c and d) could improve security, but could not verify that a problem exists in the first place.

3. c. The only real solution is to move the files to an operating system that supports security, such as Windows 2000. The user should be educated to avoid saving local copies of the files.

Case Study: Create a Tree

Create a Tree Answer # 1

Less Secure	More Secure
LM	NTLM
NAT	Proxy Server
HTTP	SSL
Standard Windows authentication	Digest authentication
Username and password	Smart cards

Highlighter's Index

Planning Network Security

Basic Security Tasks
Authentication
Controlling access to resources
Auditing resource access
Encryption

Business Requirements
Needs of management
Needs of users
Company structure
Size and locations

Technical Requirements
Connectivity and bandwidth
Performance
Administration

Company Information
Information flow
Product life cycle
Decision making

Designing Basic Security

Operations Masters

Schema master

Acts as the authority for changes to the Active Directory schema (the specification of the object types and properties stored in the Directory). One server per forest acts as the schema master.

Domain naming master

Manages additions, deletions, and changes to the domains contained within the Active Directory forest. One server per forest acts as domain naming master.

Relative ID master

Manages the identifiers used to associate objects with containers and allows objects to be moved between containers. One server per domain acts as relative ID master.

PDC emulator

Emulates a Windows NT 4.0 PDC for compatibility with older systems. One server per domain acts as PDC emulator.

Infrastructure master

Manages associations between users and groups. One server per domain acts as infrastructure master.

Authentication Methods

Clear text
LM and NTLM
Kerberos
Digest authentication
Smart cards
RADIUS
Certificates
SSL

Certificate Authority Roles

Enterprise root CA

If you are using Active Directory, this is the master CA. It issues the certificates for the enterprise subordinate CA servers, so its security must not be compromised. Otherwise, your whole certificate system can be compromised by hijacked or impersonated CA servers. The enterprise CA requires both Active Directory and Windows 2000 DNS.

Standalone root CA

If you're not using Active Directory, this is the master CA. It issues the certificates for the standalone subordinate CA servers, so its security must not be compromised. Otherwise, your whole certificate system can be compromised by hijacked or impersonated CA servers.

Enterprise subordinate CA
Receives its authorization certificate from the enterprise CA and can issue certificates to users. An enterprise root CA can be responsible for many enterprise subordinate CA servers.

Standalone subordinate CA
Receives its authorization from the standalone root CA or another standalone subordinate CA. It can issue certificates to users or issue a certificate to authorize other standalone subordinate CA servers.

Encrypting Filesystem (EFS)

EFS Terminology

File encryption key (FEK)
A key that is associated with a particular user account.

Recovery agent key
The recovery agent key is also used to encrypt and decrypt files along with the FEK. If the FEK is unavailable, the recovery agent key can be used to decrypt the file.

Data recovery field (DRF)
The section of an encrypted file that contains information regarding the FEK and recovery agent keys.

Public key
The key that is used to encrypt files. It is stored within the files it has encrypted.

Private key
The key that is used to restore encrypted files. It is kept private and is used to restore files that were encrypted with its matching public key.

Key store
The location where private keys are stored.

Protected storage service
Generates a master key that is used to encrypt a user's private key.

Master key
An EFS system key that encrypts the user and recovery keys so that either key can recover the file.

System key
An optional security measure that can be used to encrypt all the master keys generated by the Protected Storage Service.

Designing Auditing

Built-in Audit Policies

Policy Name	Events Tracked
Audit account logon events	Success and failure
Audit account management	Success
Audit directory service access	Success and failure
Audit logon events	Success and failure
Audit object access	Success and failure
Audit policy change	Not defined
Audit privilege use	Not defined
Audit process tracking	Not defined
Audit system events	Success and failure

Events to Audit

Logon and logoff
Account changes
Policy changes
Active Directory
Access to objects
System events

Securing Network Services

DHCP and Dynamic DNS

Client OS	With DHCP	Without DHCP
Windows 9x	DHCP server updates both the A and PTR records.	No dynamic updating is available.
Windows NT	DHCP server updates both the A and PTR records.	No dynamic updating is available.
Windows 2000	Client updates A record only, DHCP server updates PTR record.	Client updates both the A and PTR records.

RIS Security

Requires PXE-enabled remote boot
Requires an RIS server
Requires a DNS server
Requires a DHCP server
Cannot upgrade from Windows 95/98/Me or NT

Designing
Security

Designing Secure Connectivity

Internet Connectivity Methods

NAT (Network Address Translation)
> NAT translates between local (private) IP addresses and public addresses. This provides a simple method of allowing Internet access and a limited way of allowing access to local resources from the Internet.

Proxy Server
> Proxy Server acts as a proxy between local computers and the Internet. The proxy's IP address is the only one exposed to the public network. Proxy Server also provides additional security features, such as customizable filters and user-based security.

VPN Protocols

PPTP (Point-to-Point Tunneling Protocol)
> A VPN protocol based on the PPP (Point-to-Point Protocol) dial-up protocol. PPTP encapsulates local data within IP packets for transmission via the public network. Windows 2000 encrypts PPTP data using MPPE (Microsoft Point-to-Point Encryption).

L2TP (Layer 2 Tunneling Protocol)
> An IETF standard for VPN tunneling. L2TP is based on a combination of L2F (Layer 2 Forwarding) and PPTP.

Windows 2000 SMB Features

Mutual authentication
> Requires both the SMB client and server to identify themselves, preventing an unauthorized node from intercepting file sharing messages

SMB signing
> Adds digital signatures to SMB messages, further preventing the possibility of unauthorized access

---

Planning IP Security

IPSec Terminology

Internet Key Exchange (IKE)
> The protocol IPSec uses to negotiate a security association (SA) between two computers. IKE also assigns a shared secret key to be used for the length of the SA.

Security association (SA)
> A relationship between two computers for the purposes of secure communication. An SA is created using the IKE protocol; the SA an IPSec connection will use is determined by negotiation between the connecting computers.

Authentication header (AH)

Allows the sender of a packet to be authenticated, but does not encrypt the contents of the packet. AH is more efficient, but less secure, than ESP.

Encapsulating security payload (ESP)

Allows for both the authentication of the sender and the encryption of the contents of the packet. ESP is more secure, but less efficient, when compared to AH.

IPSec Modes

- Transport mode: The packet itself is sent across the network
- Tunnel mode: The packet is encapsulated inside another packet and sent through a VPN tunnel

Common TCP/IP Ports

Port	Program or Service
21	File Transfer Protocol (FTP)
23	Telnet
25	Simple Mail Transfer Protocol (SMTP)
79	finger
80	WWW
750	Kerberos

Index

We'd like to hear your suggestions for improving our indexes. Send email to *index@oreilly.com*.

About the Authors

Michael Moncur is a freelance author and consultant in Salt Lake City, Utah. He is the owner of Starling Technologies, a company specializing in network consulting and web content development, and he is certified as both a CNE and an MCSE. He is the author of several books on NetWare, NT, and the CNE and MCSE programs, including *NT Network Security* and *CNE Study Guide for IntranetWare* (Sybex/Network Press), and the bestselling *MCSE: The Core Exams in a Nutshell* (O'Reilly).

Paul Murphy is a freelance author and training manager for Dreamscape OnLine, a Syracuse, NY, Internet service provider. He has been teaching classes on the Internet, HTML, operating systems, and Microsoft Office since 1996. Certified as an MCSE, he has worked as a technical reviewer for O'Reilly's MCSE series.

Colophon

Our look is the result of reader comments, our own experimentation, and feedback from distribution channels. Distinctive covers complement our distinctive approach to technical topics, breathing personality and life into potentially dry subjects.

The animal appearing on the cover of *MCSE in a Nutshell: The Windows 2000 Exams* is an African elephant (*Elephas maximus*). Elephants are the world's largest terrestrial animals, striking not only for their great size (4–6 tons), but also their trunk. The trunk is used for both smell and touch, as well as for picking things up and as a snorkel when swimming. The most important use of the trunk is obtaining food and water. Another distinguishing feature is the tusks, modified incisors of durable ivory, for which man has hunted the elephant nearly to extinction. Like right- or left-handed people, elephants favor one tusk.

Elephants spend most of their day—up to 17 hours—preparing and eating their food, which consists of several hundred pounds per day of bamboo, bark, grass, roots, wood, and other vegetation. They generally sleep standing up for short periods. Elephants also take frequent baths in water or mud, and, when the weather is hot, fan themselves with their ears. They can trumpet loudly, and also often make a kind of relaxed purring or rumbling noise.

The lifespan of an elephant is about 40 to 50 years, though a few live into their sixties. They have keen hearing, and can learn verbal commands, increasing their popularity as circus stars and beasts of burden. Elephants have also been used in war, mostly notably by the Carthaginian general Hannibal.

Elephant cemeteries, where old and sick elephants congregate to die, are a myth. Experiments have proved that they are not afraid of mice, but do fear rabbits and some dogs. They have no natural enemies apart from man.

Catherine Morris was the production editor, and Paulette Miley was the copyeditor for *MCSE in a Nutshell: The Windows 2000 Exams*. Linley Dolby was the proofreader. Rachel Wheeler, Claire Cloutier, and Catherine Morris provided quality control. Pamela Murphy wrote the index. Interior composition was done by Molly Shangraw, Gabe Weiss, and Catherine Morris.

Ellie Volckhausen designed the cover of this book, based on a series design by Edie Freedman. The cover image is from *The Illustrated Natural History: Mammalia*. Emma Colby produced the cover layout with QuarkXPress 4.1 using the ITC Garamond Condensed font. Melanie Wang and David Futato designed the interior layout based on a series design by Alicia Cech. Anne-Marie Vaduva implemented the design in FrameMaker 5.5.6. The text and heading fonts are ITC Garamond Light and Garamond Book. The illustrations that appear in the book were produced by Robert Romano using Macromedia FreeHand 8 and Adobe Photoshop 5. This colophon was written by Nancy Kotary.

Whenever possible, our books use a durable and flexible lay-flat binding. If the page count exceeds this binding's limit, perfect binding is used.

How to stay in touch with O'Reilly

1. Visit Our Award-Winning Site

http://www.oreilly.com/

★ "Top 100 Sites on the Web" —*PC Magazine*
★ "Top 5% Web sites" —*Point Communications*
★ "3-Star site" —*The McKinley Group*

Our web site contains a library of comprehensive
product information (including book excerpts
and tables of contents), downloadable software,
background articles, interviews with technology
leaders, links to relevant sites, book cover art,
and more. File us in your Bookmarks or Hotlist!

2. Join Our Email Mailing Lists

New Product Releases

To receive automatic email with brief descriptions
of all new O'Reilly products as they are released,
send email to:
ora-news-subscribe@lists.oreilly.com
Put the following information in the first line of your
message (*not* in the Subject field):
subscribe ora-news

O'Reilly Events

If you'd also like us to send information about trade
show events, special promotions, and other O'Reilly
events, send email to:
ora-news-subscribe@lists.oreilly.com
Put the following information in the first line of your
message (*not* in the Subject field):
subscribe ora-events

3. Get Examples from Our Books via FTP

There are two ways to access an archive of example
files from our books:

Regular FTP

* ftp to:
  ftp.oreilly.com
  (login: anonymous
  password: your email address)
* Point your web browser to:
  ftp://ftp.oreilly.com/

FTPMAIL

* Send an email message to:
  ftpmail@online.oreilly.com
  (Write "help" in the message body)

4. Contact Us via Email

order@oreilly.com
To place a book or software order online. Good
for North American and international customers.

subscriptions@oreilly.com
To place an order for any of our newsletters or
periodicals.

books@oreilly.com
General questions about any of our books.

software@oreilly.com
For general questions and product information
about our software. Check out O'Reilly Software
Online at **http://software.oreilly.com/** for software
and technical support information. Registered
O'Reilly software users send your questions to:
website-support@oreilly.com

cs@oreilly.com
For answers to problems regarding your order
or our products.

booktech@oreilly.com
For book content technical questions or
corrections.

proposals@oreilly.com
To submit new book or software proposals to our
editors and product managers.

international@oreilly.com
For information about our international distributors
or translation queries. For a list of our distributors
outside of North America check out:
http://www.oreilly.com/distributors.html

5. Work with Us

Check out our website for current employment
opportunites:
http://jobs.oreilly.com/

O'Reilly & Associates, Inc.
101 Morris Street, Sebastopol, CA 95472 USA
TEL   707-829-0515 or 800-998-9938
       (6am to 5pm PST)
FAX   707-829-0104

TO ORDER: **800-998-9938** • **order@oreilly.com** • **http://www.oreilly.com/**
OUR PRODUCTS ARE AVAILABLE AT A BOOKSTORE OR SOFTWARE STORE NEAR YOU.
FOR INFORMATION: **800-998-9938** • **707-829-0515** • **info@oreilly.com**

International Distributors

http://international.oreilly.com/distributors.html

UK, EUROPE, MIDDLE EAST AND AFRICA (EXCEPT FRANCE, GERMANY, AUSTRIA, SWITZERLAND, LUXEMBOURG, AND LIECHTENSTEIN)

INQUIRIES
O'Reilly UK Limited
4 Castle Street
Farnham
Surrey, GU9 7HS
United Kingdom
Telephone: 44-1252-711776
Fax: 44-1252-734211
Email: information@oreilly.co.uk

ORDERS
Wiley Distribution Services Ltd.
1 Oldlands Way
Bognor Regis
West Sussex PO22 9SA
United Kingdom
Telephone: 44-1243-843294
UK Freephone: 0800-243207
Fax: 44-1243-843302 (Europe/EU orders)
or 44-1243-843274 (Middle East/Africa)
Email: cs-books@wiley.co.uk

GERMANY, SWITZERLAND, AUSTRIA, LUXEMBOURG, AND LIECHTENSTEIN

INQUIRIES & ORDERS
O'Reilly Verlag
Balthasarstr. 81
D-50670 Köln, Germany
Telephone: 49-221-973160-91
Fax: 49-221-973160-8
Email: anfragen@oreilly.de (inquiries)
Email: order@oreilly.de (orders)

FRANCE

INQUIRIES & ORDERS
Éditions O'Reilly
18 rue Séguier
75006 Paris, France
Tel: 1-40-51-71-89
Fax: 1-40-51-72-26
Email: france@oreilly.fr

CANADA (FRENCH LANGUAGE BOOKS)
Les Éditions Flammarion ltée
375, Avenue Laurier Ouest
Montréal (Québec) H2V 2K3
Tel: 00-1-514-277-8807
Fax: 00-1-514-278-2085
Email: info@flammarion.qc.ca

HONG KONG
City Discount Subscription Service, Ltd.
Unit A, 6th Floor, Yan's Tower
27 Wong Chuk Hang Road
Aberdeen, Hong Kong
Tel: 852-2580-3539
Fax: 852-2580-6463
Email: citydis@ppn.com.hk

KOREA
Hanbit Media, Inc.
Chungmu Bldg. 210
Yonnam-dong 568-33
Mapo-gu
Seoul, Korea
Tel: 822-325-0397
Fax: 822-325-9697
Email: hant93@chollian.dacom.co.kr

PHILIPPINES
Global Publishing
G/F Benavides Garden
1186 Benavides St.
Manila, Philippines
Tel: 632-254-8949/632-252-2582
Fax: 632-734-5060/632-252-2733
Email: globalp@pacific.net.ph

TAIWAN
O'Reilly Taiwan
1st Floor, No. 21, Lane 295
Section 1, Fu-Shing South Road
Taipei, 106 Taiwan
Tel: 886-2-27099669
Fax: 886-2-27038802
Email: mori@oreilly.com

CHINA
O'Reilly Beijing
SIGMA Building, Suite B809
No. 49 Zhichun Road
Haidian District
Beijing 100031, P.R. China
Tel: 86-10-8809-7475
Fax: 86-10-8809-7463
Email: beijing@oreilly.com

INDIA
Shroff Publishers & Distributors Pvt. Ltd.
12, "Roseland", 2nd Floor
180, Waterfield Road, Bandra (West)
Mumbai 400 050
Tel: 91-22-641-1800/643-9910
Fax: 91-22-643-2422
Email: spd@vsnl.com

JAPAN
O'Reilly Japan, Inc.
Yotsuya Y's Building
7 Banch 6, Honshio-cho
Shinjuku-ku
Tokyo 160-0003 Japan
Tel: 81-3-3356-5227
Fax: 81-3-3356-5261
Email: japan@oreilly.com

SINGAPORE, INDONESIA, MALAYSIA AND THAILAND
TransQuest Publishers Pte Ltd
30 Old Toh Tuck Road #05-02
Sembawang Kimtrans Logistics Centre
Singapore 597654
Tel: 65-4623112
Fax: 65-4625761
Email: wendiw@transquest.com.sg

ALL OTHER ASIAN COUNTRIES
O'Reilly & Associates, Inc.
101 Morris Street
Sebastopol, CA 95472 USA
Tel: 707-829-0515
Fax: 707-829-0104
Email: order@oreilly.com

AUSTRALIA
Woodslane Pty., Ltd.
7/5 Vuko Place
Warriewood NSW 2102
Australia
Tel: 61-2-9970-5111
Fax: 61-2-9970-5002
Email: info@woodslane.com.au

NEW ZEALAND
Woodslane New Zealand, Ltd.
21 Cooks Street (P.O. Box 575)
Waganui, New Zealand
Tel: 64-6-347-6543
Fax: 64-6-345-4840
Email: info@woodslane.com.au

ARGENTINA
Distribuidora Cuspide
Suipacha 764
1008 Buenos Aires
Argentina
Phone: 5411-4322-8868
Fax: 5411-4322-3456
Email: libros@cuspide.com

O'REILLY®

TO ORDER: **800-998-9938** • **order@oreilly.com** • **http://www.oreilly.com/**
OUR PRODUCTS ARE AVAILABLE AT A BOOKSTORE OR SOFTWARE STORE NEAR YOU.
FOR INFORMATION: **800-998-9938** • **707-829-0515** • **info@oreilly.com**

O'REILLY®

O'Reilly & Associates, Inc.
101 Morris Street
Sebastopol, CA 95472-9902
1-800-998-9938

Visit us online at:
www.oreilly.com
order@oreilly.com

O'REILLY WOULD LIKE TO HEAR FROM YOU

Which book did this card come from?

_____

Where did you buy this book?
- ❏ Bookstore
- ❏ Direct from O'Reilly
- ❏ Bundled with hardware/software
- ❏ Computer Store
- ❏ Class/seminar
- ❏ Other _____

What operating system do you use?
- ❏ UNIX
- ❏ Windows NT
- ❏ Other _____
- ❏ Macintosh
- ❏ PC(Windows/DOS)

What is your job description?
- ❏ System Administrator
- ❏ Network Administrator
- ❏ Web Developer
- ❏ Programmer
- ❏ Educator/Teacher
- ❏ Other _____

❏ Please send me O'Reilly's catalog, containing a complete listing of O'Reilly books and software.

Name _____ Company/Organization _____

Address _____

City _____ State _____ Zip/Postal Code _____ Country _____

Telephone _____ Internet or other email address (specify network) _____

Nineteenth century wood engraving
of a bear from the O'Reilly &
Associates Nutshell Handbook®
Using & Managing UUCP.

BUSINESS REPLY MAIL

FIRST CLASS MAIL   PERMIT NO. 80   SEBASTOPOL, CA

Postage will be paid by addressee

O'Reilly & Associates, Inc.
101 Morris Street
Sebastopol, CA 95472-9902